CONTESTED
GROUND

CONTESTED GROUND

Collective Action and the Urban Neighborhood

JOHN EMMEUS DAVIS

Cornell University Press

ITHACA AND LONDON

First published 1991 by Cornell University Press.

International Standard Book Number 0-8014-2215-9 (cloth)
International Standard Book Number 0-8014-9905-4 (paper)
Library of Congress Catalog Card Number 90-42034
Printed in the United States of America
Librarians: Library of Congress cataloging information appears on the last page of the book.

*For William Mallory and
Maurice McCrackin,
who never stopped trying.*

Contents

PART III   *Urban Theory and Practice*

Acknowledgments

This book has benefited greatly from comments and criticisms offered on earlier drafts by Fred Buttel, Pierre Clavel, John Forester, Chuck Geisler, Christopher Gunn, John Logan, Kirby White, and Brett Williams.

The generous assistance of many people who live and labor in Cincinnati's West End must also be acknowledged. Without their willingness to open their doors, share their stories, and offer their scrapbooks, letters, and organizational documents for my inspection, my study of their neighborhood would not have been possible. Special thanks go to the Dominican Sisters of the Sick Poor, to St. Joseph's Parish, to the Community Church of Cincinnati, and to the Community Land Cooperative for their logistical and emotional support of my endeavors. My appreciation is extended as well to the Institute for Community Economics in western Massachusetts for nearly five years of remarkably rewarding work—one of them in Cincinnati.

Finally, I must acknowledge the multicolored generosity of Bonnie Acker in every aspect of the manuscript's physical production. For the hours of map-making, for the days of proofreading, for the weeks of typing, for the months of sustenance, and for good-humored forbearance throughout it all, I can only express my heartfelt gratitude.

Faith can do some amazing things, but without a bulldozer some mountains just never get moved.

J.E.D.

Burlington, Vermont

Part I

COLLECTIVE ACTION IN THE PLACE OF RESIDENCE

1

Do Communities Act?

Even in big cities people continue to act collectively at times
on the basis of common territory: the people of a neighborhood resist urban renewal, white homeowners band together
to resist black newcomers, disputes over the operation of
schools bring geographic groupings clearly into view. Perhaps
we can dispose of these cases as exceptions, or as residues of
the past. Still, their very existence identifies the need for a
better understanding of the conditions under which collective
action on a territorial basis occurs.

—CHARLES TILLY (1974:212)

"Do communities act?" Tilly's well-known question was rhetorical
from the beginning. He never really doubted that "collective action
on a territorial basis" can and does occur, even in the most highly
urbanized and industrialized regions of the United States. Indeed,
when he first raised the question, American cities were just emerging
from a period of political protest, popular mobilization, and social
conflict as intense as any they had ever known. The "very existence"
of such collective action, most of it organized on the territorial basis
of the residential neighborhood, provided ample evidence that "communities" were continuing to act. Confronted with this political reality, Tilly gave a quick and positive answer to his original question
("Of course communities act. At least some communities act some of
the time") and set out in search of when and why.

I plan to embark on a similar search. Before I begin, however, I
must note that many other theorists of collective action would have
answered Tilly's question in a far more ambiguous and far less positive manner. There exists, in fact, a large body of social theory that
says that people do *not* act collectively on the basis of common terri-

3

tory. Several generations of sociologists, for example, in contrasting the magnitude, mobility, diversity, and individualization of the modern urban neighborhood with the intimacy, stability, and homogeneity of the "pre-modern" village or clan, have concluded that urban neighborhoods no longer contain the primary bonds of kinship and sentiment that make community—and community action—possible. Neither do these neighborhoods still contain the productive enterprises that once joined people in secondary bonds of common labor. The typical urban neighborhood, in the classic description of Tonnies (1963:227), has been seen as a site impoverished of communal bonds where "individuals or families are separate entities, and their common locale is only an accidental or deliberately chosen place to live." There is little basis in such a fragmented, denuded locality for solidary action.[1]

Another body of social theory has acknowledged that solidarities can still arise within the place of residence, but has argued that the interests on which such solidarities are based must originate *outside* the neighborhood. Social relations of race, religion, ethnicity, and especially class engender cleavages and conflicts in the larger society, which are manifested locally—fractures that appear in residential neighborhoods simply because these are sites where particular races, religions, nationalities, or classes are spatially segregated and socially concentrated. People who inhabit the same locale do act collectively at times, but they do so on the basis of material and political interests that are "displaced" from somewhere else.[2]

In sum, the question of whether "communities act" is given short shrift by numerous theorists, who either *deny* that local solidarities can have a basis other than the shared sentiments and common values of "community" or *dismiss* locality-based action as a pale reflection of cleavages and conflicts existing throughout the larger society. "Geographical groupings" may come into view, but they are ex-

1. This theme of "community lost" is deeply rooted in the work of the founders of sociology: Marx, Tonnies, Durkheim, and Weber, in particular. More recent expressions can be found in the work of Park (1952), Redfield (1941), Wirth (1938), Nisbet (1953), Stein (1960), Warren (1963), and Janowitz (1952). A variation on this theme, which documents the survival of communal bonds in modern cities but asserts that they have been "liberated" from the spatial constraints of the local neighborhood, has been developed by Melvin Webber (1963; 1964).

2. Nowhere is this sort of "explanation" of locality-based collective action more fully developed and systematically applied than in neo-Marxist urban theory. See, in particular, Harvey (1981:115), Castells (1977; 1978), Dunleavy (1979; 1980), and Clarke and Ginsburg (1975:4). A general review of this literature can be found in Jaret (1983).

plained away as transitory residues of a premodern, pre-urban past, or as locational expressions of interests and solidarities originating outside of the residential neighborhood.

Tilly was uncomfortable with such theoretical attempts to explain—or, rather, to avoid explaining—the persistent occurrence of collective action that is territorially based. So am I. My own position, based on fifteen years as a community organizer and neighborhood planner, is that geographically defined populations *do* act collectively on the basis of interests and solidarities that are endemic to the locality itself. Place-bound "communities" *do* act—sometimes out of a common interest in improving local safety, services, or amenity; sometimes out of a special interest in protecting local property values; sometimes because not to act is to acquiesce in the community's own destruction. So often does the residential urban neighborhood serve as a seedbed for collective action that much of contemporary political life simply becomes unintelligible without some understanding of the interests, groups, and conflicts of the "homeplace." As Katznelson (1981:210) observed: "It must be apparent to every student of city life that the development of urban protest has been a major characteristic of political life throughout the West in the past quarter of a century. It is also clear that these movements belong to a family of cases. They have organized at the place of residence, not at work."

The theoretical and empirical challenge of this "family of cases" is not to explain them away, but to examine when they happen, how they develop, and why. The challenge, as Tilly suggested, is not to reinterpret the collective action of territorially based "communities" as something else, but to achieve a better understanding of the conditions under which such collective action occurs.

Understanding the conditions under which "communities" do or do not act is only part of the problem, however. Just as important are the cleavages and conflicts *within* these communities. Any number of groups may organize, act, and interact within a single residential neighborhood. When these groups manage to pool their resources in a common endeavor, then "communities act." But this is not the only form that territorially based collective action can take, nor is it the most common. These groups may act separately—or in twos or in threes—instead of acting together as a single "community." They may interact *conflictually*, instead of acting *cooperatively* toward a common goal.

As useful as Tilly's question may be, therefore, in reopening an investigation that much social theory has considered closed, a more fundamental question is why and how collective action of any kind arises within the geographical boundaries of the residential neighborhood. What is there about the common territory of the homeplace that provides a basis for the formation and development of politically active groups? This is not to ignore the possibility of *community* action, where a number of locality-based groups act in concert, but it is to postpone Tilly's original question until later. The prior question is why any such groups exist at all.

THE SEARCH FOR LOCALITY-BASED INTERESTS

To revise the question in this way is to shift attention away from instances in which disparate groups in the same locale join together in common cause, and to focus instead on the interests and conditions that engender these groups in the first place. It is to assume that people who share a common relation to the place of residence—a place where they have their homes, raise their children, and relate to each other more as neighbors than as coworkers—can and do forge solidarities on the basis of interests that are inherent in that relation to that place.

This is not an assumption that is widely shared, as I have already said. I am hardly alone, however, in seeking to explain collective action within the place of residence in terms of material interests that are indigenous to the locality itself. The most relevant work, in this regard, has been done by students of urban political life who have recognized, along with Tilly (1974:222), that "the chief things members of all sorts of communities have in common is investment in the same territory—in land." Even in an urban society, land remains what Molotch (1976:309) has called "the basic stuff of place." An urban neighborhood, therefore, is first and foremost a tract of land on which people labor and live. Yet, for most localities, where there has been a steady "emptying out" of extractive, industrial, and even commercial functions, land is less a site for productive labor than it is a place to live. The "basic stuff" of the residential neighborhood, for most urban residents, is "domestic property"—land and buildings that are used (or useable) for shelter.

No matter, then, that contemporary urban neighborhoods have lost many of their communal bonds and productive functions; people still invest themselves, their fortunes, and their futures in the domestic property of these places of residence. They have an interest in what happens to that property, as well as an interest in what happens to the neighborhood in which their property is located. People with a similar investment in the same territory have similar economic and political interests. These common interests of property and place provide a basis for collective action even in the most communally and productively denuded locality.

Many studies of neighborhood activism have implicitly acknowledged the role of such material interests in the appearance and mobilization of local groups. These studies have variously treated neighborhood activism as a collective response to the threatened security of tenants (Dreier, 1982b; Barton, 1977, Hartman, 1984), the threatened property values of homeowners (Agnew, 1978; Cox, 1978; Ineichen, 1972; Blum and Kingston, 1984), or the threatened safety, services, aesthetics, or amenity of the neighborhood as a whole (Cox, 1982; Cox and McCarthy, 1980; 1982; Ley and Mercer, 1980; O'Brien, 1975). Since many of these "threats" come from outside the locality, provoking a high degree of solidarity among the neighborhood's residents and groups, it is not surprising to find that most studies of neighborhood activism follow Tilly in concentrating on instances in which a territorially defined population mobilizes as a single "community," acting together to defend its common interests against external disruptions or dangers.

A few studies, however, have called attention to the fact that locality-based interests of domestic property create a basis not only for collective action by those who inhabit residential neighborhoods, but for social cleavages and political conflicts among them as well. Perin (1977), for example, has detailed the many economic, social, and political differences that exist between the renters and owners of domestic property. Agnew (1978) has studied homeowner opposition to the siting of public housing. Auger (1979) and LeGates and Murphy (1981) have noted the bitter confrontations that often occur among various residential groups in neighborhoods undergoing gentrification. Cox (1981) has described the inevitable tension and conflict existing in residential neighborhoods between those for whom the "communal living space" has meaning and use as a "community" and those for whom its meaning and use is that of a "commodity."

Implicit in these latter studies is the proposition that people with different relations to property and place will have different economic and political interests. Given an external threat affecting all who occupy the same territory, these differences may be put aside and a unified "community" may form and act. More typically, in any neighborhood having a degree of diversity in the kinds of relations that people bear to property and place, these differences will constitute multiple bases for the formation of multiple interest groups, each acting collectively and consciously in pursuit of a different set of goals. Since the interests and goals of these groups will often be at odds, intergroup conflict may be much more common than intergroup cooperation in the political life of many urban neighborhoods.

Provocative though these neighborhood studies may be in acknowledging the existence of locality-based interests and in describing the appearance of locality-based groups, they fall short of providing a theoretical framework within which the formation, development, and conflict of these groups might be better understood. Despite identifying economic, social, and political cleavages that commonly exist within the homeplace, these studies do not look closely enough at how such cleavages are created—how locality-based groups are structurally differentiated from one another. Despite describing the kinds of "threats" that typically engender locality-based action, these studies offer little insight into how people become conscious of their locality-based interests, how neighborhood groups come into being, and why they develop or decline. Finally, despite acknowledging the high incidence of internal tension and conflict that often exists in residentially diverse neighborhoods, these studies do not delve deeply enough into the structural origins of such conflict. They tend to explain intergroup conflict in terms of the antagonistic attitudes, lifestyles, or social attributes (race, national origin, etc.) of the groups' members, instead of looking to the same social relations and "objective" interests that constituted and differentiated these groups in the first place.

Some of the same theoretical shortcomings mar the recent efforts of Logan and Molotch (1987) to fashion a "political economy of place." Yet their work deserves a closer look because of its laudable attempt to explain the politics and conflicts of American cities in terms of an underlying structure of "urban property relations."

Molotch (1976) had previously described the political landscape of the American city as "a mosaic of competing land interests capable of strategic coalition and action."[3] He had argued that the growth and development of urban areas can be largely understood as a product of these land-based interests, politically mobilized in citywide "growth

---

3. For an earlier discussion of the pivotal role of land-based interests and land-based interest groups in urban politics, see Form (1954).

coalitions." By means of these strategic alliances, "otherwise competing land-interest groups collude to achieve a common land-enhancement scheme," seeking to "use government to gain those resources which will enhance the growth potential of the area unit in question" (ibid.:311).

Building upon this concept of the "city as a growth machine," Logan and Molotch discover an "inherent contradiction" between politically mobilized growth coalitions and the communal fabric of residential neighborhoods. Whereas growth coalitions are made up of "entrepreneurs who strive for financial return" from urban real estate, the residents of local neighborhoods "use place to satisfy essential needs of life" (1987:2). It is the conflict that exists between the "pursuit of exchange values" by entrepreneurs and the "maximization of use values" by neighborhood residents that determines the shape and development of the modern American city. It is the underlying tension between exchange and use that determines the "political dynamics of cities" and the "patterns of neighborhood life," including the collective action of residents in defending themselves against "exchange value threats" from real estate entrepreneurs.[4]

Although Logan and Molotch go further than most students of neighborhood activism in looking to "urban property relations" for an explanation of urban political action, their analysis is less appropriate to the politics of the homeplace than to larger, citywide phenomena like urban development, urban renewal, and the stratification of urban neighborhoods. Questions pitched to a more "micro" level of analysis such as how and why groups might form, or groups might act, or groups might collude (or clash) *within* these neighborhoods are barely addressed. This is partially a matter of focus, a decision by the authors *not* to grapple with the same questions that concern us here, but Logan and Molotch leave out of their theory important elements that render it incapable of answering such questions, even if they are asked.

The most significant of these omissions are the "land interests" and

---

4. Other theorists have noted the significance of "exchange" and "use" in shaping the political dynamics of urban neighborhoods, including Cox (1981), Saunders (1978; 1981), and Mollenkopf (1983; 1981a; 1981b). Mollenkopf, in particular, anticipates Logan and Molotch's thesis in arguing that "cities concentrate and contain two kinds of relationships: those of production and economic accumulation and those of social interaction and community formation. By appreciating the strong but asymmetric and ultimately antagonistic interdependence between accumulation and community, we can clarify the duet between urban growth and crisis" (1981:319–20). Mollenkopf's work will be discussed in greater detail in Chapter 12.

"land interest groups" that Molotch once deemed so essential to any understanding of urban political life. Despite their announced intention of creating an "interest driven social construction of cities" (ibid.:4), Logan and Molotch say remarkably little about what these interests might be or how they might differentiate one urban group from another. They mention a "pecuniary interest" in higher rents that is apparently shared by all real estate entrepreneurs, but give scant recognition to the many ways in which the property relations and the property interests of various groups of entrepreneurs might differ: those of landlords versus developers, for instance, or of developers versus bankers.[5] When their attention turns to people who are not entrepreneurs, their analysis suggests that neighborhood residents may have hardly any "interests" at all—let alone any interests that might distinguish one residential group from another. The patterns and politics of residential neighborhoods have more to do with "sentiments," "attachments," "emotional meanings," and "networks" of support, than with material interests that people possess because of their relation to property and place.

Adding to their confusion over property interests is their neglect of how and why such interests sometimes engender collective action. For Logan and Molotch, a "coalition" of entrepreneurs and a "community" of neighborhood residents arise automatically out of the necessary structures of interest and sentiment in which each of these groups are embedded. No distinction is drawn between these objective structures of the urban place and the conscious, contingent expression of these structures in organized groups. Solidarity is simply presumed. Scant attention is paid to how uncertain such solidarity can be, how precarious. Scant attention is paid to the formation and survival of urban groups.

Finally, in couching their analysis solely in terms of the dichotomy between those who pursue "exchange values" and those who protect "use values," Logan and Molotch overlook the theoretical and empirical reality of competing land interest groups existing on both sides of

---

5. The "social typology of entrepreneurs" provided by Logan and Molotch distinguishes three types of entrepreneurs not on the basis of competing land interests, but on the basis of accidental or intentional strategies for "generating material gain from place." Rather than saying how the interests of a landlord might differ from those of a developer, for instance, this typology can only say that some ("serendipitous") landlords and developers inherit property, some ("active") landlords and developers seek to acquire property on the edge of a gentrifying area, and some ("structural") landlords and developers lobby for government investment in the areas in which their property is located.

this political divide. They mention in passing "growth trade-offs" and "differential material interests" (ibid: 97), but we hear almost nothing about factions and tensions within the ranks of the growth coalition. They mention "exchange value interests" that sometimes make homeowners behave differently from renters in neighborhoods undergoing social and economic change, but we hear almost nothing of intergroup conflict among neighborhood residents. Ignoring those studies of neighborhood activism that discovered multiple cleavages in the place of residence and multiple bases for group formation and political action, Logan and Molotch return to the doubtful assumption with which we began, the notion of a unified, undifferentiated "community" acting harmoniously in common cause. This is a step backward.

TOWARD A THEORY OF LOCALITY-BASED COLLECTIVE ACTION

Despite overlooking many of the structural and organizational prerequisites for an adequate theory of locality-based action, these earlier studies point the way toward such a theory by acknowledging both the material existence and political significance of locality-based interests. Indeed, it is precisely what they overlook that sets the stage for my own attempt to examine and explain the kinds of collective action that residential neighborhoods regularly exhibit and engender. My research agenda is shaped and guided, accordingly, by three interrelated questions.

The first of these asks what the territorial origins might be for the social and political *differentiation* of urban neighborhoods. The research question is essentially this: what is the material base within the place of residence for the "objective" interests that structurally divide one group from another even before the members of these groups have become politically aware of their interests and even before they have organized to defend those interests?

The second question pertains to the *genesis and development* of collective action. A valid theory of collective action, in Tilly's (1978: 60) words, must be able to account for the "comings and goings" of the groups involved. The second research question asks, therefore, under what conditions do locality-based groups form, act, and develop; conversely, under what conditions do such groups fail to form, fail to act, and decline or disappear?

The third question pertains to the *production and patterning of intergroup conflict*. It asks what the territorial basis might be for the tensions and conflicts that so frequently arise among the organized groups of the homeplace. This is not to ignore that locality-based groups often act in concert, nor that "communities" as a whole can sometimes be the actors. It is, however, to make a conscious decision to focus more on the interests, issues, and ideas that divide these groups than on those that draw them together. Intergroup cooperation will not be missing from my analysis, but it will not receive the sort of emphasis that previous studies of neighborhood activism have typically accorded it.

I have consciously made other decisions of definition and focus in posing—and, later, in addressing—these three questions. Several should be acknowledged from the start. First, I have sought to avoid the biases, ambiguities, and confusions attendant upon the sociological use of "community" by using the term as sparingly as possible.⁶ I have usually chosen to speak, instead, of the "neighborhood" or the "locality," preferring their connotations of physical, spatially defined sites where bonds of sentiment and solidarity may or may not be present. Territoriality is presumed. Solidarity is left problematic. On those occasions when "community" *is* used, I have in mind that social complex of shared meanings, sentimental attachments, and interpersonal networks of recognition and reciprocity that are slowly established among the proximate inhabitants of a common territory.

My focus here will be on the *urban* neighborhood, where there tends to be a higher degree of diversity in the kinds of tenurial and functional relations that people bear to domestic property than is typically the case in suburban neighborhoods and rural towns. This is not to conclude that the theoretical framework developed here can be applied only to "residentially diverse" neighborhoods of the inner city. But since this *is* the setting that provides both the context and case for the present study, modifications in the framework may be necessary before it can be applied more widely.

6. Commentaries on the problematic use—and misuse—of "community" in theory and research can be found in Effrat (1973), Hillery (1955), Plant (1978), D. Clark (1973), Stacey (1969), Dennis (1968), and Williams (1976). Aside from an express desire to avoid the many confusions of "community," I make little use of the term for the simple reason that I focus on the *material interests* that people possess by virtue of their relation to a common locale, not on the sentimental attachments that they have by virtue of their relations with each other. The "community" that most concerns me here, therefore, is the one that Weber defined as the neighborhood group, that is: "every permanent or ephemeral community of interest that derives from [the] physical proximity . . . of households settled close to one another" (Roth and Wittich, 1978:361).

I must also note my decision to concentrate upon group formation, collective action, and intergroup conflict among the *indigenous* population of the place of residence. My primary focus, in other words, is on those individuals and groups who reside within the geographic boundaries of a specific locale. Only indirectly or secondarily do I deal with individuals and groups who have a financial stake in the locality's real property but do *not* reside within its borders. The behavior of these nonresidents, whether collective or individual, is an object of study only to the extent that it affects the interests of locality-based groups for better or for worse.

Similarly, what Pahl (1975:241) has called the "encapsulating social structure" within which the people and property of the place of residence are situated is an object of study only to the extent that locality-based interests are threatened, sustained, or enhanced by it. My focus is on the locally manifested *effects* of this larger structure of markets, politics, and laws, not on the origins or inner workings of that structure. Aside from considering the ways they affect local interests and local groups, therefore, I have very little to say about the general development of capitalist markets in land, housing, labor, and capital; the operation of the modern state; or the evolution of American property law.

The book is divided into three parts. Part I combines theoretical materials drawn from Marx's conception of "material interests" and from the neo-Weberian conception of "housing classes" in proposing a general framework within which locality-based collective action can be examined and explained. Part II applies this theoretical framework to an analysis of group formation and intergroup conflict in the West End, a residentially diverse inner-city neighborhood in Cincinnati, Ohio. Part III evaluates and refines my proposed framework in light of the Cincinnati case study. Finally, consideration is given to some of the implications that this new approach to locality-based action may have for the theory of urban development, the theory of capitalist reproduction, and the practice of neighborhood politics and planning.

One final caveat. The theoretical framework developed here attempts to root the collective action and political conflicts of residential neighborhoods in an indigenous structure of domestic property relations. No claim is made, however, that this can be or should be the *only* approach to the study of locality-based action. Nor do I claim that the interests, groups, and conflicts that are engendered by relations of domestic property encompass *all* the collective behavior and political antagonisms arising within the place of residence. When people act collectively on the basis of a common territory, they do so because of the interests they share with those who live nearby. Not all of these interests originate in the various relations that people bear to the "basic stuff of place."

On the other hand, many do—and even when neighborhood groups form and act on the basis of interests originating in "external" relations of race, class, religion, ethnicity, and so on, local interests of land and housing may still be a factor in cementing solidarity or in spurring a group into action. A better understanding of locality-based action begins with a better understanding of the material origins and collective outcomes of these locality-based interests of domestic property. Such is the thesis of the chapters that follow.

2

Marxist Perspectives on
Locality-based Action

> A valid theory of collective action must explain the comings
> and goings [of collective actors]. It must also explain why
> some groups never show up at all. Part of the explanation lies
> in the organizational problems we will take up later. But part
> of it surely resides in the fact that groups have varying inter-
> ests in collective action.
> —CHARLES TILLY (1978:60)

A valid theory of locality-based action must explain why groups form
(or fail to form), why they act (or fail to act), and why they conflict
(or cooperate). At the center of each of these problems, in nearly all
theories of collective action, is the concept of "interest." *Conscious*
interests are said to provide "a means of linking up the problems of
group formation with objective factors in the social structure"
(Balbus, 1971:158). *Shared* interests are said to provide the "glue"
that holds a group together, a means of linking individual needs and
desires with collective goals. *Threatened* interests are said to provide
the impetus that sets a group in motion. *Conflicts* of interest are said
to predispose or orient the actions of one group to another in a competitive, contentious, or rancorous way. Theoretically, whenever
groups are involved, interests and action go hand-in-hand.

Any attempt to fashion a new understanding of locality-based action—one purporting to explain the formation, mobilization, and
conflict of groups in the place of residence—therefore must begin
with an adequate conception of locality-based interests. A conception
of *interests* that is "adequate" to the task of explaining the "comings
and goings" of collective actors must take account of both the "sub-

15

jective" and "objective" aspects of interests. It must acknowledge various kinds of "instrumentality." It must allow for the possibility that people may be mistaken about their interests. It must allow the outside observer to assess what the interests of a group might be. Lastly, and most importantly, an adequate conception of *locality-based* interests must root these interests in the concrete relations that different people bear to the property and place of the residential neighborhood. A bit more should be said about each of these tests of adequacy before we turn to a theory of interests and action that meets all of them—except for the last.

The etymology of "interest" derives from the Latin, meaning in part "to be between."[1] To speak of an interest, therefore, is to denote a two-termed relationship between a subject—that is, a person or group of persons—and a substantive in which that subject "has an interest." Who has an interest in what? is the defining question whenever an issue of interest is raised. This relationship between a "who" and a "what" varies along a continuum that moves between the "subjective" and the "objective." At the "subjective" end of the continuum, the relationship consists of a psychological or intellectual perception, attitude, or attraction that someone has toward something. A person (or group) is said to "have an interest" in something because he or she consciously considers that something to be absorbing, desirable, or worthy of pursuit. At the "objective" end of the scale, the substantive affects the person (or group) whether he or she is aware of the effect or not. A person (or group) "has an interest" in something because his or her well-being is diminished, sustained, or enhanced by it. An adequate conception of interest will reflect this complex reality, defining and using the term in such a way as to acknowledge both its "subjective" and "objective" attributes.

Second, while it can be said that people have both noninstrumental and instrumental interests, it is primarily the latter that will concern us here. The "what" in which a person (or group) "has an interest" is a means to the satisfaction of some primary need, final good, or ultimate end. It affects a person's well-being, for better or for worse.[2] There are two different kinds of instrumental interests. One is what Wall has called "entrepreneurial interests":

1. This discussion of "subjective" and "objective" meanings of interest is based upon Flathman (1966:15–17).

2. Thus, while one can be said to have an interest in such ultimate ends as "life," "liberty," or "happiness," these noninstrumental interests will concern us less than the instrumental means by which "life," "liberty," "happiness"—or some other ultimate end—might be defended or pursued.

We often speak of a person's interests meaning the projects, enterprises, or states of affairs in which he has a stake and from which he expects to derive some advantage or benefit. In this sense, I might have an interest in an oil company (e.g., an investment), or as a trade unionist, I shall have an interest in preserving the solidarity of the members of the union. These are my interests because if the projects or enterprises are successful, the results will be to my advantage. Let us call this the *entrepreneurial* sense of "interest." (Wall, 1975:489)

There are also instrumental interests that might be called "strategic interests." These refer to events, actions, or policies that affect the stake which a person (or group) already has in a project or enterprise. Thus, just as one can be said to have an (entrepreneurial) interest in a piece of property, one also has a (strategic) interest in zoning ordinances, tax codes, and the actions of one's neighbors—all of which can diminish, sustain, or enhance the advantage or benefit of that property.

The temptation is great to refer to "entrepreneurial" interests as economic interests and to refer to "strategic" interests as political interests. More often than not, these will be accurate descriptions. However, since one's stake in a state of affairs is sometimes not purely "economic" and since the events affecting that stake are often not only "political," these labels are probably more confusing than helpful. The only point that really needs to be made here is that the instrumental character of interests should be acknowledged and that different kinds of instrumental interests should be distinguished in any conception of what an "interest" is.

Third, an adequate conception of "interest" must allow for the fact that people may sometimes be mistaken about their interests.[3] Both ordinary discourse and social theory make a common distinction between what people think their interests might be and what they *really* are. Similarly, people may want what is not in their interest or may not want what is in their interest. The possibility that people may be mistaken, confused, or ignorant regarding their own interests is a necessary element in defining what an "interest" is and in explaining how interests might lead to collective action—or inaction.

Finally, an adequate conception of "interest" must be researchable "on the ground." There must be some way for an outside, "uninterested" observer to decide what the interests of a person (or group)

---

3. This test of adequacy is insisted upon by Barry (1965:179; 1969:164), Connolly (1972:472–74), and Wall (1975:497), among others.

might be. Furthermore, since individuals may be mistaken about their interests, the determination of interests should be based on evidence not solely dependent on the subjective assessment of the "interested" parties.

These first four tests are most successfully met by a conception of interests that Marx made the cornerstone of his theory of collective action. Although Marx's focus on class interests makes his theory somewhat less successful in explaining cases of group formation and intergroup conflict that arise outside of the social relations of the workplace, there is still much to be learned from his particular conception of interests and action. Indeed, even with its "inadequate" treatment of interests (and groups) that are indigenous to the place of residence, there is much in Marxist theory that will later prove useful in developing a new theoretical framework for the study of locality-based action.

CLASS INTERESTS AND COLLECTIVE ACTION

The Marxist conception of "interest" lies toward the "objective" end of our definitional continuum. Subjective perceptions and desires are not disregarded, but neither are they given the theoretical primacy accorded them by other theories of interest and action.[4] In the Marxist conception, conscious wants are a consequence, not a condition, of interests. Or, as Marxists themselves might put it: interests, subjectively perceived, are contingent upon interests, objectively constituted. The prior, objective status of "interest" combined with its "collective" and "relational" attributes makes the Marxist conception of "interest" unique. These attributes also make for a theory of interest and action that is designed, rather specifically, to explain group formation, group mobilization, and above all intergroup conflict.

Interests, for Marx and his followers, are "objective" in a struc-

4. At least three other conceptions of "interest" fall further toward the "subjective" end of the continuum: interests regarded as the enacted preferences of political groups, a conception associated with the Pluralists; interests regarded as the conscious wants of individuals, a conception associated with the Utilitarians; and interests regarded as justifiable claims, a conception associated with the "Legalists." A review and critique of the Pluralist approach to interests and action can be found in Balbus (1971), Connolly (1972), Bachrach and Baratz (1962), and Lukes (1974). The Utilitarian approach is presented in Bentham (1948), Barry (1962; 1965; 1969), and Connolly (1972). The "Legalists," a label of my own choosing, are represented by Benn (1960), Fried (1963), Held (1970), and Plamenatz (1954; 1963). A detailed discussion of all three conceptions of "interest" appears in Davis (1986:42–59).

tural, material sense. They are the epitome of what were earlier called "entrepreneurial interests"—that is, the stake one has in a particular state of affairs, the advantages (and the disadvantages) that inhere in a particular enterprise or position in which one is "invested." In the Marxist case, these entrepreneurial interests originate in the social divisions created by the underlying economy. They inhere in the social position that one happens to occupy vis-à-vis the means of production: owning or not owning productive property; controlling or not controlling the process of production. Interests, in other words, are inherent in the "objective" position that one occupies, not in the "subjective" wants, preferences, or perceptions of the incumbents of that position. This distinction has been described well by Dahrendorf:

> By postulating interests that are given and conditioned by positions, we encounter once again a problem which we must now face squarely. In everyday language, the word "interest" signifies intentions or directions of behavior associated with individuals rather than positions. It is not the position, but the individual who is "interested in something," "has an interest in something," and "finds something interesting." . . . Interests would seem to be psychological in the strictest sense. Yet the proposition of certain antagonistic interests conditioned by, even inherent in, social positions contains precisely this apparently meaningless assertion that there can be interests which are, so to say, impressed on the individual from outside his participation. (Dahrendorf, 1959:174)

These entrepreneurial interests are not only "objective"; they are "communal" (or "collective") as well. Individuals who share the same "life situation," by virtue of sharing the same relation to the means of production, have a similar stake in "contemporary bourgeois society." They are also similarly affected by events that enhance, sustain, or erode this material stake. Those who are similarly situated and similarly affected, in this regard, constitute a collectivity that is known as a "class." Members of the same class situation have a common set of economic and political interests—whatever their individual wants might be and whether they perceive this commonality or not. Individuals who make up a class are "objectively" related to one another because of the interests they share.

Interests also relate one *class* to another. The interests that inhere in various social positions—that is, in various "class positions"—are, in Marx's mind, intrinsically precarious and contentious. Whatever advantages a class may enjoy, entrepreneurially or strategically, may be put at risk by the actions of another class. Whatever advantages a class may gain are gained at the expense of others. As Ollman (1976:123) has pointed out, "What satisfies the interests of one group in a class divided society is invariably taken, more or less forcibly from other groups, so that Marx's notion of 'interest' should also be understood as 'interests hostile to those of other groups.'" Thus interests are *relational*, across class lines, connecting and orienting one class to another in a threatening, antagonistic way. These interests are *antagonistically* related, moreover, even if neither class is conscious of its hostile relationship with another.[5]

Interests conceived in this particular way lend themselves easily to an explanation of collective action. Class positions imbued with a set of advantages (and disadvantages) that are both "collective" and "relational" have an inherent action orientation. The incumbents of these positions have a predisposition to act collectively and conflictually that is "given and conditioned" by the structural position itself. Thus:

- An interest is a collective advantage, one that is common to all who share the same "life situation." People whose interests are common are predisposed to act together.
- An interest is a precarious advantage, one that is vulerable to erosion or attack. People whose interests are threatened are predisposed to mobilize in their defense.
- An interest is also a contentious advantage, one that is wrested from other groups. People whose interests would be preserved or promoted are predisposed to collide and conflict with other groups.

There is no guarantee, however, that groups (i.e., classes) will form, mobilize, or conflict. Structurally generated "objective" interests, inhering in social positions, precede any "subjective" awareness that the incumbents of those positions might have of them. People who share a common relation to productive property may fail to perceive their common interests—or threats thereto. They may fail to recognize their common enemy and never organize or mobilize to defend their interests. Therefore, even though objective interests may bestow a cer-

---

5. It is because interests are contentious—even if groups never actually contend—that Marx is able to say that the bourgeoisie "stands in opposition to the proletariat even before it has organized itself as a class in the political sphere" (from *Die Moralisierenda Kritik and the Kritische Moral*, translated by Dahrendorf, 1959:14).

tain predisposition to act collectively and conflictually, it is not until the incumbents of a class position become conscious of their interests that they can act like a class. It is not until the interests of a particular class position become the conscious wants of those who occupy that position that a class can be said to exist at all, organizationally or politically. Class consciousness converts a commonly situated collectivity (a "class-in-itself") into a politically organized class (a "class-for-itself"). In effect, it is consciousness of interests that are objective, collective, relational, and antagonistic that makes collective action (and class conflict) both possible and probable.

Marx fully recognized that people may be fundamentally mistaken and systematically misled concerning their own interests. Consciousness may be confused, diverted, or manipulated. Nevertheless, he seeems to have had insufficient appreciation for how difficult this so-called conversion process might be. As Weiner (1981:88) has noted, the process whereby a collectivity constitutes itself as a consciously organized political force "represents a Konstitutionsfrage that is neither formally developed by Marx nor easily reconstructable from the Marxian corpus."[6] Marx does suggest that there are *technical* conditions (such as advanced communications systems), *social* conditions (such as the proximity of numerous workers in modern factories), and *political* conditions (such as a nonrepressive liberal state) that facilitate the development of class conscousness. He also predicts that worsening economic conditions will pressure members of the working class into recognizing their common class interests: entrepreneurially, a recognition that their well-being is jeopardized by the cyclical crises and exploitative relations of capitalist society; strategically, a recognition that capitalism itself must be overthrown if their well-being is ever to be secured. Aside from these suggestions, however, Marx says little about *how* a similarly situated collectivity becomes a consciously organized class.

He also says little about how his theory of interests and action might be applied to the analysis of collective action occurring *outside* the place of work. Marx's conception of "interest" is closely tied to his conception of "class," with the latter defined almost exclusively in terms of productive property. It is the common position that people occupy in relation to the means of production—owning or not owning productive property; controlling or not controlling the labor pro-

6. Elster (1985:367) offers a similar assessment: "Marx did not give much thought to the problems of providing microfoundations for collective action."

cess—that determines their common interests and their common orientation to political action. Class formation and class conflict are both engendered by relations of production.

What is problematic about this is the observed fact that groups in residential urban neighborhoods frequently form and fight along lines that have very little to do with productive property. These groups are not classes, according to Marx, for they are engendered by relations of distribution and consumption, not by relations of production. But what are they? And how does one explain their "comings and goings"? Marx's theory of class formation and class conflict provides few satisfactory answers.

THE DISPLACEMENT OF CLASS STRUGGLE

A serious attempt to provide these answers has been made in recent years by a number of neo-Marxist scholars seeking explanations for political movements that are essentially *urban* and typically *residential*; movements that are organized, in Katznelson's words (1981:210), "at the place of residence, not at work."[7]

The context and cause of such political action, according to these neo-Marxists, is the same accumulative process and class struggle that Marx had discovered underlying the social relations of the capitalist economy. Their assertion is that neither capitalist accumulation nor class struggle is confined to the workplace alone. The built environment of urban neighborhoods can also serve as a source of profit, a site of accumulation. Consequently, neighborhoods can also become sites of class struggle when the workers who reside there collectively resist capitalist efforts to extract rental profits, convert the locality to more profitable uses, and/or reduce the level of public funding for social services, public transportation, education, housing, and other items of "collective consumption."

Collective action may be organized at the place of residence, therefore, but it is "displaced" from somewhere else. In the words of Harvey (1981:115): "This leads us to the notion of *displaced* class struggle, by which I mean class struggle which has its origin in the

7. A general review of neo-Marxist urban theory can be found in Jaret (1983). The analysis of urban politics specifically in terms of the contradictions, cleavages, and conflicts created by consumption processes that have become "collectivized" through public funding and state intervention can be found in Castells (1977; 1978) and in Dunleavy (1979; 1980).

work process but which ramifies and reverberates throughout all aspects of the system of relations which capitalism establishes." These urban movements may appear in the homeplace, but it is not where they are thought to originate. Groups form, act, and fight on the basis of solidarities that arise within the urban neighborhood, but the interests on which these solidarities are based originate in social relations that lie *outside* of the neighborhood. People who inhabit the same locality may act collectively, but they do so on the basis of material and political interests that are not indigenous to the locality itself.

Locality-based struggles over both the built environment and collective consumption may sometimes become, in Harvey's (ibid.:118) description, a "springboard for class action," functioning to deepen class consciousness and to exacerbate the underlying tensions between capital and labor. Castells (1978) has even raised the possibility of such struggles resulting in broad, anticapitalist alliances among the residents of urban neighborhoods. More typically, however, Harvey, Castells, and other neo-Marxists speak of the *danger* of locality-based action in functioning not to reinforce class struggle, but to divert, divide, obscure, and suppress it.

The danger, to put it simply, is that locality-based action will take on a life of its own, breeding social divisions, political conflicts, and ideological definitions of social reality that are unrelated to the "true" structure of capitalist society. Thus, instead of replicating the cleavages of the workplace, new cleavages may be created in the homeplace. Instead of reinforcing and furthering the class conflict between capital and labor, locality-based groups may fight with each other or with the state. Instead of class consciousness, "a consciousness of place, 'community consciousness,' may emerge as a powerful force which spawns competition among communities for scarce public funds and the like" (Harvey, 1978:32). Since such a result can only undermine working-class solidarity and divert attention and resources away from the struggle to overcome capitalist domination, neo-Marxists tend to regard most locality-based action with suspicion and to relegate both its causes and its effects to the realm of "ideology" and "false consciousness."

This tendency is especially pronounced in their treatment of collective action by working class residents who happen to be homeowners. Beginning with Engel's discussion of the "housing question,"[8] most scholars in the Marxist tradition have dismissed individual home-

---

8. See both Engels (1935) and Angotti (1977).

ownership, and any movements or conflicts surrounding it, as merely "ideological." They do so because they regard the conditions of a homeowner's material existence to be no different from the conditions that objectively constitute the material situation of any other member of the working class. The "objective" interests of every worker who inhabits a place of residence are the same—that is, interests that are constituted by and reducible to the worker's relation to the means of production.[9] Political differences and collective action that are based on *other* interests are based on a "subjective" misunderstanding of social reality. This misunderstanding, this false conception of one's "real interests," makes homeowners unwitting parties to the protection and reproduction of capitalism, rather than participants in the organized resistance to capitalist relations.

The problem with this neo-Marxist treatment is that it suffers from the same class bias that is found in Marx himself, an assumption that all political events must have a class basis or class orientation. Katznelson, Gille, and Weir (1982) have argued that racial conflicts, for one, cannot be treated in this way. I contend that territorial conflicts are similarly misinterpreted if economic classes are the only, or primary, units of analysis. Consequently, I suggest that what Katznelson, Gille, and Weir have to say about group formation and political struggles on the basis of race is also pertinent to collective behavior on the basis of place:

> Urban struggles are seen [by neo-Marxists like Castells] as an aspect of class struggle. One of two interpretations are possible, each unsatisfactory. Either all urban movements are thought to be class movements, or all urban struggles, whatever their basis, are automatically assimilated to the category [of] class struggle. The first is empirically wrong; the second, by begging too many questions, is theoretically impoverished. When struggles change their historical forms, they are not the same struggles. . . . It is one thing to say that race conflicts express and work themselves out according to some features of the logic of capitalist development, but it is quite another to treat all conflicts as class antagonisms. (Ibid.:221)

---

9. It is not only the collective action and political conflicts of homeowners that are explained by and reducible to the structural cleavage between capital and labor. The struggles of tenants are also treated this way by most neo-Marxists. Clarke and Ginsburg (1975:4) provide a perfect example of this perspective: "The housing struggle analyzed objectively is a struggle between capital and labor over the provision of housing, even if it is a struggle which is diffused both by the fragmentation of capital and by the fragmentation of the working class."

To suggest, in a similar fashion, that collective action may sometimes have a nonclass, territorial basis is not to argue that urban localities are autonomous from capitalist relations of production or that locality-based action is unaffected by capitalist accumulation and development. Neither the place of residence nor the collective action organized there can be divorced from the "encapsulating social structure." But localities also contain social structures of their own, resulting in situations in which the social relations of the homeplace do not exactly replicate those of the workplace. As a result, the social groups, political movements, and urban conflicts that emanate from the residential neighborhood will usually have a "logic" that is somewhat different and somewhat independent from the "logic" of class struggle and capitalist development. Locality-based action has a "historical form" all its own. To understand it, as Katznelson (1981:204) has argued, we will "badly need objective classifications of the social relations of residence communities of the kind that [Erik Olin] Wright has provided for the active labor force." I agree.

A RECONSIDERATION OF MARXIST THEORY

Despite these problems in applying Marxist theory to locality-based action, there is much in this theory's approach to interests and action that is worth keeping. There is an "adequate" conception of material interests, regarded as relational advantages that inhere in structural positions and imbue those positions with an action orientation. There is a general model of collective action, describing how such interests may lead to group formation and intergroup conflict. Furthermore, since the Marxist agenda for the study of collective action "on the ground" follows essentially the same sequence as the theoretical model that purports to explain it, there is a set of guidelines that the "uninterested" researcher may follow in seeking to explain how and why collective action occurs.

This analytic sequence begins with structurally generated interests, existing before groups or wants are formed, before mobilization or conflict occurs. The study of collective action begins, in other words, with the entrepreneurial interests that a collectivity already has by virtue of its particular relation to the society's material base.

Next, there is an analysis of strategic threats to those interests—or strategic opportunities to enhance them—that exist by virtue of a collectivity's position vis-à-vis productive property *and* by virtue of that collectivity's relations with other collectivities and classes.[10]

After assessing the entrepreneurial and strategic interests that are part of a collectivity's social position, an analysis is made of the "conversion process" whereby: (1) objective interests become (or fail to become) subjective interests; (2) a collectivity becomes (or fails to become) an organized class; and (3) the action orientation that is inherent in objective interests—predisposing the incumbents of social positions to organize and mobilize in collective defense of their interests—becomes (or fails to become) realized in collective action and class conflict.

What limitations exist in applying this otherwise solid framework to the study of *locality-based* action arise mostly from the Marxist insistence on defining "interest" primarily in terms of "class," while defining "class" exclusively in terms of productive property. If, however, the Marxist conception of "interest" could be cut loose from the Marxist conception of "class," a theory of locality-based interests and locality-based action might be fashioned out of the theoretical and analytical framework already provided by the Marxist model of collective action.

The challenge, in such a case, would be to find a way of retaining Marx's notion of an objectively constituted social formation with a material base (which is what is generally meant by "class"), while removing the theoretical bias of a necessary connection with productive property. Objective interests, rooted in the property relations of the homeplace rather than in those of the workplace, could then be used to explain the formation, mobilization, and conflict of locality-based groups. Since this is precisely the challenge that the neo-Weberian conception of "housing classes" has attempted to meet, it is to this modification of Marxist theory that we now turn.

10. This assessment of strategic interests might also be described, as Peter Saunders (1979:45) does, as "the achievement of benefits and the avoidance of costs in any particular situation." These costs and benefits—or threats and opportunities—accrue to a particular social position, according to the Marxist, because of *"contradictions"* in the structure of capitalist production and *confrontations* between economic classes. The interests of a class are beneficially or adversely affected, therefore, by both its relation to productive property and its relation to other classes.

3

Weberian Perspectives on Locality-based Action

> It is still worthwhile asking whether there are not certain fac-
> tors among those specifically from an *urban situation* which
> structure the world of social relations. . . . It seemed to me
> that there were, and that they were underrated in two types
> of sociological writing. One was that which claimed that
> there was no such thing as urban sociology. The other was
> the kind of Marxism which insisted that all other conflicts
> were ultimately traceable to and explicable in terms of the
> conflict between capital and labor in industry. The concept of
> housing classes was intended to pose questions and help the
> way towards a more precise delineation of the social structure
> and conflicts of the city.
>
> —JOHN REX (1971:295)

During the 1970s, several British sociologists proposed a new approach to the study of group formation and intergroup conflict in
residential urban neighborhoods. Drawing upon a Weberian conception of "class" while invoking Marxist images of "class interests,"
"class consciousness," and "class conflict," they argued that social
relations in urban settings are structured not only by relations of production, but by relations of consumption as well. Class cleavages and
class conflict are structured not only around the ownership and control of productive property, but around the ownership and control of
domestic property—land and buildings that are currently used for
shelter. Tenure-based divisions in residential neighborhoods, moreover, are as likely to engender collective action and intergroup conflict as are production-based cleavages in the world of work. This

27

new approach to locality-based action and locality-based conflict was the theory of "housing classes."

Some of the theoretical aspirations of this neo-Weberian approach were to fall short of their mark, particularly the attempt to construct a consumption-based model of class. Nevertheless, there is much to be learned from a line of argument and analysis that sought to discover *within the locality itself* a material basis for the interests and politics of the homeplace.

HOUSING CLASSES: REX AND MOORE

John Rex and Robert Moore were among the first theorists to argue that Weber's conception of class might be appplied to an analysis of social conflicts that are primarily urban, residential, and racial in character. They wrote: "We follow Max Weber who saw that class struggle was apt to emerge wherever people in a market situation enjoyed differential access to property and that such class struggles might therefore arise not merely around the use of the means of industrial production, but around the control of domestic property" (1967:273).

Employing this Weberian conception of "class," Rex and Moore concluded that the structure of social relations in English cities had two main determinants: differential access to employment and differential access to housing. Just as industrial classes emerge out of the former situation, "housing classes" may emerge out of the latter.

What sort of access one has to domestic property determines one's membership in a housing class. People enter the housing allocation system with certain subjective preferences and with certain material advantages. Where allocation is made by the housing market, the size and the reliability of one's income determines access. Where allocation is done by the public housing bureaucracy, *lack* of income and length of residence determine access. There will be, therefore, "as many classes in the city as there are kinds of access to the use of housing" (ibid.:274).

Rex and Moore were not content merely to describe a static model of local stratification, however, for their goal was to discover the basic process underlying urban social relations—the structural dynamic shaping and constituting urban society. They wanted, in other words, to develop not merely a model of class, but a model of class *conflict*:

"As in Marxist sociology, the notion of a housing class leads one to ask whether class-interests or 'objective class position' lead or do not lead to the formation of classes for themselves, i.e. collectivities having some degree of class subjective indentification by members, some common values, and an orientation to conflict with other classes" (Rex, 1971:295). Building on this analogy, they concluded that among the multiple housing classes that they discovered, "there is a class struggle over the use of houses and . . . this class struggle is the central process of the city as a social unit" (ibid.).

Retaining a Marxist notion of materially based "objective class positions," while removing the Marxist bias of productive property, Rex and Moore claimed to have created both a new model of class and a new model of urban conflict. Their critics were quick to question whether they had accomplished either.

Housing classes are differentiated, according to Rex and Moore, not on the basis of the advangages (or disadvantages) that people possess by virtue of their tenurial relation to domestic property, but on the basis of either the income that people earn through their relation to the means of production or the qualifications that people have by virtue of their relation to the housing bureaucracies of the state. This raises a serious question. If housing classes are constituted entirely by relations that are *prior* to the structure of housing ownership and control, then how can one theoretically justify a separate, relatively independent system of housing "classes"?

One cannot, concluded Haddon (1970), Saunders (1979:1978), and other critics, because this is not a model of class at all. What Rex and Moore describe is a hierarchy of housing *status* groups, not a system of housing *classes*. An individual's ability to consume a particular type of housing is "an index of achieved life chances, not primarily a cause" (Haddon, 1970:132). Access to domestic property reflects one's class situation; it does not constitute it.

Even more problematic was Rex and Moore's model of class conflict. They see housing classes being led into conflict by their "class-interests." Yet whatever antagonism exists among the classes they describe originates *not* in the objective interests of different property positions, but in the subjective preferences of individuals seeking the same form of housing tenure. Conflict arises because the most desirable housing, topped by the single-family, owner-occupied "suburban ideal," is always in short supply, forcing individuals with the same preferences to compete with one another for whatever "scarce and desired" housing may be available. Thus, for each kind of housing at each level of the tenure hierarchy, "conflict" occurs among all who are seeking access there.

This is very different from saying that there is conflict between different tenure groups—that is, between different housing classes: "Indeed the conflict would seem to be more likely *within* one of these 'classes' rather than between it and another. This would more appropriately be termed market competition: thus those on local authority waiting-lists, for example, are competing with each other and not with those seeking with limited capital to own their own houses who may be in competition with those having more capital" (Pahl, 1975:243). Given such a model of market (and bureaucratic) competition, one based upon the subjective preferences of individual housing consumers, Rex and Moore could simply not be credited with a model of housing class conflict analogous to the interest-based model of Marx.

DOMESTIC PROPERTY CLASSES: PETER SAUNDERS

Ten years after Rex and Moore presented their provocative hypothesis, a more adequate theory of housing classes came from one of their most perceptive critics. Peter Saunders (1978) argued that domestic property *can* be a basis for class formation and that a Weberian conception of class *can* be used to analyze urban social relations. His reading of Weber was very different from Rex and Moore's, however, and yielded a very different theory of domestic property classes.

Rex and Moore had focused their class analysis on people's differential *access* to domestic property in a market (or bureaucratic) situation. Saunders emphasized the differential *possession* of property having a market value. Saunders pointed out that Weber drew a distinction between "acquisition classes," whose members possess skills or services that can be exchanged for income in the marketplace, and "property classes," whose members possess forms of property that can be exchanged for income.[1] In the latter case, one's class situation is defined by one's relation to property—owning or not owning a resource that is usable for profitable returns, using or not using the resource in this accumulative way. The question for

---

1. Among the kinds of property that members of a "property class" may possess, such as "productive establishments, warehouses, stores, agriculturally usable land," Weber includes "domestic buildings" (Gerth and Mills, 1958:182).

Saunders was whether housing is "property" in this Weberian sense. If domestic property could be shown to be a source of income—"a source of real accumulation"—then Saunders believed that domestic property could be a basis for the formation of property classes.

Real accumulation is available to the owners of domestic property, Saunders claimed, because land and housing values tend to rise faster than the general rate of inflation, mortgage rates tend to lag behind increases in general interest rate, government subsidies and tax allowances transfer wealth from the public-at-large to private property owners, and owners can increase the value of their property by expending their own labor on rehabilitation and improvements.[2] Because of these factors, the ownership of domestic property can offer access to significant wealth accumulation.

Having demonstrated that domestic property can indeed be used to generate real income, Saunders could argue that housing is not merely "an index of achieved life chances," but a form of "property" that can causally affect those "life chances." He was able to argue, in other words, that domestic property is the basis for a Weberian model of property classes, differentiated according to ownership and utilization.[3] One either owns domestic property or one does not. If one does, one uses it either for shelter (accommodation) or for profitable returns (accumulation). This leads to a trichotomous model of property classes, made up of (1) owners who use their property for accumulation, (2) nonowners who use "their" property for accommodation, and (3) owners who use their property for accumulation and accommodation. Or, as Saunders described these three classes: "suppliers" of domestic property; tenants; and owner-occupants.

Within each of these classes, Saunders identified various subdivi-

2. These arguments for the accumulative potential of domestic property appear in Saunders (1978:244–45; 1979:88–93). The later discussion is the more fully developed of the two.

3. For Weber, the *function* of property—that is, the use to which it is put—is as important in distinguishing one property class from another as *tenure*—that is, whether the property is owned or not owned by the "class" in question. Thus, after listing various kinds of property that are "useable for returns," Weber says that "all these distinctions differentiate the class situations of the propertied just as does the 'meaning' which they can and do give to the utilization of property, especially to property which has money equivalence" (Gerth and Mills, 1958:182; Roth and Wittich, 1978:928). Saunders may have this in mind when he abruptly declares that homeownership "functions both for use and for accumulation" (1978:246), and then employs the utilization of property as the primary axis along which property classes are divided. This is conjecture, however, for Saunders neither cites Weber at this point nor does he say why he has gone beyond Rex and Moore's focus on forms of tenure to include different functions of property in his model of class.

sions or strata.[4] Thus, within the class of "suppliers"—a class that he also refers to as "private capital"—Saunders distinguished between finance capital ("engaged in lending money for home purchase, housing development, and housing improvements"), industrial capital ("engaged in the construction of housing"), commercial capital ("engaged in the market distribution of housing"), and landed capital ("both landowners and rentiers such as private landlords"). Within the tenant class, he distinguished between tenants in private housing and public housing. Within the homeowner class, he distinguished between mortgage holders and outright owners.

Saunders was not entirely comfortable with Weberian class analysis, however, despite the fact that he had just employed it to distinguish three domestic property classes and various subdivisions. His dissatisfaction arose because his primary analytic purpose had been not to describe local stratification, but to examine and explain local class relations. Specifically, Saunders wanted to understand "political struggles which are constituted around tenurial divisions." He wished to develop not merely a model of class, but a model of locality-based conflict. He could not do this, he believed, within a purely Weberian perspective, because Weber's conception of class (in contrast to that of Marx) is "descriptive rather than analytical, static rather than dynamic, positional rather than relational" (Saunders, 1981:139). Nor did he want to make the same mistake as Rex and Moore, whom he criticized for defining housing classes in terms of the subjective preferences of individual consumers rather than in terms of the "objective material situation of different tenure groups" (Saunders, 1978:237).

Thus, while he cited Weber in arguing that domestic property can be the basis for "objectively constituted social formations" known as "housing classes," Saunders turned to Marx in developing a conflict model of collective action, structured around interests that are objective, collective, and relational.[5] Those who share a common relation

4. These "sub-divisions" are described in detail in Saunders (1979:94–95), from which the quotations used here are taken. They were first introduced, but not fully discussed, in Saunders's earlier article (1978:246).

5. What I am suggesting is that Saunders utilizes a Weberian conception of "class" to define domestic property classes, but then he adopts a Marxist conception of "interest" to make these classes more analytical, dynamic, and relational. This conceptual shift is not acknowledged by Saunders, perhaps because he does not recognize any difference between the Weberian and Marxist conceptions of "interest." (On the other hand, it is hard to understand how Saunders could recognize that Weber's classes are "positional rather than relational" without also recognizing that Weber conceives of interests more in terms of *relative* advantages than *relational* advantages.) There is also reason to believe that Weber's own conceptions of "interest" and "class" may have been more closely linked to the kind of *competitive* process described by Rex and Moore than to the kind of "objective conflict of class interests" described by Saunders (cf. Barbalet, 1980).

to domestic property are said by Saunders to have a common set of "specific economic interests." These shared interests, which are inherent in a collectivity's "material situation"—inherent, that is, in its specific tenurial and functional relation to domestic property—are "objectively different and conflicting" in relation to the interests of other collectivities. Consequently, one collectivity cannot pursue its own interests without threatening those of another. "Threats to the domestic property interests" of any commonly situated collectivity may prompt its members to become conscious of their common interests and to act collectively in their defense. As property classes organize themselves into distinct political forces, the "objective conflict of class interests" existing in embryo between them becomes manifest in overt political struggle.

Saunders devoted particular attention to the political organization and mobilization of his "middle class" of owner-occupiers. He refuted political theories of the Right and Left that have typically regarded owner-occupation as either "a diffusion of capitalist property rights" or "a strengthening of 'false consciousness' among the proletariat." He argued that "owner-occupation provides access to a highly significant accumulative form of property ownership which generates specific economic interests which differ both from those of the owners of capital and from those of non-owners" (ibid.:234). These economic interests of owner-occupiers are not only "different" than those of private capital and those of tenants; they are "conflicting" as well. Since threats may come from either side, owner-occupiers may find themselves in conflict with private capital *or* with tenants. Similarly, they may forge temporary political alliances with either group in opposing threats that are posed by the other.[6]

Saunders had only just finished this three-class model, however, when he began finding fault with it. Indeed, in 1979, he put forward several arguments that he believed repudiate the entire theory of domestic property classes. First, the neo-Weberian approach is "dependent upon the continuation of specific conditions which are external to the analysis itself" (Saunders, 1979:98). The conditions that allow domestic property to be a source of accumulative wealth—policies of the State, in particular—are contingent upon historical, political, and bureaucratic phenomena that lie outside of the property class model.

6. At this point, Saunders's analysis of homeowner conflict with capitalists and tenants is derived more from Parkin's (1979) theory of "class strategies" than from Marx's theory of class conflict. According to Saunders, homeowners adopt a strategy of "solidarism" when they act to compel concessions from private capitalists; homeowners adopt a strategy of "exclusion" when they act to repel threats from tenants. Interclass conflict is explained in terms of "class strategies" not antagonistic class interests.

Should these conditions change, so that homeownership no longer serves as a profitable source of income, then Saunders argues that "the logic of the Weberian position is that the different tenure categories would no longer constitute distinct property classes, but could only be represented as specific political interest groups" (ibid.).

The second weakness in his own neo-Weberian approach, says Saunders, is that the model is "essentially static." He agrees with Bell (1977) that class "ought to be treated as a relational concept." It is not enough to show that property classes have distinct interests. A model of class conflict must portray antagonistic interests. Theoretical adequacy demands, a "necessarily antagonistic relationship" among property classes—a relational antagonism that Saunders does not discover in his own model.

Finally, he criticizes his own neo-Weberian model for failing to show how the property classes of the homeplace articulate with the economic classes of the workplace. How, for instance, is the house-owning factory worker to be classified "in terms of the overall class system"? Furthermore, if we allow for class structuration through homeownership, how are we to treat the possession of other forms of property, such as works of art, insurance policies, or annuities, which may also be important means of wealth accumulation? These questions can never be answered satisfactorily, Saunders suggests, unless the intermesh between property classes and economic classes can be fully specified. Since the model of domestic property classes does not—probably cannot—specify what this connection might be, the model itself must be rejected.

SAVING SAUNDERS FROM SAUNDERS: GERALDINE PRATT

Geraldine Pratt (1982) suggests that Saunders was premature in rejecting his own model of domestic property classes. If we refine and extending Saunders's original conception, she argues, the model can be made to withstand his later critique.

Pratt begins her rebuttal of Saunders's self-critique by noting that the accumulative potential of domestic property is less contingent and less transitory than Saunders thinks. Although she concedes that the tax subsidies and fiscal policies of the State contribute greatly to making domestic property a profitable investment, she notes that land shortages and fluctuations in private interest rates are important as well. The relative scarcity of domestic property and the impossibility of recouping rates of interest that exceed the rates of a long-term mortgage add considerable value to domestic property. As for the tax and fiscal policies that add so much to housing profits, Pratt insists that Saunders is wrong to dismiss them as temporary historical flukes. These policies favoring the owners of domestic property have not only lasted for over forty years, they have created a self-sustaining constituency of their own—making their repeal very difficult and highly unlikely.

Pratt next identifies a source of housing class conflict that Saunders ignores, refuting his claim that the model is static. Once Saunders concedes that "class ought to be treated as a relational concept," he becomes troubled by the fact that two of his classes, owner-occupiers and tenants, are *not* antagonistically related (Saunders, 1979:96). Pratt, on the other hand, argues that the public policies that make domestic property a source of accumulative wealth do so by effecting massive income transfers from society as a whole (including tenants, of course) into the pockets of owner-occupiers. Presumably, tenants would have an interest in ending or altering such policies and owner-occupiers would have an interest in protecting them. Thus, "an important source of conflict between tenants and house owners centers precisely on such government policies" (Pratt, 1982:489). This conflict is "indirect," for it is "mediated through the state," but it is an antagonistic relationship nonetheless.

According to Pratt, there is also a more "direct" source of conflict between owner-occupiers and tenants. When homeowners act individually to reap the highest market gains from the resale of their houses or when they act collectively to restrict the development of multi-family apartments in their neighborhoods, the aggregate effect is to inflate rents and reduce the availability of tenant housing. More directly still, when homeowners move into a neighborhood in which tenant housing has predominated, they are able to use their greater market power to displace tenants residing there. Inflated rents, shortages of rental housing, and gentrification occurring neighborhood-by-neighborhood make locality-based conflict between owner-occupiers and tenants a familiar and frequent fact of contemporary urban life.

As for Saunders's third criticism of domestic property classes, Pratt agrees that other forms of property may serve as sources of income and that the relationship between property classes and economic classes needs to be specified. She believes, however, that neither of these concessions necessarily invalidates the neo-Weberian model.

After all, the model makes the claim that domestic property is particularly important in structuring class relations, not that domestic property is the only source of property leading to wealth accumulation or the only factor in class structuration. Property classes based on the income potential of annuities or insurance policies, for instance, would no doubt complicate class analysis, but "the logic of domestic property classes would remain intact" (ibid.:493). Furthermore, while it is important to specify what the relations might be between property classes and economic classes, these relations are "open and empirical ones—not ones that a priori invalidate the domestic property class analysis."

Rebutting each argument in Saunders's self-critique, Pratt concludes that his criticisms are "weakly sustained" and that "tenurial divisions *can* form the basis of property class formation, in the Weberian sense of the term class" (ibid.:482). Saunders's original theory of domestic property classes should *not* be rejected.

DOMESTIC PROPERTY CLASSES: A RECONSIDERATION

Throughout her rebuttal of Saunders's self-critique, Pratt's attention is focused on the income potential of domestic property and the conditions, conflicts, and relations surrounding this accumulative element. The model of domestic property classes that she is intent upon defending requires such a focus. I would argue, however, that the usefulness of this model in explaining the cleavages and conflicts of residential neighborhoods is severely limited by its narrow focus upon *economic* interests to the virtual exclusion of all other material interests of domestic property. Indeed, the inadequacy of Saunders's original conception of property interests—an inadequacy that Pratt incorporates into her own modifications—calls the entire model into question, at least as it applies to the locality-based politics of property and place.

Saunders (and, by incorporation, Pratt) originally argued that any collectivity's tenurial and functional relation to domestic property "objectively separates" its housing interests from those of any other. At one point, singling out the differences between the owners and nonowners of domestic property, he enumerated the material advantages of the former tenurial position that are lacking in the latter: greater choice over where to live and the form of accommodation in which to live; greater control over the use of domestic property; and the power to dispose of property through inheritance or sale (Saunders, 1979:84). These "beneficial aspects of owning a house" are declared to be insignificant, however, in structuring housing classes or housing class conflict:

> Although all of this is of undoubted significance in affecting both the life style and life chances of the owner-occupier as compared with the tenant, none of it warrants the identification of house ownership as a basis for class formations in either the Weberian or Marxist sense of that term. It is therefore necessary to go beyond factors such as these and to consider in more detail what is entailed in the right of beneficial use. In other words, it is important to analyze whether the benefits enjoyed by the owner-occupier also extend to financial gain and wealth accumulation. (Ibid.)

As crucial as various "beneficial aspects" of a property position might be in distinguishing the "life style and life chances" of one collectivity from another, they do not constitute or differentiate domestic property classes. Only economic interests can do that; the entreprenurial opportunity for financial gain and wealth accumulation that is present (or absent) in one's relation to domestic property. Only what is popularly known as "property values" can be a basis for class formation and class conflict. Other benefits (or costs) inhering in one's property position—in short, other interests—are excluded from domestic property class analysis.

Such a narrow conception of class *interest* creates serious problems for Saunders's model of class. It creates problems that are more serious still for his model of conflict. These are highlighted, not resolved, by Pratt's modifications.[7]

If economic interest—specifically, the entreprenurial stake that one has in housing equity—is the only basis for differing one class from another,[8] then it is difficult to see how Saunders can claim that

---

7. This is not to dispute Saunders's—and Pratt's—contention that Weberian class theory *requires* such an exclusive focus upon economic interests. I merely suggest that the economic interests of domestic property are too fragile a reed to support an entire theory of urban social relations.

8. Equity may not be the only economic interest that people have in domestic property, as I shall argue in the next chapter, but it *is* the only one that has a place in the neo-Weberian model that is under discussion here. Thus Saunders and Pratt define the accumulative potential of domestic property solely in terms of the "increase in money value of housing" (Saunders, 1978:243), "gains in property values" (Saunders, 1979:84), and "capital gains" (Pratt, 1982:497).

private capital and owner-occupiers are two different classes. After all, they are both tenurially positioned to enjoy the benefits of "financial gain and wealth accumulation" from domestic property. On the basis of economic interests alone, private capital and owner-occupiers would seem to be of the *same* domestic property class (though perhaps of different strata or "fractions") But Saunders assigns them to different classes, after noting that domestic property "functions both for use and accumulation." Whatever accumulative (or economic) interests private capital and owner-occupiers may share, their use interests are different. Consequently, Saunders asserts that their class situations are different. The problem with this assertion is that use interests *cannot* be the basis for class formation within the Weberian scheme that Saunders has adopted. The entrepreneurial stake that one has in accommodation may differentiate lifestyles and life chances, but it cannot differentiate property classes. Saunders's trichotomous model of class, in short, is undermined by his narrow specification of what a class interest might be.

His trichotomous model of conflict, moreover, is jeopardized not only by the exclusion of use interests from the analysis, but by the fact that the economic interests that *are* included are treated nonrelationally. In the abstract, Saunders is squarely within the Marxist tradition in positing interests that are objective, collective, and relational—that is, class interests that are "objectively different and conflicting" relative to those of another class. In practice, however, when it comes time to discuss the "objective conflict of class interests," which Rex and Moore are criticized for *leaving out* of their analysis, Saunders uses Parkin's notion of "class strategies" to explain the "dynamic aspects" of his model, not Marx's notion of class interests (cf. footnote 6, supra). There are hints that classes sometimes act collectively in defense of threatened property values—or, at least, that owner-occupiers do—but Saunders gives little indication that property values are inherently precarious or that one class can realize financial gains from domestic property only at the expense of others. Lacking a relational concept of property interests, he is correct in criticizing his own model for lacking a relational concept of property classes.

Pratt's analysis of conflict is somewhat superior in this regard. The rising property values of the owners of domestic property are directly related to the rising housing costs of nonowners. The property values of owner-occupiers are vulnerable to erosion or attack by the development of multifamily housing by private capital or by the efforts of tenant advocates to eliminate exclusionary zoning and other forms of spatial separation. The homes of tenants are vulnerable to loss as private capital and would-be homeowners, lured into tenant-dominated areas by the prospect of housing bargains and future profits, intentionally or unintentionally fuel gentrification. In each case, the economic interests of various classes are "objectively different and conflicting." In each case, classes are drawn into conflict *because* of their precariously contentious interests.

This represents an improvement over Saunders's model of conflict, because Pratt shifts the analysis away from *strategies* of property classes that are already consciously organized and politically active and toward *interests* of tenurial positions that are antagonistically related, even if classes never actually form or conflict.[9] Nevertheless, Pratt's discussion of gentrification also reveals the limitations of a model of housing class conflict that rests upon economic interests alone. The pursuit of profits may indeed be one of the factors prompting owner-occupiers to settle in neighborhoods with a high proportion of rental housing, and these economic interests may also prompt newcomers to perceive the indigenous tenant population as a threat to their property values. On the other hand, owner-occupiers may also be individually attracted into a neighborhood and collectively drawn into conflict with private capital or with tenants for reasons that have less to do with an economic interest in financial gain and wealth accumulation than with a use interest in pursuing or preserving a stable, safe, and pleasant place to live. Their interest in accommodation may be more important than their interest in accumulation in explaining their individual or collective actions, as well as conflictual interactions with other classes.

On the tenant side, locational conflicts such as gentrification are largely inexplicable without reference to use interests. Possessing no accumulative stake in housing, tenants organize and mobilize on the basis of accommodative interests alone. It is their secure use of shelter that is threatened by the creeping conversion of a neighborhood's rental property into condominiums, cooperatives, or single-family owner-occupied housing. It is their interests in use that binds them

---

9. It should be acknowledged, however, that this relational conception of property class interests is not as explicitly drawn nor as centrally placed in Pratt's analysis as the discussion here might suggest. Furthermore, as the next chapter will indicate, there is much more that Pratt could have said about the relational character of equity, but did not, that would have strengthened considerably her model of class formation and class conflict.

together and orients their collective action toward conflict with those who would cause their displacement. Furthermore, even when gentrification is not an issue, tenants often act collectively to improve the amenity of their surroundings or to defend their neighborhood against threats arising from private developers, public programs like urban renewal, or any number of other sources. Neither Pratt nor Saunders can adequately account for such collective action, since a collectivity's interest in the appreciating equity of domestic property is the *only* basis for class formation and mobilization that they acknowledge.

Use interests are also essential in explaining the frequent resistance of indigenous homeowners to gentrification. Since their property values are often positively affected by the influx of affluent newcomers, the basis for collective, conflictual action of long-time homeowners against the "gentry" cannot be attributed to the narrowly defined economic interest proposed by Saunders and Pratt. Furthermore, like the neighborhood's tenants, long-time owner-occupiers will occasionally find themselves in conflict with private developers, public planners, and any number of other groups over issues other than gentrification, issues that may also affect their property values only indirectly. The security or amenity of property and place, the ability to use and develop property in accordance with one's own desires and needs, the "home rule" that residents are collectively able to exercise over the future development of their neighborhood—threats to any of these "use interests" may politically mobilize homeowners just as quickly and surely as any threat to their equity stake in domestic property.

My basic objection to the theory of domestic property classes proposed by Saunders and modified by Pratt, therefore, is that an interest in equity is the only interest that is causally significant. Other interests of domestic property, which may also be causally related to the differentiation of locality-based groups and the generation of locality-based conflict, are overlooked. So intent are Saunders and Pratt upon constructing a model of *class*, faithfully following the rigid lines of a Weberian blueprint, that they wed themselves to a definition of *interest* that is simply too narrow to account for the multiple cleavages and conflicts of residentially diverse neighborhoods. Their exclusive focus on financial gain and wealth accumulation, moreover, tends to undermine the model of class and conflict that they do construct.

There is reason to agree with Saunders (1984), then, when he later concludes that the analysis of locality-based struggles in the "consumption sector" should go "beyond housing classes." The attempt to construct a neo-Weberian model of class, according to Saunders, "elides the analytically distinct spheres of consumption and production"; it is inappropriate and confusing to apply a conceptual tool that was developed specifically to analyze relations constituted in the sphere of production to examine and explain "relations constituted through processes of consumption, even when (as in the case of home ownership) private ownership of the means of consumption may function as a source of revenue" (ibid.:206).[10] Saunders's argument, in effect, is that the concept of "class" is stretched too far when applied to the cleavages and conflicts of consumption sectors like the residential neighborhood. While not disputing this assessment, I believe that focusing on this concept of domestic property "class" prevents the concept of domestic property "interest" from being stretched *far enough* to explain how these locality-based cleavages and conflicts arise. I agree that this model of class should be abandoned.

What should *not* be abandoned is the attempt to construct a model of collective action on the basis of people's tenurial and functional relation to domestic property. In this regard, there is much in the neo-Weberian approach worth saving. Beginning with Rex and Moore's idea that "the control of domestic property" may constitute a basis for the differentiation and conflict of urban groups, continuing with Saunders's notion of "objectively different and conflicting" interests that inhere in a collectivity's "material situation" vis-à-vis domestic property, and ending with Pratt's attempt to describe a relational conflict of economic interests between homeowners and tenants, the theory of domestic property classes establishes a structural basis *within the locality itself* for the social groups and social conflicts that tend to proliferate there. Arising from the locality-based relations of domestic property, these cleavages and conflicts reflect "a significant divergence of real material interests" (Saunders, 1978:247). They can neither be dismissed as "false consciousness" nor trivialized as "displaced class conflict"—pale reflections of the cleavages and conflicts of the workplace. Even the neo-Weberian emphasis upon financial

---

10. This does not mean that Saunders embraces, in the end, the neo-Marxist attempt to explain locality-based conflict in terms of the production-based interests and action of economic classes. Domestic property *does* objectively separate the economic and political interests of different tenure groups (Saunders, 1979: 97). These interests can be the basis for group formation and intergroup conflict in urban settings, political struggles that have a life and significance of their own, apart from the conflict between capital and labor.

4

Domestic Property as a "Bundle of Interests"

Any given parcel of land represents an interest and any given
locality is thus an aggregate of land-based interests. That is,
each landowner (or person who otherwise has some interest
in the prospective use of a given piece of land) has in mind a
certain future for that parcel which is linked somehow with
his or her well-being. . . . We need to see each geographical
map . . . not merely as a demarcation of legal, political, or
topographical features, but as a mosaic of competing land
interests capable of strategic coalition and action.

—HARVEY MOLOTCH (1976:310–11)

The Marxist theory of collective action suggests that objective, relational interests may be the basis for group formation and intergroup
conflict. The neo-Weberian theory of Saunders and Pratt suggests that
such interests may inhere in the tenurial and functional relations of
domestic property. Combining these theoretical strands, we are led to
the proposition that the cleavages and conflicts of residential neighborhoods may be explained, to one degree or another, by the different
and conflicting interests that people have in a neighborhood's land
and buildings. A better understanding of the conditions for collective
action on a territorial basis begins with an understanding of the "interest mosaic" that domestic property engenders.

We pick up where Saunders and Pratt leave off. The particular
strength of the neo-Weberian approach was to rest its model of consumption-based cleavages on "an objective assessment of class interests" (Saunders, 1979:94). Its particular weakness was to restrict this
"objective assessment" to a single interest, the appreciating equity of
domestic property. Saunders (ibid.:84), especially, acknowledged

43

other "beneficial aspects" of domestic property, but even though these were said to be of "undoubted significance in affecting both the life style and life chances" of one group as opposed to another, they were excluded from a class analysis focused exclusively upon "financial gain and wealth accumulation." Without the constraints of a class model, however, these other benefits (and costs) of one's "material situation" can be readmitted into the analysis of group formation and intergroup conflict and given equal weight with whatever economic interest a person (or group) may have in equity. Furthermore, without the constraints of a Weberian conception of "class," a Marxist conception of "interest" can be more freely applied, both to the analysis of equity and to other entrepreneurial interests inhering in various property positions. Particularly important are a conception and analysis of domestic property interests that capture their *relational* character, for it is the contingent, precarious, and contentious nature of these interests that bestows an action orientation upon different property positions, drawing one property interest group into antagonistic relation with another.

These essential characteristics will be examined more closely later on in discussing what it means to say that domestic property interests are "material," "objective," "collective," and "relational," and that such interests impose an "action orientation" upon various property positions. Let me begin, however, by adding a handful of interests to the single interest proposed by Saunders and Pratt.

DOMESTIC PROPERTY INTERESTS

On the most general level, there are only two domestic property interests: accommodation and accumulation. People may have an entrepreneurial and strategic interest in the use value of domestic property, utilizing residential land and buildings for personal accommodation, or they may have an interest in the exchange value of domestic property, utilizing residential land and buildings for financial gain and wealth accumulation. Depending on their tenurial and functional relation to domestic property, therefore, some people will have an accommodative interest in housing, some will have an accumulative interest, and some will have both.

Accommodation and accumulation can be more accurately described, however, as categories or clusters of property interests. They are ways of generally characterizing two different sets of material interests that people possess by virtue of their particular property positions. Three "accommodative" (or "use") interests can be distinguished: security, amenity, and autonomy. Likewise, three "accumulative" (or "exchange") interests can be distinguished: equity, liquidity, and legacy. These half dozen domestic property interests do not exhaust the field; each could be subdivided again and again to yield an ever-longer list of interests, some of which may have special political significance in certain situations. These six, however, describe the principal lines of demarcation that will most often be found within a locality's "interest mosaic" and, as I shall argue in the next chapter, the principal lines of social cleavage that will most often differentiate the "interest groups" within a locality's population.

Equity

Since "property values" figure so prominently in the neo-Weberian perspective that serves as our theoretical point of departure, it is appropriate to begin with a discussion of equity. Thus do we acknowledge a certain continuity with the work of Saunders and Pratt, even as we leave them behind, for I shall attribute a relational character to this economic interest that neither of them fully developed and then proceed to other interests of exchange and use that neither of them recognized.

Equity refers to the unencumbered value inherent in land and buildings. In a market economy, equity is the fair market value placed on a parcel of real property minus any debt that encumbers that property; hence, it is the value that exists once a mortgage, a lien, or any other liability has been paid off (or subtracted). Part of this property value is created by the dollars and labor of the individual owner (or occupant), an investment of wealth and sweat that is poured into the property over a period of time to purchase, build, maintain, and improve it. Another part, often the larger part, is less a product of the owner's (or occupant's) investment than a gratuitous windfall bestowed by the surrounding society. This "social increment" is a function of numerous factors: urbanization and the economic development of an entire region (Yearwood, 1968:22; Harvey, 1974:240; Engels, 1935:23); public investment in neighborhood services, facilities, and infrastructure (Roweis and Scott, 1978:71; Mollenkopf, 1981a:329; Perin, 1977:160; Cox, 1981:434); public subsidies to property owners in the form of tax benefits, mortgage underwriting, and below-market mortgage rates (Saunders, 1979:91–92; Pratt, 1982:489; Harvey, 1974:243; Stone, 1978); and the relative scarcity of land, housing, and favorable locations (Pahl, 1975:276–77, 291, 293; Carey, 1976:257; Harvey, 1974:240, 243–45; Edel, 1977:4–5; George, 1975). Socially generated equity is also a function of the general amenity of a parcel's locality. As Cox (1981:434) has noted, "A variety of property-value studies . . . find that such resources as school quality, public safety, quiet, and even views of Pacific sunsets are indeed reflected in house values." Whether created by the personal labor and monetary investment of the property's owner or by the investments, policies, and development of the surrounding society, equity accrues to individual parcels of real property and belongs to whomever owns that property. Indeed, in the United States, equity is popularly known and commonly defined as "the owner's interest."

Domestic property, therefore, can be regarded as a kind of financial repository, where a certain level of personal savings and publicly created wealth are embedded in residential land and buildings. Unlike a savings account at a local bank, however, the financial stake that one may have in domestic property is neither protected nor predictable. Equity in land and buildings is not a private, autonomous transaction between owner and owned, where a dollar in is always a dollar out. Equity is, instead, a relational advantage that is largely contingent upon the "transactions" of many other actors. To paraphrase Carey (1976:257), that which gives value to domestic property is social, not individual.

Contingent upon so many people, upon so many factors in the surrounding society, equity is intrinsically precarious. That which gives value can also take value away should circumstances change. Even that equity which an individual creates and nurtures by his or her own investment can be wiped out by changes in the maintenance or amenity of proximate parcels of domestic property, by changes in the level (or kinds) of private and public investment in the surrounding neighborhood, by changes in the local economy, or by changes in the public policies of local, state, or federal governments.[1] One's equity, in short, is precariously related to the actions of others, near and far. An entrepreneurial interest in the equity of one's *own* parcel of domestic property carries with it, therefore, a strategic interest in the equity and use of *surrounding* parcels, in addition to a strategic interest in numerous other factors that may affect one's financial stake for

1. It is worth noting that public investment, like private investment, can fluctuate for a given locality, sometimes creating equity, sometimes destroying it. There is public disinvestment, just as there is private. As Perin (1977:160) has pointed out, "Not only bankers redline: municipal governments do, too."

better or worse. Molotch describes this relational character rather well:

> One has interest in an adjacent parcel, and if a noxious use should appear, one's own parcel may be harmed. More subtle still is the emergence of concern for an aggregate of parcels: one sees that one's future is bound to the future of a larger area, that the future enjoyment of financial benefit flowing from a given parcel will derive form the general future of the proximate aggregate of parcels. (Molotch, 1976:311)

Since equity may be "harmed" as well as enhanced, it is not only a precarious advantage, but often a contentious one as well. The financial benefit that one group of people may hope to enjoy from their parcels may be easily threatened by the "noxious use" that others have planned for adjacent or proximate parcels. Thus, in precariously relating the financial future of one's own parcel to another, equity may also contentiously relate one local interest group to another.

Liquidity

On the most basic level, liquidity is synonymous with "ease of sale," the facility with which one can convert a parcel's equity into cash. Liquidity is more than "salability," however, because domestic property may also produce a stream of income *without* being sold. Residential land and buildings, for instance, may generate a cash income from monthly rents. They may be used for collateral, permitting the owner to raise cash for personal use or profitable investment. They may be used as an annuity; that is, the equity that has accumulated in a parcel of property may be converted into an annual income for the property's owner, even if the owner continues to inhabit the house.[2] Domestic property may also be used as a tax shelter, reducing the property owner's tax liability on income derived from other sources.[3]

Liquidity is clearly related to equity. Although that relation is seldom directly proportional, it is generally true that the higher the equity, the greater a property's income potential; the lower the equity, the lower the income potential. Anything that affects the equity in a

2. Originally developed to help elderly homeowners to realize an immediate cash benefit from the equity that is "locked up" in their homes, financial arrangements of this sort are becoming more and more common.

3. Discussions of the size and significance of this "tax break" can be found in Parcel (1982:199), Achtenberg and Marcuse (1983:216), and Dolbeare (1986).

parcel of domestic property will usually affect the income that can be realized from that parcel.[4] Liquidity, therefore, is precariously contingent upon the same sorts of social factors as equity.

Liquidity also has a life of its own. There are factors that affect liquidity rather differently than they affect equity, and the two may sometimes be inversely related. Favorable tax breaks, public rental subsidies, and overcrowding of rental property in a tight housing market can generate a stream of income that is much higher than a neighborhood's severely depressed property values would seem to allow. Conversely, it is possible for a property with a high value, in which an owner has a large equity stake, to be unsalable or unrentable because of high interest rates, high vacancy rates, the low amenity of the surrounding neighborhood, or the low status of the surrounding neighbors. Public restrictions such as rent control, anticonversion ordinances, and zoning may also limit the income that can be derived from a parcel of property that is otherwise very valuable.

Aside from the fact that equity and liquidity can vary somewhat independently, they should be treated as separate property interests for the simple reason that domestic property is financially used in two very different ways. It can be used to accumulate wealth through appreciating property values, a benefit realized upon the property's sale. Or it can be used to generate a stream of income, a benefit realized throughout the property's tenure. These different uses reflect different ways that people respond to the financial potential of local land and housing. They represent two different relational advantages that inhere in one's tenurial and functional relation to domestic property.

Legacy

Domestic property is an inheritable estate. It is often the single most valuable possession passed from one generation to another. Since inherited property may be used for personal shelter by one's heirs, just as it may be exchanged for income, there is reason to consider legacy as much of a "use interest" as an "exchange interest." Indeed, many homeowners who bequeath domestic property to their children do so in the hope that one of their children will personally occupy the house.

4. Feagin (1982:42) suggests that the opposite may also be true, that the more a property changes hands—in other words, the greater its liquidity—the more its value may increase.

Such a legacy of use, however, is not as common in the United States as it once might have been, or as common as it tends to be in other countries.[5] More typical at present, though hard data are difficult to find, are cases in which the bequeathed property is quickly sold and the proceeds divided among several heirs, or the property is rented, providing the heirs with a steady income. In short, it is frequently the *exchange* value of domestic property, not its use value, that is the greater interest of those who bequeath the legacy and, probably even more frequently, of those who receive the legacy.[6]

Though closely related to the equity and liquidity of domestic property, legacy for good reason can be regarded as a separate property interest: first, because there *is* the potential for one's heirs to inhabit the property; second, because the very *futurity* of the interest casts the property's profitability in a different light; and third, because some factors, such as public tax policies, affect legacy differently from equity and liquidity. Consequently, an overriding interest in legacy may lead one to act more readily in improving or defending the amenity of the property and locality that one's hiers may someday inhabit. It may lead one to ignore short-term threats to equity or liquidity that might instantly mobilize those with *less* of an interest in legacy. An interest in legacy can also bestow a strategic interest in policies affecting trusts and estates that may temporarily overshadow any similar interest in policies affecting capital gains or annual income. In short, legacy may involve a person (or group) in a set of relationships and bestow an action orientation that is rather different from the relational ties and action orientation of equity or liquidity.

5. The remarks of Pierre Schafer, secretary-general of the French National Federation of Promoters and Builders, are instructive in this regard. He notes that "the great difference between France and America is that in France the home is the patrimony, it is what a man will leave to his children, it is *immortal*. In America, a man's home is a consumer good; he uses it like other consumer goods and buys a new one when he is tired of this one" (Mayer, 1978:5). Similarly, when a house is inherited, it is commonly treated as a disposable consumer good by a person's heirs, rather than a "patrimony" that must be inhabited by them and later passed along to their children.

6. Legacy might also include the notion of domestic property serving as a kind of "insurance policy" against the ruining effects of future disability, disasters, or old age, a homeowner's "legacy" to himself or herself. While such an expanded notion of legacy tends to blur the line between legacy and the other two exchange interests, homeowners in countries like the USA with relatively low expenditures for social welfare frequently regard their domestic property as a financial hedge against future calamity. Such an interest in "legacy" may have political consequences that are very different than those that flow directly from a property owner's interest in equity or liquidity. See, for example, Kemeny (1980; 1981).

Security

With security, we turn from interests of exchange to those of use. If *exchange* depends on domestic property being "worth something," *use* depends, first and foremost, on the property being safely and predictably "with someone." It depends on someone having a secure hold over whatever housing he or she occupies. Security refers to the confidence that one has in that "hold." One's access to shelter is stable. One possesses what Hartman (1984) has called "the right to stay put."

Even more basic than security of tenure, but closely related, is the security of physical safety. Domestic property shelters one from the weather, shields one from the lawless, and, if there is a garden, nourishes one as well. This is the primary interest that most of humanity has in domestic property. Tawney said it well:

> As far as the mass of mankind are concerned, the need which private property other than personal possessions does still often satisfy, though imperfectly and precariously, is the need for security. To the small investors, who are the majority of property owners, though owning only an insignificant fraction of the property in existence, its meaning is simple. It is not wealth or power, or even leisure from work. It is safety. (Tawney, 1920:72)

Security as physical safety is a function, in part, of the structural condition, state of repair, and architectural design of the property itself. In this respect, security and amenity (another use interest) go hand-in-hand. Security is also a function, however, of the *social* climate from which the occupant of domestic property seeks shelter. A milieu in which assault, arson, or theft is common jeopardizes the physical safety of the occupants of even the most structurally sound dwelling. Security as safety does not stop at one's front door, therefore. The security of domestic property and the security of the surrounding place are interrelated.

Security of tenure is even more a function of this interrelationship of property and place. While stable and predictable access to domestic property is largely dependent upon the legal arrangements under which one's occupancy and use are secured, one's ability to "stay put" is also affected by local and extralocal factors that may make security a precarious advantage indeed. Cycles of private investment, disinvestment, and reinvestment, for instance, not only raise and lower the exchange value of domestic property in a given locality, but often exert tremendous displacement pressures on renters and home-owners alike. Abandonment and redlining on one side of the cycle, and gentrification, condominium conversions, and office building development on the other, can threaten whatever tenurial security the indigenous population of a residential neighborhood might have (Hartman, 1984; LeGates and Hartman, 1981; Smith, 1982).

Public investment—and disinvestment—in a neighborhood can also jeopardize security. The kind of massive removal of thousands of residents typical of the urban renewal and highway construction programs of the 1950s and 1960s is less common today, but direct government-initiated displacement still occurs in many public works projects. Furthermore, as Hartman (1984:303) has pointed out, "a great deal of ostensibly private-sector displacement is supported by or [is] the indirect result of government policies, programs, or actions." Low-interest loans for downtown redevelopment or housing rehabilitation, tax policies that encourage luxury renovation of historic buildings, landlord-tenant laws that permit easy evictions, or credit laws that permit easy foreclosures are only a few of the factors that may adversely affect residential security—whatever the form of legal tenure under which a parcel of property is held.

I do not deny that different tenurial arrangements provide different degrees of security. But residential security, like the interests of exchange already discussed, is also a social product of the parcel's neighborhood and society. Security is not merely a relative advantage, secured by law, but a relational advantage, made precarious by its contingency upon many social factors. Furthermore, to the extent that one's security can be undermined or threatened by other actors, near and far, as they avidly pursue their own economic or political interests, security is not only a precarious advantage, but a contentious one as well.

Amenity

Amenity refers to the quantity and quality of one's living space. At its most basic level, amenity is a matter of sound housing in good repair. It is what housing activists and public health officials have long sought to achieve via health, safety, and building codes seeking to improve the sanitation, ventilation, structural strength, fire retardance, and state of repair of the nation's housing. Amenity and security overlap at this point.

Amenity has many gradations, however, and quickly rises beyond health and safety. It includes a broad range of quantitative and qualitative variations in the size, style, layout, design, and decoration of housing, as well as broad variation in the acreage, topography, vegetation, and other physical attributes of residential land. All of these make a parcel of domestic property more or less comfortable, pleasant, and appealing. All are part of a property's amenity.

Amenity, like security, has a large locational component. The amenity of one's personal living space is inseparable from the safety, health, beauty, and general ambience of the communal living space—that is, one's neighborhood. This locational component also includes the availability of essential services and the proximity of jobs, stores, recreational facilities, and the like.[7] Public services, in particular, tend to be delivered on a neighborhood-by-neighborhood basis in the United States. "Since the quality and quantity of these services varies considerably from one neighborhood to another, the nature of the public services that an individual receives is dependent in large measure on which neighborhood he lives in" (O'Brien, 1975:9). Amenity varies from place to place, then, as much as it does from one property to another.

Thus, even though amenity is undoubtedly a function of individual efforts and tastes—a private transaction between the resident and the residence—it is also a social, relational advantage. It is a function of the building codes by which municipalities regulate the health and safety of private residences and public places. It is a function of zoning regulations and subdivision controls, regulating density, lot size, building size, and the development of new land. It is a function of the locational decisions of private capital in siting factories, commercial centers, and residential developments, as well as those decisions of public officials in providing public facilities and social services.

Closer to home, amenity is precariously contingent upon what neighbors are doing with *their* property and what is happening in the neighborhood as a whole. The amenity of personal living space rises and falls in accordance with that of the communal living space. The *lack* of neighborhood amenity has, in fact, come to be seen as a type

---

7. The proximity of people who share racial, ethnic, religious, or class characteristics, as well as the proximity of kith and kin who may be relied upon for mutual aid and emotional support, must also be included within the locational component of amenity. Despite the tendency of many sociologists to portray the modern urban neighborhood as a "community of limited liability" (Janowitz, 1952), a "community without propinquity" (Webber, 1963; 1964), or a "community liberated" (Wellman and Leighton, 1979), the proximate presence of people like ourselves and/or people with whom we have built sentimental bonds of reciprocity and trust remains an important part of the "quality of life" of the places in which we live.

of "housing deprivation." Drawing upon U.S. Census data, Achtenberg and Marcuse (1983:205) conclude: "Today, neighborhood conditions are the most serious problem of housing quality. In 1979, 73 percent of all renters and 62 percent of all homeowners found their neighborhoods to be deficient in one or more respects." An earlier study, by Frieden and Solomon (1977:133), discovered that "four million households in 1973 were living in adequate housing, not overcrowded, at rents within their means, but found public services or street conditions so objectionable that they wanted to move from the neighborhood." They go on to say: "In some cities, what used to be a 'housing shortage' has now turned into a 'neighborhood shortage.' There the problem for many people is not simply finding a decent house, but finding one in a neighborhood with adequate streets, schools, and public services."

Amenity encompasses, therefore, both the individual and the social, both private space and public space. As much as the other interests of domestic property, amenity is precariously—and contentiously—contingent upon the general future of the parcels and place surrounding one's own parcels of domestic property.

Autonomy

Autonomy refers to both the degree of control that one is able to exercise over domestic property and the degree of individuation that domestic property "impresses" upon its residents. Autonomy as *control* is essentially a matter of one's ability to use, shape, and develop his or her personal living space independently of the dictates of another. This interest is captured nicely in the remarks of a homeowner who was asked by Rakoff to contrast renting an apartment with owning a house:

> Well, if you live in an apartment and there are things that really bug you, you don't ever get into the thought of changing them. . . . Where, if you're in a house, and that wall really bothers you, you can always take it out, you know. This kind of thing. You can get personally, more personally involved, I think, in a house that you own, because there is always the possibility you can change it. There's a control there; whether or not you use it doesn't matter. It's there. (Rakoff, 1977:99)

Autonomy as *individuation* refers to the contribution that domestic property makes to personal privacy, power, and identity. The homeplace functions for many persons as a "realm of personal control in a world where he or she generally feels impotent" (ibid.:101). It is a private, separate sphere, providing "some insulation against the cruel self-images imposed by capitalism" (Cox, 1981:433).[8] Domestic property may also function as a status symbol, raising or lowering personal esteem in the eyes of oneself and one's neighbors. As Logan (1978:407) has pointed out, "a home is not just where you live; it is a location in a well-developed status ecology." Part of the stake that one may have in a parcel of domestic property is the prestige associated with occupying a distinctive house or residing in a highly regarded neighborhood.[9] In all of these ways, autonomy and identity tend to become tightly intertwined.

On a more macro level, the autonomy of domestic property has been associated with the political independence of individuals and the "home rule" of local areas. The notion that personal control over domestic property provides a basis for an independent, self-governing citizenry is a recurrent theme of political theory and popular belief. In ancient Greece, for example, only those men who had a private space—"a house with slaves and women, in which basic necessities of life were taken care of and to which one would retire from the public sphere in order to 'refuel'" (Van Gunsteren, 1979:261)—were allowed to be free citizens. In early America, there was common acceptance of the view that "propertied men differed in kind from unpropertied men" (Scott, 1977:75). The former were believed to possess a moderation of desire, a freedom of thought, and an independence of political judgment lacking in those who owned no land. Only landowners were permitted to vote.

Although the United States long ago extended the franchise, there is still a cultural tendency to associate autonomy in the private realm of domestic property with independence and participation in the public, political arena. Those who exercise greater control over their private space, by virtue of *owning* domestic property, are believed to participate more freely and fully in the locality's public affairs.[10] Perin

8. A detailed review of the "housing and identity" literature can be found in Duncan (1982:111–14, 120–22). See also Gray (1982:283).

9. There is an obvious overlap here between autonomy and amenity. Indeed, it will sometimes be hard to say whether an individual (or group) is "interested" in preserving or promoting the amenity of property and place primarily because of the comfort, safety, or pleasantness that this might afford, or because of the prestige or particularity that might be lost or gained.

10. Counterposed to this "popular belief" in a necessary link between property ownership and political participation—in America, a belief rooted in the political thought of Thomas Jefferson—is another political tradition, rooted in the thought of Marx. This latter tradition associates the ownership of domestic property with political quiescence. An introduction to the Marxist prespective on homeownership can be found in Engels (1935), Angotti (1977), Clarke and Ginsberg (1975), Harvey (1978), and Kemeny (1980).

(1977:56) has described this lingering ideological association between homeownership and citizenship in the starkest terms: "Homeowners are full-fledged citizens. Renters are not."

Personal autonomy has also extended into the political realm in the guise of "home rule." A social counterpart to the personal control that individuals exercise (or would like to exercise) over their own living space is found in the collective control that most America communities seek over the future development of their communal living space. Planning, zoning, and land-use restrictions of every stripe are popularly regarded as *local* prerogatives, and any delegation of land-use control to authorities far removed from the local level tends to be routinely denounced and vigorously resisted.

Of all the interests of domestic property, however, autonomy would seem to be the least social, the least relational. The degree of privacy and control that one enjoys over domestic property seems solely a function of one's personal, tenurial situation. Yet it is also true that autonomy is regularly affected by the surrounding social environment. Autonomy of use and development is partially a function of whatever land-use controls, building codes, rental guidelines, or anticonversion ordinances happen to be in effect, now or later. Autonomy of use and development may also be contingent upon the social relationship that exists between the property owner and a third-party lender. Most mortgage and development loans carry some stipulation of prior inspection and approval by the lender for any major changes that the property owner may later plan for the mortgaged parcel. The latitude that an owner has in using his or her property is even a function, in small measure, of neighborhood norms— the expectations that one's neighbors may have concerning the maintenance, design, and function of domestic property (cf., Galster and Hesser, 1982). As for nonowners, whatever privacy or control they possess may be mostly a function of their lease agreement, but the terms of that tenurial arrangement are themselves, to a greater or lesser degree, a social product of the landlord-tenant laws and regulations surrounding rental property.

Autonomy is a "relational" advantage, then, in the sense that the degree of control that one is able to exercise over a parcel is contingent upon numerous social factors. Autonomy is as much a precarious product of the social environment as it is a legal prerogative of the property's tenurial situation. Furthermore, to the extent that part of its precariousness is due to the political activity of other groups pursuing *their* advantage, to the detriment of one's own, autonomy is also inherently contentious. An interest in autonomy, therefore, not only draws one into relation with various policies, institutions, and norms that delimit one's privacy and control over domestic property, but draws one into relations with social groups that may threaten the autonomy that one already has.

A "BUNDLE OF INTERESTS"

These six relational advantages of domestic property might be treated analytically as housing preferences (or "values"); housing services (or "utilities"); or, in the jargon of real estate law, as "sticks" in the "bundle of rights" associated with any parcel of real property. I prefer to treat them as "interests." Within the Marxist meaning of that term, the attributes that make them "interests" are their material, objective, collective, and relational character, as well as the action orientation that they bestow upon different domestic property positions.

To say that these six advantages are *material*, first of all, is to claim for equity, liquidity, legacy, security, amenity, and autonomy little more than that they originate in relations that surround a physical entity—land and buildings used for shelter. In addition, with the possible exception of autonomy, they all affect the physical or economic well-being of those who have a personal stake in such property. Social cleavages based on these interests, therefore, reflect real differences in the physical and economic circumstances of different populations, not merely differences in ideology or status. As Saunders described these "material" differences for one such population:

> Owner-occupiers, for example, form a distinct sectoral interest not because as property owners they mainly *believe* that they have the same sort of stake in the capitalist system, nor because their lifestyle (e.g., suburbanism) leads them to *claim* a superior status to that of non-owners, but because the objective conditions of their material existence are such as to drive a wedge between their interests and life-chances and those of non-owners. (Saunders, 1984:207)

These six advantages are *objective* in the sense that one's position in relation to domestic property carries a probability of particular benefits, a susceptibility to particular costs, and a propensity to act in certain ways that inhere in the position itself, regardless of whether the incumbent of that position is aware of this state of affairs. One's property position is a combination of tenure and function: the legal arrangement by which one's use of a parcel is temporarily or permanently secured, and the particular accumulative or accommodative use to which the property is actually put. Different tenures and functions combine to yield different sets (and levels) of the six advantages previously discussed. These advantages represent the current stake that one has in domestic property. They are what has been called "entrepreneurial interests."

Since property interests originate in one's tenurial and functional relation to domestic property, not in one's "subjective" attitudes toward it, a person (or group) does not need to be *aware* of his or her entrepreneurial stake or of the precariousness or contentiousness of that stake, for someone else to gauge what those interests might be. It is not even necessary for a person to want those interests, or to defend or pursue them, for an outside observer to assess both the entrepreneurial interests of his or her property position and the relation of those interests to social factors that may threaten or enhance them. There will be times, in fact, when an outside observer can make a judgment of a person's (or a group's) entrepreneurial and strategic interests that is more accurate than that which is made by the "interested" party. Therefore, the six interests of domestic property are "objective" in a double sense. They inhere in one's "objective" relation to land and buildings used for shelter, and they can be "objectively" assessed by an uninterested observer.

To assert that domestic property interests are *collective* is not to embrace the dubious thesis that interests are structural properties of collectivities, having nothing to do with individual actors.[11] Interests are collective only in the sense that people who share a common relation to domestic property are presumed to share a common set of interests. These common interests are a latent, relational bond, existing among similarly situated individuals, which *may* become the basis for solidarity and collective action among persons who are otherwise isolated and very different.[12] Whether they *do* lead to group formation

11. Criticism of this thesis can be found in Giddens (1979:189). See, as well, Saunders's (1979) critique of Poulantzes' structuralist contention that class interests contain *no* individualist elements.

12. For Marx, common material interests are the *only* basis for solidarity in a capitalist society where the individual is "separated from the community, withdrawn into himself, wholly preoccupied with his private interest and acting in accordance with his private caprice." Under capitalism, "the only bond between men is natural necessity, need and private interest, the preservation of their property, and their egoistic persons" (Marx, 1972a:41). Although my own view is far less extreme, since I would readily acknowledge the continued existence (and political significance) of sentimental bonds among the proximate residents of modern, urban neighborhoods, the kinds of material bonds that Marx emphasized will draw most of my attention in the present study.

and mobilization will depend upon multiple conditions of consciousness and organization to convert this latent bond into a collective political reality.

I have spoken of equity, liquidity, legacy, security, amenity, and autonomy being *relational* in several ways. I have indicated, first and foremost, that these advantages are "social," that they are contigent upon and conditioned by numerous factors in the social environment surrounding any parcel of domestic property. Persons do, of course, have an individual stake, a "private interest," in using and enjoying whatever domestic property is at their disposal. But that stake is invariably defined, limited, threatened, or enhanced by the market forces, public policies, and social conditions of the encapsulating social structure. Marx's comments in *The Grundrisse* are particularly relevant, in this regard:

> The point is . . . that private interest is itself already a socially determined interest, which can only be achieved within the conditions established by society and through the means that society affords, and that it is thus linked to the reproduction of these conditions and means. It is certainly the intent of private individuals that is at stake; but its content, as well as the form and the means of its realization, is only given by social conditions independent of all these individuals. (Marx, 1971:65–66)

I have also spoken of an interest's relational character as being "locational," indicating that equity, liquidity, legacy, security, amenity, and autonomy are not only a function of the domestic property in which one has a stake, but of the locality in which that property is situated. Some of the most important "social conditions" affecting domestic property interests, in other words, are those that are closest to home, those that are associated with the parcels and actions of one's neighbors. To paraphrase the passage from Molotch (1976: 311), quoted earlier, one's future is bound to the future of a larger area, since the enjoyment of financial benefit and personal use flowing from a given parcel of domestic property will derive from the general future of the proximate aggregate of parcels. The relational advantages of domestic property link together neighboring parcels and neighboring actors in a "community of fate."[13] Those who have a stake in *property* have a stake in *place* as well.

13. "Community of fate" comes from Logan (1978), although the way that the term is used here differs from Logan's focus upon the chance for social mobility associated with a given locality. My own use of the term is closer to that of Blum and

The relational character of domestic property interests is also evident in what I have repeatedly described as their "precariousness" and "contentiousness." They are precarious because their very contingency upon so many "social" and "locational" factors makes them intrinsically susceptible to fluctuation, erosion, or loss. But these factors must not be reified. The precariousness of one's property interests is not merely a matter of blind, "natural" forces taking their inevitable toll upon the fragile advantages that one may hold. Rather, it is primarily a consequence of other actors pursuing *their* advantage at the expense of one's own. Interests may be jeopardized, in other words, by the actions of others. Conversely, one's own actions, in defending or promoting one's property interests, may jeopardize the interests of others. Thus people may find themselves antagonistically related, even if they neither recognize nor want such enmity, simply because of a different and conflicting stake in domestic property. Their interests are objectively contentious.

The relational advantages of domestic property, therefore, both embody and establish a number of social relationships: between a parcel of property and the economic, political, legal, and social structures surrounding the locality; between one parcel and the "proximate aggregate of parcels" within the locality; and between one person and another having a common or conflicting stake in domestic property. To have an interest in a parcel of domestic property, within a specific territorial space, is to become enmeshed in a complex web of local and extralocal relations that affect one's advantage, for better or worse, and that "orient" one's behavior in a particular way.

The *action orientation* that these interests bestow upon various property positions reflects the propensity of people to act in defense of their own well-being. To the extent that one's well-being is tied to his or her entrepreneurial stake in domestic property, whatever happens to threaten or, possibly, to enhance the equity, liquidity, legacy, security, amenity, or autonomy of a persons's property position will tend to prompt an active response from the "interested" party. The likelihood of such action, particularly defensive action, is made greater (and somewhat predictable) by the precariousness of these domestic property interests.

Kingston (1984:175), who speak of homeowners sharing "an important economic fate with their neighbors" because of the sensitivity of their property values to changes in the neighborhood's social environment. A similar idea is expressed by Qadeer (1981) who speaks of a "web of externalities" in describing the economic, social, and functional "interlinkages" that exist among individual parcels of urban land.

These interests bestow not only a propensity to act, but a propensity to act with or against other people. There is a latent tendency for the incumbents of the same property position, sharing a common set of interests, to act *collectively* in defense (or enhancement) of those interests. Similarly, there is a latent tendency for the incumbents of different property positions, having antagonistic domestic property interests, to act *contentiously* in defense (or enhancement) of their respective interests.[14] Whether this dual "orientation" of personal behavior actually leads to collective action and intergroup conflict will depend on many conditions of consciousness and organization. Even when people's interests are threatened, there is no certainty that they will act collectively or contentiously—or even that they will act at all. There is only a *possibility* that they will behave in this way, though that possibility is made more probable by the property interests that are theirs.

In the end, it is this probability of patterned and predictable behavior that provides the principal reason for treating the six relational advantages of domestic property as a "bundle of interests," rather than preferences, utilities, or rights. To regard these advantages as property *interests*, within the Marxist meaning of that term, is to discover a means by which collective action and intergroup conflict *on a territorial basis* might be explained. Various theoretical links between these locality-based interests and locality-based action can be inferred from the preceding discussion, summarized as follows:

- Because these interests are *precarious*, people will tend to act.
- Because these interests are *material*, people will tend to act somewhat predictably, along lines prescribed by their personal stake in domestic property.
- Because these interests are *social* and *locational*, people will tend to act strategically, responding to changes in specific economic, political, legal, and social factors to which their interests are intrinsically related.
- Because these interests are *collective*, people will tend to act cooperatively in relation to those with a similar stake in domestic property.

14. However, property interests that are "different" are not always "antagonistic." Nor will the incumbents of different property positions inevitably be on opposite sides of every political issue. Cooperation, rather than conflict, is occasionally possible *across* the political divide created by different property positions and interests.

- Because these interests are *contentious*, people will tend to act conflictually in relation to those with a different stake in domestic property.
- Because these interests are *objective*, the propensity to act in any of these ways will inhere in a person's (or a group's) tenurial and functional relation to domestic property. This "action orientation" is, in Dahrendorf's words, "impressed on the individual" by whatever property position he or she currently occupies.

These relationships do not by themselves explain either the formation or behavior of locality-based groups. They do establish an essential theoretical connection between the property and polity of the place of residence: linking a locality's material base with the differentiation and political action of its indigenous groups; linking the spatial and the social. Interests of equity, liquidity, legacy, security, amenity, and autonomy provide a means of comprehending why the *territory* of a common locale can sometimes become a seedbed for collective action. They provide, in short, the raw materials for a theoretical framework capable of explaining group formation and intergroup conflict in the residential urban neighborhood.

5

The Differentiation of Domestic
Property Interest Groups

> By what justification are the social relations of work given a
> special or privileged status with respect to other sets of social
> relations that are also structured in class ways, including the
> social relations of community? . . . What is clear is that work-
> place *and* residence-community relations are shaped (to a
> large but contingent degree) by the dynamics of capitalist ac-
> cumulation, and that together with political relations they
> constitute the lived, experienced world of capitalist societies.
> . . . [W]e badly need objective classifications of the social re-
> lations of residence communities of the kind that Wright has
> provided for the active labor force.
>
> —Ira Katznelson (1981:203–4)

Collective action, originating within the geographical boundaries of
local residential communities, has many causes, conditions, and consequences. No single model of collective action can explain them all. I
would argue, however, that many of the groups and conflicts that
arise within the place of residence can be explained, to one degree or
another, in terms of the multiple cleavages that originate and coalesce
around material interests of domestic property. This chapter will map
these property-based "fault lines" in the sociopolitical landscape of
the residential urban neighborhood. The next chapter will show how
consciously organized, politically active groups sometimes form and
sometimes fight within the lines of these objective, structural boundaries differentiating one domestic property interest group from another.

PROPERTY-BASED CLEAVAGES OF THE
HOMEPLACE: TENURE AND FUNCTION

Domestic property constitutes the material base of the place of residence, just as productive property constitutes the material base of the
place of work. Physically, domestic property is land and a set of structural improvements, having a spatial location in a specific locality.
Socially, domestic property is tenure and use. It embodies a set of
social relationships, combining a specific form of tenurial control
with an accommodative and/or accumulative function. Different com-
binations of tenure and function create politically significant social
cleavages within residential neighborhoods, bestowing different interests on different collections of people and differentiating one collectivity from another. Different property positions, in short, create a
material basis for what I shall refer to as different "property interest
groups." How these groups are objectively differentiated is the problem at hand.

Tenure creates a fundamental social cleavage within most residential neighborhoods, defining the interests of all who have any kind of
stake in domestic property. Conceived quite simply, tenure creates a
dichotomous division between the propertied and the propertyless.
People either own land and buildings that are used (or usable) for
shelter, or they do not.

While this may be a significant first step in describing the social
cleavages of a given locality, the owner/nonowner dichotomy ignores
the real-life complexity of property tenure itself. The personally exclusive, relatively permanent, and legally defensible rights of use, development, and disposition typically associated with the "ownership" of
real property can be split among several different parties, each possessing a different "stick" in the parcel's "bundle of rights." Thus a
bank that holds a mortgage or lien on a parcel of land, a developer
who holds a financial interest in an apartment complex that has been
syndicated among multiple investors, or a resident who holds a limited equity share in the propertied assets of his or her housing cooperative are all "owners" of one or more property rights, despite the fact
that their ownership stake is much different than that of, say, the
owner-occupier of a single-family suburban house.

Tenurial relations also may vary greatly among those who do *not*
own real property. Thus the week-by-week occupant of a lodging
house, the private tenant with an annual lease, and the public tenant
of a metropolitan housing authority, are all nonowners, but the legal

arrangements under which they occupy and use their residential spaces are very different indeed. They each have a slightly different entrepreneurial stake in domestic property.

My point is that the tenurial relation of owning or not owning domestic property can assume many forms, creating multiple divisions among social groups. A simple division between owners and nonowners, therefore, captures neither the complexity of property tenure nor the diversity of social cleavage that may exist within a residential neighborhood.

By contrast, a functional division adds both complexity and diversity to the objective differentiation of property interest groups. Whereas every parcel of domestic property is, by definition, usable as personal shelter, any parcel may also be used as a source of income and wealth. Indeed, the personal use that some people make of a given parcel may be *exclusively* financial, not residential at all. In terms that I have previously employed, domestic property may serve either an accommodative or accumulative function. It may also serve both at the same time. If locality-based cleavages are drawn along these functional lines, then *four* property interest groups are demarcated: "owner-occupiers," who use domestic property for both accommodation and accumulation; "property capitalists," who use domestic property only for accumulation; "tenants," who use domestic property only for accommodation; and the "homeless," who use domestic property for neither accommodation or accumulation. These property interest groups can be portrayed schematically as in Figure 1.

Even though this four-fold demarcation is drawn according to a collectivity's functional relation to domestic property, tenure is not entirely missing. The former division between owners and nonowners, for example, is implicit in the cleavage between those for whom housing is used (or usable) for accumulation and those for whom housing has *no* accumulative function—that is, between owner-occupiers and

Accumulation

		Yes	No
Accommodation	Yes	Owner-occupiers	Tenants
	No	Property capitalists	Homeless

Figure 1. The functional differentiation of property interest groups

property capitalists, on one side of the accumulative divide, and tenants and the homeless on the other. Domestic property can only function for accumulation for those who have some sort of "ownership" stake in residential land and buildings.

Tenure also combines with function in differentiating various interest groups *within* the four already distinguished by their relation to accommodation and accumulation. The previous discussion of property tenure suggested that the legal arrangement under which housing is held and used, by owners and nonowners alike, can vary in rather basic ways. These tenurial variations, combined with several functional variations in the way in which property is actually utilized for shelter and financial gain, constitute an objective basis for major subdivisions among owner-occupiers, property capitalists, tenants, and the homeless. Each of these subdivisions embodies a different tenurial and functional relation to domestic property. Each bestows a different set of domestic property interests. Each is, in effect, a different "domestic property interest group."[1]

These interests and groups are what Weber would have called "ideal types" (cf., Roth and Wittich, 1978:19–22). They are approximations of concrete historical phenomena, classificatory abstractions of real-life events. So many "real" variations in tenure and function may exist within any given locality, however, that even an "ideal" classification of "objectively different" property positions can become hopelessly complex, multiplying the number of interests and groups to the point of absurdity. Theoretical parsimony and analytic practicality require that a line be drawn somewhere, limiting the analysis of property interest groups to those that are relevant and necessary.

A judgment has been made, therefore, to subdivide the interests of

1. By referring to these objectively constituted social formations of the homeplace as "interest groups," rather than "classes," I am attempting to avoid both the economic bias of the Weberian perspective and the productive bias of the Marxist perspective. "Interest group" also serves to focus the analysis of group formation and collective action precisely where I shall want to focus it, on the *interests* of domestic property. There is a problem, however. Because "interest group" is a term that has long been associated with the pluralist theory of interests and action, there is a danger of "domestic property interest groups" carrying a connotation of (1) interests that are consciously articulated, enacted preferences, rather than objective, relational advantages, and (2) groups that are products of the political process rather than products of a locality's material base. The solution to this potential problem is merely to insist on the particular conception of domestic property interests that has been developed heretofore, one that is closer to the theory of Marx than to the work of pluralists like Arthur Bentley, David Truman, Nelson Polsby, Edward Banfield, and Robert Dahl. The interest groups of this chapter, in other words, must not be divorced from the property interests of the previous chapter.

domestic property no further than the *six* presented before and to subdivide the interest groups no further than the *ten* to be presented here. Although not a line that is arbitrarily drawn—based as it is upon an extensive literature on locality-based action, the testimony of experienced informants, and my own experience in many residential neighborhoods—this is a tentative classification. Its adequacy in accurately describing politically significant social cleavages within the place of residence will be put to the test in the case study of Cincinnati's West End. Afterward, the merits of this ideal classification of interests and groups will be reconsidered.

OWNER-OCCUPIERS

I shall begin the examination of the domestic property positions that may exist within a residentially diverse neighborhood by describing the tenurial and functional relations, the domestic property interests, and the various property interest groups that make up the general category of "owner-occupiers." *Tenurially,* all of these groups may be characterized as "owners." Since we have already seen how slippery a concept "ownership" may be, however, this tenurial relation should be described more fully. Thus to say that owner-occupiers "own" domestic property is to assert that (1) they hold legal title to exclusive use of a parcel for as long as they might wish (assuming, of course, that all financial obligations are met) and (2) they hold legal title to all or part of the parcel's unencumbered value. *Functionally,* all owner-occupiers make current use of a parcel of domestic property for personal shelter; this parcel is usable, moreover, for financial savings and financial gain. Their functional relation to domestic property, in general, is *both* accommodative and accumulative.

Given their tenurial and functional position, owner-occupiers will typically—that is, ideal typically—have an *entrepreneurial* stake in domestic property that includes all six of the property interests described in the previous chapter. They will likewise have a *strategic* stake in any public policies, market forces, and social events that affect these relational advantages for good or ill.

The property position of all owner-occupiers is not exactly the same, however. There are significant tenurial and functional variations that objectively differentiate one group from another and that significantly alter the entrepreneurial and strategic interests that each group may hold. I shall posit three such property interest groups: the owner-occupiers of "social property," "household property," and "acquisitive property."

The owner-occupiers of *social property* are differentiated from the other two owner-occupier interest groups by a tenurial arrangement that (1) contractually places a "social" limit on one or more of the entrepreneurial interests that owner-occupiers typically have in domestic property and that (2) organizationally connects one parcel of domestic property to another in a network of legal, financial, and/or administrative interdependence. What is "limited," most frequently, is equity. The owner-occupier is usually permitted some return on his or her original investment in domestic property, but the level of that financial gain, coming from the resale of the property, is held *below* the market value. The primary purpose of this equity limitation is to discourage speculative investment in housing in order to maintain affordability for future generations of homeowners.[2] Additional restrictions may sometimes be imposed that limit the latitude that owner-occupiers have in mortgaging, subletting, or transferring their property (liquidity), in bequeathing their property to others (legacy), or in redeveloping their property in any major way (autonomy).

The responsibility for enforcing these social limitations usually lies with a parent organization that acquired, developed, or constructed the housing. This organization typically retains a financial stake in the owner-occupiers' property and may provide management or social support services. Owner-occupiers, in turn, typically exercise a degree of policy or programmatic control over the parent organization. Thus, in addition to the "social" limitations that are placed upon their property interests, there are "social" bonds that are forged between owner-occupiers and their parent organization and, via that organization, between one owner-occupier and another. Limited equity housing cooperatives and community land trusts are common examples of such social property arrangements in the United States.

Subject to none of these contractual limitations on their property interests and legally, financially, or administratively tied to *no* other parcels of property via a parent organization, the other two owner-occupier interest groups clearly occupy a different tenurial position

2. A fuller discussion of various purposes and models of equity limitation and a more detailed look at the "social property" tradition can be found in Davis (1984). Community land trusts and limited equity cooperatives are also discussed in Institute for Community Economics (1982) and Kirkpatrick (1981).

than the owner-occupiers of social property. If it is tenure that differentiates the owner-occupiers of social property from the owner-occupiers of both household property and acquisitive property, it is function that differentiates the latter two groups from one another. Whereas the domestic property that these groups own and occupy is fully usable for both accommodation and accumulation, what distinguishes one group from another is the personal and political primacy that is given to each of these functions.

The owner-occupiers of *household property* have a relation to property and place that is currently devoid of nearly any commodity concerns. This means *not* that they are objectively "uninterested" or subjectively unaware of the value their property might have in exchange, but that they are so completely committed to living where they are and using their property for their own accommodation that equity and liquidity are largely irrelevant to their personal circumstances. Legacy, too, may have more meaning as a residence that their children will inhabit than as a cash windfall that will eventually be distributed among absentee heirs. Such a functional relation to domestic property carries with it a strategic orientation that gives little political weight or recognition to local or extralocal threats to interests of exchange. The owner-occupiers of household property are more likely to act collectively only in defense (or pursuit) of security, amenity, or autonomy for themselves and their neighbors.

By contrast, the owner-occupiers of *acquisitive property* have an overriding strategic interest in anything that affects their property values. They do, of course, have an interest in the security, amenity, and autonomy of property and place, since this is where they personally live, but even these use interests have an accumulative function. A threat to the amenity of the neighborhood, for example, may have more personal and political relevance for this interest group as a threat to the liquidity and equity of their property than as a threat to the personal comfort of themselves or their neighbors. Their property may function necessarily for shelter, but it is also a means by which income, wealth, and social mobility might be secured. This acquisitive use of domestic property functionally differentiates the owner-occupiers of "acquisitive property" from the owner-occupiers of "household property."

Admittedly, these can be very fluid categories. Individual owner-occupiers may move back and forth between a functional relation to domestic property that emphasizes the "household" one year and "acquisition" the next. Many factors will affect which group a homeowner will occupy and whether there is movement from one to the other. Some of these factors, such as individual housing preferences or personal ambition, are a matter of choice, making membership in one or the other homeowner group rather voluntary. Many other factors are largely outside of the homeowner's choice or control. For example, Connerly (1986) has found that low-income, black, and elderly residents are more likely to have strong social ties to their neighborhoods and are less likely to move away. Shlay and DiGregorio (1983) and Feit and Peterson (1985) have noted the same pattern among "neighborhood women," who typically display less readiness than men to relocate, even when an opportunity exists for profitable gain from the sale of their homes. It is reasonable to assume that homeowners with these particular economic or social characteristics would be more likely to occupy the "household" group than the "acquisitive" group and would be less likely to move into the latter.

I suggest that, because of the nonvoluntaristic nature of most of the factors affecting homeowner membership in these interest groups, most localities have a relatively stable population of owner-occupiers who relate to their property not as a commodity but as a home. There will often be, in addition, an identifiable population of owner-occupiers for whom the liquidity and equity of their property are paramount concerns. Drawing a distinction between owner-occupiers of household property and those of acquisitive property is an attempt to describe these too very different functional positions, even while acknowledging that many owner-occupiers will be sometimes part of one property interest group and sometimes part of the other.

PROPERTY CAPITALISTS

The property interest groups of private capital, like those of the owner-occupiers, exercise a degree of tenurial control over the use of domestic property and possess a claim against the value of domestic property such that they must be included among the "owners" of domestic property. It is not tenure, therefore, that differentiates private capitalists from owner-occupiers, but function. The functional relation of property capitalists to domestic property is almost exclusively an *accumulative* one. People can and do use the property possessed by capitalist interest groups for personal accommodation, but the use to which the property is put, by and for private capital, is income generation and wealth accumulation. The principal interests of property capitalists are those of exchange, liquidity and equity in particular.[3]

Function also differentiates the various property interest groups of private capital from one another. While tenurial distinctions do exist among them, their property positions and property interests are distinguished primarily by the different functional relation that each bears to domestic property—that is, the different financial use that each group makes of the domestic property within its possession. There are four private capital interest groups: landlords, financiers, developers, and speculators.

Landlords put their property to use generating a current stream of income. Every landlord seeks to attract income *directly* in the form of rents and *indirectly* in the form of tax allowances such as the deduction for depreciation. It can be said, therefore, that liquidity is their main entrepreneurial and strategic interest. Even so, most landlords will also have an interest in equity because they expect someday to realize substantial capital gains and because they hope to borrow on the basis of their present holdings. Or they may expect appreciating property values to permit them to charge even higher rents.

Landlords may have an interest in the amenity of their holdings as well. This interest is somewhat peripheral because amenity is relevant to the individual and collective action of landlords only insofar as amenity affects liquidity and, perhaps, equity. If a stream of income derived from a parcel of property can be sustained without preserving the property's amenity, or if the equity embedded in the parcel continues to grow even when amenity declines, most landlords will have little or no strategic interest in maintaining, repairing, or improving their property. On the other hand, should the deterioration of their property threaten their income or equity, amenity may become the basis for individual or collective action. Thus, unlike the owner-occupier who will have an entrepreneurial and strategic interest in the amenity of his or her home *regardless* of its effect upon liquidity or equity, the landlord will have an interest in amenity *only* to the extent that liquidity and equity are affected.

The other property interest group with a primary interest—one

---

3. Legacy is included among the financial interests of only a small subset of property capitalists: individual landlords or developers who hope to bequeath their holdings to selected heirs. Most of the members of private capital interest groups are corporations, legal "persons" who never die. Legacy, therefore, cannot be seriously counted among the interests of private capital, even if it is an exchange interest that is usually attributed to the owners of domestic property.

could almost say an exclusive interest—in domestic property as a current source of income is the one I shall call the *financiers*. This group includes institutions and individuals that provide the acquisition, construction, and mortgage financing for domestic property. They differ from landlords both tenurially and functionally. The financier's "ownership" of domestic property takes the form of a mortgage or lien, constituting a legal claim against the property's value and allowing a degree of control over the property's use and development.[4] Since the financier has the right to enforce this claim, to the point of eventually seizing the property under specified conditions of default, financiers have a strategic interest in seeing that the equity and amenity of the mortgaged property are preserved. These interests are "peripheral," however, to their primary interest in liquidity. The financier's functional relation to domestic property is that of a third-party investor, one who expects to reap a stream of income in the form of regular payments of interest. This entrepreneurial stake in the stream-of-income liquidity of domestic property—property that is "owned," except for the financier's lien, by some other party—is what distinguishes the financier's property position from those of other property interest groups.[5] It is also what strategically "orients" their individual and collective behavior in dealing with public policies, market forces, or other groups that may affect their liquidity.

The remaining two property interest groups of private capital have a primary material and political interest in equity, not liquidity. The entrepreneurial stake that they have in domestic property—and the action orientation that is inherent in such a stake—is a function of rising property values, a function of the appreciating price of domestic property as a market commodity.

Developers are the first of these groups. Typically, the developers of housing are short-term owners, holding property only until a buyer

4. Calling this claim "ownership" is somewhat problematic. A financial institution holding a mortgage on a parcel of property does not hold the kind of equity share or proprietary control that is normally ascribed to "ownership." On the other hand, because the financiers' entrepreneurial stake can be bought and sold on the secondary mortgage market and because their stake can be converted into exclusive control over the property's use, equity, and disposition in the event of foreclosure, it makes more sense to include financiers among the ranks of the "owners" than among the ranks of the "nonowners" of domestic property.

5. The financiers' overriding interest in liquidity includes not only an entrepreneurial and strategic interest in a property's stream of (interest) income, but an interest in the property's ease of sale. No financial institution wants to hold foreclosed property for very long. Financiers have a stake, therefore, in assuring the ongoing "salability" of any domestic property on which they happen to hold a mortgage.

can be found.[6] They will sometimes function as landlords, during the transition period between the completion and sale of a housing project. More characteristically, however, their functional relation to domestic property is that of designers, packagers, contractors, and builders of structural improvements. Their material advantage lies in the appreciating value of the land and buildings into which they pour their capital and labor, expecting the build-up of equity to far exceed the value of their total investment. So precarious is this entrepreneurial stake, contingent as equity is upon a multitude of fluctuating local and extralocal factors, that developers will have a strategic interest in anything that affects local property values. Furthermore, since developers must pay a premium for short-term construction financing, they have an interest in the quick "salability" of their property once construction (or reconstruction) is completed. This aspect of liquidity can be added to equity in distinguishing the developers' property position.

Finally, there are the *speculators*. Like developers, this property interest group has a primary interest in equity. Unlike developers, however, this group produces none of the equity itself. Indeed, it produces nothing at all. It merely waits, profiting from the equity build-up produced by the investment, growth, and development of the surrounding society. Speculators reap the equity produced by others, gathering the fruits of their watchful waiting at the moment of sale.[7] The investor who buys raw land on the urban fringe in anticipation of metropolitan growth, selling when the expanding city pushes the value of the property upward; the investor who buys an abandoned or occupied building in a marginal neighborhood in anticipation of gentrification, selling when affluent homebuyers at last "rediscover" the neighborhood—both are familiar examples of speculators. Less obvious members of this property interest group, because they themselves seldom *own* the property they sell, are the brokers of real estate. Like a school of pilot fish, they live off the activity of others,

6. "Ownership" can vary greatly for this property interest group, depending upon the many financial, legal, and administrative arrangements under which housing development can occur.

7. Feagin (1982:42) describes the nonproductive nature of speculation well when he writes: "Speculation in real estate—including land and buildings on that land—is a different sort of capital venture than investment in machinery. Real estate speculation is not productive, that is, it does not increase the goods and services available in the society." Similar views on the negative role of speculators can be found in Yearwood (1968), Carey (1976), and George (1975). Harvey (1974:242),·by contrast, discusses the "positive service" that speculators perform in the capitalist economy. A laudatory portrait of real estate speculation is presented by Wolf (1981).

feeding on the equity created by those who *do* own domestic property and feeding on the equity created by society as a whole.[8] Along with other members of this property interest group, they are partners in a general campaign to push property values to their highest possible level. Their financial gain is the greatest when the price of property is the greatest. All speculators are alike in this regard. Their advantage lies in appreciation. Their financial well-being and their strategic orientation to action are both derived from an overriding interest in equity.

TENANTS

Just as the property interest groups of private capital are differentiated from those of owner-occupation by a functional relation to domestic property that is primarily, often exclusively, accumulative, the property interest groups of tenants are differentiated from both of these other categories by a functional relation that is exclusively accommodative. The land and buildings that tenants occupy are used by them for shelter not exchanged for income or capital gains. Tenants are also differentiated from the interest groups of private capital and owner-occupation by a tenurial relation of "nonownership." They hold only a single "stick" in a property's "bundle of rights," the right to occupy property for a contractually limited period of time.

Given their functional and tenurial relation to domestic property, security is the primary entrepreneurial interest that is shared by all tenants, followed closely by an interest in the amenity of their dwellings and surroundings. Contingent as both of these advantages are on the actions of landlords; policies of federal, state, and municipal governments; and unpredictable fluctuations in local housing markets, the material stake that tenants have in domestic property is very precarious. Just *how* precarious will depend, in part, on their particular

8. The tenurial relation that brokers bear to domestic property is as problematic as that of the financiers. Like the financiers, real estate brokers do not "own" property in the same sense that owner-occupiers, landlords, developers, and other speculators do. They *do*, however, have a contractual claim against a percentage of the property's total resale price. They may also be granted a degree of proprietary control over the property during the period in which the property is offered for sale, particularly if the former occupants have already vacated the building. While neither of these rights is equivalent to the "ownership" that we normally associate with those who hold the deed to domestic property, such rights lend some credibility to the suggestion that the brokers' tenurial relation is something more than that of such "nonowners" as tenants or the homeless.

tenurial situation. Variations in tenure will set security and amenity at different levels, making different tenants more or less susceptible to any threats that may arise to these interests and creating, thereby, different orientations to action. These tenurial variations create an objective basis for multiple tenant interest groups, each having a slightly different entrepreneurial and strategic interest in security and amenity.

The most basic tenurial division among tenants, however, is the one between private tenants and public tenants. These are the only two tenant categories that I shall include in this tentative classification of locality-based interest groups, though it is important to acknowledge that various subdivisions within these groups will often be politically relevant "on the ground."[9]

Private tenants are tenurially related to a parcel of domestic property that is privately owned by an individual or a corporation. The cost and supply of such housing are determined by the private market in real estate (though public policies may impose a degree of cost control). Tenant access is obtained through that market, with rental housing going to whomever can pay the market price. Short-term security is contractually guaranteed by a lease agreement. Long-term security is unavailable, except where rent control or stringent "just cause" eviction statutes have made tenancy unusually secure. Amenity is a consequence of the tenant's lease, which sets the level of landlord responsibility for ongoing maintenance and repair, and of building codes, tax incentives, and landlord-tenant laws, which affect the property's habitability.

The private tenant also possesses a degree of autonomy that the

9. A strong case could be made for treating at least one of these subdivisions as a separate property interest group. I refer to tenants who occupy apartments that are privately owned but publicly regulated either through long-term rent stabilization agreements with the federal government (under HUD's 221(d)(3), 202, or Section 8 Existing, Substantial, or Moderate Rehabilitation programs, for example) or through rent control ordinances of the municipal government. The incumbents of such a property position, who might be called "social tenants," have interests that are somewhat different from those of both the private tenants and the public tenants. I have chosen not to treat these tenants as a separate property interest group for two reasons: (1) those federal programs that attached long-term subsidies to rental units are being phased out in favor of subsidies that "belong" to the individual, "private" tenant, and (2) municipal regulation of rental markets through "rent controls, eviction protections, and habitability guarantees are," as Appelbaum and Gilderbloom (1986:168) have noted, "minimal to nonexistent in most places." Still, it should be acknowledged that there *will* be localities where "social tenants" constitute a numerically large, politically significant, and objectively separate property interest group—and should be treated as such, both theoretically and practically.

public tenant seldom has. Since access to the dwelling is won by ability to pay, limits are placed on the landlord's scrutiny of the prospective tenant's personal life. Since use of the dwelling is secured by contractual agreement, limits are placed on the landlord's right to enter the tenant's private space.[10] Private tenants may even be granted the right to renovate the interior of their dwellings to suit their own wishes or needs, though this prerogative is more often retained by the landlord. Indeed, residential autonomy of this sort is more characteristic of the tenurial situation of the owner-occupier.

Public tenants, by contrast, are tenurially related to a parcel of domestic property that is publicly owned by a state or metropolitan housing authority.[11] The cost and supply of such housing are both determined by public policy. Tenant access is regulated and obtained through other public policies, with housing going to those who can meet certain legislative and bureaucratic criteria of need. Security can be long-term, lasting as long as the tenant's income and personal circumstances fit the criteria for eligibility. Amenity is largely a function of the public subsidies poured into the property for ongoing maintenance and modernization and of the allocation of such funds by the housing authority itself. When these subsidies are unavailable, the amenity of public housing declines.

Autonomy, on the other hand, can be almost totally absent. Since access to public housing is won on the basis of need, the prospective tenant's income, occupation, education, dependents, personal property, and personal habits are closely scrutinized by the housing authority. Once admitted into public housing, tenants are subjected to a formal review of their personal circumstances once or twice a year, since the housing authority must recertify their eligibility.[12] Housing

10. Both of these limitations on the landlord's right to invade tenant privacy may, of course, be regularly violated and irregularly enforced. I do not claim that tenant autonomy is never threatened, but that a degree of autonomy is provided and presumed in the tenurial situation itself. It is part of the tenants' entrepreneurial stake in domestic property and a source of strategic action and political conflict with those who would threaten what little autonomy tenants may have.

11. The publicly subsidized tenants of housing that is owned and managed by private landlords have a tenurial and functional relation to domestic property that is closer to the property position of "private tenants" than to that of "public tenants." Tenants whose rent is partially subsidized by federal programs such as Section 8 are *not* included, therefore, among the "public tenants" described here.

12. Less formal, but no less intrusive, is the sense that most public tenants have that housing authority personnel—and informants among the tenants themselves—monitor their behavior, watching for violations in eligibility or occupancy. Such violations may result in quick eviction.

authority personnel often assume the right to enter any tenant's apartment, even when tenants are not at home. Tenants are required to seek prior approval for any changes they might wish to make in the color, layout, or fixtures of "their" apartments. While such approval is customary for private tenants as well, public tenants confront a more complicated, lengthy approval process, along with a greater risk of higher rents, fines, or evictions if the review of their renovation request uncovers violations in their current use of the unit. It is easier and more prudent, therefore, for the public tenant to make no changes or improvements at all. As for the autonomy associated with "citizenship" or "status," public tenants are viewed by their neighbors—and often by themselves—as politically marginal and socially dependent wards of the state, inhabiting housing with the least prestige.

THE HOMELESS

Strictly speaking, it might be argued that the tenurial and functional position of the homeless gives them no property interests at all. They are differentiated from other property interest groups by a tenurial relation that conveys no legal interest in domestic property and by a functional relation that is neither predictably accommodative nor financially accumulative. This suggests that they have no entrepreneurial stake in domestic property whatsoever, and certainly no political interests. They are akin, in this regard, to Marx's description of the "lumpenproletariat"—"living on the crumbs of society, people without a definite trade, vagabonds, people without a hearth or a home."[13]

Nevertheless, although the benefits of this property position are practically nonexistent, the costs are multiple, material, and oppressively borne by all who share the same situation. Lacking any material advantages by virtue of their transient relation to domestic property, the homeless can be said to share a set of disadvantages bestowed upon their objective position by public policies, market forces, and the social actions of their propertied neighbors. These disadvantages—every bit as "objective," "material," "collective," and "relational" as the advantages of those who inhabit or profit from

---

13. This description is found in Marx's *Class Struggle in France*. The quotation appears in Ollman (1968:575).

domestic property—also bestow an "action orientation." The homeless may not have an entrepreneurial stake in domestic property, but
they surely have a strategic interest in avoiding the burdens that accrue to their property position. They have an overriding interest in
security.[14]

Even with their transient and tentative relation to domestic property, the homeless vary in their tenurial situations. At one extreme are
the "vagabonds," "bag ladies," and "street people," who may liter-
ally have no place to go at night. At the other are the occupants of
boarding houses, those who occupy a room under a license for a week
or month at a time.[15] Between these extremes are the transient residents of shelters, "flop houses," and single-room occupancy hotels.
Together, they constitute the property interest group of "the homeless."

Major social and political cleavages crisscross the ranks of all who
have a material stake in the domestic property of a common locale—
cleavages that are themselves created by multiple differences in property tenure, function, and interest. These crosscutting cleavages of
domestic property differentiate *ten* locality-based interest groups
(summarized in Figure 2).

Not every neighborhood will have every one of these social formations. Indeed, it is only within the residentially diverse neighborhoods
of major metropolitan areas that all ten are occasionally found. On
the other hand, any neighborhood that has domestic property as its
material base will contain at least one of them. Most neighborhoods
will contain several, reflecting the very different relations that different members of the same locality currently bear to land and buildings
that are used (or usable) for shelter.

14. For this property interest group, more than any other, an "action orientation"
is seldom mobilized to produce collective, political demands. Security for the homeless
is a strategic interest that usually makes an appearance in the political arena, if at all,
only because others have promoted this interest on behalf of the homeless.

15. The residents of a boarding house are tenurially distinguished from tenants by
the fact that the latter, in holding a lease, have a legal interest in property; the former,
in holding a license, do not. As described by *American Jurisprudence Legal Forms*,
1972: "It is often difficult to distinguish between a license and a lease, but if it is
recognized that lodgers, transient hotel guests, and boarders in a boardinghouse are
regarded as licensees, and [that] residents of an apartment house under contract . . .
are regarded as tenants, the distinction becomes clearer. A fundamental distinction
between the tenant and the licensee is that the tenant has a legal interest in the possession or right to possession of property for a period specified, while a licensee merely
has permission to do acts on property in possession of another, which acts, without
the license, would constitute trespass."

Tenurial relations	Do not own domestic property (Nonowners)			Do own domestic property (Owners)						
Functional relations	Neither accommodation nor accumulation (Homeless)	Accommodation (Tenants)		Both accommodation and accumulation (Owner-occupiers)			Accumulation (Property capitalists)			
Domestic property interests	(Security)	Security Amenity	Security Amenity Autonomy	Security Amenity Autonomy Legacy (Liquidity) (Equity)	Security Amenity Autonomy Legacy Liquidity Equity	Equity Liquidity Amenity Autonomy Security Legacy	Liquidity Equity (Amenity)	Liquidity (Equity) (Amenity)	Equity (Liquidity)	Equity
Domestic property interest groups	Homeless	Public tenants	Private tenants	Social homeowners	Household homeowners	Acquisitive homeowners	Landlords	Financiers	Developers	Speculators

Figure 2. Domestic property interest groups

These "domestic property interest groups" exist only in embryo. They are objectively constituted social formations that may or may not eventually develop into consciously organized, politically active groups. How such groups actually form and why such groups occasionally fight on the basis of those interests that differentiate one social group from another are the problems to which we now turn.

6

Group Formation and Intergroup Conflict in the Urban Neighborhood

> A fully developed theory of the origins of interest groups and interest conflicts—in short, a fully developed theory of political change—can only be developed within the framework of a theoretical analysis which . . . [manages] to distinguish between objective and subjective interests and to theorize about their interrelationship.
>
> —ISAAC BALBUS (1971:171–72)

The theoretical task now before us is akin to that which earlier faced Rex and Moore, Saunders, and Pratt once each had finished differentiating a full complement of "housing classes." None of these theorists was content with merely a static model of local stratification. Each wanted to develop a dynamic model of collective action, seeking, in particular, to understand the causes and course of "class conflict" in the place of residence.

I have a similar aspiration. Even though I have left behind their preoccupation with "class" while treating property interests in a different manner altogether, I share with the neo-Weberians a desire to move beyond a static model of social differentiation. What is needed for a better understanding of locality-based action and conflict is not only an objective classification of the multiple, material bases for group formation, but a dynamic analysis of why groups actually form, how groups organizationally develop, and why they conflictually interact.

This chapter proposes a theoretical framework within which each of these latter issues may be systematically addressed. This framework has two components: a three-stage model of collective action, depicting the genesis and development of locality-based groups, and a two-by-two typology of intergroup conflict, describing the production and pattern of political friction among organized property interest groups of the residential urban neighborhood.

THE GENESIS AND DEVELOPMENT OF DOMESTIC
PROPERTY INTEREST GROUPS

"Objective" interests of domestic property, inhering in the various tenurial and functional positions that people occupy vis-à-vis the material base of the place of residence, precede any "subjective" awareness that the incumbents of those positions might have of them. People who share a common relation to domestic property may or may not perceive their common interests. They may or may not perceive any threats to those interests, arising out of the relational character of their material advantages. They may or may not recognize the antagonism or compatibility of their interests in relation to those of other people. Until they do, however—until the incumbents of a property position become conscious of their interests—they cannot and will not collectively or contentiously act like a property interest group, even if they are predisposed toward such collective behavior by their "objective" interests. In short, it is only when the "objective" interests of a property position are converted into the "subjective" wants and collective goals of those who occupy that particular position that a commonly situated collectivity can become a politically active group.

This conversion process is a necessary condition of locality-based action. It is not sufficient, however. Consciousness must be combined with *organization* for collective action to occur. Groups form and groups act not only because their members recognize common interests, but because certain social, political, and technical conditions permit individuals to pool their resources in pursuit of common ends, on behalf of common interests. The genesis and development of consciousness and the genesis and development of organization go hand-in-hand. They are interdependent, complementary "moments" in the production and maintenance of collective action.[1] Thus, even though

1. In philosophy, "moment" refers to any one of the constituent elements of a complex phenomenon. In popular usage, "moment" has the dynamic connotation of a definite point in a series of events. Both meanings have relevance in speaking of consciousness and organization as two interrelated "moments" in the genesis and development of collective action.

it is convenient to consider them separately, in assembling the elements of a locality-based model of collective action, it is well to remember that these "moments" are never separate in the actual event of group formation and collective action.

Three Stages of Housing Consciousness

Theorists working within the Marxist tradition have commonly assumed a one-step conversion process in explaining the interrelationship between "objective" interests and "subjective" interests. They have assumed, in other words, that a group (that is, a "class") that has become aware of itself, recognizing a common situation that differentiates its interests, attitudes, and style of life from those of other groups, will have also become aware of the antagonistic relation between its interests and those of other groups. Even more, they have assumed that a "disadvantaged" group that has become aware of both a separate identity and antagonistic interests will have become aware of the need to transform the structural basis of property and power in order to defend its interests against the depradations of "privileged" groups. As Giddens (1973:113) has observed, "In Marx's writings (although not in those of Lenin) the emergence of revolutionary class consciousness is assumed to be a direct outcome of, if not wholly indistinguishable from, consciousness of conflict of class interest." In sum, what has become manifest to the politically conscious members of a collectivity, according to these theorists, is not only a set of common interests, but a set of common enemies and a structure of systematic threat and exploitation that must be overturned if their common interests are to be secured.[2]

It should be obvious, however, that the latent, unrecognized interests of objective positions seldom become the manifest goals of a revolutionary group in a single leap of political awakening and awareness. A group may become conscious of class differentiation and class identity *without* perceiving the relational character of its class interests. Likewise, a group may be aware that its interests are both precarious and contentious—and may even engage in overt political conflict with other groups—without perceiving or accepting the need for

2. The extent to which Marx himself actually subscribed to this one-step conversion process remains an issue of considerable controversy, Giddens's remarks notwithstanding. Sabia (1988), for instance, has argued rather persuasively that Marx considered revolutionary consciousness and revolutionary organizations to be later products of a long process of evolving solidarity and escalating struggle within the workers' "places of work, residence, and recreation."

revolutionary action. It seems reasonable, therefore, to posit at least three levels of political consciousness in the development of property interest groups, three different ways in which property interests may become manifest to a commonly situated collectivity.

The most rudimentary level of housing consciousness may be referred to as "*collective consciousness*," or "interest group identity." It corresponds to Giddens's (1973:112) concept of "class identity," implying a "cognisance of characteristics which separate the class of which one is a member from another or others." Collective consciousness carries an awareness of one's particular position vis-à-vis domestic property, accompanied by a recognition that others possess the same property interests. There is also recognition, as Giddens suggests, of the ways in which these common interests *differ* from those of other groups (although there is scant recognition of the ways in which these common interests might be precariously, contentiously related to the interests and actions of other groups). Collective action that is made possible by this level of housing consciousness will tend to focus on (1) activities that socially celebrate and solidify the common identity of a domestic property interest group and (2) activities that marginally improve the property and place in which its members have a common stake.

The second level of housing consciousness is characterized by the intrinsically political recognition that interests are not only objectively different from one domestic property position to another, but objectively conflicting as well. This may be referred to as "*conflict consciousness*." It presumes an awareness of the contentious character of property interests, such that one group protects or pursues its own advantage(s) only at the expense of another group—or groups. Any threat to one's interests, therefore, is perceived as originating in the antagonistic relations between differently situated, differently "interested" groups. One's interests are precarious because of the "visible hand" of opposing groups, in other words, not because of the "invisible hand" of the marketplace (or any other impersonal economic, social, or political factors). Collective action that is made possible by this level of housing consciousness will tend to focus on activities that politically defend or promote one group's property interests in the face of attack or opposition by another group. Furthermore, since an awareness of interests (and groups) that are antagonistic can provoke an awareness of those that are compatible, conflict consciousness will tend to spawn collective action that builds bridges to potential allies, even as it raises walls and mounts assaults against proven enemies.

The third level of housing consciousness may be referred to as "revolutionary," "structural" or "*radical consciousness.*"[3] It involves a perception of existing property relations as inherently inadequate, inequitable, and/or illegitimate, regarded as such because they fail to meet the accommodative or accumulative aspirations of a given population. Radical housing consciousness recognizes that an overall reorganization of the structures and rules governing the possession and use of domestic property is necessary if the well-being of a particular group is to be secured. Collective action that is made possible by this level of housing consciousness will tend to focus less on the militant defense of one's current stake in domestic property, therefore, than on the construction of new sets of tenurial and functional relationships that secure new sets of property interests.

These *multiple* levels of housing consciousness mean that the "conversion process," in which a group's objectively constituted interests become its subjectively recognized goals, may be a more complicated matter than the Marxists' two-tiered transition from a "class-in-itself" to a "class-for-itself." The creation of housing consciousness may involve not only the conversion of the objective interests of a property position into the subjective goals of an interest group, but the development of that subjective recognition. Thus an awareness of interests that are held in common may develop into an awareness of interests that are positioned and patterned for conflict; which may develop, in turn, into an awareness of the need for structural change if the advantages that a group precariously possesses (or ambitiously desires) are to be secured.

There is no guarantee, of course, that any such progression will occur.[4] Individuals may remain entirely unaware of their common interests. If they do become conscious of common interests, there is no assurance that they will soon become conscious of antagonistic rela-

---

3. Despite its connotation of cataclysmic upheaval, "radical" or "revolutionary" housing consciousness need not embrace a vision of violent, sudden, or society-wide change. All that is implied by this level of consciousness is a recognition of the need for a sweeping reorganization in the institutional mediation of domestic property. It is important to note, moreover, that all of these levels are "politically neutral"; that is, I do not assume that only groups with "liberal" or "progressive" politics will ascend to conflict or radical consciousness nor that such politics will necessarily be nurtured by these "higher" levels of housing consciousness.

4. There is no guarantee that the evolution of political consciousness, in the "real world," will always follow the orderly, unidirectional sequence of this theoretical model.

tions with other property interest groups or that they will ever become conscious of the possibility and necessity of radical change. Each transition to a different level of housing consciousness is dependent upon a host of empirical conditions that may or may not be present in a given locality.

These conditions of consciousness foster what Weber referred to as the "transparency of the connections between the causes and consequences of the 'class situation'" (Gerth and Mills, 1958:184). What is made "transparent" in the case of property interest groups are the connections inherent in the "situation" of a particular property position: the connections between an individual parcel of domestic property and the "proximate aggregate of parcels" within the locality; the connections between the property and place of the residential neighborhood and the social structure surrounding that locality; and the connections between one collectivity and another, having conflicting (or compatible) interests. The instability of one's property position or external threats to one's property interests tend to make such connections more apparent and may engender housing consciousness. Stability, ideology, or tenurial mobility, on the other hand, tend to mask such connections, making housing consciousness very difficult to achieve. These and other "empirical conditions of consciousness" will be examined more closely in Chapter 11, after we have had a chance to see them "in action" in Cincinnati.

Three Stages of Housing Organization

Three kinds of consciousness have been proposed, implying three different kinds of locality-based collective action. What is missing from this model, however, is the other "moment" of collective action, namely the genesis and development of organization. Individuals who have become aware of their collective interests must still find a way of pooling their resources in defense or pursuit of those interests. They must find a way of transforming a fragmented collectivity with conscious interests into an organized group with common goals. If they do not, then they will remain what Morris Ginsberg termed a "quasi-group":

> Not all collectivities or aggregates form groups. Groups are masses of people in regular contact or communication, and possessing a recognizable structure. There are other aggregates or portions of the community which have no recognizable structure, but whose members have

certain interests or modes of behavior in common, which may at any time lead them to form themselves into definite groups. To this category of quasi-groups belongs such entities as social classes which, without being groups, are a recruiting field for groups. (Quoted in Dahrendorf, 1959:180)

Each locality is a "recruiting field for groups." The tenurial and functional relations of domestic property differentiate a number of quasi-groups, each with a characteristic set of objective property interests. If these "latent" interests become "manifest," then organized interest groups may emerge. Then again, they may not, for there are social, political, and technical conditions that *intervene* in this process of group formation. There are "empirical conditions of organization," just as there are "empirical conditions of consciousness," affecting whether domestic property interest groups actually form and, if they do, whether they last.

Although I shall refrain from discussing these empirical conditions in any detail until after the case study, I can say that my assumption is that the genesis and development of property interest groups will depend upon such social conditions of organization as the proximity and homogeneity of local populations, such political conditions of organization as a low incidence of competing issues and groups, and such technical conditions of organization as adequate resources and competent leaders. When these conditions are present, different types of housing consciousness can engender different types of locality-based organization. When they are absent, even high levels of consciousness cannot sustain a housing organization. I shall posit three levels of organization: the "housing improvement group," the "conflict housing group," and the "radical housing group."[5]

The locality-based organization spawned by "collective consciousness" is a *housing improvement group*. (When its activities are focussed on improving conditions throughout the locality, this organization may also be called a "neighborhood improvement association.") At this level of housing consciousness, there is the rudimentary realization that individuals are similarly situated in relation to property and place and similarly affected by the benefits or costs that accrue to their particular property position. They recognize that even though

5. These three "types" of organization represent, in fact, different stages in the formation and development of a domestic property interest group. "Housing" is used here as a convenient, shorthand substitute for both land and buildings that are used (or useable) for shelter.

little can really be done to shape the larger market, state, or social forces that generate such benefits or costs, benefits can be maximized, costs can be minimized, and life can be made more pleasant for all by improving the amenity of property and place. This is precisely the sort of collective activity that characterizes the housing (or neighborhood) improvement association. Collective action by these locality-based groups tends to take such familiar forms as the restoration and rehabilitation of local housing; the mobilization of volunteers to clean up lots, fix up parks, or maintain community gardens; and the routine participation of neighborhood representatives on various planning, educational, and service delivery boards of the municipal government. Collective action is also designed to consolidate and celebrate the new-found identity of this housing group, typically expressed in social gatherings, community fairs, and mutual aid in times of personal crisis.

The *conflict housing group* is organized when domestic property interests are perceived to be threatened by another group. Consciousness of these antagonistic relations engenders collective action that is oppositional and confrontational in character. Typically, a conflict housing group will engage in activities that systematically protest, ridicule, disrupt, restrain, or block individual or collective action by members of another property interest group (or by government officials perceived to be acting in the interest of an antagonistic group). Rent strikes, anti-redlining campaigns, and public demonstrations that vigorously oppose private or public development are familiar forms of such action. Ironically, cooperation may be as characteristic of this housing group as conflict. Consciousness of "enemies" tends to make one increasingly conscious of actual or potential "friends." Therefore, a conflict housing group will tend to act cooperatively in relation to groups with compatible property interests, even as it is acting conflictually in relation to groups with antagonistic interests.

Finally, consciousness of the possibility and need for structural change in domestic property relations can engender a *radical housing group*. What distinguishes this radical group from the conflict group is not entirely a matter of tactics. Although the radical group may engage in a kind of alternative, institution-building that the conflict group eschews, *either* group may militantly confront targeted opponents in a conscious attempt to extract political or economic concessions. What is different are the kinds of concessions that are demanded and the uses to which these concessions are put. The conflict group strategically acts to defend (or enhance) entrepreneurial advantages that its members already possess. The radical group strategically acts to secure advantages that its members never had. Furthermore, since these new advantages presumably cannot be obtained for these people under the tenurial and functional structures that now prevail, a new structure of property relations must be introduced. Typically, collective action by a radical housing group is designed either to permit a neighborhood to implement a new set of tenurial and functional relations itself or to force the State to intervene to fundamentally change the rules of the game under which domestic property is owned and used. The implementation of various limited equity housing models, like cooperatives or community land trusts, would be examples of the first type of collective action. The imposition of rent control or a confiscatory tax on speculation would be examples of the second.

A Three-Stage Model of Collective Action

The housing improvement group, the conflict housing group, and the radical housing group are products and partners of three different levels of housing consciousness. When consciousness and organization combine, collective action is the complex product of both. The genesis and development of locality-based collective action, therefore, can be described and explained by means of a three-stage model that incorporates both of these "moments," combining different levels of housing consciousness with different types of housing interest group. This model is depicted schematically in Figure 3.

Three assumptions are operating here. First, this model assumes an "objective" basis for collective action—namely, the existence of similarly situated, similarly interested collectivities ("quasi-groups") that are constituted and differentiated by a particular tenurial and functional relation to domestic property. Second, this model assumes that *both* consciousness and organization must be present for these objectively constituted social formations to become collectively active interest groups. Third, this model assumes that consciousness is the prior "moment" in collective action. The conversion of latent interests into manifest interests "pushes" a quasi-group into becoming a property interest group, engaged in the collective improvement of property and place. The development of collective consciousness into conflict consciousness "pushes" an improvement group into becoming a conflict group. The development of conflict consciousness into radical consciousness "pushes" a conflict group into becoming a radical group.

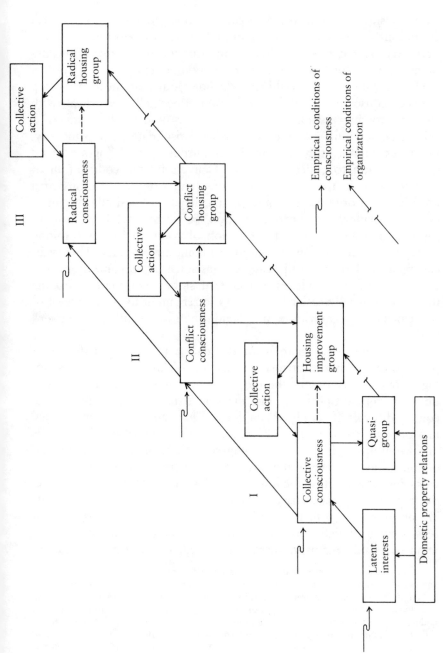

Figure 3. Genesis and development of locality-based Action: a three-stage model

Collective action

Radical housing group

Collective action

III

Radical consciousness

Conflict housing group

Collective action

II

Conflict consciousness

Housing improvement group

Collective action

Collective consciousness

Quasi-group

I

Latent interests

Domestic property relations

Empirical conditions of consciousness

Empirical conditions of organization

Consciousness is not a sufficient cause in this progression—empirical conditions of organization are required for each transition—but it is necessary, and it *is* first. Changes in consciousness provide the dynamic impetus for changes in organization and action.

Having said this, I should quickly point out that the relationship between consciousness and organization is normally reciprocal, with each reinforcing the other.[6] At each of the model's three stages, a shared perception of common interests consolidates group identity, mobilizes support for organizational purposes and programs, and gives direction to collective action. Conversely, the codification of consciousness in the internal structures and external relations of a locality-based organization, and the participation of similarly "interested" individuals in the organization's collective activities tend to foster and sustain a shared perception of common interests among those who share a common relation to domestic property. This cyclical, reciprocal relationship among consciousness, organization, and collective action introduces a degree of stability or inertia into the model. It is usually easier for a group to remain at its present level of consciousness, organization, and action than to ascend to a "higher" level.[7]

At the same time, there is an element of instability, a degree of precariousness, that is intrinsic to each level. This is not a self-sustaining system. Every one of the model's stages requires multiple conditions of consciousness and organization if it is to be attained and, equally difficult, if is to be maintained. What can be easily overlooked in a diagram such as Figure 3, where the direction of development is uniformly upward, is that changing conditions of consciousness and organization can reverse the direction of interest group development. Consciousness can become less radical, less contentious, or less collective than it once was. Organizations can retreat from a radical housing program, a conflict program, or an improvement program—or cease acting altogether. By specifying the conditional nature of consciousness and organization, by acknowledging the fragility of com-

6. This reciprocal relationship is represented in Figure 3 by a broken line, connecting consciousness and organization at Level I, II, and III.

7. This inertial tendency may be reinforced by any or all of the following: (1) the consciousness of many (or most) of a group's members may lag far behind that of its leaders; (2) consciousness may change more easily and quickly than an organization's ability to change its mission, activities, internal structures, and external relations; and (3) empirical conditions of organization that are available at "lower" stages of development—financial resources or a political climate of permissibility, for example—may become unavailable at "higher" stages (for example, when the action of a conflict group or radical group provokes repressive reactions from local elites).

mon purpose and collective action, this model is made capable of explaining the genesis and development of collective action and its demise. This locality-based model of collective action may explain not only why groups form, why they act, and how they develop, but why they fail to form, fail to act, decline, or disappear.

THE PRODUCTION AND PATTERN OF LOCALITY-BASED CONFLICT

The model before us can be combined with the earlier analysis of tenurial and functional cleavages, differentiating one locality-based collectivity from another, to explain the formation and collective action of various property interest groups. This same combination can be used in examining and explaining social relations *between* groups.

The origins of intergroup conflict or cooperation lie in the same interests of domestic property that originally constituted the groups themselves. These interests are contentiously (or compatibly) related long before groups ever form or act. This a priori alignment of what Saunders once called "objectively different and conflicting" interests has the political effect of orienting locality-based collectivities toward each other, predisposing their social interaction toward conflict. When this predisposition is made manifest in the consciousness and organization of different property interest groups, particular patterns of locality-based conflict tend to emerge.

The origins of intergroup conflict lie, first of all, in the objective incompatibility of "use" interests and "exchange" interests. Although it is true that interests may sometimes complement each other across the use/exchange divide—high amenity enhancing equity, for example—interests of use and interests of exchange represent alternative functions of domestic property that are, under most circumstances, fundamentally at odds. Accommodation and accumulation are not only different functions; they are antagonistic. Each may impede the other—and often does. Each may undermine the other—and often does. Thus public policies or social actions that promote and protect domestic property as a residential resource, by granting legal or political primacy to security, amenity, or autonomy, will tend to restrain the use of property as an accumulative commodity. Conversely, policies or actions that create new opportunities for a stream of income or capital gains from domestic property, enhancing its accumulative potential, will tend to threaten the security, amenity, or autonomy of those whose relation to domestic property is primarily accommodative.

The latent antagonism that exists between accommodation and accumulation is reflected in a general pattern of political alignment that places property interest groups with an entrepreneurial stake in security, amenity, and autonomy in antagonistic relation to groups with an entrepreneurial stake in equity and liquidity. Examples of such oppositional relations are many: speculators, developers, and acquisitive homeowners promoting their equity interest at the expense of private tenants, the homeless, or prospective buyers of household property; financiers withholding loans for amenity improvements from owner-occupiers in redlined areas; the owner-occupiers of social property impeding the property acquisition and equity buildup of speculators by decommodifying domestic property; private tenants protecting the security of their housing by agitating for rent control at the expense of the landlords' liquidity. Additional examples are easily found. In each case, across the use/exchange divide, the incumbents of property positions with accommodative interests and the incumbents of positions with accumulative interests are predisposed to act oppositionally toward one another.

A second pattern of intergroup conflict is produced by the incompatibility of specific accumulative interests among the property interest groups of private capital. While it is true that all of these private capital interest groups have a common interest in maximizing financial returns to domestic property as a market commodity, their interests collide when each attempts to maximize their profits at the expense of the others. Thus landlords, attempting to realize a stream of income from past investments in the built environment, may impede the plans of developers and financiers to redevelop an area for new investment. Speculators, pushing the price of property higher and higher, may make it impossible for developers to acquire land for new construction or to acquire buildings for renovation. The interest of financiers in obtaining maximum interest on their loaned capital may be incompatible with the landlords' interest in acquiring additional holdings or in maintaining the amenity of present holdings. High interest rates may also make it impossible for developers to begin new projects or to find buyers for completed projects. Despite a shared interest in accumulation, therefore, each of these private capital interest groups will frequently find their property interests objectively, contentiously in opposition with those of another capitalist group.

A third pattern of intergroup conflict is unique to the contradictory property position of owner-occupiers. Saunders was essentially correct in politically locating owner-occupiers between tenants and property capitalists, though he failed to identify the basis for clashes that often erupt between owner-occupiers and tenants, on one side, and between owner-occupiers and private capitalists, on the other. The incompatibility of accommodative and accumulative interests provides the piece that is missing from Saunders's analysis. Having an entrepreneurial stake in accumulation, owner-occupiers are antagonistically related to interest groups with an exclusive interest in accommodation. Having an entrepreneurial stake in accommodation, owner-occupiers are antagonistically related to interest groups with an exclusive interest in accumulation. Across the use/exchange divide, therefore, they can find themselves in political conflict on two fronts at once.

What neither Saunders nor Pratt recognized, however, was that there is also an objective basis for interest group conflict *within* the owner-occupier "class." The differences in tenure, function, and interest that objectively divide the owner-occupiers of social property, household property, and acquisitive property from one another may politically divide them as well, predisposing one group to collide contentiously with another. Two examples should suffice. In creating a limited-equity enclave of decommodified domestic property, the owner-occupiers of social property may function as a stabilizing, obstructionist counterweight to the appreciating property values of the other two owner-occupier groups. Conversely, the owner-occupiers of *acquisitive* property, who are aggressively "interested" in maximizing the equity and liquidity of their property, may induce changes in the price of land and buildings or changes in the amenity of property and place that inevitably threaten the security of the other two owner-occupier groups (by causing a rise in their property taxes, for example). In both cases, the interests of these different owner-occupier groups are economically and politically opposed, creating a basis for conflict among them. It may be useful to note, moreover, that the owner-occupiers of household property inhabit the same sort of political "middle ground" between social property and acquisitive property that owner-occupiers as a whole inhabit between tenants and property capitalists. The property interests of these household homeowners may conflict with those of either of the other owner-occupier groups, contentiously orienting the collective action of this middle group, sometimes one way and sometimes the other.

A final pattern of locality-based conflict may be less a product of objective differences in property interests than of subjective differences in the perception of those interests. The three-stage model of collective action suggests that property interest groups may differ not only on the basis of their particular relation to domestic property but on the basis of their particular level of consciousness and organization. These latter differences, I would argue, may produce significant variations in intergroup conflict, just as they produce significant variations in collective action. Thus it is not only the compatibility or incompatibility of their objective interests that determines the degree of harmony or hostility between two property interest groups, but the match or mismatch of their respective levels of organizational development. Groups fight (or cooperate), just as they form and act, not only because they have different property interests but because those interests have become the conscious goals of organized groups at different levels of development. Objective interests and subjective goals are the twin ingredients from which locality-based conflict is produced and patterned. This two-termed relationship is schematically portrayed in Figure 4.

Intergroup conflicts that occur across the use/exchange divide or among the interest groups of private capital or among the interest groups of owner-occupation are produced by objective differences in domestic property interests. As such, they would lie within Cell A or Cell B, on the *left* side of the table. Dividing such conflicts between Cells A and B acknowledges that interacting interest groups may be at different or at similar levels in their organizational development. It also implies that intergroup conflict that is based upon "objectively different and conflicting" interests may somewhat vary, depending upon the comparative developmental levels of the conflicting groups. The sort of variation that is introduced must remain an open question for now—answered, perhaps, by the case study that follows.

Comparative Property Interests

		Different	Same
Comparative Levels of Consciousness	Different	(A)	(C)
	Same	(B)	(D)

Figure 4. A typology of intergroup conflict

What also remains to be seen is whether locality-based conflicts appear within cells on the *right* side of the typology. That differences exist in the conscious goals of organized interest groups is an explicit assumption of the three-stage model of collective action. Whether such "subjective" differences can be the basis for intergroup conflict even when groups have the same objective interests (which would be the case within Cell C) can only be answered by examining actual instances of interest group conflict in a given locality. My hypothesis would be that subjective differences *can* provoke conflict between similarly "interested" groups—or between organizations representing the same interest group.

About conflicts in Cell D, there is very little that can be said—at least by a model of group formation and collective action that is built upon relations of domestic property. Intergroup conflicts in Cell D would occur despite the fact that the property interests and political consciousness of two interacting, organized groups are the same. Their antagonism would have nothing to do with the property positions or property interests of the two groups, but would originate somewhere else: perhaps in racial, ethnic, religious, or class differences; or perhaps in social differences between two organizations competing for the same constituency on the same turf. Conflicts of this sort are not denied by the model of property interest groups developed here, nor does the existence of such racial, ethinic, religious, class, or turf conflicts repudiate a domestic property approach to the study of locality-based action and locality-based conflict. Property interests are not the *only* explanation and cause of group formation, collective action, and intergroup conflict in residentially diverse neighborhoods. In fact, even when groups do form on the basis of domestic property interests, they may sometimes collectively act and conflictually interact on the basis of interests and issues that are only marginally related to their objective and subjective interest in domestic property. Cell D is a clear reminder of this.

APPLYING THE THEORETICAL FRAMEWORK

The origins of interest groups and interest-group conflicts within the place of residence—in short, a fully developed theory of locality-based action—can only be developed within a framework that manages to distinguish between objective property interests and subjective property interests and to theorize about their interrelationship. The three-stage model of locality-based collective action and the typology of intergroup conflict posited here are the beginnings of such a framework—tentative answers to the original question of how and why communities act?

As I have indicated, there is still much to be done before this theoretical framework may be considered complete, particularly with regard to the specification of various "empirical conditions" underlying the genesis and development of consciousness and organization. Enough is in place, however, to take these "ideal" conceptions of property interests and collective action out of the classroom and into the field, examining an actual case of group formation and intergroup conflict in a residentially diverse urban neighborhood.

The research agenda is dictated by the framework itself. Such a framework suggests that an understanding of locality-based action will depend upon an analysis of (1) objectively constituted property positions existing within a locality; (2) entrepreneurial interests, currently possessed by various "quasi-groups" (by virtue of their property positions); (3) strategic threats to those property interests—or opportunities to enhance them—arising from the relational contingency, precariousness, and contentiousness of the interests themselves; (4) empirical conditions of consciousness and organization existing inside and outside the locality; (5) collective activities and organizational development of various domestic property interest groups; and (6) social relations of conflict (and cooperation) existing among these organized groups. The researcher can begin an investigation at any point on this casual chain, but neither the description of locality-based action nor its explanation can be considered complete until he or she has moved analytically backward and forward along its entire length.

The coming case study of Cincinnati's West End should give a clearer idea as to whether this research agenda and the theoretical framework behind it actually provide a better understanding of locality-based collective action. A single case cannot establish the validity of this framework, of course, but it *can* test its plausibility—and fill in a few of its missing pieces.

Part II

COLLECTIVE ACTION IN CINCINNATI'S WEST END

7

The Besieged Community: Building and Bulldozing, 1800–1965

> I had a preacher friend in my youth, and I heard him say
> once at service that "Cincinnati should not be called the
> Queen City; it should be called the Peacock City. It loves its
> plumage—the arts, the sciences, music! But it hasn't any
> concern about these ugly feet that are planted in the West
> End of the city.
> —MAURICE MCCRACKIN (1982:95)

> The southern part of the West End, we moved into that area
> and it became a very important area for us. . . . Are you famil-
> iar with Southside Chicago? It was our Southside.
> —RICHARD LEWIS (interview, 1985)

The West End of Cincinnati, Ohio, is a residentially diverse, inner-city neighborhood with over one hundred and fifty years of history. Thirteen thousand people currently inhabit the neighborhood's 6,400 housing units, located on approximately four hundred acres. Most of the neighborhood's housing is tenant-occupied, evenly divided between the privately owned units of indigenous and absentee landlords, and the three publicly owned projects of the Cincinnati Metropolitan Housing Authority. The portion of the neighborhood's housing that is not rental property is evenly divided between traditional homeownership and social property. The former is divided between homeowners who have lived in the West End most of their lives and those who have recently entered the neighborhood—restoring its historic buildings, profiting from its low-cost property, and gentrifying several of its residential blocks. The West End's social property is divided between the occupants of the Park Town Cooperative and the "resi-

99

dent owners" of the Community Land Cooperative. All but a small percentage of the neighborhood's present population is black. A majority of its people are poor.

These tenurial and functional boundaries, dividing one set of residents from another, represent important social and political divisions as well. Group formation in the West End has tended to occur within these boundaries; intergroup conflict has tended to occur across these boundaries. Indeed, by the 1980s the West End had become a "fractured community"—internally divided among a handful of locality-based groups, organized along political lines laid down by the social cleavages of domestic property. The West End had also become a "contested community"—conflictually divided among organized groups whose material interests of domestic property are both different and antagonistic. These locality-based groups, especially their formation, development, and conflicts, are the ultimate focus of the West End study.

They will not be the initial focus, however. The locality-based action of today has its precursors and, to a large extent, its origins in the neighborhood's recent and not-so-recent past. The West End "community" that currently "acts" with so many voices, each attempting to shout the others down, once spoke with a single voice. There were, to be sure, differing interests of domestic property that existed then, just as now. But for ten years, from the mid-1960s to the mid-1970s, these cleavages were bridged and these groups were united in a new-found solidarity of race and place. The many groups that made up the "mobilized community" of this period defended their common interests in the face of threats and opposition from outside of the West End. They fought the political elites of City Hall and the economic elites of private capital instead of fighting each other. They fought to redress the grievances of the neighborhood's past and to participate in designing the neighborhood's future. They were somewhat successful in both of these struggles. Then the conditions that had engendered and sustained these struggles changed, and the "mobilized community" of the 1960s became the "fractured community" and the "contested community" of the 1980s.

Long before the community acted in any of these ways, however, it was acted upon by outside groups that alternately viewed the West End as either a source of private profit or an impediment to public prosperity. Acting singly and together, these interest groups of private capital first joined with city officials and public planners to build the West End into a densely settled slum of some 67,000 people housed on nearly 800 acres of land. These same groups later acted to re-develop the neighborhood into a commercial zone of interstate highways and industrial parks, erected around a residential remnant with one-half the acreage and one-fifth the population that the West End had before.

It was in response to these depredations and disruptions that the beleaguered residents of the West End began acting collectively, consciously, and contentiously in political defense of common interests of property and place. Even today, much of the locality-based action and locality-based conflict that exists in the neighborhood has its roots in this "besieged community," built and bulldozed by the powers-that-be many years before. The study of the present begins in the past.

BUILDING THE WEST END, 1800–1900

The original settlement of Cincinnati was established in the early 1790s on a flat, seven-square-mile valley shelf bounded on the south by the Ohio River, on the west by Mill Creek, and on the other two sides by steep hills, rising to an average height of three to four hundred feet. These natural features both defined the new city's boundaries and constricted outward expansion for its first one hundred years. Not until the construction of five inclined planes in the 1870s and the development of electric trolleys in the 1880s did Cincinnati's population spread beyond the crowded Basin onto the surrounding hills.[1]

Despite its tightly circumscribed land base, Cincinnati experienced rapid growth in its economy and population during the 1800s. By mid-century, the city had become the major machine-tool manufacturer in the West. It also led the nation in the production of finished clothing, beer, ale, and whiskey. Its extensive packer industries of meat, hides, tallow, and soap earned the city the name "Porkopolis," while its dominant commercial position in the steamboat trade of the Ohio River attracted the more glamorous name, "Queen City of the West."

This economic boom lured thousands of people to Cincinnati. Between 1820 and 1860, only New York and Philadelphia grew at a

---

1. Primary sources for this brief history of Cincinnati and the West End in the period before 1900 include Miller (1972; 1982), Taylor (1979:16–76), and Fairbanks (1981:17–20).

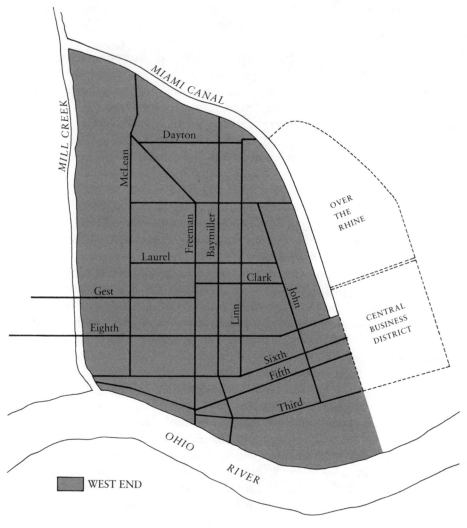

Figure 5. West End, circa 1890

faster rate. By 1860, with a population of 160,000, Cincinnati was the sixth-largest city in the United States. Before 1820, most immigrants were of English and Scottish descent; after 1820, Irish and Germans were predominant, with the latter making up over a third of the city's population by 1860. Blacks, migrating from the South, were also drawn to Cincinnati, particularly by the promise of relatively stable jobs in the steamboat industry. The city had only 690 blacks in 1826, but that number grew to 3,731 by 1860. Many of these newcomers, black and white, settled on the periphery of the central business and commercial district in an area between Western Row (Central Avenue) and Mill Creek (see Figure 5). This area became known as the West End.

Changes in the city's economy and population brought a real estate boom to the West End, beginning in the 1830s, that was to transform the residential and industrial structure of the entire area. At the lower tip, in the "bottoms" along the Ohio River, a black community arose that was derogatorily known as "Little Bucktown," or the "Swamp." Pushing against Little Bucktown, to the west and north, was a district of newly arrived Irish settlers. A little higher up, on Third Street, an affluent neighborhood that had pre-dated the 1830s boom expanded along Fourth and Fifth streets. Between Sixth and Laurel streets, "a diverse conglomeration of lower- and middle-class Cincinnatians overran the farms, factories, and cemetaries and established their homes and institutions" (Miller, 1982:54).

The greatest transformation occurred in the upper West End, an area that had been previously occupied by dairies, farms, and truck gardens. Slaughterhouses, soap factories, and tanneries began to appear after 1815. Such industrial development soared between 1830 and 1875. By the latter year, the upper West End had three meat-packing plants, eight machine shops, two carriage manufacturers, a brewery, a Singer Sewing Machine factory, and numerous producers of soap, oils, and candles. Tenement houses for workers appeared throughout the district. On Dayton Street, at the top of the West End, a group of wealthy beer brewers, pork packers, and factory owners built lavish three-story houses. This area, developed between 1850 and 1890, became known as "Millionaires' Row."

As the city's population continued to grow and as its business district pushed westward, the lower West End (below Fourth Street) began filling up with railroad tracks, terminals, warehouses, and hotels. At the same time, the entire West End was becoming one of Cincinnati's most densely settled areas, with more than its share of tenement houses. From 1869 to 1879, tenement houses throughout the city increased from 1,410 to 5,616, leading one observer to note in 1870 that "there is no city in the United States in which a larger proportional population is crowded into tenement houses—than Cincinnati" (quoted by Fairbanks, 1981:17). Many of these tenements were located in the West End.

The residential pattern in the West End—and in most of the city's twelve wards—was one of "mixed" neighborhoods, integrated racially and economically, even when different blocks within these neighborhoods were organized along racial, ethnic, or economic lines: "Distinct though these neighborhoods and ethnic colonies were, no invincible barriers separated them. For example, Millionaire's Row on Dayton Street in the west end was only a stone's throw from the workers' tenements sections." (Taylor, 1979:35–36).

The crowding of pre-1900 Cincinnati was not conducive to social harmony, however, even if "no invincible barriers" existed between racial, ethnic, and economic groups. As different groups were pressed against each other and were periodically displaced in the competition for increasingly scarce commercial, industrial, and residential sites, violence flared. Intergroup conflict became a familiar part of Cincinnati life in the middle and late 1800s. Race riots occured in 1829, 1836, 1842, and 1863. The 1836 riot was confined to the lower West End, involving the black and Irish residents of the Ohio River bottom section. Antiforeign and anti-Catholic outbursts occurred in the early 1850s. Cincinnati's most serious urban disorder, the Court House Riot of 1884, killed fifty people and injured another two hundred.

Cincinnati's crisis of spatial congestion and social conflict was partially alleviated after the mid-1880s by the development of electric trolleys, allowing the city's burgeoning population to scale and settle the eastern and northern hills.[2] The exodus from the Basin was led by the wealthy, who established properous residential neighborhoods on the hilltops overlooking the city, and by the larger industries that gradually moved from the West End and Over the Rhine to the Mill Creek industrial belt, several miles to the north.[3] Although the upper West End was to retain a large diversified assortment of light industry

2. With the introduction of electric transit up and over the hills, Cincinnati expanded from 22.20 to 35.27 square miles between 1880 and 1900. It covered fifty square miles by 1920.

3. One of the companies that left the Basin was Proctor and Gamble. After a fire in 1884, Proctor and Gamble moved from 830 and 832 Central Avenue on the northeastern edge of the West End to Ivorydale in the Mill Creek industrial belt.

into the twentieth century, the lower West End lost all but three of its factories and nearly half of its commercial establishments in the 1880s and 1890s.

By the turn of the century, the affluent enclaves in the lower and upper West End had been abandoned by the wealthy. The brick and masonry homes of the lower West End, around Fourth, Fifth, Sixth, and Seventh streets, were divided into flats and then rented out to the neighborhood's new residents, immigrants from southern and eastern Europe, many of whom were Jews, and blacks from the expanding ghetto at the southern and western edge of the West End. The mansions of the upper West End, in the Dayton Street area, were turned over to middle-class homeowners, some of whom had lived in the lower West End. These families were white, as were most of the residents of the upper West End. Thus, while the lower West End was becoming a black, residential neighborhood with an ever-increasing proportion of low-income tenants (black and white), the upper West End remained a predominantly white, middle-class and lower-middle-class area of mixed uses—industrial, commercial, and residential.

Whatever the differences between the upper and lower West End, the tenement districts of both areas had begun to deteriorate badly by the turn of the century, along with much of the rental housing not built of masonry. The absence of sanitary facilities was common, and overcrowding was on the rise. Much of the lower West End, and probably a third of the upper West End (below Armory), had begun to take on the characteristics of a slum.

THE MAKING OF A SLUM, 1900–1930

As new neighborhoods opened up on Cincinnati's hilltops, as many industries moved outside of the city, and as housing conditions in the city's original downtown neighborhoods declined, "every inner-city resident with the economic means to do so left the Basin area" (Taylor, 1979:125). Almost half of the city's population resided in this downtown "Basin" in 1900. Twenty years later, the proportion stood at just over a third. Although every ethnic, racial, and income group was represented in this exodus, the demographic shift of whites from the Basin to the hilltops was the most extreme. Between 1900 and 1930, the number of whites living in other sections of the city increased by 36 percent, while the Basin was losing 27,398 whites—a decrease of 18 percent (see Table 1).

Table 1. Downtown population by area and race, 1900–1930

	1900			1910			1920			1930		
	Black	White	Total	Black	White	Total	Black	White	Total	Black	White	Total
City of Cincinnati												
Population	14,482	312,148	326,630	19,639	332,543	352,182	30,079	348,401	378,480	47,818	376,612	424,430
(percent)	4	96	100	6	94	100	8	92	100	11	89	100
Basin (incl. West End)												
Population	9,542	148,788	158,330	12,481	135,912	148,393	20,284	116,933	137,217	33,299	121,390	154,689
(percent)	6	94	100	8	92	100	15	85	100	22	78	100
(percent of city)	66	48	48	63	40	42	67	33	36	70	32	36
West End												
Population	3,604	32,612	36,216	8,647	50,518	59,165	17,207	36,799	54,006	29,332	17,543	46,875
(percent)	10	90	100	15	85	100	32	68	100	63	37	100
(percent of Basin)	38	22	23	69	37	40	85	31	39	88	14	30
(percent of city)	25	10	11	44	15	17	57	11	14	61	5	11

Source of population data: Taylor (1979:128–29).

Nevertheless, the total population of the Basin's neighborhoods remained fairly stable during this thirty-year period for the simple reason that migration into the Basin kept pace with migration out of the Basin. These inner-city neighborhoods, with their high concentration of tenements, shacks, and subdivided two- and three-story houses, contained the city's most inexpensive housing. Furthermore, despite the departure of many industrial and commercial firms, the Basin still contained numerous plants, factories, shops, and stores—all within walking distance of the Basin's residents. For newcomers to Cincinnati, most of whom arrived with few resources and no immediate prospects for employment, the Basin was the only area in which they could afford to live.

The West End was the inner-city area that absorbed most of these migrants. At the beginning of the 1900s, with an ample supply of cheap housing throughout the neighborhood, with many places of employment in the upper West End, and with the railway station (where the majority of the city's newest residents disembarked) in the lower West End, the neighborhood attracted low-income newcomers of both races. Between 1900 and 1910, the white population in the West End grew by 22,949 people, an increase of 63 percent; the black population grew by 5,043, a 140-percent increase. These additions increased the neighborhood's density while creating severe overcrowding in its tenements. They also signaled a coming change in the neighborhood's racial composition. Although still a predominantly white neighborhood in 1910, with whites making up 85 percent, the West End was fast becoming home to more of the city's blacks. By 1910 only 6 percent of the city's population was black, but 44 percent of the black population lived in the West End.

The migration of rural, southern blacks to northern urban centers, which had begun as a trickle in the 1880s, became an inexorable flood after 1910. Some blacks headed straight for Cincinnati, hoping for jobs in the city's long-established light industries of clothing, shoe, printing, liquor, and soap, or in the city's newer mechanical, chemical, iron, and steel industries. Others, originally headed elsewhere, stayed in Cincinnati because they could not afford to move on (Taylor, 1979:86–99). The city's black population grew by 28,179 between 1910 and 1930. By the end of this period, blacks made up 11 percent of Cincinnati's population.

As the northern migration continued, the West End filled up with newcomers who were too poor to live anywhere else and with longtime residents who were too poor to leave. The neighborhood became more impoverished and more black, particularly at its lower end. Although a large Jewish community remained in this part of the neighborhood well into the 1920s, most other whites either retreated to the upper West End, moving above the "natural" divide of Laurel Street, or fled the neighborhood altogether.[4]

During the twenties, the West End became the center of Cincinnati's black community. Of the city's 47,818 black citizens, 33,299 lived in the downtown neighborhoods of the Basin, and 88 percent of these residents were concentrated in the West End. The combination of (1) a burgeoning black population, (2) increasing barriers to black settlement in outlying areas, and (3) a developing black bourgeoisie with few opportunities for employment or advancement outside of the downtown ghetto caused the energies of the black community to turn inward. A lively cultural, religious, and social life was created in the lower West End for the thousands of blacks who settled there:

> [The lower West End] was the heart of the community, the old black West End, which built up with the immigration from the South. . . . The railroad station was down there, at Third and Central. . . . A lot of people came in by train. The people came in and saw other blacks and settled around the railroad station. . . . Our churches were there. The churches became the Hull Houses, the settlement houses for the blacks that were coming in: Union Baptist and Antioch and Zion Baptist. . . . Our schools were there: Stowe School, Jackson School, Sherman School. Then the Catholic schools: St. Ann's and DePorres. . . . Our social clubs were there. Our hotels: we had the Sterling Hotel. Our main places of entertainment: there were several night clubs, but the Cotton Club had New York-style shows, complete with chorus lines, big bands, comedians, singers, tap dancers. You'd see a complete show. (Lewis interview, 1985:364–65)

In addition to these traditional religious, educational, social, and recreational institutions, a new kind of black organization began to appear in the West End after 1910, the civic and reform group.[5] Some of these organizations—such as the NAACP, the Negro Civic Welfare Association, and a Cincinnati branch of Marcus Garvey's Universal Negro Improvement Association—were devoted primarily to racial improvement, civic pride, race uplift, and social justice for Cincin-

4. In 1918, 55 percent of the city's 19,000 Jews still lived in the West End. By 1930 only 5 percent of the city's Jewish population (which had reached 20,000) remained in the West End (Miller, 1982:65).

5. Details of the organizational structure of the West End during the period 1910–1930 are drawn from Miller (1982:70–73) and Koehler (1983:101–45).

nati's black community. Other civic and reform groups dealt primarily with neighborhood improvement, concentrating upon the deplorable housing, health, and recreational conditions in the West End. In the mid-1920s, a number of these neighborhood improvement associations were organized, including the Baymiller Improvement Association and the Central Avenue Improvement Association. Racial improvement and neighborhood improvement were not easily separated, however, despite the intention of these local groups to focus on one or the other. With nearly two-thirds of Cincinnati's black community located in the lower half of a single neighborhood, the politics of race and the politics of place tended to overlap.

This was also true in the upper West End. The white residents above Laurel Street, no less than their black neighbors to the south, were concerned with the improvement of their neighborhood, their housing, and their opportunities for economic and social advancement. These concerns spurred the formation of numerous locality-based organizations:

> [I]nhabitants enjoyed but marginal economic security, for strikes, layoffs, industrial accidents, depressions and absence of old age and other welfare programs clouded their lives with the fear of poverty. Their half-way position in the process of assimilation intensified their sense of insecurity, as did their residence on or near the cutting edge of the slums. . . . Threatened by poverty and absorbtion into the expanding slums, . . . residents assumed a defensive position which expressed itself in a passion for organizational affiliation. (Miller, 1972:61)

This sense of economic and residential insecurity made the upper West End one of the most politically unpredictable and volatile sections of the city, and "in times of economic stress, social tension, or industrial conflict, many of its inhabitants made easy prey for religious and racial bigots" (ibid.:62). Consequently, to the neighborhood improvement associations; building associations; fraternal, ethnic, and mutual benefit associations of the area; white West Enders added a "racial improvement association" of their own, the Ku Klux Klan. It is estimated that city membership in the Klan reached fifteen thousand during the early 1920s. There is evidence that the upper West End—and the minority white community in the lower West End—"made a disproportionate contribution to the membership rolls of the hooded society" (Miller, 1982:76).

As white and black West Enders distributed themselves among various civic organizations for the betterment of their neighborhood or for the betterment of their races, other organized groups were actively pursuing economic interests that were to threaten the well-being of all West Enders, regardless of race. These included (1) real estate brokers and financiers, who blocked the migration of blacks out of the Basin; (2) landlords and developers, who converted the Basin into a profitable slum; and (3) business-men and industrialists, who coveted the residential lands of the West End for uses other than housing. The actions of these capitalist interest groups in the decades after the turn of the century, along with the inaction of public officials, created the conditions that turned the West End first into a ghetto, then into a slum, and finally into an officially designated "blighted area" that was to bring a bulldozer to many a door.

By 1930, 70 percent of Cincinnati's black population lived in the downtown neighborhoods of the Basin. Nine out of ten of these black, inner-city residents were concentrated in the lower end of the West End. The creation of this black ghetto was due, in part, to factors suggested earlier: the presence of cheap housing, the proximity to places of employment and commerce, the location of the railroad station at the neighborhood's southern end, and the proclivity of newly arrived immigrants to settle near others like themselves and near institutions serving their religious, material, and social needs. Although they provide a certain commonsense explanation for the tendency of black immigrants to settle in the West End, these factors do not provide sufficient explanation for the tendency of blacks to remain there. They do not explain the concentration of blacks in a single area and the persistence of this ghetto over time.

The West End ghetto was created, first, by an opportunity structure that froze black workers at the bottom of the occupational ladder. Between 1910 and 1930, despite the fact that the number of black industrial workers grew by 5,673, only 2 percent of them were able to find jobs in classifications other than laborer; indeed, during this period, 77 percent of *all* black employees in Cincinnati's industries were classified as "laborers" (Taylor, 1979:104). Trapped in low-paying, dead-end jobs, most blacks found themselves trapped in the low-rent housing of the Basin as well.

Second, blacks who did have the income to leave the Basin were systematically blocked from doing so by financial institutions that refused to lend them money for the purchase of homes and by white neighborhoods that refused admission to black homeowners.[6] These

6. Faced with the refusal of banks and building and loans to provide money to purchase homes, blacks organized two building and loan associations of their own. The first, the Industrial Federal Savings and Loan Association, was chartered in 1919.

racist attitudes were given institutional force in 1921 when the city's best-organized housing interest group, the Cincinnati Real Estate Board, adopted segregation as its official policy, enlisting its members in the cause of ghettoization: "No agent shall rent or sell property to colored in an established white section or neighborhood and this inhibition shall be particularly applicable to the hilltops and suburban property" (quoted in Fairbanks, 1981:115).

Though confined to the Basin and increasingly concentrated in a single section of a single neighborhood, Cincinnati's black population continued to grow. Since developers believed that they could not make a profit building units for people who earned only $1,200 per year (the average annual income for black Cincinnatians in 1910), no new housing was built downtown. The result was a housing shortage in the lower West End that produced severe overcrowding for the neighborhood's blacks and a booming real estate business for the neighborhood's landlords: "The overcrowding lured greedy speculators to the West End, who traded and bought tenements, raised rents, and reaped the economic benefits while Negroes suffered. Rents, which tripled in some instances between 1918 and 1922, produced doubling and tripling in some West End flats and some truly extraordinary cases of congestion" (ibid.).

Every available structure was converted into rental property in order to house the soaring black population. Houses were subdivided again and again. Many of these rental units were located in tenements built before the Civil War and lacking indoor toilets, catch basins, and an indoor water supply. These aging structures deteriorated quickly with more intensive use. It was not only the pre–Civil War housing that deteriorated, however, because more and more of the Basin's landlords simply stopped putting money into maintenance and repair:

> [L]andlords rationalized that they could not maintain the existing quality of their rental property and still make a profit. Hence, they adopted a policy of keeping overhead down by ignoring local housing and sanitation codes, and making only essential repairs on the ancient buildings. When these structures could no longer generate a profit, the property was sold, the building razed, and the land converted to commercial and/or industrial use. (Taylor, 1979:134)

Forty years later, after making 650 home loans, totaling $1.8 million, the president of Industrial Federal described the mortgage situation of blacks as follows: "We have had to supply a market most other building and loans have refused. . . . We haven't made much of a dent in the Negro housing problem. It would take $10 million to do that" (*Post and Times-Star*, June 6, 1959:9).

The actions of these landlords was tacitly condoned by the city's economic and political leaders. Financial and industrial elites were all too happy to have tenements razed and the land converted to commercial or industrial use. Public officials, nearly all white, had no desire to antagonize the white residents of neighborhoods outside of the Basin by encouraging black settlement there. Neither did political leaders of the 1920s believe that it was the public's responsibility to provide or administer better housing for low-income people. Consequently, Cincinnati's economic and political leaders viewed the landlords of the Basin's rental property as "the unofficial administrators of housing for the poor," and by not enforcing housing and sanitation codes, gave them great leeway in operating their downtown "housing program" (ibid.:134–35).

True, some concern was voiced about the West End becoming a danger to public health. The mortality rate among West End blacks from tuberculosis alone reached eight hundred per one hundred thousand during the 1920s, a rate four times as high as that of whites.[7] Acknowledging the danger of such diseases to the general public, the city employed a team of health and housing inspectors to eliminate the most pestilential housing. But their numbers were few, their powers were slight, and their backing was practically nil. The city's leading housing reformer at the time noted gloomily: "Conditions in the Basin area were appalling. The some half dozen inspectors couldn't begin to force compliance with the law and nobody seemed to care, certainly not the chief officials of the city government. The judges in the municipal court were not really interested either. They listened to the wealthy landlords, so that these men could and did get away with years of delay" (Marquette, 1972:42).

Not all of the housing in the lower West End became dilapidated, however, and not all was owned by landlords. One historian, examining a section of the lower West End that later became known as Queensgate II, noted, "There were, in fact, many substantial citizens in the neighborhood. . . . One check in the 1920s revealed 202 Negro property holders in Queensgate II" (Miller, 1982:69). Here and there in other parts of the West End, blacks also began to purchase homes.

By the mid-1920s, despite the area's many economic and residential problems, a degree of occupational and residential differentiation had begun to develop in the black portion of the West End. Most workers, male and female, were in menial, low-paying jobs at the bottom

7. Marquette (1972:43); Tillery (1971:9).

of the city's occupational ladder, but a black bourgeoisie of clergy, teachers, doctors, porters, musicians, and small businessmen had begun to develop. Most residents were tenants, and many lived in dreadful housing, but some were gradually becoming homeowners. Equally important, the West End possessed a diverse, highly developed institutional matrix of churches, clubs, associations, and neighborhood-based organizations dedicated to improving the circumstances of the area's residents. As the decade progressed, there was ample reason to believe that a healthy dose of housing reform, rational planning, and public assistance might still salvage the West End as a viable residential community: "[M]ost of the West End, to be sure, was a slum, but it was neither stagnant nor yet doomed to inevitable decline. A balanced assessment of the forces of flux in the 1920s would have to conclude that options remained, that the vital undertow of optimism was not unwarranted" (Miller, 1982:73).

REFORMERS AND PLANNERS, 1925–1948

Cincinnatians who lived outside of the Basin felt no such "vital tow of optimism" when surveying conditions in the West End. Their assessment excluded any appreciation for the social differentiation, institutional diversity, and interpersonal networks that were developing amidst the decaying structures of this overcrowded neighborhood. They saw only the slum, nothing of the social order behind it. Home to the city's most notorious red-light district, the most dilapidated tenements, the most impoverished residents, and some of the city's most unsanitary living conditions, the West End seemed to the citizens of Cincinnati's hilltops a virtual cesspool of crime, dependency, and disease. It is not surprising, therefore, that as various movements for governmental reform, housing reform, and city planning got under way—movements originating on the hilltops, not in the Basin— the eradication of the West End slums rose higher and higher on the public agenda.

Would-be reformers of the Basin's housing conditions had pursued several strategies before the 1920s.[8] Their earliest efforts placed an emphasis on regulating tenements through building and sanitation codes. Later, under the leadership of the Better Housing League,

8. Details of early housing reform efforts in Cincinnati are drawn from Fairbanks (1981:30–81), Taylor (1979:141–61), Marquette (1972:44–58), Miller (1972:3–4), and City Planning Commission (1925:50–51).

formed in 1916, housing reformers expanded their regulatory approach to include "preventive care"; that is, they sought to protect outlying residential areas from the kind of density and deterioration common to the Basin, using zoning to limit the areas where multi-unit housing could be built. The city's first zoning act passed unanimously on April 1, 1924.

Other housing reformers threw their energies into convincing Cincinnati's industrialists to construct "model housing" or "new towns" for their workers, or focused on supporting Cincinnati's growing number of savings and loan associations. Others became ardent supporters of government reform, reasoning that less corruption among the city's public officials would mean better enforcement of existing housing codes.[9]

Housing reformers became increasingly disillusioned with such piecemeal approaches to the housing problem and began advocating a more comprehensive approach, one that "acknowledged that housing was inextricably linked to neighborhood and city-wide problems and needed city-wide solutions" (Fairbanks, 1981:43). They began lobbying for comprehensive city planning. Partially as a result of their efforts, Cincinnati's first city plan was completed in 1924 and adopted by the city council the next year, making Cincinnati one of the first municipalities in the nation to have an official city plan. But if housing reformers had hoped that this plan would provide a citywide solution to the Basin's housing problems, they were to be woefully disappointed.

The 1925 City Plan acknowedged that, "so far as wage earners are concerned," the "housing problem" is "more pressing than it has been at any time in the past, and there are fewer vacancies, more bad housing conditions and a far greater degree of room overcrowding." (City Planning Commission, 1925:50–51). Housing conditions in the western end of the Basin were said to be especially bad: "In the west

9. Corruption, in fact, was a mainstay of Cincinnati politics until the mid-1920s. The concentration of people in the inner city, most of them poor, newly arrived, and marginally employed, had allowed "Boss" George B. Cox to fashion a powerful system of patronage and political control (cf. Miller, 1972:4). This increasingly corrupt Republican machine dominated Cincinnati politics from the 1880s to the 1920s. Finally, in 1924, a coalition of "good government" Republicans, Democrats, and independents created the Charter Party, won a majority of seats on the city council, and established a city manager form of government with a nine-member council elected at large. These reforms broke the back of the Republican machine by removing both patronage and precincts from city politics. They also broke what little grip on political power the West End might have had. After the reforms of 1924, candidates for city council were elected by and accountable to *all* of the city's residents, more and more of whom lived outside of the Basin. No one spoke exclusively or primarily for the West End.

end most of the oldest and more unsanitary tenements are occupied by colored people, where they often live six, seven, eight, and even twelve people in a single room. These slum conditions could be much improved if the City had available even normal means for their control."

This last sentence held the hint that one or more recommendations were about to be made for providing the city with the "means" to improve slum conditions. Not so. Neither the city planning commission that prepared the 1925 plan, nor the city council that approved it were willing to acknowledge that the public sector had any responsibility for eradicating slums or for providing shelter for those who inhabited those slums. Therefore, except for the enforcement of zoning and the provision of parks, playgrounds, and community centers, the plan proposed no role for the public in solving the "housing problem in Cincinnati."

The solution lay, instead, in the "natural" market forces of the private sector. Left alone, these natural forces would both remove the tenements and slums of the inner city and relieve the citywide shortage of affordable housing. According to the 1925 plan, the problem of the Basin's slums would be eventually solved by the "invasion of industry and business" (ibid.:6). The entire West End, the plan predicted (and hoped), would be converted from a residential neighborhood into a commercial and industrial district.[10] The problem of affordable housing, on the other hand, would be "solved" by the private production of upper-income homes, with older units filtering down to lower-income people: "[I]t is obvious that new houses can not be built directly for wage earners, and that the only way housing accommodations can be provided for them is by relieving the pressure higher up. In other words, as fast as the families in better circumstances move out of the older tenements and houses, they will become available for housing the lower wage earners" (ibid.:51). Thus, as one set of market forces cleared the downtown Basin of slums, another set would open up affordable, secondhand housing for the thousands of former slum dwellers who had been displaced by the spread of industry and business.[11]

10. In anticipation of—and to encourage—this commercial and industrial "invasion," the city planning commission zoned nearly all of the West End either "Industrial B" or "Business A."

11. The 1925 plan estimated that 67,000 people would eventually be forced out of their West End tenements into low-cost housing outside the Basin. Although this took much longer than the planners had predicted, requiring as it did the combined forces of the public and private sectors, between 57,000 and 67,000 people were eventually pushed out of the West End. It took nearly sixty years to meet this 1925 planning objective, but it *was* met.

Despite this plan, an increasing number of public officials, housing reformers, and city planners had lost faith in these "natural" market forces by the 1930s. The onset of the Great Depression had halted industrial expansion, all but ended new housing production, and undermined general confidence in private-sector solutions to public problems. Many of these problems were getting worse. In the West End, a twenty-year decline in population, which had led the city's planners to hope that the area's chronic overcrowding was being eased at last, abruptly turned around. Black migration—and even a modest white migration—into the West End caused the size and density of the neighborhood's population to climb. And, by 1933, much of that population was unemployed. Throughout the city, unemployment for whites reached 28 percent; unemployment for blacks was nearly double that figure, 54 percent (Tillery, 1971:31).

Many of these impoverished people could only afford the cheap housing of the West End. A survey of West End residents, conducted during the Depression, found that 48 percent of the families earned between five and twenty dollars a week; nearly 12 percent reported no income at all. The same survey, examining housing conditions in the West End, found that two-thirds of the area's units were in only "fair condition," needing repair; an additional 10 percent were badly deteriorated and structurally unsafe. Nevertheless, *all* of these dwellings were occupied (Hamilton County Department of Public Welfare, 1933).

As Cincinnatians lost confidence that the private market would clear the slums and provide affordable housing, housing reformers took the initiative in proposing a public solution to the problem. They argued that the powers and resources of government should be mobilized to raze the slums and to erect decent, affordable public housing. In 1929, Cincinnati's Commission of Health observed that "nothing short of a huge development will relieve the situation of the West End within a reasonable time, a consummation that we look forward to devoutly" (quoted in Fairbanks, 1981:130). Several years later, the Executive Secretary of the Better Housing League, Bleeker Marquette, proclaimed that the only solution to the slum problem was to "tear down those areas and rebuild them along modern, well-planned lines (ibid.:156)." Around the same time, a new lobbying group formed to pressure the city into applying for federal public housing funds, made available under the National Industrial Recovery Act of 1933. This group, made up mostly of members of the Women's City Club and the Better Housing League, was named the Citizen's Committee on Slum Clearance (ibid.: 145–46; Marquette, 1972:83).

As the public housing bandwagon gathered momentum, the city planning commission developed a new plan for the West End. This 1933 Basin District Redevelopment Plan, in a marked departure from the Official City Plan of 1925, proposed to replace 145 city blocks in the West End and Over the Rhine with sixteen superblocks of low-cost housing, built around open parks, schools, and community centers. The city's planners seemed no longer to believe that commercial and industrial expansion would eliminate the area's slums or that affordable housing would be forthcoming outside of the Basin. Instead, the slums of the North and West Central Basin would be replaced by a modern, well-planned, residential community, built with public encouragement and support.[12]

City officials and local housing reformers moved quickly to put the machinery in place for slum clearance and public housing.[13] The Cincinnati Metropolitan Housing Authority (CMHA) was created on November 22, 1933, three months after the Ohio legislature passed the nation's first housing authority law. The CMHA's first meeting was held on December 9. Five days later, it submitted a preliminary proposal to the Public Works Administration (PWA) in Washington, requesting $22 million. Basing its grant request on the Basin District Redevelopment Plan, already in hand, the CMHA proposed to begin residential redevelopment of blocks C, D, E, J, K, and L, an area bounded by Freeman, Liberty, Central Parkway, and Clark (see Figure 6). Informed by PWA officials that Cincinnati would be granted only $6 million, the CMHA scaled down its project plans, eventually proposing blocks D, E, and K for demolition and new construction. On October 9, 1934, the authority began securing options for the purchase of property in these blocks.[14]

12. On the other hand, the planners were not prepared to abandon entirely their belief that the West End should be redeveloped for industrial use. The area below Seventh Avenue, home to the city's worst slum and 13,000 of its poorest residents, was not included in the residential redevelopment plan. Neither was the area west of Freeman Avenue. The commission decided that both of these areas—later known, respectively, as Queensgate I (or Kenyon-Barr I) and Liberty-Dalton—should be redeveloped for commercial and industrial uses.

13. Details of early public housing development in Cincinnati are drawn primarily from Fairbanks (1981:159–86).

14. Included in the CMHA's original request for $22 million had been a proposal to build a vacant-land housing project north of Cincinnati, providing low-cost housing for blacks unable to find room in the new projects of the West End. Implicit in this proposal was an acknowledgment by the CMHA that West End redevelopment would not rehouse as many people as it would displace. Granted only $6 million, the CMHA decided to go ahead with its West End plans even though replacement housing was known to be unavailable for many of the blacks who then resided within the target blocks.

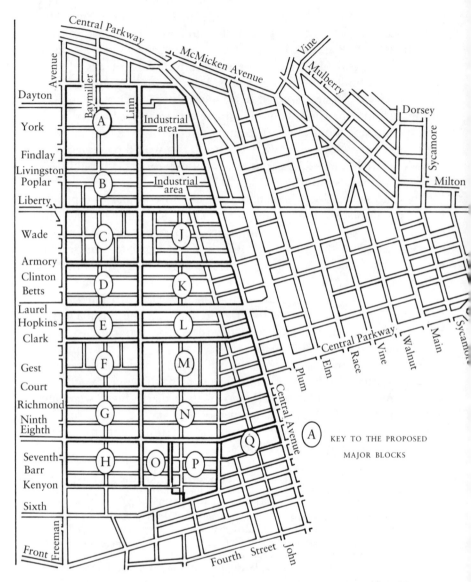

Figure 6. Target blocks of Basin District Plan (Source: City Planning Commission, 1933; CMHA Papers, Cincinnati Historical Society)

Almost immediately, the CMHA encountered resistance from residents west of Linn Street, those living in blocks D and E. Property owners complained, on the one hand, that the prices being offered for their parcels were too low and, on the other hand, that their property should not be taken at all, since their neighborhood was not a slum. In fact, a quarter of the 1,012 dwellings that the CMHA proposed to demolish in blocks D and E were owner-occupied, and housing conditions *were* better in this area than in most of the other blocks included in the 1933 Redevelopment Plan. Residents suspected that the real reason blocks D and E were being given such high priority by the CMHA had less to do with the condition of the area's housing than with its location along Laurel Street, the main approach to the city's newly completed railroad station (Union Terminal). The beautification of this avenue had been advocated for years by Cincinnati's cultural, economic, and political leaders, leading the residents of blocks D and E to complain that their homes were being sacrificed to satisfy someone else's aesthetic ideals. Such grievances prompted the formation of the West End Property Owners Association, composed mainly of property owners from blocks D and E.

Confronted with the public protest of the property owners association and the refusal of its members to sell their property, the CMHA began considering a change in its redevelopment plans. On February 26, 1935, a request was sent to the PWA to relocate the proposed clearance site to blocks J and K, an area east of Linn and north of Laurel. Not only were there few residents from this site who were members of the West End Property Owners Association—indeed, 91 percent of them were tenants—but the CMHA discovered that the absentee owners were willing to sell at the prices being offered for their property.[15] Furthermore, given the increasingly politicized context of this site selection decision, it was probably not insignificant that blocks J and K contained a higher concentration of blacks than blocks D and E. Blacks would be politically easier to displace than whites.[16]

15. Part of the conflict between the CMHA and the property owners of blocks D and E arose out of the former's insistence on using the 1931 tax appraisals in pricing the latter's property. The Depression had greatly reduced property values; in some cases, the 1931 tax appraisal was 50 or 60 percent of the 1927 appraisal. The property owners of blocks D and E, therefore, believed that the low price being offered to them by the CMHA was "taking unfair advantage of them during a period of temporary disaster" (Fairbanks, 1981:172). Apparently, the absentee landlords of blocks J and K had no such complaints and were willing to sell at the currently appraised price.

16. There is a measure of conjecture in this. After all, the CMHA was also hesitant to displace too many blacks, fearing that they would scatter further north and turn the upper West End into the same kind of slum as the lower West End. (This was one of

Permission was given by the PWA for the site switch, the property was acquired and cleared, and on February 13, 1936, construction began on Cincinnati's first public housing project—Laurel Homes.

Although 769 black families (comprising 61 percent of the site's original occupants) were displaced by the construction of Laurel Homes, CMHA decided that its first slum clearance project would be for whites only. When Cincinnati's black community learned of this, it began pressuring the housing authority and city council to admit blacks to Laurel Homes. CMHA resisted throughout 1937, hoping that the PWA would approve its request for additional funds to build an all-black public housing project south of Laurel Street (renamed during this period, Lincoln Park Drive). When this proposal was not approved, the CMHA finally bowed to public pressure and decided that 30 percent of the 1,200 units would be reserved for blacks. On August 22, 1938, the first tenants began moving into Laurel Homes.

City officials persisted in trying to secure a black housing project for Cincinnati. On December 27, 1939, the U.S. Housing Authority agreed to grant the CMHA a $5.371 million loan for slum clearance and housing construction in sections L and M of the West End. By May 1941, the CMHA had acquired all of the land in this area and demolition of approximately four hundred buildings had begun. Blacks started moving into the completed project, named Lincoln Court, on December 11, 1942.

The construction of Laurel Homes and Lincoln Court completely transformed a twenty-two-block area east of Linn Street, stretching from Court Street on the south to Liberty Street on the north. Approximately 750 two-, three-, and four-story tenement houses, small businesses, churches, and shops were demolished, making way for eighty-two interconnected four-story brick apartment buildings. No doubt reflecting the influence of the 1933 Redevelopment Plan, these apartment buildings were arranged around open courtyards, creating self-contained "superblocks." With far less coverage than the twenty-two blocks they had replaced, these superblocks provided more light, air, and recreational space; moreover, with fewer housing units and with fewer people packed into each building, these superblocks eased

---

the reasons given by CMHA officials for not begining their slum clearance projects where housing conditions were the worst.) On the other hand, block-for-block sites D and E had a much higher proportion of white residents than sites J and K. These areas west of Linn Street were eventually cleared in the 1950s, but it did not happen until they had become much blacker—and, I would argue, much more politically vulnerable—than they had been in 1934.

the area's chronic overcrowding. Population density was reduced from 72 families per acre to 47.4 (Fairbanks, 1981:329).

Herein lay a problem for the rest of the West End, however, because Laurel Homes and Lincoln Court eliminated more housing than they created. While there are conflicting accounts of the numbers actually displaced, it can be estimated that between 3,000 and 4,500 families were moved off these sites to make way for the construction of 2,264 units of housing.[17] At least 2,000—and perhaps as many as 3,000—of these displaced families were black, but only 1,319 black families were admitted into Laurel Homes and Lincoln Court. To make matters worse, these projects were reducing the total number of housing units in the West End while the neighborhood was adding about 10,000 people to its population, most of whom were black. By 1942, housing conditions were so bad in the West End that over 4,200 black families applied for space in Lincoln Court even before it opened (ibid:328). By 1944 overcrowding was so rampant that 20 percent of all black families were estimated to have doubled up (Fairbanks and Miller, 1984:197). A census survey, published that same year, found that 82 percent of all black families living in the West End were housed in units that failed to meet minimal metropolitan standards (Fairbanks, 1981:349).

The completion of Laurel Homes and Lincoln Court, while improving the housing conditions for some, worsened conditions for many more. These slum clearance projects also furthered the ghettoization of the West End. As CMHA officials struggled to relocate thousands of people displaced by their projects, they faced particular difficulty in finding satisfactory housing for black families. They solved the problem of low vacancy rates by persuading landlords who were renting to whites in racially mixed neighborhoods to rent to blacks instead (ibid.:325). Thus, rather than working to integrate all-white or mostly white areas, the CMHA converted neighborhoods that were already integrated into all-black areas. The integrated blocks of the middle and upper West End were not overlooked by the housing authority's relocation staff. This relocation policy combined with black migration into the neighborhood and white flight to cause the West End's white population to plummet after 1940.

17. Varying estimates of the number of families relocated have been reported by Fairbanks (1981:305, 322, 327), the *Cincinnati Post* (December 26, 1940:13), the *Cincinnati Times-Star* (August 5, 1950:11), and Jenkins (1974:23). The low estimate of 3,000 families comes from Fairbanks and the newspapers, who rely on CMHA sources. The high estimate of 4,500 families comes from Jenkins, who relies upon data from the National Association of Housing and Redevelopment Officials.

As World War II drew to a close, a number of public officials, city planners, and business leaders began to worry about Cincinnati's postwar development. Not least among their concerns was the immediate prospect of employing and housing 50,000 servicemen who would soon be returning to Greater Cincinnati. But they were equally disturbed by the longer-term trend of inner-city deterioration and suburban growth. The city was losing both population and industry to the suburbs. Its central-city real estate values were stagnant. Its housing was old and, in core neighborhoods like the West End, badly deteriorated. Its transportation system could not handle the growing number of automobiles. Its hospitals, schools, parks, libraries, and airport were in need of massive capital improvements.

Despite these signs of economic stagnation and decline, the city's political leaders showed little inclination either to commit public funds to the city's revitalization or to champion a new development agenda. The Republican-dominated city council prided itself on Cincinnati's low bonded indebtedness and its low tax rate. Year after year, it refused the request of the city planning commission to revise the 1925 City Plan and to create plans for the redevelopment of the older portions of the city.[18] In short, those who were concerned about the city's stagnation and decline encountered a political establishment that neither recognized the problem nor seemed willing to solve it.

Faced with this deadlock, a group of private business leaders, representing the city's largest industrial, financial, and commercial firms, came together in December 1943 to organize the Citizens Planning Association for the Development of the Cincinnati Area (CPA). The immediate objective of this new organization was "to urge Council to vote funds for the making of a master plan." Its larger purpose was to support "every movement of a broad nature that is for the improvement of living and business conditions in the Greater Cincinnati area" (Stimson, n.d.:14). During the next four years, the CPA was successful in mobilizing corporate and business support for the preparation of a new master plan and for the passage of a $41 million bond issue for school improvements. More importantly, through its active speakers bureau and a monthly newsletter with a selected circulation of seven thousand, the CPA gradually built the basis for a "growth coalition" that was willing to use the powers and resources of government to redevelop Cincinnati's urban core.

The first fruits of the association's lobbying efforts came in the

18. Cf. Stimson (n.d.:8–11), Fairbanks (1981:368–669), Fairbanks and Miller (1984:20), and Marquette (1972:59).

form of an appropriation of $100,000 by the city council on February 16, 1944, to fund a master plan. A division of city and metropolitan planning was created within the city planning commission to undertake this task. Having achieved its primary goal, the CPA turned its attention to publicizing the studies that were soon being produced by the division, in order to create a favorable public climate for the plan's reception. Relations between the CPA and the master plan staff were cordial and close throughout this planning process.[19] The plan itself was released in parts over a two-year period as the studies on its various phases were completed. In all, there were fifteen monographs, plus a summary volume. By mid-1947 ten of the monographs had been printed and distributed to the public. The entire master plan was completed the next year and officially adopted on November 22, 1948.

The 1948 Master Plan was, at once, a very conservative and very radical document. Its conservatism, like that of the 1925 plan, came in its refusal to tamper with the fundamental market forces that were presently shaping the city's development. Nowhere was this more apparent than in the 1948 plan's residential strategy. As reported by the master plan monograph, *Residential Areas*, most residential construction in the Cincinnati metropolitan area was occurring outside of the city proper. Almost none was occurring in the inner city. This trend was expected to continue, with "the greatest growth in population . . . expected to take place in the major peripheral communities" (City Planning Commission, 1946:76). Far from being disturbed by such suburbanization, however, the plan expressed a certain relief that there was so much land for development still available in the city's outlying areas. The only public intervention that was warranted was the construction of a multilane highway system to serve these areas.

If the plan was not prepared to interfere in the process of suburbanization, neither was it willing to resist what it called the "force of circumstances" that produced residential deterioration and racial segregation. Resurrecting the filter-down thinking of the 1925 plan—but applying it this time around to neighborhoods, instead of houses—the

19. Contributing to the closeness of this relationship was the revolving door that existed between the staffs of the two organizations. Malcome Dill was chosen as the CPA's first executive secretary in 1944. After a short tenure at the CPA, Dill was hired by the city planning commission as its chief of planning and design. In May 1947, Sherwood Reeder, who had served as director of the planning commission's master plan division, was named as executive secretary of the CPA. Upon Reeder's departure from the planning commission, the job of directing the final phase of the master plan's preparation was assigned to Malcome Dill (Stimson, n.d.:16, 32).

1948 plan advanced a theory of neighborhood "life cycles" to explain the decline of older residential areas like the West End. According to this theory, neighborhoods go through a period of growth and development, followed by a period of stability. Then, gradually, "a complex of factors comes into play which begin to cause the neighborhood to decline." What are these factors? According to the 1948 plan:

> Homes depreciate in value—partly because they are by their very nature wasting assets, and partly because the newer homes being built further out tend to make them obsolete in size, design, appearance, and layout. The children of the initial home owners grow up and leave the neighborhood, and the parents have less need of the home. As a consequence, the sale of homes begins to rise again, with changes in the type of population coming into the neighborhood, and with the gradual shift from owner to tenant occupancy, accelerated perhaps by the conversion into smaller apartments of larger homes for which there is a slow market. (ibid.:17–18)

From this point, according to the 1948 plan, the neighborhood rapidly deteriorates and eventually reaches obsolescence. As the oldest neighborhoods approach the "end of their life cycle," poor and black residents start moving to adjacent neighborhoods that are themselves beginning to decline. Thus, just as houses abandoned by higher-income people filter down to the poor, so do neighborhoods that have reached the end of their days.

The 1948 plan accepted as a given both the immutability of this process and the inevitability of its product—namely, a pattern of racial and economic segregation of residential neighborhoods in varying stages of decline. There was no suggestion that intervention might change either the process or the product. Since there was little that anyone could do about such "natural" forces as houses depreciating, children leaving home, and houses changing hands in "a slow market," blight and segregation must be "natural" too. Fairbanks and Miller (1984:208) were among a handful of later critics who recognized this conservative, almost fatalistic bias: "Thus the residential strategy of the 1948 Master Plan aimed to perpetuate and perfect past patterns of urban growth and the familiar form and structure of the metropolitan area, including its social and racial geography."

On the other hand, from the point of view of the West End, the 1948 plan was not conservative at all. Basing its conclusions on a 1939–1940 citywide survey of housing conditions, which found

19,550 of the West End's 21,184 dwelling units to be "deteriorated" and another 1,257 to be "declining," the 1948 plan recommended the "redevelopment" of the entire neighborhood. What was meant by "redevelopment" was no less than the "complete demolition of buildings and restoration of the cleared land to the market under whatever controls have been adopted by the public authorities concerned for the specified area" (City Planning Commission, 1948:70).

Part of this cleared land would be devoted to new housing and part to industry. Although the 1948 Master Plan adopted roughly the same boundaries that had been laid out by the 1933 Redevelopment Plan, in apportioning the area between residential and industrial development, there was a major change. The 1948 plan proposed to build a super highway along this boundary line, the Mill Creek Expressway (see Figure 7). Blocks lying north and east of the Expressway would be "redeveloped" for residential use. Blocks lying south and west of the expressway, the Kenyon-Barr and Liberty-Dalton areas, would be cleared of their houses, churches, and neighborhood businesses and "redeveloped" for commercial and industrial use.[20]

As the plan readily acknowledged, such redevelopment would result in the displacement of thousands of families, most of them poor and most of them black. In fact, when the redevelopment proposed for the West End was added to that proposed for the Basin's other central-city neighborhoods, the plan predicted that the population of the Basin would "decrease to less than half of its present population" (City Planning Commission, 1949:78). Anticipating such massive displacement of the poor, the plan endorsed the expansion of Cincinnati's public housing program, albeit in a rather oblique way: "Housing must be provided for low income families displaced by redevelopment activities [who] cannot hope to secure standard accommodations either through new private construction or in existing homes" (ibid.:81).

Thus, even though the authors and sponsors of Cincinnati's master plan were unwilling to restrict suburbanization or to reshape the city's "social and racial geography," they stood ready to use the full

20. While the planners were content to permit and even to encourage the suburbanization of the city's population, they were less sanguine about the emigration of its *industry*. According to the master plan study, *Industrial Land Use: Present and Future* (City Plannning Commission, 1946b), two alternatives were open to the city if it wished to provide future industrial sites and prevent the relocation of existing plants: either annex areas outside of the city or redevelop areas inside of the city. The master plan of 1948 recommended the second in proposing the industrial redevelopment of substantial sections of the West End.

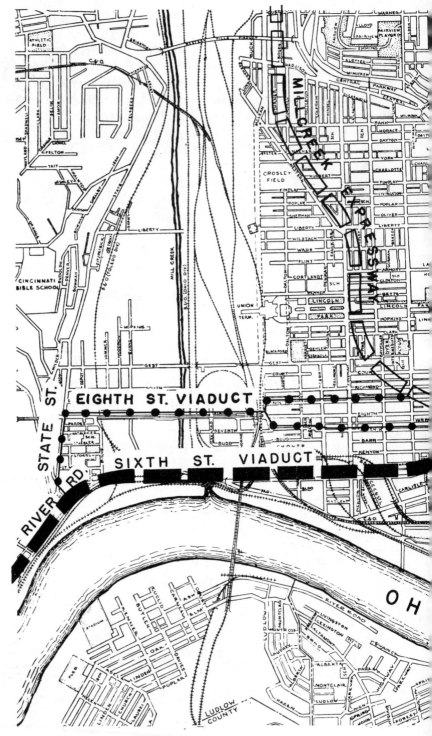

Figure 7. West End route of Mill Creek Expressway (Source: 1948 Master Plan)

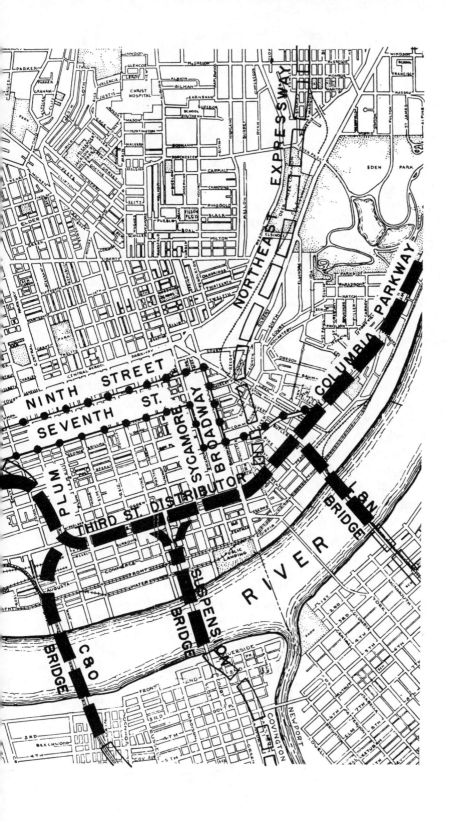

powers and resources of government to raze and redevelop the city's deteriorated core. They were willing to remake the West End in its entirety. To that end, the 1948 Master Plan was to serve as a blueprint for most of the neighborhood's future development.

URBAN RENEWAL, 1948–1965

Although the blueprint was there by 1948, it would take the city a few more years to bring together the structural prerequisites for the kinds of massive redevelopment envisioned by the master plan. Urban development on such a scale required: (1) millions of dollars in financing, (2) the executive capacity to carry out the project, and (3) enough replacement housing to accommodate the thousands of people displaced during and after redevelopment. Assembling such resources required a political consensus lasting many years that united political, business, and industrial elites around an aggressive redevelopment agenda. But by the mid-1950s all of these pieces had been put into place and Cincinnati had launched one of the nation's earliest and largest urban renewal programs.[21]

The organization that took the lead in forging and maintaining this pro-development consensus was the Citizens Planning Association. After the completion of the 1948 Master Plan, the CPA reconstituted itself as the Citizens Development Committee (CDC), adopting as its goal the full implementation of the plan's proposals. Counting among its membership many of the presidents and directors of Cincinnati's major banks, businesses, and industrial corporations, the CDC was extraordinarily successful in mobilizing business support for various bond issues, infrastructural improvements, and slum clearance projects that were the mainstay of the city's urban renewal program. While most of the CDC's time, effort, and money during its first ten years was spent promoting the expressway system that had been laid out in the 1948 plan, urban redevelopment was high on its list of priorities. Indeed, the organization worked tirelessly during its twenty-year existence to assure that the city had enough funds and executive staff to make its urban renewal plans a reality. So committed was the CDC to urban renewal that it even supported the expansion of public housing—despite being "opposed to public housing in

21. In January 1955, the *Bulletin* of the Citizens Development Committee noted with pride, "Except for Pittsburgh, New York, and Chicago, Cincinnati now leads all other cities in its work on urban redevelopment."

theory" (Stimson, n.d.:77). The CDC and the business community that it represented did not want the proposed highway system and the redevelopment of the central city to be stymied by the lack of relocation housing. Support for public housing, therefore, seemed a small price to pay for assuring the implementation of the major features of the 1948 Master Plan (cf., Fairbanks, 1981:373, 381).

The funds for Cincinnati's urban renewal program were to become available through a combination of federal programs and local bond issues. The Federal Housing Act of 1949 (along with its 1954 amendments) provided grants and loans for the purchase, clearance, and residential redevelopment of "blighted areas." The Federal Highway Act of 1956 provided 50-50 financing, along with the state, for the construction of the interstate highway system—of which the Millcreek Expressway was to be a part. Locally, bond issues were to provide most of the municipal share of urban renewal financing. Though always an arduous process of convincing local voters to approve any new bond package, the Ohio legislature made the passage of such referenda easier to achieve. After a statewide lobbying effort, led by Cincinnati public officials and the CDC, the legislature voted in 1949 to reduce the favorable percentage required to pass a bond issue from 65 to 55 percent (Stimson, n.d.:47). Helped by this legislative change, Cincinnati's city council won approval for major bond packages in 1950, 1954, and 1956. A large portion of these funds was earmarked for expressways, public improvements, and urban renewal projects in the West End.

The executive machinery that was required for urban renewal was threefold: redevelopment officials needed powers of eminent domain to acquire the necessary real estate; the city needed a central agency to carry out the redevelopment program; and the city needed detailed development plans for each project area. These elements fell into place even more quickly than did the funding. The Ohio Redevelopment Act was passed on June 29, 1949, (two days before the Federal Housing Act), granting cities the power to acquire property in "blighted areas" by purchase, gift, exchange, or eminent domain.[22] The act also permitted cities to designate an existing office, commission, or department of the city to act as the primary redevelopment

22. The Ohio Redevelopment Act defined a "blighted area" as "an area within the corporate limits of a city in which a *majority* of the structures is detrimental to the public health, safety, or welfare by reason of age, deterioration, overcrowding, faulty arrangement, lack of ventilation or sanitary facilities, or any combination of these factors" (City Planning Commission, 1951:18). By these criteria, as the 1948 Master Plan had suggested, the entire West End could be considered a "blighted area."

agency. On May 1, 1950, the Cincinnati City Council created an "urban redevelopment division" within the city planning commission that was given overall responsibility for planning and implementing the city's urban renewal program. Within ten months, this division had identified fifty-four "project areas" of four or more acres that were "blighted" and in need of "treatment"; twenty-seven of these were in the West End. The planning commission selected ten project areas from this original list and instructed the urban redevelopment division to prepare definite plans for the redevelopment of each. On May 21, 1951, detailed development plans for six of these ten project areas were submitted to the planning commission for approval. All but one were located in the West End—128 acres of densely populated land that was now targeted for total clearance and redevelopment (City Planning Commission, 1951:18–21).

Providing replacement housing proved to be a more intractable problem than acquiring the funds or establishing the executive machinery for urban renewal. From 1950 to 1970, the construction of the Millcreek Expressway (I-75) and the city's urban renewal pro-

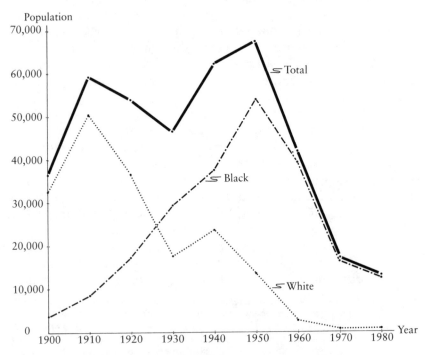

Figure 8. West End population, 1900–1980 (Source: U.S. Census)

gram eliminated between 13,147 and 22,354 low-cost dwellings in the West End, displacing a predominantly black, low-income population of between 50,561 and 54,471. Residential redevelopment of West End sites that had been cleared by urban renewal produced only 1,038 units, housing 3,152 people. During a twenty-year period, therefore, the West End lost three quarters of its population. With the eradication of so much housing, this loss of population was permanent (see Figure 8).

Before development plans for urban renewal could be approved, both the Federal Housing Act of 1949 and the Ohio Redevelopment Act required a finding by the city council that displaced families could be rehoused "in the project area or in other areas not generally less desirable . . . and at rents or prices within the financial means of the families displaced from the project area." Consequently, the prospect of eliminating so many units of housing and displacing thousands of families from the West End, most of whom were black and poor, posed an enormous problem for city officials.

This was a problem, in fact, that was never solved, merely finessed. Estimates of the numbers to be displaced were kept artificially low or simply suppressed.[23] Public predictions of an expanding supply of low-cost units in private housing were groundless.[24] Announced plans for additional units of public housing failed to materialize.[25] Official assurances of generous relocation assistance were promises meant to be broken.[26] The truth was that there were almost no vacancies in

23. An example of data being suppressed is found in a November 19, 1956, letter from the CDC's executive secretary to the chairman of the CDC's urban redevelopment committee, following the barely successful passage (56.41 percent) of the 1956 urban renewal bond issue: "The Urban Renewal Committee had withheld results of a thorough study of the relocation problem at the request of the bond campaign committee. The Committee will now complete this study which shows convincingly that there will be a minimum of 1,200 non-white families ineligible for public housing" (CDC Archives, box 25, folder 6).

24. Redevelopment officials based their faith in the private housing market on little more than several conversations with local builders and on a market survey that showed a substantial market for new, moderately priced housing for blacks (Fairbanks, 1981:393).

25. CMHA's inability to provide as much relocation housing as intended was due largely to factors beyond its control. From 1944 to 1951, new construction of public housing in Ohio was all but halted until the state's supreme court issued a ruling that allowed municipalities to grant tax exemption to public housing projects. When the CMHA attempted to resume construction of new units, it found its efforts repeatedly frustrated and blocked by neighborhoods that refused to allow public housing—particularly black public housing—to be located in their midst.

26. As Bleecker Marquette of the Better Housing League was later to admit: "It was a great mistake to give so little attention to the question as to what would happen

Cincinnati's existing supply of housing that were within the financial means of the families that were to be displaced. Furthermore, neither the private market nor the CMHA offered any realistic prospect of expanding that supply fast enough or fully enough to replace the 13,000 to 22,000 units that were to be demolished. Critics like Joseph B. Hall pointed out, after the fact, that little replacement housing was available anywhere for those displaced by urban renewal:[27]

> The relocation wasn't planned well. The program provided for relocation but the facts of the situation were that no properties would be available anywhere, old or new, at the rentals that were being paid by people in those terrible run-down homes whose condition should have been corrected by the building codes, but were not. So the answer was that two or three families would move together into a place to be able to afford it and that automatically developed new slum conditions. (Joseph B. Hall, quoted in Stimson, n.d.:76)

This citywide dearth of replacement housing did nothing to deter the planning or approval of Cincinnati's urban renewal program. When the first two project plans were submitted to the city council— both of them in the West End—it quickly determined that there *was* a feasible plan for the relocation of the families then residing on these proposed redevelopment sites. On September 5, 1951, the council approved the plans for Laurel-3 and Richmond-1. The city's urban renewal juggernaut was under way.

The project areas designated Laurel-3 and Richmond-1 covered forty-seven acres of the West End, a twenty-block area lying west of Linn Street (see Figure 9). Contained were the blocks that had been known to the planners of the 1930s as D and E, where residents had successfully resisted the city's efforts to clear their neighborhood for public housing. They were less successful this time around, despite a spirited defense. At two public hearings on the city's plans for Laurel-3 and Richmond-1, residents of these areas registered vigorous opposition to the city's urban redevelopment plan. Failing to persuade

---

to the families to be displaced. A relocation office was set up but the cost of moving was the responsibility of the displaced people. There was no help given the families after they moved, no follow up, no assurance that they got housing of acceptable standard and certainly many did not" (Marquette, 1972:117–18).

27. What lends this criticism of the city's relocation efforts particular veracity—and irony—is that Joseph B. Hall, president of the Kroeger Company, was the chairman of the CDC's urban redevelopment committee during the 1950s. Few people in Cincinnati did more than the members of this committee to assure that there would be no political obstacles to the full implementation of the city's urban renewal plans.

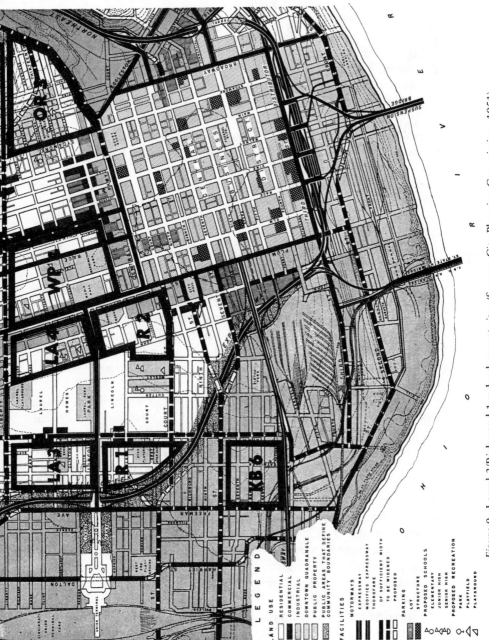

Figure 9. Laurel-3/Richmond-1 redevelopment sites (Source: City Planning Commission, 1951)

the city council not to approve these plans, the area's residents joined with a majority of Cincinnati's electorate in voting against the 1951 bond issue that would have provided $1.35 million for the Laurel-3/ Richmond-1 project. Citywide, 58 percent of the votes cast in this referendum were against the bonds for Laurel-3; 61 percent were against the bonds for Richmond-1. The executive secretary of the CDC, after his organization had publicly backed the campaign to approve this urban renewal bond issue, correctly analyzed the cause of its defeat in a letter written one week after the referendum:[28] "As expected, major opposition came from tenants of slum areas who were not satisfied that suitable accommodations would be provided when they would be displaced, together with real estate and building and loan interests who still contend that public housing is to occupy a significant part of the program."

Despite this set back, the city found an inventive way to go ahead with the Laurel-3/Richmond-1 project. Its one-third share of the project's cost was put up in the form of "noncash credits." By expanding a school, improving parks and streets, and widening Linn Street within the Laurel-3/Richmond-1 area—improvements that were financed by bonds that the voters had previously approved—the city was credited by the U.S. Housing and Home Financing Agency with enough expenditures to qualify for the entire federal match (Stimson, n.d.:77).

Acquisition of property within the two project areas began at the end of 1952. Relocation of the area's 1,617 families proceeded slowly, however, primarily because of the difficulty of finding homes for the 1,200 black families. By the end of 1955, only half of the parcels in the tract had been acquired and only a sixth of the residents had been relocated.[29] Nevertheless, because city officials were eager to show progress, dozens of Cincinnati's political and economic leaders were gathered together on October 3, 1955, to attend a ceremonial "House Razing" at 833 Lincoln Park Drive. The invitation from the city manager read in part: "The occasion will celebrate the demolition of the first of the 540 structures to be cleared in the redevelopment of the combined Laurel-3, Richmond-1 slum clearance project. . . . The ceremony marks the realization of another major feature of Cincinnati's master plan and is an indication of the new spirit of progress so evident in Cincinnati today."

28. Letter from George Haywood to Joseph Hall, November 14, 1951 (CDC Archives, Box 25).
29. *CDC Bulletin* 13, no. 1, February 1956:5.

It took until the spring of 1959 to clear the entire Laurel-Richmond tract. A contract was awarded to the Reynolds Aluminum Corporation to construct a 323-unit middle-income housing cooperative on the Laurel-3 site, a project known as Park Town. The Hamilton Corporation won the contract to develop 288 moderately priced rental units on the Richmond-1 site, an apartment complex that was given the name Richmond Village. Both were completed by 1961. Neither housed people of the economic class that had been displaced. As the head of the Better Housing League later recalled, this result was hardly an accident:[30]

> I felt, and I am more sure than ever I was right, that some provision should have been made to enable at least those who wanted to go back in the renewal area to do so. This would have meant, of course, some public low rent units. I made a strong case for this. But I didn't have a ghost of a chance of having my proposal accepted. Some leaders in the power structure were violently opposed. (Marquette, 1972:118)

In the meantime, planning for Cincinnati's second urban renewal project, Kenyon-Barr, went into its final stages. The 1948 Master Plan had proposed driving the Millcreek Expressway through the center of the lower West End and razing every one of the 3,100 buildings located there. By 1956, detailed plans had been developed, plotting the route of the expressway and designating the boundaries of a 435-acre tract for clearance and redevelopment (see Figure 10). That same year, Cincinnati voters narrowly approved (56.41 percent) a $41 million bond issue, of which $15.5 million was for expressway construction and $9 million was for slum clearance in Kenyon-Barr. The *Master Plan for the Redevelopment of the Kenyon-Barr Urban Renewal Area* was published in 1959.

The Kenyon-Barr plan proposed the complete eradication of the neighborhood that had housed Cincinnati's oldest black community. Ten thousand families still lived there, crowded into 2,800 buildings.

---

30. At another place in his memoirs, Marquette describes in greater detail the reaction of one of these members of the "power structure" to Marquette's suggestion that housing should be built in the West End for families displaced by urban renewal: "One of the strong minded and somewhat arrogant members immediately opposed the idea so bitterly that he threatened that if I succeeded he would have the area replanned so that nothing but industry could be located there" (1972:64). Nevertheless, the CMHA did succeed in building an additional 436 units in the West End, around the same time that Park Town and Richmond Village were opening. This project, Stanley Rowe, cleared four residential blocks west of Linn Street, between Poplar and Liberty. Two thirteen-story buildings (primarily for the elderly) and a small number of freestanding duplexes were built on the site. Stanley Rowe was dedicated on June 11, 1964.

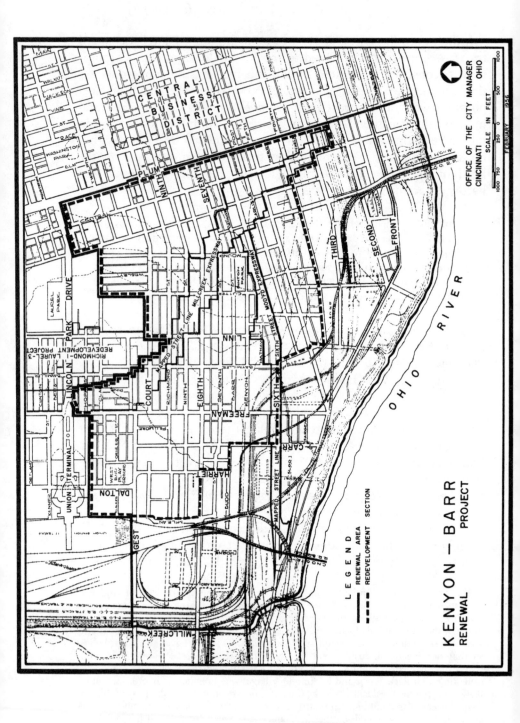

KENYON — BARR
RENEWAL PROJECT

LEGEND

——— RENEWAL AREA
- - - REDEVELOPMENT SECTION

OFFICE OF THE CITY MANAGER
CINCINNATI   OHIO

SCALE IN FEET

1000 750   250 0   500   1000

FEBRUARY 1956

These same structures contained some five hundred shops, missions, churches, and other nonresidential facilities. Scattered throughout the neighborhood were three hundred commercial and manufacturing establishments.[31] The Kenyon-Barr plan proposed to redevelop this entire area along lines originally suggested by the 1948 Master Plan: commercial and industrial uses in the 296 acres below the Millcreek Expressway; mixed-income residential use above the expressway. Planners designated the area that was planned for industrial development, Kenyon-Barr I (later renamed Queensgate I). The 117-acre site that lay above the expressway was designated Kenyon-Barr II (later renamed Queensgate II).

Despite the number of dwellings and businesses to be eliminated and the number of people to be displaced—five times as many as those displaced by the city's first urban renewal project—little resistance came from the neighborhood.[32] Indeed, as a local minister recalled, the 1956 bond issue would not have passed without the *support* of West End residents:

> The people in the suburbs voted it down. They didn't want the black and the poor moving in *their* direction. But the people in the downtown area were a real voting block. They voted themselves out of their homes and invited the bulldozer in. [But] they didn't know what was happening to them. . . . I remember hearing at the time that the people down there were promised that they'd have the first chance to come back and they would be helped to be resettled. All that was paper stuff. It was just an inducement to get the area cleared. (McCrackin interview, 1985:374)

This inducement worked partly because the housing in the area was truly dreadful. Only four of the neighborhood's 2,800 residential structures were without building code violations; all but twenty-three

31. Data on population and land uses in the Kenyon-Barr area are drawn from the Kenyon-Barr master plan (City Planning Commission, 1959:1).

32. *Outside* the neighborhood, the Kenyon-Barr plan had a host of critics. D. Reid Ross, who replaced Bleeker Marquette as the head of the Better Housing League, argued that relocation housing wouldn't be adequate, either in quantity or in quality, for those displaced by the project. Theodore Berry, Cincinnati's leading black politician, was said to fear that "with less and less housing available to Negroes, landlords are profiting on what remains." J. Austin White, an investment broker, threatened to halt the Kenyon-Barr project through legal action. Voicing the concern of many suburbanites who voted against the 1956 bond issue, White predicted that those displaced from Kenyon-Barr would create "more transition neighborhoods" and threaten property values (*Post and Times-Star*, "West End Slum Is Doomed, But Where Do People Go?" November 2, 1959:14).

had several structural problems; 70 percent were deemed to be fire hazards; half had inadequate sanitary facilities; two-thirds were over-crowded (City Planning Commission, 1959:2). The promise of better housing was undoubtedly attractive. Then too, the residents of this inner-city slum had not the resources, the information, or the time to evaluate other courses of action:

> There was a lack of information. That's one thing with poor people, particularly when you're poor and you're black and you're not into things, is that information flows slowly. The information might come out, but the digestion of that information—what it means—is slow. I used to hear the old men at Sinton Park arguing about different things. Some of 'em would say, "We're all going to have to move. They're going to take all this." Others would say, "No way! They can't take all this. It'd take too much money." Back and forth. It was that kind of trauma in the neighborhood. It was like the "knock on the door" I guess. Really. Like in the Holocaust. They'd knock on your door and tell you you're going to have to move in 30 days. (Lewis interview, 1985:366–67)

At the suggestion of federal officials, the city decided to execute the Kenyon-Barr urban renewal plan in phases, over a period of years. The industrial redevelopment of Queensgate I was to be carried out first, to be followed immediately by the residential redevelopment of Queensgate II. Acquisition of property in Queensgate I began in earnest in 1960. By 1962 a quarter of the area had been acquired and cleared (Stimson, n.d.:1962). That same year, while continuing to acquire the rest of the tract, the city began selling off parcels of Queensgate I, mostly to commercial firms involved in wholesaling, warehousing, and industrial and construction supply. In all, it was to cost the city and the federal government $43 million to acquire, clear, and redevelop Queensgate I for industrial use. The land was resold to private corporations over a ten-year period for only $7.8 million. The cycle was completed in September 1972.[33]

Throughout the 1950s and 1960s, therefore, the bulldozer of urban renewal continued the transformation of the West End that had begun long before with the first slum clearance project of the 1930s. By 1965 the area south of the expressway (Queensgate I) had been cleared of houses and was being gradually resold to commercial and industrial developers. The area west of the expressway (Liberty-

33. *Cincinnati Post*, August 29, 1973:9.

Dalton) was being targeted for a similar fate. What remained of the West End, as a residential neighborhood, was confined to a four hundred-acre enclave lying between Interstate 75 (Millcreek Expressway) and Central Parkway. Much of this area stood as a monument to thirty years of city planning and urban redevelopment. Going or gone were the overcrowded, aging, and frequently dilapidated dwellings of yesteryear. Park Town and Richmond Village provided new housing for five hundred middle-class and lower-middle-class families. Stanley Rowe Apartments, built by the CMHA soon after Park Town and Richmond Village were opened, provided 436 units of brand-new elderly and family housing. On the other side of Linn Street, Laurel Homes and Lincoln Court provided another 2,300 units of public housing. Further south, Queensgate II awaited clearance and redevelopment for a mixed-income residential community.

Surveying this scene in the early sixties, the editor of the *Cincinnati Enquirer* (June 22, 1961:12) enthusiastically noted that "substantial chunks of the rundown, crumbling blocks are gone and shining new neighborhoods are taking their place." He urged the denizens of Cincinnati's hilltops to go witness the "New West End" for themselves: "The West End traditionally is off the beaten path for most suburbanites, but a visit there today can be stimulating and exciting for any citizen who is interested in his 'city of tomorrow.'"

One person who apparently took this editorial advice was Howard Morgens, the president of Proctor and Gamble: "The difference between the way the West End looks now and the way it did before is unbelievable. I just like to go there occasionally because I remember the way it was when we used to go through it to the Union Terminal" (quoted in Stimson, n.d.:83). Morgens, of course, had special reason to make periodic pilgrimages to the "new" West End. As a long-time member of the CDC's Executive Committee, he had helped to make this "miracle" happen.

What was almost forgotten in the celebration of the city's success in transforming the West End was that, after thirty years of city planning and urban redevelopment, very little of the West End remained. Half of its residential acreage had been lopped off. Two-thirds of its housing had been eliminated. Three-quarters of its population had been permanently displaced—forcibly scattered to Avondale, Evanston, Mount Auburn, and a half dozen other outlying areas. The slums of the West End were finally gone, but so too were most of the people and most of the institutions that had made the neighborhood the social, cultural, and political center of Cincinnati's black community.

The destruction of that community had little place in either the "city of tomorrow" boosterism of the city's editors or the self-congratulations of the CDC's businessmen and bankers. It loomed large, however, in the collective memory of Cincinnati's blacks. For them, the "shining new neighborhoods" of the West End were a tarnished reminder of homes, neighbors, and a vital community—lost forever. Time gradually embellished this memory, which grew more poignant as the fresh experience of the slums receded and the area's first public housing began to decay. For a rising generation of black leaders, the "New West End" was to become a symbol of pain inflicted and promises broken by a white establishment determined to rebuild the old West End in its own image. By the mid-1960s, these new leaders had come to the fore, and the West End was mobilizing to defend and develop itself on its own terms. The era of metropolitan planning, housing reform, and urban renewal had passed. The era of neighborhood protest and participation had begun.

8

The Mobilized Community: Protest and Participation, 1965–1975

It was the tenor of the times. Martin [Luther King] was doing his thing. White folk were going to continue doing what they were doing. And we did what *we* had to do: Y'all not going to move us out and put no new ball field over here. Bullshit! *This* is what y'all going to do. This is what y'all going to do or we're going to block the streets; we're going to demonstrate in the streets.

—JEROME JENKINS (interview, 1985)

On Thursday evening, January 12, 1965, West End residents gathered at the Inspirational Baptist Church to discuss ways of resisting the city's recently announced plan to demolish two densely populated residential blocks in the Liberty-Dalton area. Crosley Field, home to the Cincinnati Reds, stood at the northern edge of this neighborhood. The city's traffic department had recommended the demolition of dozens of nearby houses to provide additional parking. Infuriated that the city would consider tearing down people's homes so a few hundred baseball fans would have less distance to walk, local residents declared that the time had finally come to fight back. They decided to picket Crosley Field on opening day.[1]

That April, as they prepared their Crosley Field protest, the leaders

---

1. The anger of West Enders was no doubt greater for the fact that this was the *second* time that local residents were being displaced for the convenience of baseball fans. The first instance of parking lot displacement occurred in 1957, an event that will be discussed later.

of the West End issued a set of demands. Going beyond the immediate objective of protecting the Liberty-Dalton area, they demanded that the urban renewal "game" be played by a different set of rules. Generally, they insisted upon neighborhood participation in all future planning and development of the West End. Specifically, they urged the city manager to create an official task force, including members of various city departments and residents of the West End, to take charge of the planning and development of Queensgate II and the West End's other residential areas. They also called upon the city council to meet on "the home territory of the residents" to discuss citizen concerns (Jenkins, 1974:57; Jenkins and Lewis, 1982:109).

Confronted with these demands on the eve of opening day, Cincinnati's political leaders promised a series of public meetings to discuss the community's grievances and were able, thereby, to persuade the residents to call off their planned protest. As one resident put it, "You don't do nothing to stop the Reds from playing on opening day. The city manager and the city council got real upset. They came down and met with us. The council as a whole came down and met with us in Sands School" (Lewis interview, 1985:363).[2]

The city council met twice with West End residents in the summer and fall of 1965. On both occasions, these elected representatives of Cincinnati's predominantly white political establishment found themselves face-to-face with the angry black memory of urban renewal:

> Attendance averaged over 200 at these sessions, and during each session irate West Enders peppered council members with hot and bitter questions about the entire renewal-removal process. The meetings climaxed with a walk-in demonstration at a regular meeting of City Council in city hall. Over 300 West End residents participated, and several interrupted the Council's deliberations to be heard. . . . After things quieted down, Council promised the West End residents that a proposal concerning renewal in the West End would be forthcoming. (Jenkins and Lewis, 1982:109–10)

This promise resulted in the West End Task Force, created in April 1966 and organized along lines similar to those proposed by West End residents the year before. Representatives from eight different West End organizations served on this task force, along with repre-

---

2. Primary and secondary sources for Chapters 8, 9, and 10 are discussed in Appendices A and B. When individuals are quoted verbatim within these chapters, page numbers refer to the four-hundred-page transcript prepared from their recorded remarks.

sentatives from half-a-dozen city departments, the CMHA, the Better Housing League, the board of education, and the archdiocese of Cincinnati (West End Task Force, 1968:6). During the next ten years, the West End Task Force came to exercise virtual veto power over all major planning and development decisions, public and private, affecting the West End. It also functioned as a planning agency in its own right. Supported by professional staff from the city planning commission and a team of planners from the University of Cincinnati, the task force produced a detailed "urban design plan" for Queensgate II (Department of Urban Development, 1972) and an overall "development plan" for the West End (City Planning Commission, 1972a). Neighborhood residents, voicing their concerns through a dozen task force representatives, were full partners in this planning process. They even became, for a time, full partners in the development process as well, participating financially and administratively in the residential redevelopment of Queensgate II.[3]

This was clearly a radical departure from the days in which tens of thousands of people resigned themselves to the demolition of their homes and the destruction of their community, yielding to a plan developed by others. The Crosley Field confrontation was a signal to the city's political and economic elites that those halcyon days were over and gone. By the mid-1960s, the West End had reached a new stage of political consciousness and organizational development. It was prepared, at last, to resist the urban renewal juggernaut. By the decade's end, it had succeeded in dramatically changing the entire game, with West End residents among the players and their local leaders among the referees. While the ingredients for this successful neighborhood revolt lay in a number of local and extralocal factors that slowly developed over a period of years, none was more important than the rise to power of the West End Community Council, a locality-based organization that managed to hold all of these ingredients together for nearly a decade.

3. Although consideration will later be given to some of the *products* of the West End Task Force, namely the two major West End plans that it produced, the planning *process* will be given little attention. The West End Task Force, in other words, will not itself be a topic of extensive discussion here. Our overall concern is the formation and action of locality-based organizations. The West End Task Force had representatives of such West End organizations among its members—the most influential of which was the West End Community Council—but half the task force was made up of representatives from city-wide organizations and municipal agencies. Furthermore, the story of the West End Task Force has been told in detail twice before (Jenkins, 1974; Miller and Jenkins, 1982).

THE MAKING OF A NEIGHBORHOOD REVOLT

Urban renewal, in many ways, created the conditions for its own demise. Outside of the West End, political support for urban renewal was eroded by the program's many successes and failures. Its success in completing Cincinnati's highway system and clearing the city's worst slums weakened the resolve of the prodevelopment coalition that had made urban renewal possible. Convinced that its job was largely done, the Citizens Development Committee disbanded in 1967. The Chamber of Commerce, which inherited the CDC's agenda and staff, was content to oversee the completion of projects already under way. It was not inclined to initiate a new round of metropolitan planning and redevelopment.

At the same time, the failure of urban renewal to produce promised jobs on cleared sites and promised housing for the thousands of families displaced finally created a political backlash, locally and nationally. For example, despite its goal of providing 16,000 jobs, the industrial redevelopment of Queensgate I created employment for only six thousand people—in part, because the city council panicked when demand for the cleared land did not approach official predictions and, unable to take the political heat, forced the urban redevelopment department to sell off the land to low-labor commercial firms.[4] This fiasco made it more and more difficult to mobilize political support for later development projects, such as the one planned for Liberty-Dalton. Then, too, the twenty to forty thousand people that the Queensgate I project had displaced had been scattered throughout the city, causing congestion, higher rents, and racial tension in a dozen neighborhoods. This undoubtedly jarred the political resolve of the city's elected officials, when faced with the prospect of further urban renewal projects.

Nationally, a Democratic administration moved to consolidate its political base among urban majorities and to contain the protest of those aggrieved by the urban renewal policies and programs of the past.[5] Beginning in 1964, housing and social services programs that were part of this Democratic strategy not only increased the resources

4. See: "Queensgate I: The Goals Didn't Match the Reality," *Cincinnati Post* (August 29, 1973:9); and Creahan (1973).

5. A more detailed discussion of the purposes and effects of this national Democratic agenda and the Republican counterattack can be found in Mollenkopf (1983), who provides a couple of excellent case studies of urban renewal in Boston and San Francisco. Other studies of urban renewal have been done by Rossi and Dentler (1961), Keith (1973), C. Stone (1976), and Friedland (1982), among others.

made available to urban neighborhoods, but mandated resident participation in the kinds of neighborhood planning, housing development, and service delivery that these resources made possible.[6] Consequently, new opportunities were created for locality-based participation in municipal planning and development at precisely the time that new resources were provided for locality-based organizations to hire staff, train leaders, and employ professional consultants, enabling these grass-roots groups to take advantage of those opportunities. As the capabilities and influence of locality-based organizations increased, the process and products of urban renewal began to change.

Locally, urban renewal created the conditions for a neighborhood revolt that slowed the progress, transformed the process, and hastened the demise of urban renewal itself. There were five such conditions. Each affected the relations and interests of domestic property. Each contributed to the genesis and development of locality-based collective action, given organizational form by the West End Community Council.

The first condition—or "ingredient"—of the West End revolt was the residue of resentment that slowly accumulated during the 1950s and early 1960s with the forced removal of one family, one building, and one business after another. The destruction of the black community that had long supported thousands of people was a traumatic event that was neither forgotten nor forgiven. With the passage of time, this collective West End memory of "community lost" became a symbol of past injustice and a source of solidarity for those who were fighting for a better future.

Second, urban renewal posed a credible threat that cut across the social boundaries separating one property interest group from another. The redevelopment of Kenyon-Barr (Queensgate I), following on the heels of Laurel-3 and Richmond-1, was a dramatic, convincing demonstration that (1) the city was prepared to use any means and to pay any amount to "redevelop" the West End, (2) such "redevelopment" would inevitably entail the "clear cutting" of entire blocks, and (3) rebuilding these demolished blocks would provide few benefits for West End residents. The city's promises of better housing and

6. The most important of these programs and mandates, in terms of their impact upon the formation and development of locality-based organizations, were those of the Office of Economic Opportunity, Model Cities, and the HUD order known as "LAP Letter 458" issued in June 1968 and requiring "maximum resident participation" in project area committees.

better jobs had worn thin by 1965, and the move to sacrifice even more West End homes and businesses merely to provide parking for suburban baseball fans was a blatant sign that the impulse behind those promises was as predatory and insensitive as ever. Faced with this immediate threat, and suspecting that the rest of the West End was targeted for the same sort of redevelopment that had leveled Kenyon-Barr, Laurel-3, and Richmond-1, the neighborhood's tenants, homeowners, landlords, and small business owners discovered a common interest in preserving what was left:

> That's what we were really dealing with: how the city was pushing us around, tearing down our houses, making us move out to places that we didn't know, and putting down this concrete, just putting down this concrete. (Warren interview, 1985:52)

> It was bad enough when they put the Expressway through portions of the community. But they took another portion, Queensgate I, and redeveloped that into industrial, primarily, and did not provide any jobs for the community. It was a slap in the face, [adding] insult to injury. They take forty thousand people out, put in industry, and we're not working there! So our objective was to draw the wagons in a circle and protect what we had left. (Jones interview, 1985:84)

Third, while the threat of urban renewal cut across the lines of property interest, there was also less of a line to cross. Thirty years of slum clearance, public housing development, and urban renewal had arrested and reversed the growth of homeownership in the West End. Owner-occupied units were demolished along with rental units. Some of these homeowners relocated within the West End, purchasing homes in Liberty-Dalton, Amory Central, and in the areas north of Liberty Street. Most did not. They moved, instead, to outlying neighborhoods where the money paid for their West End homes would go further. Tenants, not homeowners, were the ones more likely to relocate within the West End, doubling up in existing apartments and richly rewarding those absentee landlords who purchased and converted owner-occupied buildings into rental housing. By 1965, only 550 of approximately 14,600 housing units in the West End were owner-occupied. With most West End residents renting rather than owning their homes, a major social cleavage did not develop within the neighborhood that might have otherwise undermined neighborhood solidarity.

Fourth, the combined effect of highway construction and urban renewal concentrated fewer people into half the territorial space. The

West End no longer contained sixty to seventy thousand people, covering some eight hundred acres of land. Nor did the neighborhood contain as many churches, stores, bars, parks, or clubs. Consequently, the people who remained in the West End interacted within a smaller physical space and shared more of the same social spaces. Such physical and social proximity was to make it easier for the neighborhood to share information and to develop a common sense of its own identity and interests.

Finally, urban renewal inadvertently provided much of the leadership for the West End revolt. The housing that was built on the Laurel-3 and Richmond-1 sites attracted a group of better educated, better paid, highly motivated people into the heart of the West End. This was particularly true in the case of Park Town, the housing cooperative constructed on the Laurel-3 site.[7] Beginning with its establishment as a no-equity cooperative in 1962, Park Town was to provide a disproportionate share of the leadership in the locality-based organizations of the West End:[8]

> I think that the people who moved in there were conscious of the trials and tribulations of the West End, probably more so than the residents themselves were aware. And because of that, you had this tremendous stir. Many of the leaders that you had pushing the West End Community Council were there. There was a lot of letter writing, a lot of pro-

---

7. Both Richmond Village and Park Town were intended to house middle-income families, but eventually housed a lower-income population. Richmond Village went into receivership soon after it was established. Many of its units eventually housed families with Section 8 certificates. The plan to establish Park Town as a middle-income, limited equity cooperative was never realized, simply because there were not enough families who were willing and able to purchase an $800 share in a housing project located in the West End. When this became apparent to the project's developers, they refinanced Park Town under the federal 221(d)(3) program, pushed the share price lower, and eliminated the occupants' right to build up equity that could be removed upon an occupant's departure. Even so, Park Town did provide newer housing with greater security and more autonomy than any renter enjoyed. There was also the prospect of the occupant's monthly charge dropping significantly when the mortgage on the cooperative was eventually paid off. This arrangement was attractive enough to recruit a better educated and slightly more affluent population.

8. Many West End leaders lived in Park Town at one time or another: Allen Davis, president, West End Community Council; Betty Warren, president, West End Community Council; William Mallory, president, West End Community Council; Harry Martin, president, West End Community Council; Bonnie Batton, president, West End Commmunity Council; Richard Lewis, director, West End Development Corporation; Jimmy Jones, director, West End Development Corporation; Jerome Jenkins, director, Seven Hills Neighborhood Houses; Pauline Robinson, organizer, West End Social Services Project; Willie Watts, director, Community Land Cooperative.

posal writing, the whole bit. Many of these people took a chance even moving to Park Town. You're coming into a community where vandalism is—heck, the insurance rate was hellish. They were taking a chance even coming here. And I guess that in itself said you had to be committed to *something*. You wanted to see something done or you wouldn't have even made the move. Many of them didn't *have* to move into this community, you know. (P. Robinson interview, 1985:48)

Added to these five conditions underlying the West End revolt was another condition not engendered by urban renewal: the black movement for civil rights. The southern civil rights movement came north following the Birmingham demonstrations of 1963, arriving in Cincinnati soon thereafter (Jenkins, 1974). Its arrival and rapid growth in the West End, which was nearly 95 percent black by that time, coincided with the maturation of the other conditions put in place by urban renewal. The local chapter of the NAACP conducted a door-to-door voter registration campaign in the West End (and in the city's other black neighborhoods) in 1963, launching a successful drive to elect the first black to city council in six years.[9] That same year, Cincinnati sent a couple of hundred people to the nation's capitol to hear Martin Luther King address the March on Washington. Fifty people went from Park Town alone (Watts interview, 1985:35). In 1964, the Cincinnati chapter of CORE organized a black boycott of the city's schools, protesting discrimination in teacher hiring and segregation in pupil placement, and later proposed a fair housing ordinance to the city council. The Park Town residents council was one of seven civic groups publicly endorsing this proposal. On March 25, 1965, CORE, SNCC, and the NAACP sponsored a protest march on City Hall, calling for passage of a fair housing ordinance, better enforcement of building codes, more black police and firemen, and an end to the city's plan to demolish West End housing for Crosley Field parking.[10] During the next two years, the civil rights movement in Cincinnati grew more militant, and racial tensions grew more intense. These tensions came to a head in the "long hot summer" of 1967 with rioting and

9. The NAACP member who coordinated the voter registration drive in the West End was Richard Lewis, who later served as an organizer for the West End Special Service Project, chairman of the Park Town board, and director of the West End Development Corporation. In Lewis's career, as in that of most of the black leaders connected with Seven Hills Neighborhood Houses and the West End Community Council, the politics of property, place, and race are intertwined.

10. This sampling of events from Cincinnati's civil rights movement is drawn from Koehler (1983:216–65).

,violence in a half-dozen black neighborhoods, including the West End.

Throughout this period, locality-based politics and racially based politics went hand in hand. As the civil rights movement took root in the West End, the interests, ideologies, and solidarities of race were superimposed upon those of property and place. Conditions and grievances created by thirty years of urban redevelopment combined with those created by two hundred years of racial oppression to provide the volatile ingredients for a popular neighborhood revolt. All that was needed was a unifying organization with adequate leadership and sufficient resources to make it happen—and to make it last. The Great Society furnished the resources. The West End Community Council furnished the leaders.

WEST END COMMUNITY COUNCIL: GENESIS AND DEVELOPMENT

The origins of the West End Community Council (WECC) are obscure. One West End resident suggests that it evolved from the Lincolnia Council, a group that was formed in the late 1930s to secure a library and better recreational facilities for the neighborhood (Payton interview, 1985:2). Another resident remembers it in 1952, but known then by the name of the West End Professional Workers (P. Robinson interview, 1985: 42). Still another remembers it in the 1950s under the name of the West End Civic Association (Mallory interview, 1985:19). The earliest mention in the Cincinnati press of a West End organization functioning *like* a community council was an announcement on August 29, 1946 of the formation of "The Negro Community Council" (*Cincinnati Times-Star*, p. 9). This group, "composed of 31 representatives functioning in the Negro community," insisted "that any proposals by other civic groups affecting the West End and Negro citizens be reviewed by our council and that our opinions and views be given full consideration before any official action is taken." The West End Community Council does not appear in the Cincinnati press, under that name, until the late 1950s.[11]

The constituency, activities, and leadership of the council before the

11. This does not necessarily mean that the WECC came into existence in the latter part of the 1950s, only that the white press did not report its existence until that time. The first time the WECC is mentioned by name is during the Crosley Field controversy of 1957–1958.

1960s are also rather obscure. Piecing together random reports and oral histories of the West End, a picture emerges of an organization not unlike the neighborhood improvement associations that existed in the West End in the early part of the century. The council apparently drew its major support from the neighborhood's small group of black and white homeowners. When the city decided to clear the Laurel-3 and Richmond-1 urban renewal sites, the homeowners in these areas took the lead in resisting the plan, joining together in the WECC to denounce urban renewal and working together to defeat the 1951 bond referendum. One participant has even suggested that the council itself originated in that struggle:

> When they were going to tear down homes to make way for Park Town, then that's when we formed the Community Council. We tried to organize to save some of the property, the people's property. . . . Of course, the staff of Findlay Street [Neighborhood House] was the main one, and the church who sponsored Findlay Street, West Cincinnati–St. Barnabus. We organized the other churches in the neighborhood and the neighborhood people. At that time, there was a different type of black clientele. They was interested, they were *motivated* in getting something for themselves. They had bought their homes and they wanted their homes saved. But we fought for it and it was a losing battle. (Lee interview, 1985:10–11)

The West End Community Council fought another battle with the city in 1957—a dress rehearsal for the Crosley Field protest eight years later. The city proposed to relocate 395 families living in the vicinity of Crosley Field in order to create 2,600 additional parking spaces by opening day, 1958. The WECC campaigned to force a city-wide referendum on the city's proposal, but the council was successful in collecting only 12,000 of the 30,689 signatures needed to put the issue on the November ballot. With this last obstacle out of the way, the city went ahead.[12]

These protests, however, were rare exceptions to the council's usual style and role. More typical in those days were activities directed toward preventing crime, providing recreation, helping neighbors, and maintaining the neighborhood base of the local Democratic Party. Looking back on this period, one of the council's later presidents—who was active in making the council a more militant, confrontational organization in the 1960s—described her predecessors of the 1950s:

12. *Cincinnati Enquirer* (August 3, 1957:14; January 31, 1958:27; February 12, 1958:6). *Cincinnati Post* (February 12, 1958:4; February 21, 1958:1).

They wanted to do things for the community. But it was a combination of a peace and goodwill society and a church missionary group. Babe West and people like that—they were very political; we had a good following for the Democratic Party. They had a West End Weekend. They'd have an ox roast and people would sit around. They'd help each other. Somebody'd die, they'd help each other. Things like that. . . . They weren't as politically oriented, in terms of making things happen in the community, as we became. . . . What was important to them was like having a good ward club and who worked on the polls and that kind of thing. . . . The activity was around, you know, "sister so-and-so is sick; we'll take her some food." We sort of moved away from that. (Warren interview, 1985:65–66)

Not only were the council's activities different in this early period, so was its leadership. Until 1963, with the election of William Mallory to the council presidency, the leaders tended to be older, homeowners, and white—despite the fact that the neighborhood was nearly 80 percent black by the middle of the 1950s.[13]

The movers and shakers at that particular time were white. Later on, blacks took over the leadership of the council. I think Mallory became president. Rev. Beck, Rev. Mitchell, and, I believe, it was then Mallory. (Lewis interview, 1985:357)

Transition to Conflict Consciousness and Organization

Mallory, a West End native residing in Park Town, was thirty-one years old when he became president of the West End Community Council. A natural politician, he spent the next three years cultivating strong vertical ties between the council and various officials and agencies in the city administration, while building the council's horizontal base in the West End. These vertical ties were forged through threat, negotiation, and compromise, beginning with the Crosley Field protest and proceeding through years of deliberation in the West End Task Force. The WECC under Mallory was instigator, participant, and prime mover in the task force planning process:

13. Two exceptions to this tendency of whites to predominate in the WECC's early leadership were William "Babe" West and Harry Martin, both black. West served for a time as the council's vice president. Martin, a talented leader who later became the head of Cincinnati's Model Cities Program, served as the council's president during the 1957–1958 petition drive to force a referendum on the Crosley Field parking plan.

I was instrumental in getting it started, to actively work with the city to plan the redevelopment of this area. That came about as a result of a confrontation with the city. We wanted to be involved in the development of the area, and I badgered the City Manager to set up this Task Force. . . . The Community Council, of course, pulled the levers. (Mallory interview, 1985:20–21)

This bid to become an active player in the city's urban renewal game would not have succeeded, however, had the council not successfully expanded, mobilized, and maintained its support in the West End. The council's ability to establish vertical ties with the city, in other words, largely depended on its prior ability to establish horizontal ties with the residential groups of its own neighborhood. Mallory had a great deal of help accomplishing this primary task.

The West End Community Council built its base of support in the neighborhood with the help of two federally assisted programs, both run from the local Seven Hills Neighborhood House.[14] The first of these programs was the West End Special Services Project (WESSP), funded by the Office of Economic Opportunity (OEO). By 1965 this project had a staff of twenty, seven or eight of whom were working full-time as community organizers in the West End (Lewis interview, 1985:360). Beginning with the door-to-door contacts already made by the NAACP during its 1963 voter registration drive—two WEESP staff members, Richard Lewis and James Rankin, had been active in that drive—these organizers recruited people into the community council who had never been active in the neighborhood before:

Our mission was to go out and organize the neighborhood. Our first mission was to strengthen the West End Community Council and organize block clubs that would feed into the West End Community Council. We did just that. We organized several block clubs: the Charlotte Street Block Club, the Dayton Street Block Club, the York Street Block Club, the Dayton-Whiteman Block Club. (Lewis interview, 1985:359)

These block clubs drew tenants and homeowners into the council from areas of the northern West End that the urban renewal bulldozer had not yet touched. But Mallory and the staff of the WESSP

14. The Findlay Street Neighborhood House, started in the upper West End by the West Cincinnati Presbyterian–St. Barnabus Church, and the Riverview Neighborhood House, in the eastern section of the city, merged in 1962 at the insistence of the Community Chest to form the Seven Hills Neighborhood Houses, Inc. The headquarters for this new administrative body was placed in Lincoln Court (P. Robinson interview, 1985:41).

were aware that the council also needed support from the areas south of Poplar Street, since half of the neighborhood's entire population was residing in Richmond Village, Park Town, and the West End's three public housing projects by the mid-1960s. Park Town was not really a problem. Many of the leaders of both the WECC and the WESSP lived there, and the WECC held its monthly meetings in the Park Town auditorium. There was no lack of involvement by Park Town residents. The residents of the other housing projects, however, were less involved in the community council. The council made a special effort, therefore, to solicit their participation in its affairs and to support issues of particular concern to public housing tenants:

> A lot of our activities were centered around the Metropolitan Housing Authority. I recall that they tried to raise the rent and we had a massive protest against that. . . . The protest against the increase in the Metropolitan housing rents involved around two thousand people. But it depended on the issue, of course. The closer the issue to the overall interests or needs of people, the greater the participation. (Mallory interview, 1985:19–20)

Beyond these efforts to expand and mobilize the council's local constituency, the organizers of the WESSP attempted to identify and develop new leadership. Potential leaders, once discovered, were put through an intensive training program, known as CHART. This was another federally assisted program, administered by Seven Hills. CHART was an acronym for "Community, Human, and Resource Training:"

> They basically learned how to run their organizations, how to delegate responsibility, how to establish goals and directions, how to work with complex organizations and systems, how to make reports to city council, how to do research that shows data, how to use the media, how to call a press conference, how to write to government officials. So, basically, we went back to the old civics class: how government works, how bills are passed, how city council works. . . . People *had* leadership ability. It was a matter of seeking those people out and saying, "Hey, you know the leadership skills that you used in running the Johnny-Boy Social Club? You can use some of that in dealing with this problem over here." (Jenkins interview, 1985:342–43)

The training, conducted in small groups, lasted eight weeks. The first group to be trained were the WESSP organizers themselves, followed by the leaders of the community council and the leaders of the block clubs being set up by the WESSP. After that, the organizers of WESSP began to recruit in the neighborhood for CHART, using the same door-to-door methods that had been employed to register voters and to pull people into the community council:

> So this young man named Artis Dawson came to my house. I was a case worker at Hamilton County Welfare. I wasn't bothering anybody. I stayed in my house. I went to work. I went to church. And, he said, "The community needs you." And I said, "Oh yeah, okay." So he told me about meetings they were having and I promised to go. But I'd never go. And he would come right back. And so finally I said, "Well, I'm just going to go over there and see what he's talking about." So I went, and I was really enthused and I was shocked at all the people. And I said, "Well, maybe I can learn something." So I started going. (Warren interview, 1985:51)

The council's campaign of constituency-building and leadership training occurred amidst the political upheaval of a threatened neighborhood defending itself against the further depradations of urban renewal, and a mobilized race asserting itself in the face of a recalcitrant white estabishment. Each of these political situations fueled the other, with the organizational development of the community council becoming a condition *and* a consequence of both.

The council's membership and influence grew, partially because the locality-based and racially based turmoil of the times presented the council with a wide array of interests and issues; and partially because Mallory and the organizers of the WEESP were politically astute enough to jumble all of these interests and issues together. They did not confine themselves to "neighborhood improvement" but thrust the council into every controversy of property, place, and race affecting West End residents. One month it would protest the planned demolition of local housing in Liberty-Dalton; the next, it would join with CORE and the NAACP to protest the city's failure to pass a fair housing ordinance or to hire black police. One month the council would demonstrate at City Hall, demanding to participate in the planning and redevelopment of Queensgate II; the next it would picket a branch bank on Linn Street, demanding the employment of black tellers. Neighborhood issues and racial issues overlapped in the work of the WECC, just as they tended to overlap in the larger society. This had the dual effect of multiplying the council's bases of support within the neighborhood and layering the bases of solidarity within the organization itself. For a time, the internal solidarity of the WECC grew just as fast as its external constituency.

Overlapping issues of race and place had the added effect of multiplying the number of contests and conflicts in which the council became engaged. The consciousness and activity of the council grew gradually more militant as the frequency of its confrontations with Cincinnati's business and political leaders increased. There were also new ideologies in the air, giving the leaders of the WECC a new vocabulary of "black power" and "community control." The riots of 1967 pushed all of this to a new level. One West End activist later wrote: "After the summer of 1967, Black Power became so respectable that practically everybody in the Black community from coast to coast became a Black Power spokesman" (Jenkins, 1974:40). The black community of the West End was no exception, and the council became an increasingly militant, conflict-oriented advocate of black empowerment and community control.

The WECC was pushed to this new level of conflict consciousness and confrontational activity not only by "external" events and ideologies but by the emergence of a new generation of leaders within the neighborhood. Mallory had stepped down from the presidency of the council to campaign for a seat in the state legislature, which he won in 1966. His place was taken by Doris Brown, a homeowner in the Queensgate II who was employed at that time as a cafeteria worker in the Cincinnati public schools. In the meantime, the CHART program began to attract and develop a younger group of potential leaders who were especially atuned to the militant rhetoric and style of the day. In 1968 one of CHART's "graduating classes" decided to take control of the West End Community Council:[15]

> They had a community thing where they were training us in leadership. They talked to us about the community and we began to think politically about it. There were seven of us in the group. I was the only female. We used to meet until one and two o'clock in the morning. We'd look at old city plans, we'd look at what City Hall had in mind for the West End; and we'd try to figure out ways to stop it. . . . So we sat down and drew up a plan. Now, first, we got to be in charge if we going to make some changes. So we decided that we were going to take over the Community Council. . . . You had to have a membership card to vote. You had to pay a dollar to be a member. But they had a weak constitution. We looked at this constitution, and anybody in the community could vote. So we went across the street to the neighborhood bar. We had about $40. We all pooled our money. So we got forty

15. The seven members of this CHART "class" were Betty Warren, Allen Davis, Warren Dennis, Johnny Jackson, Raymond Jackson, Nate Barnett, and Gerald Winstead (Warren interview, 1985:51, 67).

people, and we bought 'em beer and enticed them to come over and
vote for us. So that's how we ousted 'em, and we took over. (Warren
interview, 1985:50, 52–53)

For the next ten years, the presidency and principal offices of the
West End Community Council were passed back and forth among the
seven members of this group. (Onlookers soon dubbed them the
"Magnificent 7.") The group was younger than the leaders they had
replaced: all except one were under thirty; the new president, Allen
Davis, was twenty-five. They were tenants or residents of Park Town,
rather than homeowners. Most important for the political development of the community council, they were willing—even eager—to
confront and antagonize City Hall, city agencies, and the white business community in ways that Doris Brown and her generation were
reluctant to. This contrast in political style is captured well in the
following exchange:

Q: Being young, did you push harder? Did you have far less fear of
being aggressive?
A: We had less fear, because we hadn't felt the weight of being black-
listed. Babe West and people like that were very astute; they knew
there were certain people's toes you didn't step on. *We* didn't care.
We'd make people mad at us. . . . The distinct difference was, the older
council moved in a more secure environment. They didn't push, and
they didn't make waves. Consequently, they didn't have all the attention from City Hall that we needed. When we took over, it was like:
"We going to get 'em!" (Warren interview, 1985:66–67)

Warren somewhat exaggerates the contrast between this new regime and the ones before. After all, Mallory's presidency had been
marked by a considerable escalation in conflict, and the organizers of
the WESSP were no less interested in confronting City Hall. Yet Warren's picture is essentially correct. The ouster of Doris Brown did
inject a new spirit of militancy. It sealed the organization's transition from a mutual-aid and neighborhood self-help association to a
politically conscious conflict group prepared to oppose and pressure the powers-that-be. This transition began with Mallory and the
WESSP, but it came to full maturity under the stewardship of the Magnificent 7.[16]

16. This is not to suggest that the election of Allen Davis and company pleased
everyone or that all of the council's members shared the conflict orientation of the
new administration. It took a while for this orientation to become general. The council's older members, in particular, were reluctant to embrace these brash young mili-
tants—a reluctance that was reinforced by the disturbing style of some of the new-

With the federally funded WESSP continuing to act as the organization's de facto staff, the council's new leadership moved on several fronts at once to consolidate its position and to put the organization on a new footing. First, recognizing the role that the CHART training had played in their own political growth, the young leaders of the WECC expanded the program to include more of the council's membership. They also arranged day-long council retreats to analyze city plans, discuss strategy, and develop their own plans and proposals for the West End's future.

Second, they introduced a degree of internal organizational discipline and structure that had seldom been seen before:

> You knew your duty. It was organized. Not to the extent the Panthers were, but the same kind of commitment. Our thing wasn't violence, but it was the same structure. . . . I took my position as serious as a job. Because people said, "Well, if you're going to be our leaders and we need to go to City Hall, then you guys better be able to speak for us intelligently and deal with what we need in the community." (Warren interview, 1985:54–55)

Third, for several years the leaders of the WECC kept the organization's members in a state of almost constant mobilization. Members demonstrated before the city council and city agencies again and again. They called news conferences. They staged protests blocking traffic on public sidewalks and streets; demanding an end to the police practice of firing indiscriminately at suspected felons in black communities; demanding an end to heavy truck traffic passing through the neighborhood.

Fourth, despite their brash, confrontational style, the new leaders were careful not to break entirely with the leaders of the past. They attempted to make a place for people like Babe West and Doris Brown. Even more important, they maintained close ties with those representatives of the West End Special Services Project, Seven Hills Neighborhood House, and the West End Community Council who were still participating in the West End Task Force—Richard Lewis, Jerome Jenkins, and William Mallory, in particular. These ties were to prove essential, not only in enhancing the new leaders' credibility with the council's older members, but in preserving the council's hard-won place in the city's urban renewal planning process. These ties were also to help pull the community council toward another

---

comers. For example, the council's new vice president was Warren Dennis: "Warren used to wear bib overalls with no shirt and Jesus Christ sandals. And he had a bush this big. And before he'd get up he'd say, 'Everyone over 30 ought to be dead.' Oh! It scared a lot of the old people in the council" (Warren interview, 1985:66–67).

stage of organizational development, even as Allen Davis and company were completing the council's transition to a conflict group.

Transition to Radical Consciousness and Organization

As of 1969 the West End Task Force (WETF) had been meeting nearly every other week since 1966.[17] Although its overall mission was planning and development for the entire West End, the Task Force devoted most of its time to setting goals for the redevelopment of Queensgate II. The future of this residential area, the virtual birthplace of Cincinnati's black community, was a concern shared not only by the diminishing number of black families still residing there but by black leaders throughout the West End and city. Several of these West End leaders, along with the man in charge of the CHART training, Paul Henry, took special pains to convey this community concern to the University of Cincinnati planning team hired to assist in designing the Queensgate II redevelopment plan. The head of this team later recalled how forcefully these neighborhood leaders made their point:

> They recounted their childhood experiences of growing up in the West End and their memories of other Cincinnati black neighborhoods, citing with affection certain stores, vacant lots, intersections, hangouts, "marvels," pathways, and structures. They also described how they had observed over the years a pattern of "rip-offs," "takeovers," and physical "intrusions" . . . all "stealing," "destroying," "changing," and "exploiting" many of the sights and sites with which they were long familiar, and all for the economic and practical benefit of the outside, established, affluent white community. . . . They then spelled out the larger meaning of their message. Though small (117 acres), the location and significance of Queensgate II was important for the overall inner-city black community in Cincinnati. It meant an immediate major investment of public and private money. Action there, with planning and construction, could boost community development morale in other black areas. The *kind* of action there could set a precedent for City

17. The West End was represented by the following people, as of 1969: Rev. Robert Beck, West End Community Council; Doris Brown, Queensgate II Community Club; Marybelle Brown, West End YMCA; Arlye Davis, West End Homeowners Association; Rose Daitsman, West End Community Council; Richard Hartke, West End Business Association; Walter Hempfling, West End Industrial Association; R. Jerome Jenkins, Seven Hills Neighborhood Houses, Inc.; Richard Lewis, Seven Hills Neighborhood Houses, Inc.; William Mallory, West End Community Council; James Rankin, Seven Hills Neighborhood Houses Inc.; Rev. Richard Sellers, West End Presbyterian Church; Georgiana Wynn, resident-at-large (T. Jenkins, 1982:84–85).

Hall and the white establishment in dealing with other black neighborhoods. If necessary to protect the black neighborhood's interest in the project, Henry added, "We could bring black leaders from all over Cincinnati to physically squat or lay on the land in Queensgate II. You can tell all of those concerned they are not dealing with just Queensgate II!" (T. Jenkins, 1982:93–94).

The attempt by the West Enders on the task force to exercise a degree of control over the Queensgate II planning process was aided by their continuing tie to the community council and by that organization's increasing pugnaciousness. Mallory and his allies on the task force often called upon the WECC to mobilize its constituency in vocal opposition to city or state proposals that would have undermined resident control over the redevelopment of Queensgate II. In 1969 alone, the community council staged three protests in defense of such resident control: halting the city's acquisition of land in Queensgate II until the new city manager ratified the task force's authority to oversee planning and development in the West End; halting the state's proposal to build a two-year technical college in Queensgate II on a site set aside by the task force for commercial development; and halting an attempt by private developers to bypass WETF review and approval of projects planned for the West End (ibid.). An increasingly militant, grass-roots organization considerably enhanced the influence of Mallory, Jenkins, and the other West End representatives on the task force.[18]

As the West End Task Force drew near to a final set of housing proposals and development plans for Queensgate II, Mallory was to call again for the support of the community council. This time, however, he had in mind a radically different role for the council. He wanted it to create a locally based, locally controlled community development corporation. It would be separately incorporated from the

18. Compared with the strident, aggressive young leaders of the WECC, people like Mallory, Lewis, and Jenkins—who held dignified positions, who were college educated, and who were somewhat older than Allen Davis and company—must have seemed reassuringly "moderate" and "responsible" to the businessmen and city officials forced to negotiate with them. This impression was undoubtedly reinforced by the appearance in the West End after the 1968 assassination of Martin Luther King of a black self-defense group calling itself the Black Turks. Attracting young blacks from the neighborhood who were too disaffected to support even the WECC, the Turks dressed in black berets and T-shirts, drilled with machetes, and talked tough to police, newspaper reporters, and city officials, who reacted (that is, overreacted) with predictable alarm. West End residents, on the other hand, appear to have regarded the Black Turks with a combination of tolerance and amusement.

WECC but directly controlled by the WECC through the power of the council to appoint a majority of the new corporation's board. Mallory's hope, in urging the council to add such a development arm, was that West End residents would gain a hand in encouraging and controlling both the redevelopment of Queensgate II and the rehabilitation of the remaining residential areas of the upper West End (Mallory interview, 1985:21). His fear, one that was shared by Richard Lewis, Jerome Jenkins, and other West Enders on the task force, was that *without* such a development capacity the carefully laid plans for Queensgate II would be gutted by the city (Jenkins and Lewis, 1982:119). The community council agreed to sponsor this spin-off organization. In May 1969 the West End Development Corporation (WEDCO) formally incorporated. Richard Lewis, one of the original incorporators, was later hired as WEDCO's first director. Betty Warren, another incorporator and an officer of the community council, was named chair of the WEDCO board.

As a first project, WEDCO acquired and rehabilitated two buildings in the upper West End using federal funds from the 221(d)(3) housing program.[19] It also acquired options to buy nearly every vacant lot in the upper West End (Johnson interview, 1985:231). These options were allowed to lapse, however, as WEDCO soon turned its entire attention to the redevelopment of Queensgate II. From the early 1970s on, WEDCO had little involvement in any part of the West End lying north of Ezzard Charles Drive (formerly Lincoln Park Drive).

The West End Task Force approved a housing plan for Queensgate II in 1970, calling for the construction of two thousand units of townhouse, garden-row, and terrace-type housing.[20] These units were to be developed for a heterogeneous population that was mixed by income and race and split between families with children and families without. WEDCO, however, had persuaded the task force to ease its restrictions on housing type and relax its insistence on the kinds of construction staging that would have guaranteed heterogeneity from the start. These changes allowed it to propose, as the first project in

19. These buildings were located at 850 Dayton Street and 1916 Colerain. They held eleven apartments between them, which were rented out to low-income families. WEDCO owned and managed these buildings for eleven years. They were later turned over to HUD.

20. These housing goals and plans and an account of their approval by the WETF appear in the Queensgate II Urban Design Plan (Department of Urban Development, 1972) and in "Housing: The Critical Nexus" (Miller and May, 1982). Additional information on the Queensgate II planning and development process was provided in interviews with Richard Lewis, Jim Jones, and Hugh Guest, taped in 1985.

the residential redevelopment of Queensgate II, a multistory residential-commercial complex for low-income families with children.[21] WEDCO, in partnership with a large developer from Washington, D.C., eventually created 348 rental units in a high-rise complex containing 40,000 square feet of commercial space. This project, named Uptown Towers, was completed in 1975.

Mallory's organizational brainchild pointed the West End Community Council in a new direction. The council's rhetoric of "black power" and "community control" had meant, heretofore, militant confrontation with city officials and business elites to demand more housing, more services, and more say by black West Enders in how these resources should be developed or delivered. The creation and early success of WEDCO gave added meaning to these concepts. Confrontation remained a part of the council's repertoire, but "black power" and "community control" were increasingly given an institutional cast by the council's leaders. They sought to establish interlocking locally-based, community-controlled institutions that might change the basic structure of housing development, service delivery, and cultural production in the West End. Engaged in this endeavor, they hardly noticed that they were gradually changing the basic structure of the community council as well.

By 1972 the community council had created three spin-off organizations: WEDCO, intended to assure, in Mallory's recollection, "community control over housing and development" (Mallory interview, 1985:21); the West End Health Center, a community-controlled clinic built with the help of Hill-Burton funds and established in spite of opposition from the city's health department (Sellers interview, 1985:39); and the Arts Consortium, a West End center for black music, art, and history founded "to pull together the culture of the submerged people, the minority folk" (Warren interview, 1985:80). Each of these organizations was separately incorporated, but each remained formally and informally linked to the WECC—at least in the

---

21. By the time WEDCO was developing its proposal for new construction in Queensgate II, the area had been cleared of all but about ninety of its original structures. The WETF had wanted *all* of the early construction in Queensgate II to be for middle- and upper-income people, as well as for the poor. WEDCO, however, believed that new construction should first provide for the area's original residents. As Richard Lewis put it, "The harsh realities of American life in this stage of history make the goal of heterogeneity just a dream and a very unstable plank in a planning platform. . . . The West End representatives' first obligation is to the people who presently live in the Queensgate II area, and to those who have been forced out by the steady deterioration of the area" (quoted in Miller and May, 1982:155).

beginning. The community council appointed a portion of each organization's board and reserved the right to review and approve major projects proposed by each. All of these organizations were further linked to the community council—and to each other—by sharing a common set of leaders, a common constituency, and a common political agenda for the West End.[22]

During the early years of the 1970s, therefore, the black leadership of the West End began to lay the foundation for an institutional network that might serve as a locality-based alternative to key development, service, and cultural institutions of the dominant society. Simultaneously, many of these same leaders were actively participating in two separate, city-sponsored planning bodies: the West End Task Force and the Resident Neighborhood Community Association, the citizen participation component of the Model Cities Program, established in 1969. The participants' hope was that both planning processes would result in greater financial and political support for the kinds of institution-building that they were undertaking in the West End. They were not disappointed. They were not prepared, however, for the unintended—and rather damaging—consequences of their success.

WEST END COMMUNITY COUNCIL: DECLINE AND FRAGMENTATION

At first, under the changing mandate of urban renewal, with additional funds from Model Cities, and with federal funds from a dozen other vestiges of the Great Society, there *was* an upsurge of financial and political support for the alternative institutions that the WECC attempted to establish. Herein lay a problem. As WEDCO, the West End Health Center, and even the Arts Consortium began to receive funding from various state and federal agencies and began to negotiate and cultivate separate relationships with city agencies, their primary relationship with the community council began to dissolve:

> What I think happened is that as WEDCO got set up with money through Model Cities and all those kinds of stuff, Model Cities re-

22. There was actually a fourth community-controlled institution that was part of this West End network, the West End Credit Union. This corporation predated the establishment of WEDCO and was created by Seven Hills, not by the community council. Nevertheless, until its demise in 1975, the credit union was a loose part of the alternative institutional network that began to arise in the West End during the early 1970s.

quired a certain allegiance that kind of superceded the allegiance to the West End Community Council. There were new reporting lines that superceded the reporting lines to the council. The health center—when they started getting that federal and state money—they had to do certain reporting to the funding agencies that superceded reporting to the community council. Unfortunately, the leadership of the council wasn't strong enough to say, "Time out! Yeah, you got to do all that, but you also got to come and tell us what you're doing." (Jenkins interview, 1985:351)

As these spinoff organizations gradually became less financially accountable to the community council, they became less politically accountable as well. They began to build their own constituencies and to hire their own staff, whose first concern was building houses, providing health care, or holding classes in arts and crafts—not furthering the political agenda of the community council. There was a drift in all of these organizations away from the highly politicized conflict orientation of the WECC and toward technical problem-solving around a specialized mission.

Meanwhile, the community council experienced a similar organizational drift. As more effort went into institution-building and neighborhood planning, less went into the kinds of grass-roots organizing, leadership training, and popular mobilization that had made the council a militant, broad-based conflict group. Part of this change was a conscious choice, since several West End leaders believed such institution-building to be a more radical, permanent political strategy than constant confrontation. But the greater part of this gradual drift toward political quiescence was due, as Jenkins suggests above, to the weakening of the council's leadership. By the mid-1970s the leaders of the WECC were "not strong enough" to hold their organization together, let alone prevent the political defection of the council's organizational satellites.

The council's leadership was slowly enfeebled by several factors, some structural and some personal. First, the proliferation of organizational commitments simply spread neighborhood leadership far too thinly. In the early sixties the community council had little competition from other locality-based organations for the small supply of talented, ambitious, civic-minded individuals with leadership ability that most neighborhoods contain. Ten years later, the community council was not the "only game in town" for West End blacks. There were a half-dozen block clubs in the upper West End and Queensgate II; there were resident councils in each of the public housing projects;

there were WEDCO, the West End Health Center, and the Arts Consortium; there was the West End Credit Union, started by Seven Hills; there were a dozen neighborhood representatives on the West End Task Force; and there were ten representatives from the West End on the Resident Neighborhood Community Association of Model Cities. Then too, nearly every federal program that served the West End had its own requirement for "citizen participation," placing additional demands on the limited time of the neighborhood's leadership:

> The generalized white society depletes black neighborhoods of its leaders. As soon as we would develop people, they'd snatch somebody and put 'em on their committee, and snatch somebody and put 'em on another committee. Because *they* didn't know how to find 'em. Basically, what happened you got a certain drain on the neighborhood group. So you'd get spread so thin you couldn't do what you were created to do. A lot of our talent got drained off. They were doing meaningful things, but the parent group suffered. (Jenkins interview, 1985:349–50)

These multiple opportunities for citizen participation overlapped with the organizational results of years of grass-roots organizing and in stitution-building to create a serious leadership problem for the community council. Increasingly, the council found itself competing with numerous other organizations for the time and allegiance of a limited pool of potential volunteers, while *all* of the West End's leaders and activists found themselves stretched and scattered to the point of ineffectiveness.[23]

The council's leadership was depleted by personal factors, as well. Some leaders, such as William Mallory and Betty Warren, continued to reside in and serve the West End, but their work took them away from the neighborhood much of the time.[24] More often, as in the cases of Allen Davis, Warren Dennis, and Richard Lewis, leaders moved

---

23. Not only the community council suffered from the depletion and overcommitment of the West End's leaderhip. Thomas Jenkins, the head of the university planning team for the WETF, was disappointed by the decreasing task force involvement by West Enders in the early 1970s—part of the reason, in his view, for the eventual failure of the WETF to prevent subsequent changes in the WETF's plan for Queensgate II (T. Jenkins, 1982:97).

24. Mallory, as a member of the Ohio legislature, worked most of the year in Columbus. In 1969 he had moved out of Park Town and purchased a house on Dayton Street. Warren continued to live in Park Town but devoted more of her time to a succession of professional, public-sector jobs outside of the West End.

out of the neighborhood.[25] This was partially a matter of individual choice and occupational mobility; talented people were offered jobs or educational opportunities in other cities or states. But the housing situation in the West End also presented a considerable obstacle to anyone interested in staying. Leaders living in public housing who managed to improve their economic circumstances were forced to move. Leaders living elsewhere in the neighborhood who sought to improve their accommodations found few attractive rentals and even fewer opportunities for affordable homeownership. So they left the West End in pursuit of housing in other parts of the city: "There was always the urge to do better, man. You know, you get people locked into the American Dream of buying a house. There was nothing down here to buy. So people left the community to buy a house" (Jenkins interview, 1985:352).

None of these factors would have been so fatally damaging to the community council, however, had they not been accompanied by massive cut-backs in federal support for community organizing and community development. Throughout the country, these cutbacks had a devastating effect on the ability of grass-roots groups like the WECC to maintain themselves. They had a similar effect on the ability of municipalities like Cincinnati to fulfill their promises that grass-roots groups would be full partners in the neighborhood redevelopment process.[26] Thus, at the very point that the West End began to exercise a modicum of control over the city's planning process and to establish an institutional infrastructure that would have allowed neighborhood participation in the development process, the federal programs that sustained the community council and made community control politically and financially possible were brought to an end.

Had funding continued for the West End Special Services Project,

---

25. Davis moved to Columbus, Ohio. Dennis went into the ministry and ended up in Atlanta (Warren interview, 1985:63). Lewis left WEDCO in 1975. He and his wife later started a school in the Cincinnati area.

26. As Mollenkopf (1983:209) has noted, this pattern was repeated in neighborhoods throughout the United States: "Ironically, just as neighborhoods had won some influence over these [Commmunity Action, Model Cities, and 1968 Housing Act] programs, the Nixon administration began its onslaught against them, including urban renewal itself. . . . Nixon moved forcefully to undermine the program base around which neighborhoods and Democratic City Halls had made their peace. From 1973 to 1975 economic recession and Nixon's New Federalism pushed subsidized housing projects towards bankruptcy, halted the construction of additional projects, terminated urban renewal, and made it impossible for local agencies and officials to deliver on their promises."

the council would have had the staff to maintain control over its spin-off organizations. Instead, the council lost most of its de facto staff and had to rely more on part-time volunteers to organize the neighborhood, mail out notices and minutes of council meetings, prepare summaries of city programs and plans, and perform the myriad other tasks needed to maintain organizational effectiveness. After awhile, fewer of these tasks got done.

Had funding continued for leadership training programs like CHART, the council might have replenished the supply of leaders that were being scattered out and siphoned off. Instead, these programs ended. After awhile, the number and quality of the new leaders appearing on the council declined.

Finally, had funding continued for urban renewal, subsidized housing construction, and the sort of commercial and residential redevelopment planned for Queensgate II, WEDCO might have built a technical staff that was capable of implementing much of the urban design plan put together by the West End Task Force for Queensgate II while creating West End housing options for the upwardly mobile black leaders who were beginning to leave the neighborhood. Instead, with the cutbacks in Model Cities and, later, in Community Development Black Grant funding, WEDCO was forced to reduce its staff every year. WEDCO went from a staff of eight in the early 1970s to a staff of five, to four, to three, to two, and finally to a staff of one (Jones interview, 1985:87–88). After 1975, with the completion of Uptown Towers and the departure of its original director, Richard Lewis, WEDCO undertook no other major construction or rehabilitation projects in Queensgate II. Nor did the city pick up the slack and attempt to implement the task force's Queensgate II plan, since federal cutbacks had paralyzed its redevelopment efforts as well. Ten years later, most of the area's cleared land was still vacant, as were most of the ninety buildings that were never razed—an outcome that the head of Cincinnati's city planning department later described as "tragic":

> I think the tragedy in the whole process is that we began to get in different administrations at the federal level and never really had a chance to pull program and resource together to make it happen. All of that came at just about the time that we were finally getting to a point of really having a social program, especially for the development of Queensgate. Just about the time we had the plan, just about the time we had agreement, just about the time the citizens bought into what it was the city wanted to do, just about the about the time [Urban Renewal Director] Peter Kory committed to making certain things hap-

pen—then all the bottom started falling out of those programs. (Guest interview, 1985:391)

Some federal funds still remained for urban redevelopment, but the West End was forced to vie with other neighborhoods for any available resources. A weakened community council, an understaffed WEDCO, and a West End Task Force whose plans seemed increasingly irrelevant to changing political and economic realities could muster less and less political support for Queensgate II. Particularly when faced with opposition from the city's business community—who preferred to see Queensgate II redeveloped for an upper-income population and wanted to see the city's diminishing federal resources devoted to downtown revitalization—the West End saw its own plans for Queensgate II slip ever lower on the city's agenda:

At the same time that we had the plan and we were beginning implementation, there was a lot of resistance from the business sector of the city. Therefore, there was a lot of pressure put on the city council to give the central business district priority in terms of resources. . . . The priorities changed, and Queensgate came out *last* in terms of priorities. (Guest interview, 1985:392)

The periodic delays and eventual suppression of most redevelopment activity in Queensgate II, due in part to the decreasing political clout of the West End, had the effect of weakening the community council even further. Leaders who had participated in the lengthy Queensgate II planning process grew discouraged. Residents who had believed that the WECC and WEDCO would soon be producing new housing grew disillusioned. Relations between the community council and WEDCO grew distant and increasingly antagonistic. There had long been some resentment within the council at WEDCO's insistence on concentrating exclusively on the lower end of the neighborhood, but the successful development of Uptown Towers had held such criticism in check. When redevelopment activity in Queensgate II began to wane, these resentments resurfaced—particularly when WEDCO decided that its next project would neither include low-income housing nor be located within the West End.

Facing reductions in funding for organizational support and project development in Queensgate II, WEDCO sought to develop other projects that might attract city support and generate a future stream of income for its own operations. In 1976 it acquired an eight-story apartment building located in the central business district. This building, "the Biltmore," was treated to a $1.2 million rehabilitation, creating twenty-four high-rent residential units and three thousand square feet of commercial space. The project took nearly five years to complete.

Council criticism began almost immediately and grew more vehement with each year of the Biltmore's development. There was resentment that WEDCO was not working within the West End. There was resentment that this downtown project had created neither jobs nor housing for West End residents. There was anger that WEDCO's new director, Jimmy Jones, seemed more intent upon following his own course rather than the one originally laid out for WEDCO by the community council.

The feud between the community council and WEDCO gained in intensity from year to year. It came to a head in the early 1980s when the council finally disowned WEDCO altogether. WEDCO, in turn, amended its bylaws to require only a single member of its board to be a member of WECC.[27] This conflict sapped the political energy and effectiveness from both organizations. Estranged from WEDCO, the community council no longer possessed the technical capacity to develop its own housing projects or monitor those proposed by the city. Estranged from the council, WEDCO no longer possessed the popular base to pressure the city into taking seriously either its project proposals or its criticisms of city proposals. In fact, once city officials became aware of the growing disarray of the community council, the internecine conflict between the council and WEDCO, and the growing distance between the council and its other spinoff organizations, they started taking the West End as a whole far less seriously.[28]

By 1980 the community council's external alliances and internal solidarity had become so badly fragmented that it had little influence

27. "Amended Code of Regulations of the West End Development Corporation," 1982. The WECC had originally been permitted to appoint a majority of WEDCO's board.

28. Nowhere was the neighborhood's diminished clout more telling and the city's newly dismissive attitude more apparent than in the redevelopment of Liberty-Dalton. The community council and the West End Task Force had long resigned themselves to the fact that Liberty-Dalton would be redeveloped for industrial or commercial use, but in the late 1960s they had forced the city to adopt a plan that "contemplated major industrial expansion in Liberty-Dalton as a means of providing a broader diversity of jobs for West End residents" (T. Jenkins, 1982:101). By 1977, however, city officials were recruiting firms for resettlement in the Liberty-Dalton area that would provide very little employment for West Enders. Promises made when the Community Council was strong were easily broken when the Council was weak, no longer possessing either the staff capacity to monitor the city's performance or the political clout to hold the city to its original commitments.

in the neighborhood, let alone at City Hall. The West End Health Center and the Arts Consortium functioned independently of the WECC, with their own funding, boards, constituencies, and organizational agendas. WEDCO functioned not only independently but in open disregard of the council's housing and development agenda. Most of the local block clubs, which the WESSP had so assiduously nurtured and integrated into the community council, were functioning apart from the WECC—or not at all.

Meanwhile, the council's membership was falling and the organization had become internally divided. No longer did the community council have a de facto staff to knock on doors and actively recruit volunteers. No longer, in fact, were there as many residents that could be recruited. The population of the West End, which had fallen from 41,929 to 17,068 during the 1960s, fell further to 13,066 by 1980. No longer did the fervor of an awakening civil rights movement or the threat of a bulldozing urban renewal program mobilize and bind together the neighborhood's residents. Both had passed by the decade's end. With the overlapping solidarities of race and place no longer present with sufficient intensity to attract a diverse set of interest groups into the council or to hold together those that were already there, the council—and the larger West End community—splintered along lines of social cleavage created by different interests of domestic property.[29]

Neither the council nor the neighborhood still possessed the kind of leadership that might have kept this from happening. Indeed, remaining leaders tended to be aligned with one set of property interests or another. Leaders spoke for older black homeowners, for tenants of public housing, or for tenants of private housing. Leaders spoke for the Park Town Cooperative or for the newly formed Community Land Cooperative. They spoke for the new landlords and homeowners, black and white, who began moving into the neighborhood in 1977, intent upon restoring historic buildings, improving the image of the upper West End, and making their fortunes in real estate. No longer did anyone speak for the West End as a single residential community.

29. These property-based cleavages had long existed just beneath the surface of the WECC's solidarity. Factions and tensions engendered by such cleavages had, in fact, occasionally appeared before 1980. But they had not mattered much because of various conditions that had allowed the WECC to knit together the scattered interests and groups of the neighborhood. When these conditions changed, the subterranean fractures of domestic property began increasingly to dominate the neighborhood's political life.

One person who briefly tried was Roger Bradley. Elected president of the WECC in 1981, Bradley attempted to return the council to its earlier conflict orientation. He was a highly vocal, highly visible native of the West End who had earned a reputation for being militantly pro-black and pro-poor.[30] On this basis he tried to reconstruct the community council, casting the organization in the political role of militant defender of the neighborhood's low-income blacks. With the exception of Park Town, nearly all of the neighborhood's residents living below Poplar Street fell into this category, as did 85 percent of the residents living above Poplar. Consequently, Bradley had a large and sympathetic audience for his attacks on City Hall, absentee landlords, and the historic preservationists who, in his opinion, were conspiring to displace low-income tenants and gentrify the neighborhood. For a time, the attendance at community council meetings was higher than it had been for many years.

At the same time that Bradley was attempting to rekindle a militant, confrontational spirit in the community council, he moved to terminate two remaining vestiges of the council's "radical" excursion into institution-building. The council's tie with WEDCO, already strained, was severed, and the West End Task Force was finally dissolved. These actions not only helped to return the council to an earlier stage of political activism, they also helped to concentrate more power in Bradley's hands. There were no longer three organizational voices claiming to speak for the West End. There was only one, the community council's, though that voice usually belonged to Roger Bradley alone.

The council's new-found vitality lasted about a year. Bradley's energy and rhetoric could not sustain an organization that did no grassroots organizing and no leadership development, an organization entirely without resources and staff (except for a part-time "neighborhood services worker" from the city's community action commission). In addition, too much of the responsibility for running the organization rested solely with Bradley and a few of his friends. When he began to lose interest toward the end of his tenure, no one waited in the wings to take over the council's leadership.

This effort to resuscitate the council was also doomed by larger events. Championing the cause of the poor by confronting City Hall

---

30. Information about Roger Bradley and the WECC under his leadership is drawn from interviews conducted in 1985 with Jim Jones, Dwight Wilkins, Diane Wright, Clinton Johnson, Norm Kattleman, and Adele Cramer. Bradley himself could not be located for an interview.

might have been politically effective when displacement was due to publicly funded redevelopment; it was less effective when the threat originated in the privately funded rehabilitation activity of landlords, homeowners, and Cincinnati's premier historic preservation society, the Miami Purchase Association. Without a development arm of its own, the council could rail against gentrification and could even impede the city's efforts to spur it on, but it could neither stop it nor provide housing for its victims. With so little impact on the neighborhood's housing problem, the council could not hold the allegiance of the poor. With so much rhetorical focus on the plight of the poor, it could not hold the allegiance of the black homeowners of the upper West End or the owners of social property in Park Town, both of whom had come to see themselves as middle class. Eventually, the council struggled to retain even the allegiance of public housing tenants whose leaders were concerned less with gentrification of the neighborhood than with the deterioration of Lincoln Court and Laurel Homes, a process that had been accelerated by the Nixon administration's onslaught on all federally funded housing between 1973 and 1975.

The community council had reached a point of factionalized disarray and political paralysis long before Bradley stepped down as president. After his departure, however, the organization slid into complete chaos. Each year, a different faction came to the fore, elected a new president, and proclaimed that the council was "on its way back." Each year, the rest of the council's interest groups banded together just long enough to neutralize—and, on occasion, to oust—the new administration. The cycle then began again:

Unfortunately, there's been no continuity of leadership. . . . The last real progressive president was Roger Bradley. That's been some time ago. He sort of faded out towards the end of his tenure. Since then, it's been people that pop up at election time and want to be president. They don't understand the roll-call of what the struggle's all about. There's no continuity of problem-solving. There's always a break. You have to do a reeducation process, and, by the time you reeducate a person, it's time for them to move on. Another person comes in. That's been the problem. (Wilkins interview, 1985:259)

You know, it's like a sinking ship. Okay, you've got a whole ship of people and all different groups all over the ship and it's well-balanced. You get somebody who navigates the ship and it runs along fine. What happens with the community council is they elect somebody, and they go to run the ship. And everybody else—the *whole* group, no matter where they are on the ship—goes to the opposite end. And the ship goes down! (Wheeler interview, 1985:221)

WEST END COMMUNITY COUNCIL: AN EXTERNALLY INDUCED "REVIVAL"

As disruptive and divisive as the council's demise has been on relationships within the West End, its most damaging effect has been on the neighborhood's external relations with City Hall. The organizational chaos of the WECC, beginning around 1981 and stretching into 1985, has left the West End without an effective, unified voice in either the city's neighborhood planning process or in its process of resource allocation. There are unusual opportunities within Cincinnati's rather elaborate structure of neighborhood support and neighborhood involvement for organizations like the WECC to affect local plans and to bargain for additional services, facilities, and funds. While critics of this participatory structure complain that it is merely a means of legitimating plans that the city has already made and of depoliticizing both the planning and budget process, the fact remains that neighborhoods that drop out of the process get left out of the planning and funding picture altogether. This is pretty much what has happened, in recent years, with the West End. One of the city's senior planners puts it this way:

> As you well know, communities in this day and age that do not have political clout or political expertise or organization—or all three—tend to get overlooked. For the last several years, the West End has been essentially ignored. Because there was no one there that we could work with. We kept trying. They would fall apart. Then they'd have these wars among themselves. Then two or three individuals would kind of surface and disappear. (Goepper interview, 1985:119)

Though it might seem that city officials would be glad not to have an active community council in the West End, this has not been the case. As much as they might dread a resurgence of the kind of politicized pro-black and pro-poor militancy that has periodically inflamed the council in the past, they are equally uncomfortable with a political vacuum. The risks of an obstructionist community council impeding the city's planning and budget process are outweighed by the risk of having no one in a volatile neighborhood with which to talk or bargain.

Abhorring the political vacuum that the council's disarray created in the West End, the city has sought to establish working relationships with other locality-based organizations in the neighborhood. Predictably, the West End organizations with which city officials and neighborhood planners have felt the most comfortable are those that have a professional staff and a middle-class membership most like themselves. For the past several years, therefore, what little public funding and planning assistance has been made available to the West End has gone mostly to the West End Health Center, the Miami Purchase Preservation Fund, and to an organization set up by the affluent newcomers to the upper West End, the Dayton Street Neighborhood Association.

At the same time, under the auspices of the city's Department of Neighborhood Housing and Conservation, an attempt has been made to reconstitute the West End Community Council as a *neighborhood improvement association*, representing all of the neighborhood's interest groups. So far, this attempt to pull together the neighborhood's various property interest groups has not succeeded. Aside from the distrust that one group has for another—after all, *they* know that their interests are incompatible, even if the city does not—the effort to revive the council has foundered on the failure of city officials or anyone else to discover a set of development proposals for the West End on which every group can agree. Nevertheless, the city is continuing to invest public funds and staff time in the pursuit of this elusive goal. The expressed hope of city officials is that, sooner or later, they and their allies in the neighborhood will succeed in developing "a really representative, recognized—'authorized,' if you will—district-based community council to negotiate with the city and to work with the city" (Goepper interview, 1985:101).

The problem with this dream of a pluralistic, broadly representative community council is that it assumes a West End "community" of common and compatible interests. Such a community no longer exists in the West End—if it ever did. Nor do the conditions exist, as they once did, that might allow the council to recruit and combine the neighborhood's multiple interest groups in a common cause of race and place. Without these conditions—some of them external to the West End, some of them internal to the neighborhood, and some of them endemic to the community council—a neighborhood organization like the WECC cannot hope to hold together a plurality of property interest groups that are not only different but opposed. Inter-

9

The Fractured Community: Property Interests and Property Interest Groups, 1975–1985

> Are wealthy white people the elite for whom the Dayton Street Neighborhood Association and the Miami Purchase Association are reclaiming the area? Don't the longtime residents have any rights? The newcomers say no. They say they are destined to reclaim and restore it for those who are able to appreciate its beauty and historic significance.
> —MAURICE MCCRACKIN ("Gentrification as a Tragedy," *Cincinnati Enquirer*, April 14, 1984)

> One of the Rev. Mr. McCrackin's favorite statements is that there are "invisible forces" supporting the Dayton Street Neighborhood Association and the Miami Purchase Association. I have heard this statement many, many times, but I have never heard who these forces are. Is this a verifiable fact or mere paranoia? If there are so many forces at work, why isn't the complete historic district renovated? Tell us who they are, Mr. McCrackin, we could use the help!
> —MICHAEL PAINTER ("Gentrification and Paranoia," *Cincinnati Enquirer*, April 21, 1984)

The existence of distinct and competing property interest groups in the West End is taken for granted by most observers, within the neighborhood and beyond. Typical are descriptions of the neighborhood's social and political order that readily acknowledge local differences of race, class, or lifestyle, but regularly distinguish its principal groups entirely in terms of their particular relation to domestic property. Sidewalk typologies like the following are not unusual:

175

There are those of us who are new in the community, whether we're white or black, who have bought and are restoring. And people who have lived here a good while, who bought back in the forties and preserved [their houses] from that point. And there are people who have rented and lived here all this time. (Kattleman interview, 1985:145)

Similar lines are drawn by one of the city's senior planners in distinguishing the "different groups of people down there:"

You've got the few remaining old-timers. Property owners. They're the folks that have been there since that was really a respectable part of the West End, when it was a very viable middle class community. Those people are pretty much up in years now. . . . You've got the few, relatively few, new people who've come in and bought and restored, mostly in the Dayton Street area. That's an easily indentified group, and it's relatively small in terms of the overall population. . . . You've got a large transient population in here, which may or may not be families, but they're transient. They come in and out. . . . Some of these buildings have been cut up and re-cut up until their density is that of a boarding house. . . . Those people are, at best, indifferent and, at worst, totally hostile to anything. They're too involved in trying to survive, I suspect, to worry about things as necessary as planning. They are seldom involved. (Goepper interview, 1985:397–98)

What is captured in these observations is the popular perception that the West End does contain a diversity of interest groups, differentiated according to each group's unique relation to domestic property. Popular wisdom is not far off the mark. Yet these sidewalk sociologists have a much harder time saying exactly how many groups there really are, why these groups came into existence, how their interests might differ, and why they act as they do. It is necessary to move beyond these casual classifications for a better understanding of the locality-based groups that exist and contend in the West End. The challenge is to look within the words of local residents, behind the actions of local organizations, and between the lines of public and private documents to discover the pattern of property interests that help to explain the "comings and goings" of these various groups.

THE RISE OF PROPERTY INTEREST GROUPS

As the West End Community Council began to unravel during the 1970s, the neighborhood was undergoing significant changes of its own. By 1980 its population had fallen to 13,076, a third of what it had been in 1960.[1] One of the neighborhood's former residential areas, Liberty-Dalton (see Figure 11), was being redeveloped by the city as an industrial park. It had been entirely cleared of all structures. Even Crosley Field was gone.[2] Another residential area, Queensgate II, had been nearly cleared of all people (with the exception of residents in the newly built Uptown Towers). Most of its land, along with most of the buildings that remained, lay empty, awaiting the next move by a city whose priorities had shifted during the previous decade. Laurel Homes, Lincoln Court, Richmond Village, Park Town, and Stanley Rowe Apartments now contained two thirds of the neighborhood's entire population and half its housing units. The other half were in privately owned buildings, either rental or owner-occupied. These last vestiges of private housing stood mostly above Poplar Street, in the areas known as Dayton-Findlay I, Dayton-Findlay II, and Brighton. Only in the upper West End did there still exist the kind of residential neighborhood that had once characterized the entire West End.

But this area above Poplar Street had also experienced major changes during the 1970s. The upper West End had long contained the most middle-class population in the entire West End—in aspiration, if not always in fact—along with the highest number of homeowners, the highest level of education, and the most people employed in a professional, technical, or managerial capacity.[3] The upper West End remained the most middle-class section throughout the 1970s, but showed signs of serious decline. The number of black homeowners dropped from 337 to 235 during the 1960s (see Table 2). By 1980 the number stood at 195. The area's population became older and poorer. By 1980 a higher proportion of the upper West End was over fifty-five (27 percent) and a lower proportion was under fifteen

1. All demographic data in this chapter, unless stated otherwise, are based upon the 1960, 1970, and 1980 U.S. Census for Cincinnati.

2. Soon after seizing the residential blocks around Crosley Field, the Cincinnati city council voted to build a new downtown sports arena on the riverfront. This vote was taken in spring 1966. Riverfront Stadium was opened in 1970. Several years later, when the city began redeveloping Liberty-Dalton as an industrial park, Crosley Field went the way of the houses and shops that had once surrounded it.

3. Park Town was the only residential area in the neighborhood with a greater proportion of its population employed in professional, technical, or managerial work and educated past the high school level. Employment for the residents of Park Town, as well as for residents of the rest of the West End, is mostly found outside of the neighborhood in hundreds of factories, offices, and stores. The principal exceptions are teachers and service workers employed in the neighborhood's schools or in a U.S. Postal Service complex located on the neighborhood's border.

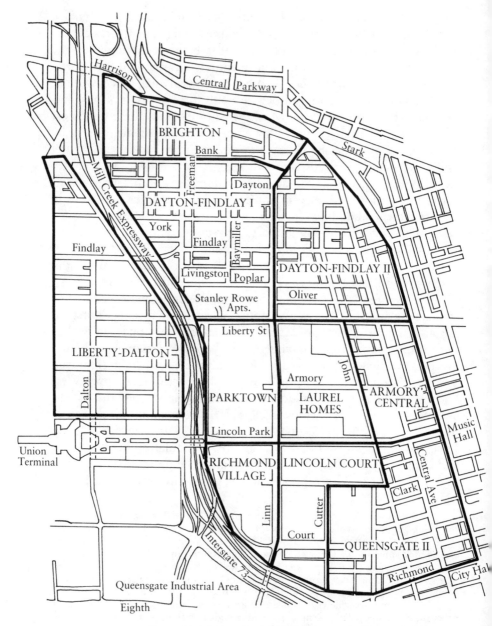

Figure 11. West End neighborhoods, 1975

Table 2. Population and housing: Upper West End,* 1960–1980

	1960		1970		1980	
	no.	percent	no.	percent	no.	percent
Total Population	10,566	100	6,073	100	4,600	100
White	1,349	13	371	6	429	9
Black	9,164	87	5,697	94	4,171	91
Professional/Managerial	97	0.9	102	2	327	7
Over 55 yrs. of age	354	3	1,411	23	1,257	27
Under 15 yrs. of age	3,659	35	2,598	42	1,147	25
Total dwelling units	3,636	100	2,481	100	2,519	100
Rental	2,946	81	1,994	80	1,752	70
Owner-occupied	375	10	247	10	239	9
Vacant	315	9	240	10	528	21
Total rental units	2,946	100	1,994	100	1,752	100
White	460	16	207	10	163	9
Black	2,486	84	1,787	90	1,589	91
Total owner-occupied units	375	100	247	100	239	100
White	38	10	12	5	44	18
Black	337	90	235	95	195	82
Total vacant units	315	100	240	100	528	100
For rent or sale	186	59	195	81	260	49
Uninhabitable	129	41	45	19	268	51
Families below poverty line:	NA		460		528	
Percent of upper West End families below poverty line:	NA			35.4		53.3

*Census Tracts 14 and 15 (Liberty-Dalton, Brighton, Dayton-Findlay I and II)

(25 percent) than at any other time in the previous two decades. There were also more families in poverty, 53 percent in 1980. The most telling indicator of the area's decline was the dramatic increase in the number of vacant and abandoned buildings. In 1970 the upper West End had a vacancy rate of 10 percent (240 units); by 1980 the vacancy rate had jumped to 21 percent (528 units), and more than half of these units were uninhabitable.

Even as these vacancy and poverty rates rose, two counter trends gathered momentum: historic preservation and gentrification. One promised to restore the the area's deteriorated buildings; the other threatened to displace the area's impoverished population. By 1980 both of these signs of neighborhood "improvement" were as much in evidence in the upper West End as the signs of neighborhood decline.

Historic preservation in the neighborhood had its start in the early efforts of the community council to save portions of both the upper and lower West End from the bulldozer of urban renewal. Realizing that the historic designation of strategic sections of the West End might prevent a repetition of Laurel-3/Richmond-1–style redevelopment in other parts of the neighborhood, the community council had endorsed the efforts of preservationists to declare several blocks of the upper West End an "historic interest area." Responding to these recommendations, the city proceeded to designate an eight-block rectangle, lying along Dayton Street and between Linn Street and Winchell Avenue, a protected "historic interest area" in 1965. This "historic interest area" was anchored by the two blocks of Dayton Street that had once been known as Millionaires' Row.[4]

In 1968, several years after the city's historic designation of Dayton Street, Cincinnati's leading preservation society—a private, nonprofit organization known as the Miami Purchase Association (MPA)—purchased an ornate, two-story structure at 816 Dayton Street. Soon thereafter, the MPA transferred its offices there and began to devote special attention to the preservation and restoration of buildings in the upper West End. In 1972, the MPA submitted a formal application to the Department of the Interior, asking that fourteen square blocks, bounded by Poplar, Linn, Bank, and Winchell, be added to the National Register of Historic Places. Approving MPA's application the next year, the department designated this area (which incorporated the city's "historic interest area") the Dayton Street Historic District.

Historic designation made it more difficult for the city to demolish buildings. Later, it even encouraged the city to provide grants and loans to the district's property owners for facade improvement and structural rehabilitation. Property owners within the district also became eligible for federal tax benefits for rehabilitation. Although few of the area's older homeowners had the savings, income, or desire to take advantage of these tax incentives, other interest groups did. These federal tax incentives, city subsidies, and prospect of sizable profits from domestic property that was underpriced made investment in the buildings of the Dayton Street Historic District an attractive proposition for a new group of acquisitive homeowners, landlords, and realtors.

Despite these attractions, new investment in the upper West End came slowly. There were two major obstacles. First, the investment

---

4. In the lower West End, the West End Task Force helped convince the city not to raze approximately ninety "historic" structures in Queensgate II. It was not until 1982, however, that an eight-block area in Queensgate II was finally designated the "Betts-Longworth Historic District."

climate was chilled by the number of dilapidated housing units and low-income blacks, crowded within and around the historic district. One West End landlord, himself a black, described the situation this way:

> The average investor figures that he can make just as much money and do just as well on his investment by going to an area where the socioeconomic structure is a little better, or a little more enticing for an investor. See, right now—hate to say it, but it's the truth—the *obstacle* is the poor people in the West End. Investors are just afraid to come to the West End and put their money in. (Lundy interview, 1985:104)

Even when investors were not scared off by the black faces, impoverished families, and deteriorating structures, they often found it extremely difficult to finance their proposed projects. This was the second obstacle to new investment in the upper West End: the neighborhood was redlined during the 1970s by banks, savings and loans, and insurance companies. Capital and insurance for West End property were, for many years, either unavailable or uneconomical.

The investment climate in the upper West End began to change in the latter half of the 1970s—partially because of the promotional efforts of Miami Purchase, partially because fewer bargains remained in other central-city neighborhoods undergoing rehabilitation and gentrification, and partially (perhaps mostly) because a number of energetic young investors were willing to use their own money to buy into the upper West End and to move there themselves.[5] During the five years before 1975, only eight owner-occupiers purchased homes in Dayton-Findlay I, Dayton-Findlay II, and Brighton. During the next five years, fifty new homeowners moved into the area. Furthermore, for the first time in more than a generation, most of these newcomers, thirty-two of them, were white.

Many of the newcomers to the upper West End, particularly those who settled on Dayton Street, shared with the Miami Purchase Association an eagerness to see the entire fourteen-block historic district restored to its nineteenth-century elegance. For some, especially those newcomers who were part-time or full-time real estate developers, brokers, and landlords, a commitment to historic preservation was combined with an expectation of substantial profit should the area ever be completely restored. It was this group, along with various developers, brokers, and landlords residing outside of the West End,

---

5. Two- and three-story brick buildings could be purchased in the upper West End for prices ranging from $7,000 to $25,000 in the late 1970s.

that took the lead in establishing the Dayton Street Neighborhood Association in 1978.

The Dayton Street Neighborhood Association (DSNA) worked closely with the Miami Purchase Association in a joint effort to improve the image of the upper West End and to promote investment in the area by financial institutions, city agencies, and new homebuyers. A $90,000 grant from the city for facade improvements in the historic district and a multi-million-dollar conversion of nearby Union Station into an urban mall of restaurants and boutiques boosted the confidence of both organizations that the West End was on the verge of turning around. The DSNA and MPA helped their own cause by launching the first in a series of annual "house tours" of the neighborhood in 1979. Each year, hundreds of visitors flocked to the upper West End, invited by DSNA and MPA to tour the historic district, inspect houses already restored, and (it was hoped) invest in houses that had yet to be rehabilitated and restored to their turn-of-the-century splendor.

These efforts to spur interest and investment in the area showed results, albeit not as quickly or abundantly as DSNA and MPA had hoped. There was a flurry of real estate activity in the upper West End between 1977 and 1982, slowed only by the leap in interest rates to 21 percent in 1980. New homeowners moved into the area in numbers that would have seemed modest elsewhere, but were quite large for the West End. Rehabilitation and repairs were undertaken on dozens of buildings.[6] Forty-four percent of the area's privately held parcels changed hands at least once during this period, a remarkable turnover for any neighborhood.[7]

After years of neglect from city officials, financial lenders, absentee landlords, and would-be homebuyers, the upper West End suddenly began looking like a reasonable place to invest—still a risk, but an attractive risk. As a reporter for the *Cincinnati Enquirer* (March 4, 1979:B1) assessed the situation: "In a city where renovation is a way of life, Dayton Street is the new frontier." In the same article, Gerald

6. Building permits for the upper West End (Census tracts 14 and 15) nearly tripled between 1976 and 1981 (Building Permit File, Office of Planning and Management Support).

7. An examination of City Hall property ownership and property tax records listing the "dates of recent sale" for commercial, residential, and vacant parcels in the upper West End (north of Poplar Street) revealed that 293 of the area's 659 listed parcels had changed hands at least once during the period 1977–1982; fifty-nine of these transferred properties had been sold two or more times. The hottest area for real estate transfers was in the Dayton Street Historic District. For example, of the fifty-nine parcels that were sold two or more times, fifty-one of them were located *within* the historic district.

Bates, a black real estate developer who moved to Dayton Street in 1977, offered an even rosier assessment:

> "The interest in this area is phenomenal," beams Gerald Bates, president of the newly organized Dayton Street Neighborhood Association. "We get all kinds of calls from people who want to move in. I can't even keep up with it.
> "If we had property becoming available, we would sell it like that," continued Bates, snapping fingers on both hands. "We're selling them at just that rate."

By 1982, however, the march of restoration and gentrification had begun to slow. Most of the prime properties on Dayton Street had been purchased, rehabilitated, and occupied by affluent newcomers to the neighborhood. Additional restoration was in progress or planned for properties on York, Baymiller, and Freeman streets, but fewer properties were immediately available for sale. Black owners held onto their homes, and absentee landlords waited for property values to rise even further. Rising property values, spurred on by private and public investment in the area, also meant that fewer bargains remained for speculative investors. Houses selling for $7,000 in the 1970s sold for $40,000 to $50,000 in the 1980s, even before renovation. Underpriced properties were still available south of York Street, but white homeowners were reluctant to move much closer to the neighborhood's all-black public housing projects. Underpriced properties were still available outside the historic district, but affluent investors, black and white, were reluctant to forego the tax benefits of rehabilitating property in a federally registered historic district. Also slowing restoration and gentrification were the exhorbitant interest rates of the early 1980s and the Reagan administration's cutbacks in housing and community development programs that the city might have used (and had started to use) to push rehabilitation.

Of equal importance was the intergroup conflict that began occurring within the West End, fracturing the community along lines of competing property interests. There were several ways in which the gentrification process was hampered by the competition and conflict of property interest groups. The mobilization of property interests in the West End contributed, first of all, to the decline and disarray of the West End Community Council.[8] With the council in chaos, the

---

8. This was a reciprocal process. The decline of the WECC made the formation and mobilization of property interest groups more possible—and more necessary. The rise of property interest groups, organized and active outside of the WECC, hastened the council's decline.

West End was routinely overlooked in the city's allocation of a shrinking pool of housing and community development funds.

Second, intergroup conflict disrupted the flow of private investment into the neighborhood and redirected the housing aims of the Miami Purchase Association. Institutional and individual investors, who were already reluctant to move their dollars or families into the neighborhood, hardly found it reassuring to learn that various West End groups were loudly and publicly opposed to Miami Purchase, the Dayton Street Neighborhood Association, and their predominately white, uniformly well-off supporters.

Finally, restoration and gentrification were hampered by the rise of another locality-based organization, pursuing a housing and development agenda that was radically different than that of either the MPA or DSNA. The organization was the Community Land Cooperative of Cincinnati (CLC). Incorporated in 1980, the CLC immediately launched an aggressive program to purchase and preserve as much low-income housing as it could before MPA, DSNA, or other investors acquired and converted it for higher-income use. It also attempted to mobilize tenants, long-time homeowners, and the tattered remnants of the West End Community Council *against* historic preservation and gentrification. By the end of its first year of operation, the CLC was acting collectively in direct opposition to the MPA and to the acquisitive homeowners and landlords of the DSNA.

In sum, by the late 1970s and early 1980s, the West End—particularly, the upper West End—experienced two contradictory trends. The neighborhood's domestic property was deteriorating, and its black population was becoming older and more impoverished. On the other hand, part of the neighborhood was undergoing rehabilitation and gradual gentrification in the name of historic preservation and financial profit.

These disruptive trends affected different people in different ways, depending upon their particular relation to domestic property. They gave rise to new property interest groups (or gave new life or new direction to old ones). Formed or reformed within the crosscurrents of the deterioration and revitalization of the neighborhood's domestic property and framed against the steady decline of the WECC, these locality-based groups became newly conscious of their separate property interests and began acting collectively, in concert or in conflict with each other, in defense of those interests. These groups, their interests, and the organizational form which the defense of such interests has taken deserve a closer look.

DOMESTIC PROPERTY INTEREST GROUPS,
1975–1985

Six locality-based interest groups—each having a different relation to domestic property; each possessing a different set of economic and political interests *because* of that relation—can be discerned among the residential population of the West End. Among those who relate to domestic property as "homeowners," in the popular sense of that word, there are the long-time residents of the neighborhood and an affluent group of newcomers. Among those who relate to domestic property as "renters," there are public tenants and private tenants. Among the residents of "social property," there are those who live in cooperative housing and those who are part of a local community land trust. Drawing on the theoretical framework proposed in Part I, this analysis will focus on the material interests that (objectively) differentiate one locality-based group from another, and the political behavior of each group in (subjectively) recognizing those interests and in collectively acting to defend them.

Homeowners, Old and New

Owner-occupied housing, excluding for now what was previously referred to as "social property," has never constituted a large proportion of the units in the West End. At its peak, in 1950, the neighborhood's 1,456 owner-occupied units made up only 7 percent of the total. Even in the upper West End, which has historically held *half* the owner-occupied housing in the West End, homeownership has stayed around 10 percent.

Despite their numbers, homeowners have always supplied a disproportionate share of the membership of local improvement associations and block clubs. Until the mid-1960s they were also disproportionately represented among the leaders and members of the West End Community Council. As the council changed from a neighborhood improvement association to a locality-based conflict group, black homeowners still involved themselves in the council's activities, even when control of the council passed to a new generation of leaders. Undoubtedly, the passion of the civil rights movement motivated many, but the primary impetus for homeowner participation in the community council was the very real threat of urban renewal. There was every reason to believe in the 1960s that the city would eventually "redevelop" every section of the West End. Black homeowners, many already displaced at least once by urban renewal, were willing to support any organization that might keep the bulldozer away.

Even so, homeowners tried to distance themselves from the growing militancy of the WECC. They were always more comfortable with the neighborhood improvement and mutual aid activities of the "old" community council than they ever were with the aggressive style and confrontational program of the "new" council:

> They set themselves apart, because they already had their homes. . . . That's where their energies were. Most of them were. Now, a lot of them are older, and have gotten by this far. I look at that too. But I honestly think that most of 'em felt: "They're just a bunch of upstarts. They're just causing trouble. I got my place, and I didn't cause no trouble, and I ain't gonna go out there and cause none, so nobody going to mess with me and my family." (Warren interview, 1985:76–77).

Nevertheless, when the city began to "mess with" Kenyon-Barr and Liberty-Dalton, homeowners added their voices to the chorus of protest from the West End and vigorously backed the WECC.[9] Despite their reluctance to participate directly in council-sponsored confrontations with the powers-that-be, homeowner support for the community council was mobilized and maintained by means of the half-dozen block clubs that had been so carefully nurtured by the West End Special Services Project. These block clubs permitted homeowners to put most of their energies into various neighborhood improvement projects. At the same time, since these block clubs fed into the WECC, homeowners lent their names and respectability to the confrontational program of the council's younger activists and leaders. These intermediary organizations allowed the homeowners to endorse and support the council's political ends without forcing them to involve themselves directly or personally in the council's militant means.[10]

Homeowners were not easily held within the orbit of the WECC, however, and their participation in the civic affairs of both the coun-

9. This flourish of homeowner activism harkens back to the struggle over Blocks D and E during the 1930s and the resistance to Richmond-Laurel in the 1950s. When threatened, West End homeowners have tended to mobilize quickly in defense of their property interests.

10. The West End Special Services Project had lent organizational support to the development of the Charlotte Street Residents Club, the York Street Block Club, the

cil and the neighborhood dwindled during the 1970s. The dark threat of urban renewal and the green promise of the civil rights movement had both passed. The number of homeowners in the West End, which had already fallen from 1,456 to 507 between 1950 and 1970, declined by another 40 percent in the 1970s. Those that remained had grown older—many had retired by 1980—and the block clubs that had sustained their civic involvement had grown moribund, partially because no group like the WESSP was still there to provide staff support. These factors, combined with the decreasing civility and diminishing effectiveness of the WECC, contributed to the decline of homeowner involvement in the community council.

As important as these demographic and organizational factors might have been in hastening the departure of homeowners from the council, they mask a more fundamental cause of homeowner defection from the council's ranks. During the 1970s, the council's membership and leadership were increasingly dominated by public housing tenants from the lower West End and by private tenants from the upper West End. The council became a forum and a voice for issues, concerns, and interests of those *without* domestic property. Neighborhood residents who owned property steadily drifted away. It was not a question of race—most of the homeowners were black, as were most of the council's members. It was not even a question of income, education, or status—homeowners differed very little from the rest of the neighborhood in these respects. The crucial difference was tenure. Because they owned their housing, homeowners had a different set of property interests than the renters who had become predominant in the community council:

> It may have been that people who own their own property—and live in those properties—they found a little more security. They're kind of indifferent to what's going on. You know, to be poor and to own your own property is saying, I guess, that you're a step above people that live in public housing. Those people [the homeowners] never get too involved—at least, they haven't. (Wilkins interview, 1985:263)

Freeman Street Residents Council, and the Oliver Street Block Club in the *upper* West End; the Sherman-Liberty Block Club in the Liberty-Dalton neighborhood; and the Hopkins Street Block Club and the Queensgate II Community Club in the *lower* West End. One other block club, the Dayton-Whiteman Improvement Association, was developed through Maurice McCrackin's Community Church. Black homeowners were the mainstay of every one of these block clubs.

Not only did the homeowners have more security than the neighborhood's renters, they had (for the most part) more commodious and pleasant accommodations. They had property that they could pass on to their heirs. They had independence from the dictates and intrusions of private landlords or CMHA officials. Some were even small landlords themselves, renting out rooms in their own homes or an apartment or two in a nearby building.[11]

As the WECC increasingly reflected its tenant constituency's concerns about rising rents, deferred repairs, impending displacement, and cutbacks in subsidies for public and private housing, homeowners worried about their rising taxes and utility bills. They complained about the inability to obtain homeowner's insurance or home improvement loans. They expressed concern about the dilapidation and abandonment of the neighborhood's housing. Such homeowner issues and concerns had diminishing priority on the council's agenda. With neither the racial solidarity of an impassioned struggle for civil rights nor the material threat of urban renewal to close the cleavage between owners and renters, the long-time homeowners of the West End withdrew their presence and support from the community council.[12]

Meanwhile, in the upper West End, a new property interest group formed within the homeowner ranks. The fifty new, owner-occupied households that were established in the upper West End in the five-year period following 1975 were headed by persons who were generally younger, better educated, and better paid than the area's other homeowners. Furthermore most were white. Yet, as different as these newcomers might have been in age, education, income, and race, they differed from the older homeowners less in their distinct demographics than in their different relation to property and place. The interests expressed by these new homeowners in speech, writing, and deed and that were embodied organizationally in the Dayton Street Neighborhood Association were not the same as those of either the older homeowners who had remained in the neighborhood or the homeowner-dominated block clubs that had once been so active in

11. In addition to having a greater stake in the neighborhood's property, homeowners had had a longer stake. In 1980 only 23 percent of the neighborhood's renters had lived in their apartments for more than 10 years, while 71 percent of the neighborhood's homeowners had more than a decade of occupancy.

12. Long-time homeowners are those owner-occupiers who occupy the thirty-nine houses in the upper West End that have been occupied by the same family for over fifteen years, and the 140 houses that have been occupied by the same family for more than twenty-five years.

the upper West End. The essential difference between these two homeowner interest groups is touched upon by William Mallory, who had become a Dayton Street homeowner himself in 1969:

> What you have here is a new group of people coming in who probably felt more geared toward their particular program—restoration. You've got real estate people, people who are concerned about development and making money. That's their goal. I think that's the major difference in terms of what we had. In block clubs, you had people concerned about the total community. (Mallory interview, 1985:21–22)

The newcomers to the upper West End, especially the organizers and leaders of the DSNA, had an investment orientation to domestic property that was seldom found among the older homeowners. As Mallory notes, many of them are "real estate people." The interests and roles of realtor, developer, landlord, and owner-occupier tend to overlap within the Dayton Street Neighborhood Association. In 1978, for example, half of the new organization's sixteen board members were realtors, developers, and/or landlords. Homeowners such as these have a different interest in domestic property—and in the neighborhood in which their property is situated—than homeowners who are not engaged in speculative investment. Even among those newcomers who own only the houses they occupy, there is more of an interest in the equity and liquidity of their property than is true for most of the neighborhood's older homeowners. The investment-oriented members of the DSNA actually seem irked by this fact:

> Q: Do the older homeowners have the same understanding or appreciation of property values [as the newcomers]?
> A: Well, they're *not* as concerned, because they pretty much figure they're here for the duration. They're not really concerned with property values. They're not going to move—until they die. This is probably (based on their economic level) as far as they're going to go. This is it. They've been here for a while, and all these houses have been in the same hands for a long time. There's very little turnover around here. That's been one problem with the neighborhood moving on. These people don't go anywhere. You don't have a natural turnover you have in other neighborhoods, where people are changing jobs and that. These people don't change jobs. If they change, they still stay here. (Hewer interview, 1985:186–87)

The property *rights* of the two homeowner interest groups are the same, since both have the same tenurial relation to domestic property.

Their *interests* are different, however, because the leaders of the DSNA have a functional relation to domestic property that is, first and foremost, a commodity relation: the property and place of the upper West End have a value to them that is measured primarily in terms of exchange, not of use. Consider these remarks by one of the DSNA's leaders:

> That's always my philosophy down here, we're either going to make a lot of money here or we're going to *lose* a lot of money. We're not going to break even, even if we stay here for a long time. And that's why you have to keep taking more risks: in order to get the neighborhood going—to get the momentum going—in order to get your property worth something. Because these houses, we've got so much money into them that we can't sell them until we fix up all the other ones. (Painter interview, 1985:144–45)

This is not to say that security, autonomy, and amenity are unimportant to the newcomers. Indeed, they would argue that they are doing more than anyone else in the neighborhood to defend and promote these interests, both for themselves and for others. They would claim that no one cares more for the use value of the upper West End. Particularly in their commitment to preserving and restoring the historic structures of the upper West End, the members of the DSNA claim a unique interest in promoting the aesthetic amenity of property and place—an interest which (they complain) the area's older homeowners seldom share:

> To them, this is just a house. To us, it's more of a cause and a thing we're trying to do. You know, preservation and all that. They don't even understand preservation, the historic concept. . . .

> One thing that's a difference, and it's created an irritation with us, is when an old homeowner makes an improvement on their house, they tend to take a very short-sighted view of that improvement. They do things that don't relate to the architectural integrity of the house. They paint them a strange color, or they'll do something strange to it that makes it look bad. . . . They'll tear down iron fences and put up chain link or something, instead of repair the iron fence. Which is an irritation. These kinds of things. . . . Like I say, to them, the house is a house. It's a place to live. (Hewer interview, 1985:185–86)

For the members of the DSNA, homes are also "a place to live"— but not *only* a place to live; perhaps not even *primarily* a place to live. The newcomers' interest in the use value of the upper West End is never far removed from a conscious, overriding interest in equity and liquidity. Their efforts to improve the neighborhood, its buildings, and its quality of life may enhance the amenity and affect the security of the upper West End,[13] but such efforts also "get your property worth something." Their efforts to restore their own houses and the other buildings of the historic district may preserve an important piece of the West End's architectural, aesthetic, and cultural past, but such efforts also enhance the marketability of the newcomers' homes—"we can't sell them until we fix up all the other ones." It is this primary interest in the exchange value of domestic property that differentiates the newer homeowners of the upper West End from the longtime homeowners.[14]

This does not mean that the older homeowners are indifferent to the cash value of their accommodations. Politically, however, they tend to place a higher priority on the use value of domestic property than on its exchange value. They will collectively organize to defend or promote security, amenity, or autonomy, as they did during the 1960s, and then fail to notice or refuse to act in response to threats to their exchange value. In fact, on at least one occasion, some of the neighborhood's older homeowners mobilized *against* a policy that promised higher property values, because greater equity and liquidity might have threatened the security and autonomy of themselves and their neighbors. This happened when the Miami Purchase Association and the city planning commission first proposed historic designation for the Dayton Street area. The preservationists and planners wanted to include an area east of Linn Street in their historic district. The homeowner-dominated block club that was then active in that area, the Dayton-Whiteman Community Association, successfully lobbied to prevent the historic designation of their blocks.[15] In the end, they

13. The neighborhood's security is affected in a positive way by the dent made in the problem of vacant and abandoned buildings—a consequence of the MPA's and the DSNA's efforts to restore the historic district. The individual security of tenants and low-income homeowners, who may be displaced by the restoration and gentrification of the neighborhood, is affected in a more negative way.

14. Lest this portrait become too one-dimensional, I should point out that the accumulative interests of the DSNA's members are tempered, to a degree that varies across the organization's membership, by property interests of accommodation and by personal sympathies for the history and people of the West End. At least one member has confessed that his own sympathies run somewhat against the grain of the DSNA's general orientation: "I, in a sense, care about the community. And I can see where somebody who had bought that property to make money off of it and to resell it won't have that same feeling. But I'm out of step with a lot of people in my feelings for community or what I want to see happen" (Kattleman interview, 1985:155).

15. As Barbara Wheeler has described it: "When they started the whole thing with

cared less about possible appreciation in their property values than about the possibility that higher taxes and speculative investors might undermine the security of the neighborhood's present residents. They also rebelled against the prospect of preservationists and planners telling them what they could or could not do with their own buildings.[16]

In 1981 as real estate activity in the upper West End hit a peak, William Mallory and Maurice McCrackin, a white minister and social activist who had lived in the neighborhood since 1946, attempted to recruit longtime residents into a new locality-based organization, intended to resist displacement and gentrification. Although open to both tenants and homeowners, the latter became the primary constituency of this new organization, named the West End Homeowners and Residents Association:

> We wanted to retain the homeowners in the area. We talked to them in terms of how they could *keep* their homes. . . . We wanted them to not feel threatened and to be pushed out of their neighborhood by real estate speculators, people coming in and saying, "Okay, I'll give you $40,000 cash." That might seem like a lot of money, but you can't buy a house with $40,000 today. So, I think it was more along those lines that we talked about a homeowners association. (Mallory interview, 1985:22–23)

This organizational initiative lasted less than a year. Perhaps Mallory and McCrackin overestimated the degree of homeowner insecurity at the changes occurring within the neighborhood. Perhaps these changes simply became less threatening, since the dreaded real estate boom never happened and gentrification slowed to a more eas-

---

the historic designation of the area, people on the other side of Dayton Street, including Dorothy Ratterman, got together and prevented it from being declared an historic area. Dorothy told me, 'Well, they never got their hands on this'" (Wheeler interview, 1985:213).

16. Historic designation, in actuality, does very little to intrude legally on homeowner autonomy. Nevertheless, the perception of long-time homeowners has been that historic designation means that "people can tell you what to do," in repairing or improving one's own house. This perception has undoubtedly been reinforced by the propensity of several MPA and DSNA members to chide their neighbors for painting their houses the "wrong" color or for making other "nonhistoric" alterations. One frequently repeated tale—accepted as gospel throughout the West End, though never fully verified—tells of a white newcomer haughtily informing a black homeowner, who was busily painting the front of her house, that she was "not allowed" to use that color in the historic district. Angered and insulted, the woman told her husband. He personally—and very publicly—completed the job that she had begun, using the color that she had chosen. The woman, so the story goes, was Representative William Mallory's wife.

ily assimilated pace after 1981. Perhaps the older homeowners no longer had the numbers or the leaders or the energy to sustain an active organization. Whatever the reason, the West End Homeowners and Residents Association soon disbanded. Since the last of the West End block clubs, the Dayton-Whiteman Community Improvement Association, also become inactive in the 1980s, older homeowners still suspicious of the MPA and the DSNA were left with no organization of their own. The politicized remnants of these "household homeowners" shifted their political support to the Community Land Cooperative, a vocal opponent of gentrification.

In summary, it was possible to distinguish two property interest groups among the neighborhood's owner-occupiers in the 1980s, although only the newer homeowners had developed and sustained an organizational capacity to act collectively and aggressively in support of their separate interests. The older homeowners drifted away from the WECC when it no longer represented their particular interests. They greeted the MPA and DSNA with suspicion and anger when they felt their interests possibly threatened by these acquisitive newcomers. Nevertheless, as a group, these older "household" homeowners have remained unorganized and politically inactive in recent years. Their interests have remained more latent than manifest—more a basis for distinguishing a *potential* property interest group than one that is consciously, collectively active.

Public Tenants

Rental housing, public and private, now accounts for 89 percent of the West End's 6,433 units. Approximately 2,675 units are in the public housing projects that are administered by the Cincinnati Metropolitan Housing Authority: Laurel Homes, Lincoln Court, and Stanley Rowe Apartments.[17] These projects contain nearly half of the neighborhood's rental housing. The other half is found in Richmond Village, Uptown Towers, and other privately owned buildings in Armory-Central and the upper West End.

The tenants of public housing have tended to be more collectively conscious, more thoroughly organized, and more politically active than the tenants of private housing—particularly in the last ten to fifteen years. The greater proximity of public housing tenants, the

17. A majority of the units in Stanley Rowe Apartments are for elderly individuals, many of them feeble or infirm. Stanley Rowe has never had a politically active residents council.

similarity of their personal circumstances, and the commonality of their tenurial and political situation vis-à-vis a single landlord have aided public housing tenants in discovering a common set of property interests and have abetted group formation.

Equally significant has been the role played by the federal government. Federal guidelines have required the participation of resident councils in the operational affairs of every public housing project. Furthermore, federal funding for the West End Special Services Project and the West End Community Council during the 1960s meant that organizers were sent into all three West End projects to encourage organizational and individual involvement by public housing tenants in the community council. Finally, federal cutbacks in financial support for public housing, beginning with Nixon's assault on the remnants of the Great Society between 1973 and 1975, pushed local housing authorities to the brink of bankruptcy and threatened the amenity and security of their tenants.

Tenant organizations formed in Laurel Homes and Lincoln Court soon after these housing projects were built. For most of their existence, these "residents councils" were local improvement associations, concerned mainly with enhancing the amenity of their surroundings. Activities such as planting flowers, cleaning up courtyards, requesting new cabinets from the CMHA, and sponsoring social events dominated their organizational agendas. Seldom did they challenge the prerogatives or policies of the CMHA. Their housing was the newest in the West End and, in the beginning, the best-equipped, best-maintained accommodations that most occupants had ever known. Tenant selection was rigorous, supervision was close, security was tight, and tenant morale was high. The residents councils and the tenants themselves saw little need for conflict with the CMHA.

When tenant dissatisfaction with the CMHA began to rise in the 1960s—as maintenance and security declined, rents increased, and the tenant population became more impoverished—the primary organizational means to express dissatisfaction was the WECC, not the residents councils. This was due partially to the grass-roots organizing of the WESSP and the WECC in the housing projects, and partially to the overlapping solidarities of race and place that gave the community council such visibility, coherence, and appeal in those days. Public housing tenants by-passed their residents councils for another reason as well. The leaders of the WECC were young, aggressive, and independent. The leaders of the residents councils were perceived as old, passive, and thoroughly co-opted by the CMHA.

The involvement of public housing tenants in the WECC, however, had a significant impact on the Laurel Homes residents council. Tenants become politically conscious and organizationally skilled by working with the WECC. After 1968 they began restructuring their own residents council at Laurel Homes. This happened while the federal government was pushing for greater tenant participation in housing authority affairs with one hand, and withholding more money for public housing operations with the other. The Laurel Homes residents council soon began clashing more frequently with the CMHA. Shirley Colburt, then secretary of the WECC and vice president of the Laurel Homes residents council, later described the latter's transition from a housing improvement association to a conflict housing group:

> It started out being a thing where you were supposed to be able to get in touch with the housing authority, sit down with them, and talk with them about whatever your concerns were. Okay, but the administration is funny. If there is a way for them to get around something, they will do it. So what we did—it was a learning process for the next five to seven years, which was a learning process for all of us—was to learn the ins and outs of all the loopholes that they got around and how they by-pass people. . . . We got to the place where we started watching what it was that we were asking for and trying to see how much of it we were getting—which made us an advocacy group because we were constantly in conflict with them over something they weren't doing that they were supposed to be doing. (Colburt interview, 1985:337–38)

Shirley Colburt was elected president of the Laurel Homes residents council in 1980. This council gradually became one of the best attended, most vocal, best led, and most influential public housing interest groups in Cincinnati. A member of the CMHA board readily acknowledges this fact:

> Laurel Homes has a strong council. People criticize Shirley Colburt because of the way she does things, but when you go to her resident council she has seventy-five to eighty people there every time. They had a snow day and even then she had fifteen people. The majority of our communities don't even *have* fifteen. She has a strong council. (Partee interview, 1985:334)

Meanwhile, another conflict-oriented advocate for public housing interests was forming outside of the West End. In 1979 a group of Roman Catholic clergy and nuns joined with public housing tenants in a CMHA project in another Cincinnati neighborhood to organize the

Public Housing Action Committee, Church and Tenants (PHACT). Becoming a citywide organization soon after its inception, PHACT organized in the public housing projects of the West End after 1980. A PHACT organizer, assigned exclusively to the West End, was hired in 1984.

From the very beginning, PHACT's style of organizing differed from that of most of the CMHA residents councils, since PHACT eschewed the role of a housing improvement association. Instead, it deliberately provoked and aggressively confronted the CMHA. Meeting after meeting, its supporters went to the CMHA board, demanding to be heard on the tenants' behalf. Time after time, they were ignored. The more the board tried to dismiss PHACT, however, the more loudly and militantly it insisted on its right to submit tenant grievances: "That's how, I think, we got to be a confrontational group. . . . We could fill the room, *pack* it with fifty, seventy, eighty people, and not be recognized" (Martinez interview, 1985:276).

Things changed in 1982. PHACT won an agreement from Cincinnati's mayor to recommend a woman resident of public housing to serve on the CMHA board of directors. In July 1982, Mary Partee, a CMHA tenant (who had once lived in Lincoln Court), was appointed to the CMHA board, along with two other new members. Later that year, after PHACT went Christmas caroling (and agitating) in the affluent neighborhoods of several CMHA board members, the CMHA agreed to meet formally with PHACT and to reevaluate objectionable CMHA policies (Martinez interview, 1985:277).

But as PHACT's influence grew, both with the CMHA board and among public housing tenants, competition with the local residents councils became inevitable. In some cases, it was peaceful, even harmonious, and encouraged individual councils to become forceful advocacy groups in their own right:

> It put a fire under 'em. Anything that's competitive makes something more effective. . . . So a lot of 'em have taken a new outlook on the kind of leadership that they're doing. Like I said, it was a challenge. That's what we needed as residents, a challenge. We've got two groups now that we can get some support from. (Partee interview, 1985:332)

In the West End, however, relations between PHACT and the local residents councils have been fraught with tension and conflict. The members of the Lincoln Court residents council, satisfied with their personal privileges and content to continue their peaceful housing improvement work, have resisted the attempt of PHACT supporters to "light a fire under 'em." Relations between the two groups have deteriorated to the point that the Lincoln Court members of PHACT have begun positioning themselves to oust the present leadership of the resident council. In Laurel Homes, where the residents council shares with PHACT the same level of conflict consciousness and organizational development, relations are no more cooperative than they are in Lincoln Court. The antagonism between these latter like-minded organizations will be explored in greater detail in Chapter 10. For now, it is enough to say that PHACT and the Laurel Homes residents council are property interest groups that militantly defend the same interests against the same opponent while contentiously competing for the same constituency.

Despite such bickering, the supporters of PHACT and the members of the Laurel Homes residents council both recognize the CMHA as their principal adversary—the main threat or greatest obstacle to the realization of tenant interests. There is also broad agreement as to what these interests are. Security is foremost. This refers to both secure use of one's private space (security against sudden eviction or a precipitous rise in housing costs) and secure passage through public space (security against assault, theft, or other crimes). Both kinds of security are believed by politically conscious tenants to be at risk because of action or inaction by the CMHA. People have been rountinely evicted from public housing for the misbehavior of their children or for misunderstandings among neighbors. They have also lost their homes for voicing opposition to CMHA practices and policies:

> The security issue, in terms of evictions, really got to be an issue when the organization got more active and out in the open. People who were members of PHACT were threatened with eviction on various occasions. (Martinez interview, 1985:278)

The other security issue, crime, is less a matter of what the CMHA does than what it does not do; that is, tenants believe that the Housing Authority does not do nearly enough to protect the people of Lincoln Court and Laurel Homes. Tenants pay, in more ways than one, for such CMHA negligence:

> They don't have no security. They don't have *no* security. We have a lot of complaints about people coming into their hallways. People come in and smoke reefer. And old ladies get robbed. And they use the bathroom in there. Then people get charged [by the CMHA] for cleaning up

the hallway. Tenants get mad about that. (Minefield interview, 1985:327)

Despite the predominance of security issues, two other interests have figured highly in the political activity of public housing tenants, the defense of amenity and the pursuit of autonomy. Since the early 1970s, the beginning of a long decline in federal funding for public housing, the amenity of Laurel Homes and Lincoln Court has been eroding. The CMHA bears little responsibility for these federal cutbacks, but as tenants have experienced the rapid deterioration of their private and public spaces, the CMHA has borne the brunt of the anger, suspicion, and opposition that these cutbacks have provoked, The CMHA managed to secure modernization money to remodel Lincoln Court around 1980. Even this served only to fuel tenant resentment. The money ran out after the completion of only a *single* block of buildings. Since the remodeled section faces Ezzard Charles Drive, a public thoroughfare running between Cincinnati's Music Hall and a refurbished Union Terminal, tenants also suspected that the CMHA was more concerned with city beautification than with housing improvement.[18]

The erosion of residential amenity, like the threat to tenant security, has spurred tenant consciousness and political activity in defense of tenant interests. It has swollen the ranks and hardened the demands of the Laurel Homes residents council and those of PHACT. Both organizations continue to fight the CMHA for better maintenance, safer basements, cleaner courtyards, and greater attention to the rats and roaches that infest every building.

The struggle for tenant autonomy, on the other hand, has yet to mature—though it is simmering beneath the surface. Except for a few leaders of PHACT, most public tenants do not yet recognize autonomy as a political issue. Public housing tenants have very little autonomy—even less, for that matter, than most tenants of private housing. Like private tenants, they cannot alter or improve their units without the landlord's permission. Unlike private tenants, however, they must submit twice a year to a thorough CMHA investigation of the ages, occupations, marital status, income, and personal property

---

18. Rumors persist, throughout the West End, that these remodeled units are destined to be eventually *sold* by the CMHA to upper-income buyers, displacing the families who are currently there. Whatever their truth, and there is no evidence that the CMHA is planning such a sale, these rumors are indicative of the suspicion with which tenants now greet any action of the CMHA.

of each family member. Public housing tenants must also permit CMHA officials to enter their homes at any time. Officials are supposed to give forty-eight hours notice before entry. Tenants claim that this requirement is often ignored:

> Q: How much control do you have over your own apartment, how much privacy?
> A: You don't have none, not really. They got a key to your apartment, and they can come when they want to come. (Minefield interview, 1985:327)

PHACT has begun to make tenant privacy an issue, demanding that more notice be given to tenants before entry. There is also discussion, among PHACT leaders, about pushing for more tenant control over their own space. For example, tenants might be allowed to improve their homes however they wish or might be rewarded for personally financed improvements by a reduction in rent. Such an expansion of tenant autonomy would radically change the tenurial prerogatives of public housing tenants and the balance of power between tenants and the CMHA. Tenant demands for a change of this sort would require a fundamental change in tenant consciousness, going beyond the recognition of the relational, precarious nature of their present interests (security and amenity) to the collective aspiration for an advantage that has never been theirs (autonomy). Public housing tenants in the West End have not yet reached this stage. There are signs, however, that PHACT may be headed in this direction. PHACT may be on the brink, in other words, of transforming itself from a "conflict housing group," defending tenant interests against erosion and attack, to a "radical housing group," pressing the CMHA for basic changes in the tenurial relation that tenants have traditionally had to domestic property.

Private Tenants

By contrast, the tenants of private housing in the West End have exhibited neither a rudimentary political consciousness of their property interests nor a propensity to act collectively in acknowledgement or defense of those interests. Individuals and institutions have advocated on behalf of private tenants—staff members of the local Legal Aid Society and various West End churches and ministries have been the most vocal of these advocates, but the neighborhood's private tenants have never banded together to advocate and agitate for themselves.

Given the succession of threats to their property interests, the lack of group formation among the tenants of private housing is somewhat surprising. Their security has been threatened again and again. During the 1950s and 1960s, for instance, urban renewal and highway construction permanently eliminated over thirteen thousand private rental units in the West End, displacing an estimated forty to fifty thousand tenants. Many other tenants lost their homes during the 1970s, as deferred maintenance and abandonment left an increasing number of rental units vacant or uninhabitable. The 1980s brought a new threat to tenant security. Historic preservation and the first wave of gentrification sparked the conversion of multi-unit buildings into single-unit dwellings and pushed private rents higher. Tenant displacement has been a product of both.

The *amenity* of private tenants has also suffered. Deferred maintenance not only increased the vacancy rate of the neighborhood's rental units, it undermined the safety, soundness, comfort, and attractiveness of units still occupied. The amenity of the neighborhood's public spaces was similarly affected. Disinvestment by private landlords, redlining by private lenders, and fewer services and subsidies from public agencies during the 1970s, turned West End areas with the highest proportion of rental housing into crumbling, rat-infested, and crime-ridden blocks.[19]

As for the autonomy of private tenants, there has probably—and ironically—been a slight improvement over the years. Landlords who are investing little to maintain properties have little interest in controlling the behavior of their tenants. Furthermore, since the majority of the West End's rental property is absentee-owned, mostly by individuals who live quite a distance from the neighborhood and who do not employ the services of a property management company, tenant privacy appears to be infrequently invaded by landlord inspection of the premises.[20] However, there is an opposite trend in those historic properties that have been recently renovated under the auspices of the

19. The exception was Census tract 2, where Park Town and Richmond Village continued to provide private rental and cooperative housing of quality and comfort, while maintaining the amenity of their public spaces.

20. A 1982 study of residential property owners in the upper West End, between Bank and Poplar Streets, revealed that 77.6 percent of the occupied buildings were absentee-owned; 60.6 percent of the area's occupied buildings were owned by parties residing in other neighborhoods of Cincinnati, in other cities, or in other states (Topps, 1982).

MPA or by members of the DSNA. There is a tendency here for close monitoring of tenant behavior, particularly as it might affect the historically significant or aesthetically unusual details of the building's appearance.

Thirty years of upheaval and change, therefore, have had a major impact on tenant interests. Like other populations in the West End, private tenants have a unique relation to domestic property and a common set of property interests. Like others, their interests have been regularly and severely threatened. Nevertheless, the neighborhood's private tenants, *unlike* the West End's other residential populations, have not become politically conscious or collectively active. Not a single organization has appeared among their ranks. Why?

Though it is usually easier to say why a social phenomenon *did* happen than why it did *not*, there are several plausible explanations that may account for the absence of group formation among the private tenants. The tenants of the neighborhood's private housing, to begin with, do not share among themselves the same similarity of circumstances shared among the tenants of public housing or among the members of either homeowner interest group. Rental property in the West End ranges from multi-unit apartment complexes to single-family detached houses, from units renting (in 1985) for $100 to $600 per month, and from single rooms in a deteriorated boarding house to luxury apartments in the renovated mansions of Millionaires' Row. Some tenants have leases; some do not. The terms of leases vary from building to building, granting their occupants different kinds and degrees of security, autonomy, and amenity. As common as tenant interests may be *in general*, therefore, the diversity of individual situations makes it extremely difficult for private tenants to recognize the basic similarity of their property position and property interests.

A second obstacle to tenant consciousness is the wide diversity of landlords in the West End. Unlike the thousands of tenants in public housing who have a single landlord, the CMHA, the thousands of tenants in private housing have a hundred different landlords. While absentee ownership is high in the West End, concentration of ownership is not. There are only nine landlords who own more than five rental properties. The largest number of residential buildings held by any one landlord is nine, with most owning only one or two (Topps, 1982; University of Cincinnati School of Planning, 1983). With so many landlords doing business in the neighborhood, not only do the terms of occupancy differ from one set of tenants to another, but individual tenants find it difficult to perceive a common tenurial relation—and a common target—in landlords *as a group*. Tenant activism, such as it is, typically involves the tenants of one unit or one building struggling against one landlord. The number and diversity of the area's landlords has discouraged a more collective approach.

There is another reason for the lack of collective tenant action: the relative transiency of the population in private rental housing. The West End has a long history as a stopping-off place, especially for those with little to spend on housing. They rent rooms or apartments for a month or a year and then move on. Not all of the neighborhood's tenants fit this pattern, not even most, but the number that do is sizeable enough to undermine whatever solidarity private tenants might have. Forging any population into a consciously organized, collectively active group is usually a slow process. It takes time to recognize common interests, to establish emotional and organizational bonds of trust, and to build attachments to property and place. Without this time, without these attachments, a threat to one's interests is more likely to provoke an individual response than a collective one— "flight" rather than "fight."[21]

Finally, the lack of tenant activism can be explained by the simple fact that there have always been *other* organizations that private tenants have relied upon to defend their interests. This has had the effect of stunting tenant consciousness, siphoning off tenant leaders, and discouraging the formation of a separate organization exclusively geared to tenants. The West End Community Council is the most significant example. Private tenants have numbered among the council's most faithful supporters and most influencial leaders since the mid-1970s. Even today, as other property groups have divided their loyalties or drifted away from the community council, private tenants still straggle into the WECC's monthly meetings. All of the council's officers (in the mid-1980s) are tenants who live in private housing. While this has tended to tilt the concerns of the WECC in the direction

21. Among the private tenants of the West End, more than among any other residential group, there exists a high proportion of people with little history in the neighborhood. In 1980, for instance, nearly a fourth of the neighborhood's private rental units were occupied by persons who had been living there for less than a year. This indicator of transiency was 20 percent higher for private tenants than for public tenants in Laurel Homes and four times higher for private tenants than for owner-occupiers in the neighborhood. When length of residence is approached from the other end, the contrast is even more striking. In 1980 only 23 percent of the units then occupied by private tenants had been continuously occupied by the same tenant for ten years or more. By comparison, 33 percent of the rental units in Laurel Homes and 76 percent of the owner-occupied units in the West End had been continuously occupied for a decade or more (1980 U.S. Census).

of tenant interests, it has also meant that tenant interests have often had to share the agenda with numerous other neighborhood issues. The council has been an occasional advocate of tenant interests, particularly during the rhetorically pro-poor regime of Roger Bradley, but it has never devoted itself solely to private tenant concerns.[22] It has done just enough to retain tenant loyalty and to discourage separate interest-group formation among private tenants—but not enough to spur tenant consciousness or independent tenant action vis-à-vis the neighborhood's private landlords.

Tenant interests have also been defended by the Legal Aid Society and by social workers from various public welfare agencies. Such advocacy, however, is invariably conducted one-to-one. There is no effort by the Legal Aid Society or by public welfare workers to bring commonly situated tenants together and so encourage a more collective perception of and solution to tenant problems.

A more collective approach *has* been promoted, on the other hand, by the clergy and laity of the neighborhood's largest churches and ministries.[23] But this too has unintentionally discouraged interest-group formation among local tenants. In January 1980 these religious leaders organized an informal association, the West End Alliance of Churches and Ministries, and began meeting each month to discuss the neighborhood's problems. Housing topped their list since they were all concerned that displacement (from both disinvestment and reinvestment) was becoming a serious threat to private tenants in their congregations. The ministerial response to this problem had long been the same sort of individual counseling and advocacy that has been practiced by the Legal Aid Society and by the city's welfare agencies, each church dealing with its own parishioners' problems in its own way. The members of the alliance sought a more collective response. They wanted to do something about tenants rights in general—perhaps even establish a tenants rights organization in the West End. Before they could act on this idea, however, another plan came

22. The interests of *public* tenants are represented with some regularity. The DSNA has also been working hard to win a place among the council's inner circle. So far, it has not succeeded. The fact remains, however, that for all of its domination by private and public tenants, the WECC is a weakly administered forum, where many interest groups contend. It may occasionally advocate private tenant interests, but this is not the same as being a private tenant interest group.

23. The Community Church of Cincinnati, York Street Methodist Church, St. Joseph's Catholic Church, the West Cincinnati Presbyterian Church, and the social services ministry of the Dominican Sisters of the Sick Poor have provided most of the leadership of both the West End Alliance of Churches and Ministries and its spinoff organization, the CLC.

before the group: the prospect of radically changing the structure of tenancy itself and giving tenants an ownership stake in domestic property by means of a "community land trust."

With the enthusiastic backing of the alliance, a community land trust was established in the West End in the Fall of 1980. This was the Community Land Cooperative of Cincinnati (CLC), organized to prevent displacement, provide housing, and maintain residential affordability—primarily for the neighborhood's private tenants. It is from this population, in fact, that the CLC has drawn the bulk of its membership. Private tenants are its main constituency. Furthermore, in recent years it has done more than any other West End group to confront various economic and political threats to tenant interests.

By creating the CLC, however, the Alliance of Churches and Ministries also added one more obstacle to tenant consciousness and tenant activism. The alliance shifted its attention away from defending the interests of private tenants, *qua tenants*. Instead of encouraging the formation of a politically conscious interest group among the neighborhood's tenants, one which was capable of defying the owners of rental property, the alliance threw its energies into establishing a form of social property that would be the basis for a new nontenant interest group. The threat to tenant interests would be removed, in other words, by lifting tenants out of tenancy and giving them a *new* set of interests. As much as the CLC has done to improve the lives of a hundred or so tenants, its political impact on tenant activism has been to provide more of an individual "exit" than a collective "voice." Group formation and political mobilization among this population have suffered accordingly.

For all of these reasons, collective action by private tenants has lagged far behind that of public tenants. Private tenants have never attained even the rudimentary level of political consciousness and organization attained by the flower-garden aficionadoes of the Lincoln Court residents council. More foreign still is the conflict consciousness of both the Laurel Homes residents council and PHACT. Private tenants have simply not discovered a commonality in their situation that would permit collective action in defense of shared interests. They have produced leaders and they have participated in locality-based organizations like the WECC and the CLC, but instead of encouraging tenant activism, these organizational affiliations have served to dilute tenant consciousness and to divert the attention of tenant leaders away from tenant interests, issues, and concerns. Private tenants do not lack people or organizations willing to speak out on their behalf, including the WECC and the CLC. They do lack their own voice and their own organization that can act on a day-to-day basis to defend tenant interests in the face of landlord opposition.

Social Property

Besides owner-occupied and tenant-occupied domestic property, there is a form of West End housing that can be described as "social property." Tenurially closer to homeowners than to renters, public or private, the occupants of social property have many of the same interests as individual homeowners. There are social limits placed upon several of these interests, however, especially upon those that are part of a property's exchange value. Also distinguishing social property from owner-occupied property or rental property is the fact that occupants of social property have an organizational relation *to each other* that is inherent in their relation to domestic property. Group formation, in other words, is a precondition of social housing, not an uncertain consequence.

There are two organizational examples of social property in the West End: Park Town Cooperative Homes and the Community Land Cooperative of Cincinnati.

Park Town was originally planned by the city's urban renewal authorities as a limited equity housing cooperative. Its organizers hoped to attract middle-income, black professionals—teachers, police, post office employees, and the like. They failed. After months of promotion, only fifty of the 323 shares (units) had been sold. One employee of the post office, who was offered a commission for every new shareholder that he was able to bring into Park Town, recalled that his coworkers were suspicious of both the cooperative arrangement and the neighborhood:

> For people who were working at the post office, they just didn't care much for the idea of the co-op. They was [also] looking at where it was, in the torn-down old West End. They had lived there all their lives. Now they wanted to leave and go out to live with the white people. They wanted to save their money to *leave*. So we fell flat on our face. (Watts interview, 1985:33)

Park Town was saved by long-term financing from the federal government under HUD's 221(d)(3) housing program. With a subsidized loan backing the project, the cost of a share decreased to $150; occupant carrying charges dropped to $70 per month. This made Park Town units affordable to many West End residents who were "poor," but employed.

By spring of 1962, Park Town was 90-percent occupied, legally established as a cooperative, and independently governed by a nine-person board, elected by the cooperative's shareholders. The cooperative's structure had been significantly changed, however, in making it affordable to families of modest means. Park Town became a *no*-equity cooperative, which is what it is today. Occupants cannot build equity based upon their purchase of a co-op share. Nor do Park Town's residents have other exchange interests. They cannot sublet their units or rent out portions of their personal space (liquidity). They also do not have a legal right to pass along their units to designated heirs (legacy).

What they do have is a degree of security, autonomy, and amenity not enjoyed by any tenant in the West End. They have a lifetime guarantee of tenure as long as their monthly costs are met (which are among the lowest for any housing in the neighborhood). They have absolute privacy in their own homes, undertake nearly any interior alteration they choose, and exercise collective control over the co-operative corporation itself. (Major improvements require the prior approval of the Park Town board.) They occupy units that can be counted among the most modern, best equipped, and best-maintained housing in the area. Park Town's public spaces, moreover, are the cleanest and most secure of any blocks in the West End.

These residential advantages, combined with careful shareholder selection by the Park Town board, have attracted and retained a population that is, for the most part, better educated, better paid, and somewhat younger than the majority in the West End. Park Town's population is also unusually stable, with a lower turnover rate than other parts of the neighborhood. Another distinctive characteristic was discussed in the previous chapter; the residents of Park Town have a remarkable record for internal solidarity and external involvement in activist organizations like the West End Community Council.

Their support for the WECC began to wane in the 1970s, however. As the passion of the early civil rights movement became a thing of the past and the principal leaders who had been involved with the WECC moved on to other things, there was little to hold Park Town residents within the council. Their property interests were less at risk than any other housing group in the neighborhood. Furthermore, their interests, education, and income made them an increasingly alien and uninfluencial minority among the low-income tenants, public and private, who were becoming dominant in the WECC. Park Town residents reacted by turning inward, putting their energies into the housing improvement activities of their own residents council and eschewing the confrontational rhetoric and politics of Roger Bradley's community council. By the 1980s only a handful of people residing in Park Town continued their membership in the WECC.[24]

Park Town's support for another West End organization, the Community Land Cooperative, has been more forthcoming in recent years. Park Town residents were among the earliest members of the CLC and have occupied key positions over the years, including the first executive director. One reason for such support may be that it has been easier for the members of a housing cooperative to understand and accept the social property arrangement at the heart of the CLC's particular approach to low-income housing. The treasurer of the Park Town board, who has also been a member of the CLC's resident applicant committee, describes the similarity between the Park Town Cooperative and the land cooperative—and the difficulty that most people have in understanding both:

> Trying to explain to Mr. Average out there why he can buy the house but not the land, or why he can't make a profit is not easy. Now, *I* understand it . . . but you take Mr. Average out there, and he's not [going to].
> Q: Is that because people are locked into one way of looking at property: you're either a renter or a homeowner?
> A: That's it! You got the idea. You got the idea. Park Town and the Land Cooperative are in between. The average person is not going to understand that. He goes into buying a house to have something for his kids or to sell for a profit. Either way, it's the same thing: looking out for the equity in it. People don't get into the [Park Town] co-op or the Land Co-op for that—they're nonprofit. They can't show a profit. And people who live there can't show a profit. (Nesbitt interview, 1985:18)

Like Park Town, the CLC embodies a form of domestic property that places social limits on certain property interests and gathers the scattered properties of its resident members under a single organizational umbrella. It does so, however, in a different way. The CLC is a "community land trust," not a "cooperative."[25] Instead of holding

24. This conclusion is based on an examination of the names and addresses on the "West End Community Council Membership List," January 13, 1982.

25. The CLC has "cooperative" in its name, rather than "trust," because Ohio law

shares in a cooperative housing corporation and a proprietary lease for the use of an apartment, CLC residents will eventually hold deeds to their individual houses (or apartments) and a long-term, inheritable lease for the use of the land beneath their buildings.[26] The CLC will hold deeds to all of this land. The land cooperative will also hold a preemptive option to repurchase any of these houses at a below-market, limited equity price, should the homeowner ever decide to leave the neighborhood.

CLC homeowners/leaseholders have the same sort of lifetime security and personal autonomy in the use of their domestic property as the resident shareholders of Park Town.[27] They have the same strategic interest in defending and promoting the amenity of their private and public space—though, for the most part, the amenity of Park Town is higher than the amenity of the property controlled by the CLC.[28]

The residents of the CLC, on the other hand, have a set of exchange interests that the residents of Park Town do not have. CLC homeowners/lease-holders may realize financial returns from equity and liquidity, and they may bequeath the right to occupy their units. Even so, as is true for all social property, these exchange interests are formally, legally limited in a way that the equity, liquidity, and legacy of the "acquisitive" or "household" homeowner are not.

Residents of the CLC build *equity* in their property, but the amount is restricted to a dollar-for-dollar return that is earned by paying off the building's original purchase price and by personally paying for

reserves the latter title exclusively for financial institutions. Despite its name, the CLC is a community land trust, not a cooperative.

26. This discussion is couched in the future tense because the CLC had yet to complete the legal separation of land and buildings in 1985, though it was in the process of doing so. CLC resident members are now leasing *both* the land and buildings. Written into their leases, however, are the same rights of security, autonomy, equity, and legacy that they will have when they have a *deed* to their houses and a *lease* for the land. In other words, the legal arrangement of their tenure will change, but they will essentially have the same set of property interests.

27. The autonomy of CLC residents is somewhat restricted, however, in a manner similar to that of Park Town's residents. The CLC has the right to inspect its residents' premises from time to time and can prohibit certain nonresidential or socially harmful uses of the residents' property. Furthermore, as in Park Town, CLC residents may renovate and decorate their units however and whenever they wish, but major improvements require prior approval by the CLC board.

28. The CLC, since the beginning, has attempted to house a population that has less income and fewer resources than the population of Park Town. To keep its housing affordable for low-income families, the CLC has purchased inexpensive, older buildings, limited their rehabilitation to necessary, structural repairs, and minimized ongoing maintenance.

any improvements.[29] CLC residents do not reap gains from the general appreciation in the neighborhood's property values. This not only keeps housing affordable for future occupants, since the CLC will resell the unit at approximately the same price that was paid to acquire it, but also removes a profit motive from private housing that pits present homeowners against all who do not currently own domestic property. Changing the homeowner's equity interest, in other words, changes his or her economic and political orientation toward the rest of the community. Two of the land cooperative's homeowners/leaseholders describe this different orientation well:

> You can't think of the Co-op, be a member, and think of money at the same time, 'cause it just don't work. You have to be interested in maintaining the land or caring about other people. . . . I don't think about trying to sell the Vine Street property and getting money. You should never think of money. You should leave [thinking about] money to the lenders—to the people who have it, who are willing to lend it to the Co-op—and think about the well-being of people, and people having a place to stay. (C. Robinson interview, 1985:290)

> It's like my house. If I put it on the open market, it will really be worth more than I paid for it. Therefore, a person that's in my same situation, with the same income I have, they may not be able to pay the higher rate for it. If I sold it back to the Land Co-op and got what I paid for it, then if they wanted it they can pay the same thing that I did. It's all in helping people. Some people don't care about helping people as long as they move along. To me, you've got to think beyond that. . . . I wouldn't say it's a "sacrifice." You're just really doing it for your community, you know, for the people in the community. (Robbins interview, 1985:247–48)

This interest in (limited) equity makes possible, in turn, an interest in *legacy* that is missing in the no-equity cooperative of Park Town. CLC residents may bequeath the equity that they have in their homes to their heirs. Alternatively, since both the deed to the house and the lease to the land are inheritable, the heirs of a CLC resident will have the option of living in the house themselves—as long as they agree to abide by the same restrictions on their property interests as those accepted by the previous homeowner/leaseholder.

29. Because the value of such equity can be eroded by inflation, the CLC is now considering a formula that would allow upward adjustments in leaseholder equity at a fixed, annual rate. This increase, however, would still be pegged far below the market rate of appreciation for property values in the West End.

CLC residents also enjoy a degree of *liquidity*, although there are limits on this property interest as well:

> Q: If you needed extra income, could a leaseholder sublet one of her rooms?
> A: Uh huh. Because I had thought about that, I had asked someone about it. . . . You *can* do that. But cannot make a profit. Like, I pay $157. If I wanted to let a sleeping room, say, I couldn't rent it to 'em for $200 a month. You can't make a profit on what you do. But you could rent it to them to help.
> Q: To help you cover your own rental costs?
> A: Uh huh. (C. Robinson interview, 1985:293)

These entrepreneurial interests form the basis for a separate property interest group—the homeowners/leaseholders of the CLC—and for the conflictual (and cooperative) relations that have arisen between the CLC and the neighborhood's other property interest groups. Yet it is also the case that group formation occurred *prior* to the discovery of manifest property interests by a residential population possessing those interests. The Community Land Cooperative came into existence, promoting a radical form of property tenure, *before* there were CLC residents to become conscious of those interests and to act collectively on the basis of those interests. How did this happen? How does it fit into the model of group formation and collective action that was proposed in Chapter 6?

The members of the West End Alliance of Churches and Ministries, who were instrumental in starting the CLC, shared not only a religious vocation, but a long history of political activism and social service on behalf of the poor. As ministers to the poor, they had constant contact with the most ill-housed, residentially insecure people in the West End. As long-time activists, they were challenged to examine systematically the housing plight of the poor and to devise whatever solutions might alleviate their distress. In both capacities, they were the first to recognize the threat that historic preservation and gentrification might pose to the property interests of the neighborhood's low-income residents:

> We could see what was happening right there on Dayton Street. Miami Purchase was becoming more and more involved in the neighborhood. Their intentions were becoming more obvious. You could see what they were doing in terms of buying up buildings. Private developers, really speculators, were moving in and sandblasting buildings. . . . We

felt there was, at that time, the very real threat that the whole neighborhood was going to be speculated on. The Union Terminal had just opened up as an urban mall. There were all kinds of concerns that the whole neighborhood was going to be changed overnight. So the idea of community control was a very interesting one. We felt that was the route to go. (Meehan interview, 1985:310–11)

A housing solution that involved "community control," however, came only after the activists of the ministerial alliance had experienced an evolution in their own "housing consciousness." Their initial response was to deal with the threat to tenant interests one-to-one, helping individual families to resist eviction, obtain subsidies, or find better housing. As they began to think in more collective terms, they began to analyze the state of rental housing, the legal rights of private tenants, and various strategies for putting legal and political pressure on private landlords. Before they could establish a conflict group that might have represented tenants in a political struggle with local landlords, they happened upon another idea. Fighting landlords, they realized, would not really solve the problem of gentrification or give long-time residents any control over the long-term development of the neighborhood. A community land trust, on the other hand, might guarantee community control *and* give tenants more tenurial advantages than tenant-rights advocacy might ever achieve.[30] This three-step progression in housing consciousness is implicit in the following description by Sister Barbara Wheeler, a member of the ministerial alliance and first president of the CLC.

Q: The alliance said that it wanted to "do something about housing." Did you talk about what that "something" might be?

A: Well, one of the first things we were involved in was getting statistics as to what kind of housing stock there was, and what people were putting up with as renters. We were more interested in the *bad* housing

30. The alliance was exposed to the idea of a community land trust by happenstance. A tenant with ten children had been evicted from her apartment and had approached Rev. Maurice McCrackin for help in finding another place. Around the same time, Chuck Matthei, a friend of McCrackin's, had come to Cincinnati for a brief visit. Director of the Institute for Community Economics, Matthei was one of the leading CLT advocates and organizers in the United States. Confronted with the problem of the evicted tenant, McCrackin convened a neighborhood meeting (that drew several key members of the ministerial alliance) to hear Matthei describe the CLT model as a possible solution to the tenant's problem—and to the general threat of gentrification. The idea immediately took root and quickly flourished (see Institute for Community Economics, 1982:91–103).

and the landlords that didn't follow through. There were eviction notices and that kind of thing.

Q: Were you discussing tenant rights work—to stop those evictions?

A: Yeah.

Q: Had you talked about cooperative housing?

A: Not at all. Not at all.

Q: Then why do you think people were so receptive to the land trust idea when it came along?

A: Well, I think all of us were at least tuned into the fact that people had rights, and the rights weren't being respected. It seemed like if they could *own* what they had, rather than just working and trying to get landlords to give them what they deserved, maybe they could say what they want. Certainly, there was enthusiasm amongst the group that was looking at tenant-rights advocacy. Rather than that, they began to look at what ownership would do. (Wheeler interview, 1985:214–15)

The decision of these religous leaders to sponsor a radical housing group, one that would not merely defend tenant interests, but restructure the basic tenurial relation that tenants would have to domestic property, emerged from (1) a growing recognition of the kind of threat facing low-income tenants and (2) a changing assessment, by experienced activists, of the political response that might be most effective in meeting that threat. Underscoring this political consciousness, however, was a shared set of religious values that found a resonance in the radical approach to domestic property embodied in the community land trust model. These values—a de facto counterideology of domestic property—provided both motivation and solidarity for the CLC's founders:

Q: Was there anything in the background of the people in the ministerial alliance that made them more receptive to the community land trust model? Was there a greater receptivity to this idea of "social property" because of their religious background?

A: Oh, I think that was *in* it. Earlier, especially, we would refer to the idea of common ownership: the earth is the Lord's and it's to be shared among us, and this is one way of really reaching a basic need of people, a right for shelter and food and clothing. This was a real motivating thing with some of us. As Barbara [Wheeler] so often says, we've got to get back to this religious motivation, to what we're committed to. It's just not getting houses; it's getting houses for a purpose, in terms of sharing. (McCrackin interview, 1985:378)

Thus, despite the lack of a personal material interest in the neighborhood's domestic property, the leaders of the West End Alliance of

Churches and Ministries reached an early understanding of the threat that was facing the property interests of their congregations, clients, and neighbors; they passed quickly through a progression of collective definitions and solutions for the problem at hand; and they decided, at last, on a course of action that would create a new set of property relations and a new property interest group in the West End. Of course, in the beginning, there was no material foundation for this interest group because the CLC had no domestic property. There *were* tenants who joined the Community Land Cooperative in the hope of becoming homeowners/leaseholders, and theirs was certainly a material interest, but the CLC was initially founded and led by people whose primary motivation was political, social, or religious, rather than material.

Within a few years, however, the CLC was an organization made up of people with a material, as well as a political, interest in social property. By the end of 1983 the Community Land Cooperative had managed to assemble a respectable property base of fourteen single-unit and multi-unit buildings.[31] The occupants of those buildings— referred to as "resident owners" within the CLC—possessed all of the entrepreneurial interests of the social homeowners of a community land trust. On the basis of those interests, the resident owners joined with the clergy and laity who had started the CLC to constitute a new property interest group in the West End. Defending and promoting those interests, organizationally and ideologically, the CLC was soon embroiled in political conflict with other interest groups and with other organizations, inside and outside the West End.

GROUP FORMATION ON THE BASIS OF DOMESTIC PROPERTY INTERESTS

By the 1980s six different sets of domestic property interests existed among the residents of the West End, providing the structural conditions for locality-based group formation and collective action. On the basis of these interests, there existed the potential for group formation among the neighborhood's long-time homeowners, the new homeowners, the tenants of public housing, the tenants of private housing, the shareholders of Park Town, and the resident owners of the Community Land Cooperative. This potential was realized to a different

31. By the end of the 1980s, the Community Land Cooperative had acquired twenty-five buildings, containing thirty-seven family-sized units.

degree and in different ways for each interest group. In the case of one, the private tenants, group formation was never realized at all.

Two of these interest groups, the long-time homeowners and the residents of Park Town, went through an organizational cycle of (1) collective action to enhance the amenity of their particular blocks, (2) collective involvement in the conflict-oriented activities of the WECC, and (3) eventual withdrawal from the council. For the residents of Park Town, withdrawal from the collective defense of property and place meant a return to their earlier housing improvement activities. Their interest group remained intact, but there was no longer a readiness or a perceived need to engage in intergroup conflict. For the older homeowners, withdrawal from the council coincided with the collapse of their block clubs and the virtual end of all collective action. They might occasionally lend individual voices or personal support to the WECC or CLC, particularly when angered or threatened by the newer homeowners, but the long-time homeowners had essentially ceased to function as a separate interest group by the 1980s.

With the mobilization of the long-time homeowners and the residents of Park Town largely a thing of the past, and with private tenants out of the picture altogether (in terms of collective action), three residential groups remained in the West End that were politically conscious of their property interests and organizationally prepared to defend and promote them in the face of threats or opposition from other groups. The public tenants of Laurel Homes and Lincoln Court were able to choose between their local residents councils or PHACT. The newcomers to the neighborhood were affiliated with the Dayton Street Neighborhood Association. The Community Land Cooperative spoke for its resident owners, defending their interests of social property. Each of these organizations, in other words, was expressly established and maintained to protect the interests of a particular property interest group.

At the same time, two other organizations claimed to represent *all* of the neighborhood's interest groups. The West End Community Council, despite its domination by public and private tenants, proclaimed its desire and right to speak for everyone in the West End, regardless of one's relation to domestic property. The Miami Purchase Association, despite a close alliance with the DSNA, proclaimed its desire to work with any group in the West End, regardless of its relation to domestic property. Both organizations claimed neutrality in their political and economic interests, even as they tended to favor some interest groups over others.

The working assumption of this chapter has been that the differentiation, formation, and collective action of these West End groups between 1975 and 1985 can be largely explained in terms of domestic property interests. The organizations that emerged during this period—PHACT, the DSNA, the CLC, and a revitalized Laurel Homes residents council—are the formal representatives of a *single* property interest group. Two other organizations, the WECC and the MPA, emerged prior to this period and have repeatedly stated their intention of representing "the community" as a whole, not any particular interest group. Yet they too have become closely associated, in perception and in fact, with one set of property interests over others. While it is unquestionably true that the social cleavages and relational advantages created by different domestic property positions do not entirely explain the existence and behavior of these locality-based organizations, they do account for much of it. The guiding assumption of the next chapter is that these same cleavages and relations also account for much of the intergroup conflict that has become so prevalent a part of the neighborhood's recent history.

10

The Contested Community:
Intergroup Conflict, 1980–1985

I'm angry at the whole audacity of the situation. The fact that
you moved to the suburbs to get rid of us. And you left me
here with *this*. Now, all of a sudden, you ain't got no
gasoline or it cost a lot to get back and forth here to your
job, so you want *this* back. And you feel you can walk in and
take it, and I have to go somewhere else. That's just
arrogance. . . . You gave it up; you abandoned it. And we've
been paying through the nose to live here. We *had* nowhere
else to go.
                        —BETTY WARREN (interview, 1985:75–76)

We get very discouraged sometimes, because things don't
seem to move as fast as we would like. And you're dealing
with a lot of factions that keep trying to put roadblocks in
your way of doing these things.
                        —DAVID HEWER (interview, 1985:166–67)

Histo Presto: Buildings of the Past Reappear People of the
Present Disappear
                        —WEST END PROTEST SIGN (1983)

The West End of the early 1980s was a scene of nearly continuous
conflict among the neighborhood's property interest groups, especially those whose interests were given an organizational and ideological form. With a few notable exceptions, most of this intergroup conflict occurred *within* the West End and was confined to the interest
groups of the indigenous population. Individual tenants did confront
their absentee landlords, individual organizations did oppose city policies or actions, the CLC did join a class-action suit against insurance

redlining, and PHACT and the Laurel Homes residents council did regularly and contentiously struggle with the "outside" forces of the CMHA. Except for these few cases, however, most of the conflicts in which the locality-based organizations of the West End became involved did *not* involve the property interest groups of private capital or property interest groups based outside of the neighborhood. Most of the conflicts were between one or more of these indigenous West End organizations.

This intergroup conflict, waged organizationally and ideologically by the property interest groups of the West End, is the subject of this chapter. The focus will be on the formal organizations of the three interest groups that have become collectively conscious of their domestic property interests and have mobilized to aggressively defend and promote them—namely, the Dayton Street Neighborhood Association, the Community Land Cooperative, and the organizations representing the particular interests of public housing tenants. Passing mention will also be made of the two West End organizations that became interest-group partisans, despite their protestations of political neutrality: the Miami Purchase Association and the West End Community Council. In each instance, I will try to demonstrate how different and conflicting interests of domestic property—manifested in each organization's professed purposes, public actions, and internal development—provide the basis for contentious (or cooperative) relations among the neighborhood's various groups.

DAYTON STREET NEIGHBORHOOD ASSOCIATION

The leaders of the DSNA never guessed that they would someday find themselves at the center of so much controversy and conflict. They established a neighborhood improvement association to encourage changes in the upper West End that, in their estimation, would benefit everyone and be welcomed by all who lived there. The original articles of incorporation of the DSNA set goals thought to be offensive to no one: "to provide housing for low and moderate income families"; "to rehabilitate housing"; and "to generally provide or assist in the providing of services to upgrade the Dayton Street, Cincinnati, Ohio neighborhood." Seven years after the association's incorporation, its founder and president still proclaimed the organization's benevolent concern for all of the neighborhood's people: "We don't want any conflict with anyone, and anyone can belong to our organization. The things that we do are things that benefit everybody. We plant trees. We clear lots. We sponsor tours. We've given visibility to the area. We've helped everybody" (Bates interview, 1985:124).

Despite the fact that "anybody can belong" to the DSNA, the people who *do* belong are primarily those from a single property interest group. The organization's membership list is not available for public inspection, but two of the men who have served as presidents have variously described the organization's members as "the younger people that are in here, that have come into the neighborhood to restore the old houses" (Hewer interview, 1985:164) and "people in the neighborhood who have moved in and bought new buildings . . . gentrifiers, as some people would call them" (Bates interview, 1985:122).[1] This is the group that is represented by the DSNA and, even though the individuals who make up this group may not want "any conflict with anyone," their interests have made conflict practically unavoidable.

The primary interests of this property group are the equity and liquidity of domestic property. Yet these interests are hardly apparent in the commitment to improving the neighborhood's *use* value that is predominant among the DSNA's founding purposes. Nor do the association's actual efforts to clean up lots, plant trees, or initiate a neighborhood crime watch indicate an overriding interest in the exchange value of property and place. Even the association's two largest projects, an annual house tour of the neighborhood's historic structures and the restoration of a stone arch marking the boundary of the Dayton Street Historic District, may be interpreted as an interest in promoting the visibility and status of their member's property, an interest that previously has been counted among a property's use interests (autonomy).

If the exchange interests of the DSNA are not immediately revealed in the organization's formal purposes and collective actions, they appear more clearly in the private conversations and private actions of the organization's members. "Private" as they may be, these are the interests that the collective action of the DSNA is meant to promote.

Since the DSNA was founded to "improve" the neighborhood, it is appropriate to ask the leaders of the DSNA what they perceive to be

1. The DSNA bylaws state, "Any person who owns or rents property in the vicinity of Dayton Street, Cincinnati, Ohio and/or is committed to the purposes of the corporation and who pays the annual dues of the corporation as established from time to time by the Board of Trustees shall be a member of this corporation."

the neighborhood's problems, and what they—and their organization—are doing to improve the situation. Two sets of problems are repeatedly identified: the deterioration of the neighborhood's historic buildings and the lack of a favorable climate for neighborhood investment. As will soon be apparent, the two are not seen as separate by the association's leaders, but as *causally* related: neighborhood deterioration is believed to be a direct result of an unfavorable investment climate.

The deterioration of the neighborhood, specifically the deterioration of its historically significant domestic property, is the most pressing problem that is recognized by the DSNA. As one of the association's leaders noted in the previous chapter, historic preservation is something of a personal and collective "cause" for the neighborhood's newcomers. They genuinely worry that a precious part of Cincinnati's past will be irretrievably lost if the buildings of the Dayton Street Historic District continue to decay. Such solicitude, however, is seldom expressed for the occupants of this built environment. Indeed, when solutions to neighborhood deterioration are discussed, it becomes apparent that the impoverished community is perceived as part of the *problem*, a social barrier to the physical restoration of the neighborhood's buildings. Or, as the association's vice president has put it, in remarks quoted once before, "The obstacle's the poor people in the West End" (Lundy interview, 1985:104).

The neighborhood's long-time residents are an "obstacle" simply because they poison the climate for outside investment in the neighborhood's domestic property. There is too much low-income housing. The population is too poor and too black. There are too many abandoned, deteriorated, and ominous-looking buildings. Would-be investors are scared away. Equity appreciation slows. Buildings are harder to sell:

> If you're selling a house, you're not just selling a house; you're selling the neighborhood. And if you're showing a white person—or even a black person—the neighborhood, and they're paying a lot of money for a house, generally they're going to want to see upper-income people living there like themselves—middle-income. If they see blacks, it's not right, but they automatically think "lower income." And they find it hard to justify spending that kind of money to live in a lower income area. (Painter interview, 1985:146)

> One of the problems we have here, the main problem, is image. We have a very bad image in the West End. If you ask someone from another part of the city about this area; "Oh, that's down there; you

wouldn't want to drive through there at night!" This type of thing. Well, it does look bad. . . . Other people are scared to death to come down here. Why is that? It's because the buildings appear bad; they look bad. They look ominous. (Hewer interview, 1985:173)

Given this definition of the neighborhood's problem, the leaders of the DSNA, both individually and collectively, have tried to create a more favorable climate for real estate investment in the West End, one that might enhance the equity and liquidity of their own holdings. Their stated objectives are three. First, they want a change in the social composition of the neighborhood, variously described as "getting The Element out" (Kattleman interview, 1985:159), or achieving a better socio-economic "balance" or "mix" (Bates interview, 1985: 127; Hewer interview, 1985:171; Painter interview, 1985:146; Lundy interview, 1985:105, 111).

Second, they want to reverse the public perception of the West End as a stagnant, frightening slum, filled with people who are becoming more impoverished and buildings that are becoming more dilapidated every year:

> We've got to create this image effect that things are *happening*. Here again, it's perceptions. If people don't *perceive* that the neighborhood's on the move, it really isn't. . . . That's why we always joke and say what we have to do is just get a bunch of the older buildings and slap a bunch of scaffolding on the front, put signs "Coming Soon," and so forth. You know, it's just what people *think*. That would create the interest and then other people will do this. It's window dressing, and it's necessary. (Hewer interview, 1985:190–91).

Finally, as both cause and effect of their other two objectives, they want to create a robust market in the West End for the rental and sale of their domestic property.

The leaders of the DSNA have recognized that they cannot improve the neighborhood's investment climate by themselves. Their individual efforts must be complemented by collective action to "sell" the West End, drawing new investors and a new socioeconomic stratum of homeowners and renters. For this, they have organized and utilized the DSNA. The association has not itself acquired or rehabilitated domestic property, even though it is so empowered by its corporate charter. Rather, it has engaged in activities designed to spruce up the neighborhood's streets and lots, increase its visibility in the public eye, and create an enticing image of an area "on the move." Cleanup campaigns, tree-planting sessions, the reconstruction of a historic arch, and free publicity from sympathetic newspaper reporters have been an important part of this "window dressing." But the association's most significant activity has been its annual tour of the neighborhood's historic structures. The tour not only generates most of the association's annual budget, but reveals most clearly the organizational purposes and property interests that lie at the heart of the association's program.

Started in 1979, the annual tour of renovated buildings in the Dayton Street Historic District is a one-day festival, typically attracting between 1,200 and two thousand people from Cincinnati's hilltop neighborhoods and suburbs. Visitors take walking tours of Dayton Street, conducted by guides from the Miami Purchase Association. Members of the DSNA open their homes to public inspection. The MPA opens its own headquarters as well, the lavishly restored Hauck House. In recent years, an exhibition of antique cars and a brass band from one of the hilltop high schools have added a special flourish.

While it might be possible to view this tour as a fairly innocuous case of local boosterism and community pride organized to celebrate an historically significant area and to raise a few thousand dollars for a local organization, its primary purpose has less to do with boasting of *past* accomplishments than with stimulating *future* investment. The intent here is not so much to enhance the status of property and place as it is to enhance the equity and liquidity of the area's real estate:

Q: What are the purposes of the annual house tour?
A: Number one is to promote the area. To get people to see what's here. To get them interested. The last tour we even took names of people that might be interested in apartments or in doing houses. When we have a house that becomes available—or an apartment available—we call those people. (Painter interview, 1985:141)

The vice president of the DSNA is more succinct:

Once a year, we have a house tour to stimulate interest from the outside and get some new investors in. (Lundy interview, 1985:106)

In short, the DSNA house tour, like its other efforts to improve the West End's "image," is designed to draw affluent homebuyers and renters into the area and to create a vigorous real estate market of appreciating values and easy sales. Interests of exchange are para-

mount in the political consciousness of the DSNA. These are the principal interests that the collective action of the organization is designed
to promote.

Intergroup Relations

The Dayton Street Neighborhood Association may not have
wanted "any conflict with anyone," but despite the assertion by its
president that "the things we do are things that benefit everybody,"
neither the DSNA nor its members have acted in the interest of "everybody" in the West End. They have acted, collectively and individually, in their own interest. Doing so, they have threatened the interests
of others. Herein lies the basis for conflict with other property interest
groups, whether the DSNA wants that conflict or not.

There is also a basis for cooperation. Members of the DSNA, several
of whom are small-time developers and realtors themselves, maintain
cordial relations with other developers and realtors active in the area.
Individual members of the DSNA have also gone out of their way
to establish friendly relations with the neighborhood's long-time
homeowners and to invite them into the association—though with
little success. As an *organization*, however, the DSNA has established
overtly cooperative relations with only two other groups: the Miami
Purchase Association and the recently reconstituted WECC.

The DSNA and the Miami Purchase Association recruit members
from essentially the same property interest group, although the MPA
draws from a wider geographic area.[2] Many of the DSNA's members
are, in fact, members of the MPA as well. Aside from sharing a similar social base, cooperation between the DSNA and the MPA has been
founded upon a shared interest in the architectural survival and aesthetic amenity of the West End's historic buildings.

The MPA's development arm, the Miami Purchase Preservation
Fund (MPPF), has taken the lead in preserving and rehabilitating such
buildings.[3] Relations between the MPPF and the DSNA have been espe-

2. The Miami Purchase Association has members from neighborhoods and towns
throughout the Cincinnati metropolitan area.

3. The MPPF is separately incorporated from the MPA, though the two organizations have boards, memberships, and budgets that partially overlap. Both organizations occupy the same building on Dayton Street. The preservation fund is the more
deeply involved in the West End. When local residents refer to "Miami Purchase,"
either to compliment or condemn, they are usually referring to an activity of the preservation fund. Any distinction between the MPA and the MPPF, however, is almost
never drawn by the long-time residents of the West End. To them, the two organizations are one and the same.

cially close. The DSNA helped the preservation fund find buyers for the twenty-three West End properties that the latter purchased in the early 1980s to prevent their demolition. The MPPF, in turn, assisted members of the DSNA in finding renters and buyers for *their* buildings (Painter interview, 1985:134–35). Both organizations, with the participation of the MPA, have cooperated in promoting the image of the upper West End as an area "on the move," particularly through joint support for the annual house tour.

There is also a degree of tension in their relationship, since the MPPF is less committed than the DSNA to changing the social composition of the upper West End. The MPPF may join the DSNA and its own organizational parent, the MPA, in attracting outside attention and investment to the neighborhood, but it gives priority to *current* residents of the West End in the disposition of its properties. Because of this policy—adopted, in part, in response to criticism from the CLC and WECC—the MPPF is forced to overlook the affluent homebuyers from outside of the neighborhood, which the DSNA would prefer to have in the West End. The MPPF is also forced to keep the price of its property low enough that the indigenous population can actually acquire it—thus undercutting the appreciating market value that the DSNA would like to create. This is not a policy that the DSNA regards with favor:

> There's still a little conflict there with that. I feel that Miami Purchase is doing a lot of good. I'm glad they're here. But they happen to be a little wishy-washy in their motives and goals. They always are trying to straddle the fence. I can see why, because they *are* in a precarious situation. Here, on the one hand they've got the Dayton Street [Neighborhood Association] group trying to promote market housing and upgrade the level. Plus, you have the other groups . . . saying that they're promoting displacement, market housing, and trying to improve the neighborhood to the point where the old-line residents will have to move out. . . . So what they end up doing, with some of the houses they've done, they turn them over, once they complete them, to some low-income person. . . . Of the things they do, that's the thing that irritates me—that it's always low-income housing. We feel that this neighborhood has *plenty* of low-income housing. It's *all* it's got. Why do we need more? For this neighborhood to survive, we need to integrate it—both economically and racially. (Hewer interview, 1985:170–71)

This disagreement over whether the indigenous population should be given first chance to acquire MPPF properties has placed a modest strain on DSNA/MPPF relations. It irritates the leaders of the DSNA that the MPPF is not as directly, primarily interested in the commodity value of local housing as they. Nevertheless, since the bulk of the preservation fund's restoration work in the upper West End *does* improve the local investment climate and *does* augment the equity and liquidity of surrounding parcels of property, the DSNA remains a staunch supporter of the MPPF. Despite some tension, they share a social base and a set of purposes similar enough to make them long-standing, reliable allies on most neighborhood issues.

The alliance between the DSNA and the West End Community Council, on the other hand, is newer and more precarious. It is probably an exaggeration to call it an "alliance" at all. A better description might be "marriage of convenience"—a political accommodation that each has made to the other, with the city acting as the go-between. Without the council's approval, city agencies have been reluctant to provide public funds for DSNA projects. Conversely, without the participation of *all* of the neighborhood's interest groups in the membership of the council, the city has been reluctant to recognize the WECC as the political voice of the West End. Given this situation, the leaders of the DSNA have joined the WECC as individuals, and the DSNA itself has become an organizational affiliate of the community council. The leaders of the WECC, in turn, take pains to mention the DSNA in any public listing of the council's constituent groups.

Historically, however, such displays of cooperation have been the exception. The property interests of each organization's principal constituency are simply too different—too antagonistic—to make for an easy alliance. As the newcomers to the neighborhood, represented by the DSNA, convert multi-unit apartment buildings back into single-family, owner-occupied housing and increase the cost of the rental housing that remains, the security of local tenants is threatened. Since tenants are heavily represented among the membership of the WECC— and predominate among the council's leadership—the antagonism between tenants and members of the DSNA casts a pall over all relations between the community council and the DSNA. As an officer of the DSNA acknowledges: "I'd say our goals pretty much conflict . . . because a lot of the upgrading of the housing we do necessarily has to displace *some* of the people—who would be more their members than ours" (Painter interview, 1985:130).

The DSNA has also irked many West End residents by displaying remarkable insensitivity to long-time residents in its sponsorship of annual house tours and in its reconstruction of a historic arch on Linn

Street. Hundreds of well-dressed, all-white tourists, entertained by an all-white band from the suburbs, is bound to irritate an indigenous population that is predominantly poor and almost entirely black. More irritating still is the association's historic arch. To the DSNA, it is an ornate reminder of the neighborhood's cherished architectural past, salvaged to serve as a boundary marker for the Dayton Street Historic District. To the long-time residents of the West End, the arch means something entirely different, as the council's newly elected president (in 1985) soon discovered:

> Do you know where that piece of mess comes from? It used to be the archway to the police department down here on York Street. That's what it is. It holds a lot of bad memories, that police department down there, for a lot of old residents. Because a lot of residents that I've talked to said that they've had relatives (or actually themselves) that have been beaten down that police department with a hose. Then taken to Central Station. So they don't have a very good view. I mean, some of 'em wanted to go up there and pull it down! (Wright interview, 1985:388)

What this means, in practice, is that despite a mutually recognized need to cooperate and despite the politely formal ties that have been established, relations between the constituencies of these organizations are marked by continuing tension and conflict. This makes the alliance that the leaders of the DSNA and WECC have attempted to build seem very fragile indeed.

Tense though relations may be, the two organizations have managed, for now, to create a thin veneer of civility and peaceful coexistence. No such accommodation has been possible between the DSNA and the Community Land Cooperative. Conflict has been the daily rule in *their* relationship.

Overt conflict between the DSNA and the CLC has taken many forms. Leaders of the two organizations have confronted each other on the neighborhood's sidewalks and on the editorial pages of the city's newspapers. In both forums, they have publicly and heatedly argued over tenant displacement, historic preservation, and gentrification. Supporters of the CLC have convinced local churches to refuse the use of their facilities to the DSNA. The DSNA and the CLC have publicly assumed opposing stands on controversial issues like historic designation for downtown neighborhoods and a zoning variance for a commercial establishment serving the West End's lower-income blacks.[4] But the most direct and most public confrontation between these organizations occurred in 1983, when the supporters of the CLC staged a televised protest of the DSNA's annual tour:

> They put signs and little cute sayings in the windows, so that people coming down on the house tour could see these things. [Let me] see if I can remember some of the things they had. One was: "Histo Presto— Buildings of the Past Reappear; People of the Present Disappear." Little sayings like that. Another one was: "Save the People, Not the Build- ings." This kind of thing. They don't like it because the house tour is something that promotes the neighborhood in negative ways, as far as they're concerned. We are bringing in people from the outside to see what we are accomplishing, and doing very successful house tours. . . . The year before, we had 1,200 people in a three-hour period. But they don't like this at all. (Hewer interview, 1985:176–77)

The people who participated in this quiet protest, loudly covered by two of city's television stations, represented both the property interest groups that have been drawn into the Community Land Cooperative. Long-time homeowners—worried that historic restoration of the neighborhod will increase their property taxes, concerned that gen- trification will displace their neighbors, and irritated at the "pushi- ness" of the DSNA in telling others how they should paint their houses or keep their yards—have responded to the CLC's call for greater "community control" and its campaign against "speculation." Private renters—concerned about displacement, threatened with rising hous- ing costs, and confronted by the prospect of never becoming home- owners themselves—have responded to the CLC's public stand against displacement and its promise of affordable homeownership for former tenants. Although tenants have been the land coopera- tive's *principal* constituency, both property interest groups have been represented in the membership, leadership, and public actions of the CLC, including its on-going struggle with the DSNA.

The basis of this conflict is the recognition by the members of each organization that the *other* organization represents a mounting threat to their property interests. These interests are in opposition at nearly

---

4. In 1982 a developer applied for permission to construct a fast-food, "soul food" restaurant on the corner of Dayton and Linn streets. The CLC, along with the WECC, supported the plan. Members of the DSNA turned out in force at a public hear- ing to oppose the construction of such an "atrocious-looking thing" on the edge of the historic neighborhood. The supporters of the restaurant brought their own busload of people to the hearing. The restaurant was eventually granted a zoning variance and constructed on the corner.

every point. The flash point, however, is between a set of property interests and organizational purposes that treat property and place as a *commodity*, and a set of interests and purposes that defend both the *use value* of domestic property and the *social community* of the West End. The collective action of the DSNA is designed to attract private investment and affluent homebuyers into the area, enhancing the equity and liquidity of its members' holdings while preserving certain historic features of the built environment. The collective action of the CLC is designed to take as much property as practically possible *off* the market altogether, preventing its purchase by outside investors and preserving its availability and affordability for the long-time residents of the neighborhood. In the actions of the CLC to defend the use interests of the indigenous population, the DSNA perceives a threat to its own exchange interests. In the actions of the DSNA to promote the exchange interests of its members, the CLC perceives a threat to the security of the neighborhood's tenants, its homeowners, and the social network that has grown up among the neighborhood's long-time residents over many years. The "commodity" interests of the DSNA and the "community" interests of the CLC are inherently incompatible.[5]

Responding to Intergroup Conflict

The continuing opposition from the CLC—and, on occasion, from the tenant members of the West End Community Council—has had a significant effect on the political consciousness and organizational development of the DSNA. Among the leaders of the DSNA, there has

5. The inter-organizational hostility engendered by this basic cleavage also spills over onto a couple of *use* interests that the members of both organizations might be presumed to share. Concerned about the *security* of their homes and cars, the threat of vandalism to vacant buildings, and the nuisance of teenagers congregating on street corners after dark, leaders of the DSNA have attempted to enlist the CLC in a neighborhood crime watch. The leaders of the CLC, however, tend to perceive such calls as further evidence of the DSNA's desire to harass the indigenous population of the upper West End and to replace it with an affluent, "law-abiding" population like itself. A neighborhood crime watch has not been established. *Amenity* has proven no more successful as a common ground (i.e., a common interest) between the two organizations. To the astonishment and exasperation of the DSNA, the CLC has resisted every effort by the newcomers to beautify the neighborhood: "They don't want the buildings to look particularly good from the outside because it would promote the neighborhood to look better, and it would promote gentrification. That's their rationalization. So the planting of trees is [also] bad. They don't like that. We've asked the Rev. McCrackin, 'Could we plant a tree in front of your house?' . . . He didn't want a tree. He didn't want any of these trees along here. He said it just makes the neighborhood look softer and nicer, and we don't want that" (Hewer interview, 1985:173–74).

been a progression of *consciousness* from the early recognition of collective interests to a later awareness of the precarious, contentious nature of those interests. There has been a parallel development of the *organization*, as it has moved from being a neighborhood improvement association, acting to enhance the amenity of property and place, to being a housing conflict group, acting to advance its particular interests in the face of opposition from other groups. A number of factors have undoubtedly contributed to these changes, but the precipitating factor appears to have been the association's ongoing conflict with the CLC—combined, perhaps, with the highly emotional attacks on DSNA members that have occasionally ignited the monthly meetings of the community council.

The political consciousness of the DSNA was grounded, almost from the start, on a relational conception of property interests. Amenity, for example, has been the focus of much of the organization's collective action, not only because historic preservation was an end in itself but because the association's members realized that improving the amenity of property and place was a way, in Painter's words, "to get the neighborhood moving—to get the momentum going—in order to get your property worth something" (Painter interview, 1985:145). Amenity was clearly related in their minds to equity and liquidity. Whether the person's property was "worth something" and whether that property was marketable largely depended upon the state of repair, the market price, and the marketability of *all* of the properties surrounding it. There was a collective recognition among the neighborhood's newcomers, in short, that their interests—their financial fates—were linked, a realization that they "were all in this thing together."

It took much longer to realize that their own interests were precariously, contentiously related to the collective interests of others—in other words, that the interests of their property group could and would be put at risk by the opposition of other groups. Indeed, since DSNA leaders thought the association's activities "benefit everybody," local opposition to the DSNA was greeted, at first, with genuine surprise. Later, as the opposition continued, a tendency grew among the association's leadership to place the blame on individual "advocates" or "troublemakers" like Mallory or McCrackin or to attribute hostility toward historic preservation to "outside agitators" from other neighborhoods. Gradually, however, came a recognition that there existed, within the West End itself, "a lot of factions that keep trying to put roadblocks in your way" (Hewer interview, 1985:167), factions that threaten the interests of the DSNA. Principal among these "factions" was the CLC.

It has slowly dawned on the DSNA's collective consciousness that the opposition from the CLC is not a matter of personal animosity or poor communications but a deep-seated conflict of interests, embodied in two diametrically opposed organizational agendas for the development of the upper West End. This realization has had several noticeable effects on the DSNA.

First, a new element of defensiveness, even of combativeness, has become apparent in the written and verbal comments of the association's leaders, regarding displacement, historic preservation, and the efforts of the CLC to preserve low-income housing in the neighborhood. Second, the DSNA has consciously and assidously cultivated defensive alliances with two organizations that might otherwise have become its competitors or opponents. In other words, without the organized opposition of the CLC, the low-income housing policy of the MPPF might have forced the DSNA and the preservation fund further apart, and the overtures of the DSNA to the community council might have been far more muted. Third, the DSNA has developed a defensive "ideology" of property and place. These ideas explain and justify the association's actions, to members and nonmembers alike. They promote internal solidarity within the DSNA. They also accentuate the external, political differences between the DSNA and the CLC, often becoming a source of intergroup antagonism in their own right. More will be said about these ideological differences later on.

In summary, persistent opposition to the DSNA's organizational advancement of its members' interests has caused the association to orient its actions more and more toward other property interest groups. Intergroup conflict or cooperation has become as much a part of the collective action of the association's leaders and members as the effort to enhance the amenity of the neighborhood's buildings, lots, and streets. Since much of this opposition has been mobilized and orchestrated by supporters of the CLC, it is appropriate to turn our attention now to the intergroup relations and organizational development of this other neighborhood group.

COMMUNITY LAND COOPERATIVE

The leaders of the CLC, at least those from the West End Alliance of Churches and Ministries, had already passed through several stages of

housing consciousness when they embraced the "radical" idea of social property. This does not mean that they had abandoned their earlier perception of a conflict of interests existing between the long-time
residents and the newcomers. Conflict consciousness remained a part
of their motivation, but it combined with a commitment to structural
change in the ownership and control of domestic property as the *principal* means of waging that conflict. Forming a community land trust
in the West End was not done *instead* of fighting the DSNA and the MPA
but *because* the struggle against these organizations required a more
effective strategy than individual counseling or tenant advocacy. The
members of the ministerial alliance who helped to start the CLC were
convinced that steadily expanding the supply of social property was
the best way to resist the wave of speculation, gentrification, and displacement that was gathering force on Dayton Street. The threat of
this wave someday crashing through the rest of the neighborhood also
propelled the land cooperative's earliest members, both private tenants and long-time homeowners, into the ranks of the organization.

The same political consciousness is evident in the CLC's founding
documents, promotional literature, and public pronouncements.
These organizational statements combine an awareness of the "radical" nature of the CLC's unique approach to tenure with a recognition that the interests embodied in this housing model are antagonistic to those of other property groups. Consider, for example, the
contents of two widely distributed CLC brochures, produced nearly
four years apart.[6] Both describe a radical model of housing tenure: an
"alternative, grassroots approach to the ownership of land and housing"; a model of "common stewardship" that permanently "removes
land and housing from the usual real estate market." At the same
time, both pieces of literature readily acknowledge intergroup conflict
as a cause and consequence of the CLC's endeavor to institutionalize
social property in the West End. Thus are described the organization's
origins in its 1984 brochure:

> For the last sixty years, Cincinnati's West End neighborhood has expe-
> rienced one wave of displacement after another. Thousands of people
> have been uprooted as hundreds of houses have been destroyed or
> priced beyond their means—as urban renewal, interstate highway con-
> struction, and absentee landlords have taken their toll. When the north-

6. The 1980 document is a five-page pamphlet, titled "Community Land Cooperative of Cincinnati: Our Story." The 1984 document is an eight-panel brochure, titled
"Community Land Cooperative in the West End."

ern part of the West End was declared an historic district, residents were threatened with a new round of displacement from wealthy investors. In 1980, the Community Land Cooperative was organized by the West End Alliance of Churches and Ministries and by local residents to resist this threat.

Even more oppositional in its language and political consciousness is an earlier CLC brochure, produced during the first year of the organization's existence:

> As Jesus began his ministry he declared that its purpose was summed up in the words of Isaiah, to preach the gospel to the poor, to heal the brokenhearted, and to set at liberty those who are bruised. There are economic captives in Cincinnati's West End, Over-the-Rhine, and in other parts of the city. There are people who are bruised and oppressed and who are looking for healing and release from their enslavement to exhorbitant rents, ruthless landlords, and heartless speculators. May the response of the people of Cincinnati to the work of the Community Land Cooperative be a ringing affirmation that they want to help release the captives and to have a part in the bringing of hope and healing to the bruised and oppressed in our city.

Intergroup Relations

Employing such language, the leaders of the CLC frequently speak of their organizational opposition to various capitalist interest groups—landlords, financiers, for-profit developers, and speculators. In point of fact, the CLC has conflictually confronted only the last two groups—and only to the extent that these interests have been represented by the DSNA. Landlords and the CLC have not done battle because the land cooperative's "resident owners" cease being tenants at the moment they inhabit CLC housing. The leaders of the CLC regularly and publicly voice their concern for tenant interests that are threatened by the landlords' interest in realizing as high a monthly rent and as high a resale price as possible. But this threat is met by "releasing" the tenant from the landlord-tenant relationship, not by resisting the landlord's exploitation of this relationship to realize liquidity and equity gains.

Financiers and the CLC have not engaged in conflict simply because the land cooperative has financed nearly all its acquisitions with grants and loans from noncommercial sources.[7] While exhorbi-

7. Most of these funds have come from religious congregations and sympathetic individuals.

tant rates of interest and restrictive lending practices such as redlining *could* provide the basis for intergroup conflict, the CLC had, as of 1985, never approached a local bank or savings and loan in pursuit of financing. The lack of contact between the two property interest groups has meant a lack of overt conflict.

The CLC has had plenty of contact, on the other hand, with for-profit "developers" and "speculators," since these groups are amply represented within the DSNA. There *are* a few outside firms employed in rehabilitating West End property for upper-income use, and there are a number of outside investors engaged in holding West End property in the expectation of speculative gains. Nevertheless, most of the for-profit "development" or "speculation" in the neighborhood is being done by members of the DSNA. They are mostly homeowners, with all of the use and exchange interests of this particular property group. But their leaders are part-time realtors and developers, as well, and most of the members of this homeowner group seem inordinately "interested" in the speculative equity of their holdings.

The overt hostility of the land cooperative's members to the "usual real estate market," expressed collectively and consciously in a vigorous campaign to decommodify domestic property and to spoil the "investment climate" of the neighborhood, has made the CLC and the DSNA implacable political enemies. This conflict has already been discussed, and little more needs to be said. Just to round out the picture, however, the CLC's perspective on its differences with the DSNA should be voiced. Consider the reflections of Charlene Robinson, for example, one of the CLC's resident owners:

> Q: What is the fight between the Co-op and the Dayton Street group all about?
>
> A: The Co-op looks at property as shelter. The upper Dayton Street group looks at it as money. Yeah, that's it. Then, in a way, the Co-op *scares* some of the upper Dayton Street people. Like Michael Painter, he's running around: "Those Sisters are buying that house over there. That Co-op! What are they doing? What are they doing?" [laughter] . . .
>
> Q: What do you think the fear of those folks on upper Dayton Street might be?
>
> A: I think that one day they might not have the control. They're using their money to get all the houses at a big price—$120,000, $160,000. The only thing that I can see is that one day they'll be afraid that there won't be any more properties for them to buy, that people will be secure in their homes and they can't come along and say, "I'll give you a hundred twenty thousand for this." The person will say, "Well, I'm not interested." And that'll be the end of their money-making venture.

It's almost like a marble game. If you get something from the game, and you decide you don't want to sell it, you say, "Well, I'll keep this." Then the other person will just have to stop. They can't buy you out.

Q: So the Co-op is sort of getting in the way of their marble game?

A: [Laughter] Yeah, that's the way I would see it. (Robinson interview, 1985:296–97)

Another perspective on the DSNA is provided by Reverend Maurice McCrackin, one of the Community Land Cooperative's founders and a long-time member of its board:

They put up this arch from the York Street police station. Then there was this interview with the treasurer of the Dayton Street Neighborhood Association. He said, in this article, that they were putting it out there because the area hadn't been called to the attention of the public as much as it should be. They wanted to mark out the area that they were "reclaiming." Reclaiming *from* whom? *For* whom? Reclaiming it for the wealthy? Reclaiming it for the descendants of the original owners? They come down here, walk through the area and look up at the facades. And there are people right under them. They're ignored. . . . I never said we shouldn't preserve the historic buildings, but not at the price of putting people out in the streets. (McCrackin interview, 1985:379–80)

If conflict has been the hallmark of the CLC's relations with the DSNA, its relations with Miami Purchase have been only marginally better. This is due, in part, to the tendency of the CLC's members to regard the interests of the MPA and the DSNA as one and the same. Thus, when supporters of the land cooperative speak or mobilize against historic preservation, gentrification, and promotional events such as the house tour, they point to the Miami Purchase Association and its preservation fund as primary culprits in the "plot" to displace the indigenous population.[8] Vonnie Robbins, a resident owner in the CLC, typifies this point of view:

8. Despite such suspicions, several leaders of the CLC decided in 1983 to cooperate with the MPPA in submitting a joint request to the Local Initiatives Support Corporation (LISC) seeking funds for the first stage of a sixteen-building renovation project. On the eve of receiving a $16,000 planning grant from LISC, the CLC suddenly dropped out of the project. A majority of the CLC board had decided that cooperative relations with Miami Purchase were politically unwise. This decision was ratified by the CLC's general membership a few days later by a vote of ninety-eight to three. There were a number of practical reasons for the CLC's withdrawal, but the main reason was political: "While the Cooperative acknowledges the role of Miami Purchase in preserving buildings in the West End that would otherwise be demolished, it sees the expansion of historic preservation as a threat to the community control of its

I feel Miami Purchase is like the upper middle class or upper class people. I feel that they want to get a different class of people down here, because they feel that a different class of people will "upgrade the neighborhood," so to speak. . . . Miami Purchase, when they talk to you, it sounds good. You know, they want to "preserve the neighborhood"; they want to "make the neighborhood nice"; make it "a safe place." They want to prevent the buildings from being torn down, and all of this. And it *sounds* good, you know. But they don't tell you about it's going to make this family have to move, or it's going to put this family out of the house, that it's going to make housing too expensive for your neighbor or your brother to afford. (Robbins interview, 1985:252–53)

The CLC's opposition to Miami Purchase originates not only in the latter's support for changes in the neighborhood's physical amenity, financial climate, and social composition that inevitably threaten the interests of the very population that the CLC is trying to serve, but in the social fact that the two organizations are committed to two very different models of homeownership for low- and moderate-income people. The social property of the CLC gives resident owners nearly all the use interests that typically accrue to homeownership in the United States, but imposes certain social limits on equity and liquidity. The fee simple ownership that is promoted by the MPPF in the disposition of its properties limits neither use nor exchange, permitting new homeowners to profit from appreciating property values.[9]

Profit-taking of this sort is regarded by the CLC as a large part of the problem facing low- and moderate-income families in finding affordable housing. The MPPF, on the other hand, regards the tenurial right to reap equity and liquidity gains as something of a "solution" to the plight of the poor. Thus, far from preventing such petty speculation, as the CLC attempts to do, the MPPF eagerly encourages it. The director of the Miami Purchase Preservation Fund acknowledges this to be one of the major differences between the MPPF and the land cooperative:

See, our ownership idea is different. As I understand it, the land is retained by the Land Co-op. It's only the building that is owned by the

---

own housing. Historic preservation often encouages speculation, which takes housing out of the reach of low-income people and leads to displacement and the gentrification of a neighborhood" (Wheeler, 1983).

9. The one limit the MPPF does impose is an easement agreement, signed by the purchasers of MPPF buildings, which requires owners to preserve the "historic character" of their buildings' exterior.

new owner. If a new owner sells that building, they can't make a profit on it. That's a different concept. Ours is more market-oriented, I guess. It's to put people in the mainstream, rather than keep them sort of out of the mainstream. In a way, I see their program as sort of, it produces shelter, but it doesn't provide any economic incentive. (Cramer interview:204–5)

This different "ownership idea," combined with the threat that Miami Purchase is perceived to pose to the CLC's constituency, has been the basis for the continuing conflict between the two organizations. The CLC has fought Miami Purchase with the same combination of verbal abuse, editorial denunciation, and public protest with which it has confronted the DSNA. Miami Purchase has largely refrained from public debate with the CLC but has begun building its own base of political support within the West End. Using the new homeowners in its recently renovated properties as an organizational core, the MPPF is quietly cultivating a locality-based constituency of its own—one that may someday defend Miami Purchase against attacks from the CLC.

In contrast to the conflict of interests that has characterized the intergroup relations between the land cooperative and both the DSNA and Miami Purchase, the CLC has discovered a certain *commonality* of interests with several other West End organizations. Its relations with these groups have been relatively cordial and cooperative. As previously mentioned, the CLC has received regular support from members of the Park Town housing cooperative and, of course, from members of the West End Alliance of Churches and Ministries. Homeowner members of the now-defunct Dayton-Whiteman Neighborhood Association, who successfully opposed the MPA's attempt to declare the neighborhood east of Linn Street a historic district in the early 1970s, were also involved in the CLC during the latter's formative years. There also has existed a degree of cooperation between the CLC and the West End Community Council—a relationship that has been far more volatile than the others.

Park Town's own brand of social property, the religious grounding of the ministerial alliance, and the interest of the former Dayton-Whiteman group in opposing historic preservation and gentrification provided the basis for each of these groups to cooperate with the CLC. The threatened interests of the neighborhood's tenants, represented so fully by the West End Community Council's members and leaders, could have done the same—that is, these interests could have cemented a cooperative relationship between the CLC and the WECC. Several attempts have, in fact, been made to establish a formal, mutually supportive relationship between these organizations. The most serious of these efforts occurred around 1982, when leaders of the CLC and leaders of the WECC met to discuss a formal alliance between the two organizations. The land cooperative's opposition to Miami Purchase and the DSNA found a receptive audience and ally in a community council that was still dominated by Roger Bradley's militant rhetoric about "rich whites taking over the neighborhood." Furthermore, since the WECC had disowned WEDCO, the land cooperative seemed to be the only chance the council might have of getting back into the housing development game. Therefore, a proposal was negotiated whereby the CLC was to become the council's de facto "development arm," and the WECC would work to secure public funds for further CLC acquisitions.[10] Before either organization could act on this joint proposal, however, the WECC elected new officers and plunged into a new round of organizational chaos. The proposal was never renegotiated or reintroduced to either board.

Despite a similar social base, therefore, the CLC and the WECC never managed to establish a working partnership. The organizational disarray of the WECC is not the only reason. The council's leaders have resented the in-roads that the CLC has made into the council's constituency, recruiting members and resident owners out of local tenant ranks, as well as the refusal of the CLC to place itself under the administrative "umbrella" of the WECC. Resentment at the land cooperative's willful independence reached a peak in 1983, when the council's new president, Bonnie Batton, publicly attacked the CLC as a "Catholic conspiracy" to acquire most of the neighborhood's property.[11] Within six months, Batton had disappeared from both the community council and the West End, but her legacy of suspicion and accusation concerning the CLC remained. Rumors persist in the council and in certain neighborhood circles that the CLC is buying up property on behalf of the Catholic Church or some other outside party.

10. The proposed alliance between the CLC and the WECC also stipulated the inclusion of a member of the WECC executive committee on the board of the CLC (Meehan and Watts, 1981).

11. Many of the funds the CLC has received for property acquisition and rehabilitation have been made available in the form of low-interest loans from congregations of Roman Catholic nuns. The CLC has tapped nonreligious sources of capital, as well, but enough funds have come from Catholic sources to inspire anti-Catholic demagogues, of which there are several in the West End.

The CLC was equally suspicious of the WECC. The land cooperative's leaders had witnessed the decline and fragmentation of the community council at close hand, and they had no desire for the council's contentious spirit to contaminate their own consensual organization. Then too, there were persistent (though unconfirmed) rumors about corruption and embezzlement within the WECC that could not be ignored by an organization like the CLC, which had to borrow thousands of dollars for its housing work. Association with the WECC might taint the land cooperative's spotless reputation. There was also a lingering resentment that the WECC had all but abandoned the upper West End to the likes of Miami Purchase and the DSNA, in earlier allowing WEDCO to concentrate exclusively upon Queensgate II. The council's recent attempts to cooperate with Miami Purchase and the DSNA also have been a source of CLC suspicion and anger.

These suspicions, resentments, and rumors aside, relations between the CLC and the WECC have been neither close nor cooperative simply because the CLC has been hesitant to ally itself with *any* organization, private or public:

> I think this goes back to the very beginning. There was that hesitancy, there was that conviction that we can do it alone. If nobody else is going to do it, if the council can't get their act together to do housing for poor folks, then we're going to do it ourselves. (Meehan interview, 1985:315)

Partially, this desire to "do it alone" was due to a justifiable pride in meeting a need for low-income housing that no one else was attempting to meet, and fighting a fight against the forces of gentrification that everyone else, including the WECC, seemed willing to concede. But the CLC had also become excessively preoccupied with internal affairs by 1984 and was giving little attention to external relations with would-be allies. Its preoccupation with internal politics, in other words, diverted the organization from the external politics of organizing the neighborhood, building alliances with other organizations, and confronting common political opponents.

Organizational Development: Straddling Stages of Consciousness

The CLC's internal focus was largely a result of organizational consolidation. As the holdings of the land cooperative expanded, its leaders were forced to devote increasing amounts of time and energy to the technical details of financing, rehabilitating, and providing management support for dozens of housing units. At the same time, the political character of the organization was taking a rather ironic turn. After years of effort to establish a radical approach to domestic property, born and bred in ongoing conflict with the DSNA and Miami Purchase, the organization itself began to exhibit the consciousness and character of a housing improvement association.

More precisely, the CLC became, simultaneously, a radical housing group, a conflict housing group, *and* a housing improvement association. Its founding members, especially those from the ministerial alliance, retained their initial radical housing consciousness. Because of them, the CLC remained committed to a housing model that provides former tenants with many of the material advantages of homeownership while assuring long-term community control over the use and affordability of domestic property. Within the leadership and membership of the CLC, there was also a group who was painfully aware of the threat to the neighborhood's long-time residents posed by the market forces unleashed by the DSNA and Miami Purchase. This faction of the leadership exerted constant pressure on the CLC to expand its holdings of domestic property and to take additional action against historic preservation, gentrification, and those who promote them.

Then there were the resident owners of the CLC. Most were conscious that they share a unique relation to domestic property, one that bestows benefits and burdens that are radically different than those possessed by more "traditional" homeowners and tenants. Most remembered the precariousness of their previous property situations and retained a lingering antagonism toward landlords, developers, and local members of the DSNA and MPA/MPPF. Nevertheless, few exhibited either a radical or conflict housing consciousness. As a group, they were less concerned with the cooperative's ability to promulgate its radical notion of social property, to expand its holdings, or to check the advance of gentrification, than they were with the amenity and autonomy of their own property. The CLC's first president reluctantly acknowledged this political fact:

> The resident owners want to learn how to take care of their buildings.
> . . . They aren't interested in the whole of the co-op. They don't care
> what other buildings we buy. . . . What they really want to know is
> how do I fix up my house? Show me how to use a screwdriver. Show
> me how I can fix light switches and put in my own switches. Show me
> how I can do my winterization. Give me money so I can paint my wall.

That's what they're really into. They're not interested in the other. Now that I've got my house, I'm interested in *my* house. Let those other folks work to get somebody else a house. (Wheeler interview, 1985:220–21)

Simultaneous incorporation of three different levels of political consciousness within the same organization led to periodic dissention in the CLC's internal relations and progressive stagnation in the CLC's external relations. Internal disagreements were numerous and sometimes acrimonious, as the CLC awkwardly tried to accommodate and cope with the radicals' commitment to social property, the confrontationalists' antagonism toward other property interest groups, and the resident owners' suspicion that the CLC board was more concerned with expanding the property and power of the organization than with servicing the property and people already in it. So completely engrossed was the cooperative in these internal controversies that it increasingly neglected most external relations, either conflictual or cooperative, with other property interest groups.

There were signs by 1985, however, that the CLC might soon emerge from its self-imposed isolation. It had hired a part-time outreach worker to do door-to-door organizing in the upper West End. It was sending teams of speakers into neighborhood churches, clubs, and associations to explain the CLC's purposes and plans. It had elected a resident owner to the presidency of the CLC board for the first time, attempting to bridge the gap between the board and the resident owner group. The CLC had also developed over the years an informal "ideology" of property and place that was gradually becoming part of the language and consciousness of the cooperative's members. As with the "ideology" of the DSNA, the cooperative's ideas about domestic property, community, and the West End's problems promoted a shared sense of identity within the CLC, while further differentiating the CLC from its organizational and ideological opponents. All of these signs suggested that the CLC might be moving beyond its preoccupation with internal affairs and was about to resume its interaction with the rest of the neighborhood's interest groups.

LOCALITY-BASED ORGANIZATIONS OF PUBLIC HOUSING TENANTS

Of the three public housing projects in the West End, two include politically active residents councils. The residents council of Lincoln Court has remained a neighborhood improvement association since its inception. The residents council of Laurel Homes, under the leadership of Shirley Colburt, has become a politically conscious conflict group, vigorously defending tenant interests in the face of threats and opposition from the CMHA. Matching the political consciousness and conflict orientation of the Laurel Homes residents council is a third tenant organization, PHACT. Although PHACT is a citywide coalition, its members are organized on a project-by-project basis and are encouraged to act locally, focusing on issues that arise out of a particular project or neighborhood. PHACT has also hired a full-time organizer, herself a resident of Lincoln Court, to organize the public housing tenants of the West End. This locality-based strategy warrants the inclusion of PHACT in any discussion of intergroup relations among the locality-based interest groups of the West End.

It should be noted, however, that neither PHACT nor the residents councils have had a great deal of contact with the neighborhood's other property interest groups. PHACT has received a degree of assistance in its West End organizing efforts from members of the ministerial alliance, many of whom are also involved with the CLC. Nevertheless, PHACT and the CLC, as organizations, have never established formal or informal relations. The Laurel Homes and Lincoln Court residents councils have been formally affiliated with the WECC, and Shirley Colburt has even served as the council's secretary, but this association with the WECC is about the only ongoing interaction, either cooperative or conflictual, that the organizations of the West End's public housing tenants have had with other locality-based organations.

The political attention of public tenants has been focused elsewhere. Nearly all of their intergroup relations have involved formal and informal interaction between the tenants' organizations and the CMHA—or among the tenants' organizations themselves. Nearly all of these relations have been conflictual.

Unlike the neighborhood's other property interest groups, public tenants have continued to devote most of their political energies and resources to defending their property interests against threats originating outside the West End. The efforts of PHACT and the Laurel Homes residents council, in particular, in attempting to organize, educate, and mobilize public housing tenants have been aimed at the CMHA, applying pressure on this public landlord to protect the tenants' security, amenity, and autonomy. Both organizations have recognized the CMHA as the primary threat to tenant interests and the primary target of collective action in defense of those interests. This ongoing conflict with the CMHA has been overt, confrontational, and very hostile.

Intergroup Relations: Lincoln Court Residents Council and PHACT

Two other conflicts have been waged in a far less open way. The first of these is between the Lincoln Court residents council and the local members of PHACT. The leaders and supporters of the Lincoln Court residents council have long recognized a common interest in enhancing the amenity of their housing project. They have acted collectively to make their surroundings somewhat cleaner, safer, and more pleasant. Concentrating exclusively on their housing improvement work, however, they have never acknowledged the precarious, contentious nature of tenant interests in relation to CMHA policies and procedures, nor have they been willing to act as an advocate for those interests.

PHACT, on the other hand, has been a conflict housing group from the very beginning of its West End campaign.[12] It has aggressively confronted the CMHA in the name of public tenants. It has vigorously recruited West End tenants, promising to fight for their threatened interests. It has fostered political consciousness-raising among public tenants, teaching them to perceive threats to their housing interests in terms of CMHA policies, not in terms of rivalries and collisions with their neighbors.[13] As PHACT has built its membership in Lincoln Court, promulgating a new perception of tenant interests and tenant problems, its supporters and supporters of the residents council have found themselves not only in competition, but in contentious dis-

---

12. PHACT was already several years old when it entered the West End around 1982. It began with one-on-one counseling and social work with individual tenants but quickly developed a more collective, confrontational approach vis-à-vis the CMHA. By the time PHACT began organizing in the West End, it was a politically conscious conflict group.

13. Political consciousness-raising of this sort has been one of PHACT's most difficult but most important contributions. As one of PHACT's founders says: "It's very hard for people to build relationships with each other in the projects, because alienation is almost in-built in the system. . . . When you're poor, people are so busy struggling and fighting to meet needs that the person closest to you is your worst enemy. It's like you're fighting so much against each other that you never see the world around you to fight where there's a problem. So, 'Working on Issues and Not Each Other,' was our motto early on, because it was such a hard thing. You didn't have to love your neighbor, but if you work with your neighbor, we can accomplish some things" (Martinez interview, 1985:274–75).

agreement. Peaceful coexistence between a conflict housing group and a neighborhood improvement association is no easy matter, even when the social base and property interests of both organizations are essentially the same.

The Lincoln Court supporters of PHACT have brought to bear increasing pressure on the residents council to ally itself with PHACT in militantly confronting the CMHA. The council's leaders have refused, stubbornly and indignantly resisting every effort to draw them into a conflict in which they have no desire to participate. Needled by the council's refusal to support their struggle, PHACT's supporters in Lincoln Court have come to recognize and criticize the residents council as a thoroughly co-opted toady of the CMHA, people who prefer planting flowers to petitioning for the redress of tenant grievances. Relations between the two organizations have steadily deteriorated to the point that members of PHACT have begun a quiet campaign to seize control of the residents council:

> Q: What is PHACT's current relation with the Lincoln Court residents council?
> A: [Laughter] Well, I won't go into names, but I think it's trying to get off its feet now. A lot of these new people that's working under Lucy Roberts, under PHACT, are getting involved with the tenant council. They're getting all these other people in there. It will be a better council. (Minefield interview, 1985:325)

The conflict between PHACT and the Lincoln Court residents council is based less upon a difference in (objective) property interests than it is upon a difference in the (subjective) perception of what those interests are and how they should be protected. This is not a clash of antagonistic interests, in other words, but a clash of incompatible levels of political consciousness, embodied in two organizations having different political agendas for the same property interest group.

Intergroup Relations: Laurel Homes Residents Council and PHACT

A similar conflict has been brewing between PHACT and the Laurel Homes residents council. There is a difference, however, for these organizations have *identical* political agendas. This is not a clash over property interests, either objectively constituted or subjectively perceived, but a struggle over turf. Two organizations with the same interests, at the same level of political consciousness, and with the same conflict orientation find themselves competing for the allegiance of the same constituency. Relations between PHACT and the Laurel Homes residents council have not reached the degree of antagonism currently evident in Lincoln Court, but there is an undertow of tension and wariness that cannot be ignored.

PHACT and the Laurel Homes residents council are quick to give each other credit for defending tenant interests. Each acknowledges that both want pretty much the same things for their members and that both are equally prepared to fight their common enemy, the CMHA, to get them. Even so, each has complaints about the other. PHACT's supporters bemoan the fact that the residents council's advocacy of tenant interests does not extend beyond Laurel Homes. They complain that the tenant leaders of Laurel Homes are reluctant to act in solidarity with the West End's other public housing residents:

> Shirley Colburt is a darn good president for Laurel Homes. She really fights for her tenants. The only thing I tell her is she thinks Laurel Homes is the only one. That's something me and her talk about all the time. I just say, "When you fight for Laurel Homes, why don't you fight for everybody?" But her main concern is for Laurel Homes. (Minefield interview, 1985:325)

PHACT's West End organizer puts it even more succinctly: "We're fighting for the *whole* community, while Shirley is only fighting for Laurel Homes" (Roberts interview, 1985:273).

Shirley Colburt, for her part, suggests that PHACT has come belatedly to a struggle that the Laurel Homes residents council has been waging for almost ten years. There is a touch of resentment that PHACT would even consider recruiting members from Laurel Homes —a case, in Colburt's mind, of attempting to organize those who are *already* organized:

> Q: Has PHACT organized a chapter in Laurel Homes?
> A: No. PHACT has never been organized in Laurel Homes. Period. You know why? Because with the residents council, there's no need for them. With the people already out there fighting for whatever it was that we needed, we always felt a group like PHACT needed us more than we needed them. We didn't make any qualms about it. There was no need for us to do that again, because we already did that. (Colburt interview, 1985:341)

Despite such private complaints and obvious tension, *public* relations between PHACT and the Laurel Homes residents council have seldom descended to outright criticism or conflict. The leaders of both organizations have displayed remarkable restraint in avoiding public confrontations. This may soon change. As PHACT secures its base in Lincoln Court, its organizers may turn their attention to Laurel Homes, increasing their efforts to build PHACT's membership there. Competing with the residents council for the allegiance of the same constituency, PHACT may find itself locked in a contentious struggle with the council's leaders.

Conflict may also arise in another way. PHACT may be on the brink of a transition to a new level of housing consciousness. Should PHACT actually move beyond a political agenda of defending property interests that tenants already have to one of promoting a significant *expansion* in the tenurial prerogatives of public tenants, the same sort of conflict that currently exists between PHACT and the Lincoln Court residents council may develop between PHACT and the residents council of Laurel Homes.[14] Opposition to the CMHA would undoubtedly continue, but intergroup conflict between PHACT and the Laurel Homes residents council would gradually grow more intense.

IDEOLOGIES OF PROPERTY AND PLACE IN THE CONTESTED COMMUNITY

There exist numerous "empirical conditions" of consciousness and organization that underlie the genesis, development, and conflict of locality-based groups such as those in the West End. The most important of these will be discussed in the next chapter. There is one condition affecting both the level of political consciousness and the degree of political conflict, however, that deserves closer attention. I have previously referred to it as "ideologies" of property and place.

These clusters of ideas define the nature of the neighborhood's problems and prospects. They explain what sort of tenurial and func-

14. Under such circumstances, supporters of the Laurel Homes residents council might accuse PHACT of gratuitously embracing a new set of issues before the former set was fully won. Supporters of PHACT, in turn, might accuse the Laurel Homes residents council of political "conservatism"—attacking the council's leaders for being insufficiently "radical" in failing to win all that they could for public housing tenants. This is all speculation, but these are precisely the kinds of accusations that have characterized the conflict between PHACT and the Lincoln Court residents council, two tenant organizations at different levels of housing consciousness.

tional relation people "ought" to have toward domestic property if the neighborhood is to prosper. They justify a specific course of collective action in solving the neighborhood's problems. Defining, explaining, and justifying a certain "commonsense" approach to property and place, ideologies of this sort play a special role in locality-based conflict. They promote solidarity among all who share this particular perspective. They accentuate the differences among various property interest groups. They clarify the impediment or threat that one group poses for the property interests of another. In short, ideologies of property and place help people to become politically conscious of both the commonality of their interests and the opposition of their interests. They contribute immeasurably to the frequency and intensity of intergroup conflict.

Ideological factors have been most apparent in the ongoing conflict between the DSNA and the CLC, each of which has developed a separate set of explanations and justifications for its particular approach to property and place. Five themes run through the ideologies of each organization. They clash at nearly every point.

Community

The conception of "community" that is articulated by DSNA leaders has less to do with local people than with local buildings. There is a cherished past embodied in the rapidly deteriorating structures of the upper West End. Unless something is done immediately, this structural "community" of aesthetic and historic significance will be irretrievably lost. The DSNA does not entirely ignore people in its conception of community, but it is to a larger network of like-minded preservationists—or to posterity, in general—that the DSNA's members feel themselves socially bonded and morally accountable. Any social community of long-time residents existing within the West End itself is either invisible, alien, or downright obstructionist in the newcomers' eyes.

The "community" of the CLC, by contrast, is conceived exclusively in terms of social interaction and affective bonds among the indigenous population of the West End. Buildings are important, but only as a means of securing a cherished future, where reciprocity and mutual aid are made possible by an abundance of social property. The built environment of the upper West End presents an opportunity to preserve the last remnants of a *social community* ripped apart by urban renewal and threatened with extinction by gentrification, while establishing an *ideal community* of neighborliness and trust. To the extent that the neighborhood's buildings embody the neighborhood's past, they are more likely to be perceived as symbols of oppression or as symbols of a community destroyed than to be treasured as precious artifacts of a golden age of architectural splendor.

Pluralism

Members of the DSNA have their own idea of an "ideal community," one that goes beyond the preservation of the built environment. They seek economic and racial diversity for the upper West End, articulating a shared vision of rich and poor, black and white, tenants and homeowners living side-by-side in perfect harmony and mutual respect. Only with such diversity, moreover, can the neighborhood ever prosper and thrive—or, as the DSNA's first president put it, "To have a good community, we have to have a mix."[15]

At present, the West End is not a "good community," in the eyes of the DSNA, precisely because there is too high a proportion of low-income, black tenants. What is needed, therefore, if this pluralist ideal is to be realized and if the neighborhood is to get "on the move" again is an infusion of upper- and moderate-income homeowners, many of whom should be white. Integration is the key to a prosperous future for all. Anyone who willingly stands in the way of this goal is not only an enemy of progress, but probably a bigot as well.

The leaders of the CLC, many of whom have spent much of their lives combatting racial and economic segregation, find themselves in the ironic position of publicly objecting to the integrationist aims and pluralist ideology of the DSNA. They argue, however, that without a prior commitment to justice, the DSNA's vision of a pluralist future is an unattainable fantasy, at best, or a deliberate obfuscation, at worst. Pluralism is only possible, according to the CLC, when the neighborhood's *least* advantaged groups have enough residential security and political clout to face the neighborhood's *most* advantaged groups on equal terms. Until that minimum level of security and power is attained, any infusion of highly advantaged newcomers must result in the defeat and displacement of less advantaged, long-time residents. Marching into the neighborhood under the banner of diversity, the members of the DSNA will produce a thoroughly gentrified, affluent neighborhood that is eventually devoid of all who are different than themselves.

15. Quoted in the *Cincinnati Enquirer*, March 4, 1979:B1.

Counterposed to the DSNA's vision of the West End as a neighborhood that is more racially and economically mixed, therefore, is the CLC's vision of a neighborhood that is more economically and politically just. Pluralism, harmony, and tolerance are fine ideals, but first comes justice—and the righteous struggle to attain it. Until a more equitable distribution of property and power is achieved, the integration of the neighborhood by affluent, white homeowners will have to wait:

> The Cooperative hopes to . . . give past and present residents of the West End greater control over the future development of their own community. The goal is not to erect barriers that *exclude* newcomers from the property and politics of the West End, but to explore more equitable ways to *include* the poor, the elderly, the young, single-parent families, and the area's long-time residents. (Community Land Cooperative, 1983:3)

The Market

The leaders of the DSNA bristle at the charge that they are personally promoting the displacement of low-income people. At times, they deny that there is any displacement at all, claiming that only *vacant* buildings are being restored. More frequently, they acknowledge that rising rents, rising property values, and the conversion of multi-unit buildings into single-family, owner-occupied housing will displace a number of families. Displacement does occur. *But it is not their fault.* They are not personally responsible. It is the invisible hand of The Market that is causing displacement, not the visible hand of the DSNA. They are merely taking advantage of opportunities created by "natural" forces that cannot be resisted or controlled.

Not only is The Market a neutral, natural force that *cannot* be controlled, it is a fair wind that *should not* be controlled. On the contrary, it should be welcomed with open arms. Part of the West End's problem is that The Market has been stifled. There is too much public housing, too much subsidized housing, and too many groups like the CLC and the MPPF not allowing The Market to operate. If the West End is ever to thrive, the private market in real estate must be revived. The Market, in short, will be the neighborhood's ultimate salvation.

By contrast, the CLC articulates an ideology that is consistently and vehemently antimarket. The problem with the West End, at present, is not too little of a market in real estate, but too much of one. Unless the rising costs of housing are brought under control, thousands of people will be displaced. This means that The Market itself is a problem and a threat—and must be controlled. Anything that disrupts the DSNA's efforts to resuscitate The Market or to improve the neighborhood's investment climate is both politically warranted and morally justified. A radical course of action is especially appropriate, given the present circumstances, one that removes land and housing from "the usual real estate market," one that terminates The Market altogether. Only then can the "good community" be created.

There is another side to the CLC's antimarket ideology. The organization's religious leaders, in particular, espouse an ethic of personal, moral responsibility in the marketplace that categorically rejects the DSNA's reification of The Market. Displacement is not the inevitable result of natural, irreversible market forces, but a consequence of personal choices by individuals who could and should have chosen differently. The market in real estate is, in the end, a "man-made" phenomenon, operating for good or for ill because of the decisions that individuals freely make. It provides a context for moral choice. It does not absolve individual (or collective) actors of culpability.

Homeownership

The leaders of the DSNA profess a fervent faith in the public benefits of private, owner-occupied housing. Homeowners are said to be a more stable population than renters, who are perceived as transients. Owner-occupied property is better maintained than rental property. Homeowners participate more fully in public affairs, working to improve the quality of life for everyone. Renters either stand by and watch or pick up and leave whenever the neighborhood faces a crisis. The "good community," in this view, requires not only a healthy racial and economic "mix," but a high incidence of owner-occupied housing.

What is there about homeownership, as opposed to tenancy, that produces such public benefits? David Hewer's succinct answer is echoed by all of the DSNA's leaders: "Commitment. That's maybe the common thing. We are committed to this neighborhood. Because we own property, we are financially committed" (interview, 1985:181).

There are two aspects to this financial commitment. First, because homeowners want their property to be "worth something," they are motivated to work harder to create the private and public conditions that will protect and enhance their equity. Second, because houses usually take time to sell—particularly if the seller wishes to profit as much as possible—homeowners will stay and fight to make the neighborhood a better place. In short, most of the residential stability, superior maintenance, and public participation attributed to homeownership is a consequence of the interest in equity and liquidity that homeowners have in domestic property. Homeownership is a boon to a neighborhood because homeowners know that sooner or later they must submit their commodity to the financial verdict of The Market.

The CLC, in its literature and pronouncements, raises a similar paean to the public virtures of homeownership. Its ideological emphasis is different, however. Rather then dwell upon the relative stability and public-mindedness of homeowners, the CLC stresses the ability of a newly propertied population to resist displacement and exert political control over the neighborhood's destiny: "Ownership and empowerment go hand-in-hand. The CLC seeks not only to give local residents an ownership interest in their own community, but to draw local residents into a cooperative process of planning and directing the future development of the West End." (Community Land Cooperative, 1983:3). The key to a better neighborhood is not increasing the incidence of homeownership, per se, but increasing the availability of homeownership for disadvantaged populations already a part of the neighborhood. Thus the total number of homeowners in the West End is less important than the number of former tenants who are empowered by becoming homeowners themselves.

Intrinisic to this theme of empowerment is a conception of homeownership that is fundamentally at odds with that of the DSNA. Homeownership, according to the CLC, can be made available to the neighborhood's indigenous population only if it is *de*commodified. Only if equity and liquidity are tightly controlled and only if domestic property is *never* allowed to return to The Market can the public benefits of homeownership be realized. Otherwise, homeownership is a zero-sum game, where the financial gains of those with property are purchased at the expense of higher housing costs for those without. A new kind of ownership is needed, therefore, one which rewards use over exchange and, in limiting the homeowner's interest in exchange, makes the remaining interests of homeownership more available (more affordable) than ever before. What the West End needs, says the CLC, is an expanding supply of "social property"—domestic property without profits; homeownership without winners and losers.

Low-income Housing

The CLC's public stance, in defending residential affordability and promoting property ownership for persons of modest means, is a political message with wide appeal in a neighborhood with as many low-income tenants, public and private, as there are in the West End. This repeatedly proclaimed commitment to low-income housing is, in fact, one of the primary justifications used by the CLC to explain, defend, and promote itself within the neighborhood and to attract support for itself from churches, religious orders, and individuals outside of the neighborhood.

The popular appeal and political usefulness of this message has apparently not been lost on the leaders of the DSNA. On occasion, they too claim to be advocates of low-income housing. It is clear, in fact, that the *idea* of low-income housing has become an important part of the DSNA's public presentation and political defense in a hostile environment. Nowhere is this more obvious than in the candid remarks of the DSNA's vice president:

> Q: If, as you say, one of the purposes of the DSNA is to provide low- and moderate-income housing, what is the difference between what you are trying to do and a group like the CLC—or, for that matter, like the WECC or the MPPF? It seems like everybody is saying our purpose is to provide low- and moderate-income housing, and yet everybody acknowledges that there is a certain amount of friction among these groups. Why the conflict, if everybody has the same goal?
>
> A: That's a good question. I'm not sure what the total answer is. But I have some ideas. I think some of the groups are—they use low-income housing as a platform to say, "Hey, this is what we stand for." (And I make no bones about it, as far as our group is concerned, this is what *we* stand for.) It sounds good and it will be accepted. Nobody's going to kick you around for saying, "I'm for the poor." That's just a springboard to do some other things. (Lundy interview, 1985:109)

After a short digression, he provides a glimpse of these "other things" that the DSNA is doing, as it publicly "stands for" low-income housing:

> I feel that in our particular organization there are some who would rather—they would like to have higher income groups down [here]. I have no problem with that, because I think it's needed. But they may not voice it, because you're just asking for trouble. But every opportunity they get, they're going to try to influence a friend that has a good

job to come down and settle in the West End. Because, basically, we're investors. We want our investment to pay off. And the way it's going to pay off is to get somebody to afford to pay more than we paid. Basically, I mean, that's the American Dream. (Ibid.:109–10)

The Political Effect of Ideologies of Property and Place

When ideologies of property and place fundamentally differ, as they do in the DSNA's and the CLC's conceptions of "community," "pluralism," "The Market," and "homeownership," they set the stage for a politically conscious and publicly rancorous clash of organizational purposes, programs, and ideals. When these ideologies basically agree, as they do in the endorsement of "low-income housing" by both organizations, they set a public standard by which each can accuse the other of ineffectiveness, perfidy, or deceit. In either case, opposing ideologies of property and place tend to intensify intergroup conflict, either igniting or fanning flames of antagonism between organizations with opposing interests.[16]

These ideologies are also politically significant in forging bonds of intergroup cooperation. Political alliances among different locality-based organizations are built not only around similar interests but around similar ideas of property and place. Indeed, since the interests of any two organizations or groups are seldom exactly the same, similarities in ideology can help to bridge the political gap that even small differences in interest might otherwise widen into conflict.

This has been true, for example, in the DSNA's alliance with Miami Purchase. The MPPF subscribes to conceptions of "community," "pluralism," and "homeownership" that are closely akin to those articulated by the DSNA. There are differences, of course, particularly in each organization's ideological commitment to The Market and in its programmatic commitments to low-income housing. But the leaders of the MPPF and the leaders of the DSNA share a perception and appreciation of the West End "community" that is focused primarily upon its physical, historical, and architectural attributes. Similar ideological themes are also sounded in the explanations and justifications of the

16. There is something of a chicken-or-egg problem here. Do ideologies of property and place help to produce political consciousness, thus igniting intergroup conflict? Or does political consciousness produce ideologies of property and place, fanning flames already ignited by the opposition of two politically conscious interest groups? This case study provides no clear answer.

MPPF's director when she speaks of homeownership in terms of "economic incentives," or when she declares: "I'm not against new people coming in that have more money; I like a *mix*; I think that's healthy" (Cramer interview, 1985:198).[17] These shared perceptions, common language, and similar ideas of property and place help the DSNA and the MPPF interact peacefully, cooperatively—despite potentially disruptive disagreements over the role of market-rate housing in the neighborhood's future.

On the other side of the DSNA/CLC divide, the CLC's ideology of property and place has had appeal not only for the neighborhood's unorganized private tenants but for other groups and organizations. Its social conceptions of "community" and "homeownership" have won the CLC a small following in Park Town, where such ideas are firmly embedded in the cooperative's basic structure. These same ideas of the social community and social property, combined with the CLC's commitment to low-income housing, have found a resonance among the religious traditions and justice ministries of the area's churches. Even the neighborhood's long-time homeowners, whose property interests are rather different than those of the CLC's resident owners and tenant members, seem to find the CLC's vision of a social community, economic justice, and empowerment more compelling than the DSNA's image of a cherished architectural past and its hope for a commodified, pluralist future. The CLC's ideology of property and place has helped to extend and to solidify its political support among all these groups.

ONE FUTURE AMONG MANY

By the mid-1980s these ideas and the conflicts surrounding them were beginning to draw all of the neighborhood's interest groups toward either the DSNA or the CLC. The community as a whole was showing signs of dividing into two political camps, each with a very different agenda for the future development of the West End. Even groups like the neighborhood's long-time homeowners and organizations like the MPPF and the WECC, each of whom would prefer to straddle the political fence, were being pulled in one direction or the other. On one

17. Cramer's remarks also illustrate the *divergence* of ideas between the MPPF and the DSNA, because she goes on to say that, while the MPPF does not want to "freeze" out affluent newcomers, neither does it want to "totally change" the social composition of the neighborhood: "I'd like people to have opportunities to stay if they want to."

side was a political commitment to the West End as a historic artifact and marketable commodity, sustained by the economic and racial diversity of its residential population. On the other stood a political commitment to the West End as a social community, sustained by the decommodification of domestic property and the just distribution of economic and political power.

These are ideological extremes, of course, staked out by two highly conscious conflict groups. No other organized (or unorganized) interest group in the West End has become as fully engaged as the DSNA and the CLC in this political struggle, nor has any other group traveled so far toward either political pole.

The political bifurcation of the West End remains, therefore, more an incipient trend than an accomplished fact. And while the future development of the West End may appear to hang in the balance between two opposing sets of organizational and ideological commitments, many things can happen to blur the edges of this dichotomous political picture. Present alliances and alignments, many quite fragile, may not persist. The members of the DSNA may tire of conflict and retreat to the suburbs. The CLC may become more of a housing improvement association instead of regaining its political stride as a housing conflict group. The neighborhood's new property owners, affiliated with the MPPF, may become a potent political force, with a local development agenda of their own. The neighborhood's longtime property owners may reemerge as a separate political entity. Public tenants, whether through the demands of PHACT or through drastic changes in federal policy, may develop a new relation to domestic property, fundamentally changing their political interests and the nature of their political participation in the neighborhood.

In short, the political landscape is littered with organized groups, emerging groups, dormant groups, unstable alliances, evolving ideologies, and volatile conditions of consciousness and organization. Given such complexity, the organizational and ideological bifurcation of the neighborhood's political life may be posed as one *possible* path of political development. It is not the *only* path that the West End—and its multiple property interest groups—may eventually take.

Part III

URBAN THEORY AND PRACTICE

11

Toward a Theory of
Locality-based Action

> At the end of his essay on the 18th Brumaire of Louis Bona-
> parte, Marx is dealing with "the most numerous class of
> French society, the small independent peasants." Marx states,
> to begin with, that these peasants, by virtue of their situation,
> their conditions of existence, their way of life, and their
> (latent) interests, constitute a "class," namely, a quasi-group.
> One would therefore expect a political organization or inter-
> est group to grow out of their midst. However, precisely this
> did not happen.... Under certain conditions, quasi-groups
> may persist as such without interest groups emerging from
> them. What are these conditions, and under which conditions
> do interest groups come to be formed?
> —RALF DAHRENDORF (1959:183)

My general thesis, throughout this work, has been that locality-based
action can be systematically examined and theoretically explained
largely in terms of the differentiation, development, and conflict of
domestic property interest groups. These objectively constituted social
formations, having a material base in the property relations and property interests of the residential urban neighborhood, provide a means
of achieving Tilly's (1974:212) original goal of "a better understanding of the conditions under which collective action on a territorial
basis occurs." They provide a means of explaining group formation
and intergroup conflict within the place of residence.

To confirm this thesis would take many more cases than the single
case presented here. Even so, the West End study does provide a socially complex and empirically challenging first opportunity to evaluate the theoretical framework that has been proposed. It also provides

257

an opportunity to refine that framework, especially with regard to the conditions under which locality-based groups come into being. Closer consideration can now be given to these "empirical conditions of consciousness" and "empirical conditions of organization," while *re*considering the "objective" differentiation of interest groups, the three-stage model of collective action, and the typology of intergroup conflict originally presented in Part I.

THE DIFFERENTIATION OF INTEREST GROUPS

An ideal classification of ten property interest groups, distinguished on the basis of objective differences in tenure, function, and interest, has been tentatively proposed as an accurate representation of major lines of social and political cleavage crisscrossing residentially diverse localities. If people do organize and act collectively on the basis of a common territory, I have argued that they will tend to do so along these structural lines differentiating one property interest group from another. I do not mean to say that local differences in class, race, religion, gender, and ethnicity cannot create social and political cleavages of their own; indeed, group formation and collective action can occur on the basis of any of these important divisions. I do suggest that the interests derived from a population's relation to domestic property will frequently—perhaps usually—provide a better understanding of the differentiation and political orientation of locality-based groups than any comparable set of common interests that these groups might have.

The West End case study has provided considerable support for this thesis. At present, the differentiation of the neighborhood's indigenous population—objectively, organizationally, and ideologically—does appear to have followed the lines laid down by differing interests of domestic property. Earlier, the fragmentation of the West End Community Council occurred along the political fault lines dividing one property interest group from another. Earlier still, when the neighborhood was built and bulldozed by private capital, these capitalist interest groups tended to form and act according to each group's particular interests in the West End's domestic property. In each period, the major lines of social and political cleavage have been pretty much what the ideal classification of property interest groups predicted.[1]

---

1. There is one actor in the West End drama that does *not* fit comfortably into my ideal classification of interest groups—namely, the Cincinnati Metropolitan Housing

Even when West End groups have put aside their differences and organized and acted in the name of racial or neighborhood solidarity, interests of property have not disappeared. They have merely over-lapped with those of race and place. This was certainly true in the 1920s, when racial improvement associations and neighborhood im-provement associations flourished side-by-side both in the black com-munity of the lower West End and the white community of the upper West End. This was true, as well, in the neighborhood politics of the West End Community Council during the 1960s and 1970s. The grievances and interests of a black community, mobilized in response to two hundred years of racial oppression, overlapped with the griev-ances and interests of a residential community, mobilized in response to thirty years of urban renewal. Differences among the various prop-erty interest groups that made up this "mobilized community" were temporarily bridged and obscured; they were not eliminated.

Overlapping issues and interests like these do suggest, however, that an important qualification must be added. Other issues, other interests, and other goals will sometimes supplement or supplant those of domestic property in the lived experience of local popula-tions. As Dahrendorf (1959:182) has warned, in the context of his own theoretical framework:

> While quasi-groups, being in the nature of a theoretical construction, are unequivocally defined, organized interest groups may supplement the interests accruing from authority structures by a multitude of other and independent goals and orientations. This is merely another expres-sion for the fact that interest groups are "real phenomena," and that like all such phenomena, they cannot be completely described by one attribute.

If "domestic property positions" are substituted for "authority structures," Dahrendorf's caveat can be applied to the theoretical framework that is being developed here. It is well to remember, in other words, that my objective classification of ten property interest groups is a "theoretical construction," built upon a single "attribute." Even when groups form and act on the basis of their particular prop-

---

Authority (CMHA). I have treated this municipal corporation, like other agencies of the city, state, or federal government, as part of the "encapsulating social structure" within which neighborhood groups form and act. While this approach may suffice for now, it is not one that I find completely satisfactory. More theoretical work is clearly needed to relate the kind of neighborhood-level analysis proposed here to more macro theories of urban development and urban government. A tentative step in this direc-tion is taken in the next chapter.

erty positions, they may also have a "multitude of other and independent goals and orientations."

These multiple "orientations" occur not only because people who occupy a particular property position are also members of a particular class, race, and religion, but because some people occupy *several* property positions at once. This is the case, for example, in the Dayton Street Neighborhood Association, where all of the officers straddle lines differentiating owner-occupiers, landlords, developers, and speculators. Some of them occupy all four positions, blurring the boundaries that my classification of interest groups has attempted to establish. When an officer of the DSNA acts in conjunction with his colleagues to improve the investment climate of the West End, he is clearly acting to enhance the equity and liquidity of his property, but is he acting as an acquisitive homeowner, an indigenous landlord, or what? My ideal classification of interest groups becomes a bit strained when faced with such complications, even though the property *interests* that underlie that classification retain most of their explanatory power.

The West End case study also reveals how problematic can be the classificatory line that has been drawn between the owner-occupiers of household property and the owner-occupiers of acquisitive property. The problem is this: despite the fact that these two groups behave politically in very different ways, they are materially advantaged in the same way; that is, each possesses the same set of entrepreneurial property interests. This raises the question of whether the six interests that have been proposed are specific enough to differentiate, objectively and materially, two locality-based groups that have differentiated themselves, subjectively and politically, in their collective actions and organizational programs.

The answer suggested by the discussion that surrounded the original presentation of these interest-group categories is that the advantages derived from one's relation to domestic property have *both* a tenurial and functional dimension. In the present case, household homeowners and acquisitive homeowners both possess the same material advantages in "owning" their homes, but they *use* their property in different ways; that is, their functional relation to domestic property is different. Obviously, since both groups are owner-occupiers, they both use their property for shelter. The acquisitive homeowners, however, also use domestic property for financial gain. This gives a political primacy to equity and liquidity that is lacking among the household homeowners. Group formation and collective action among the acquisitive homeowners tend to be engendered more by threats to erode or opportunities to enhance the equity or liquidity of their property. Group formation and collective action among the household homeowners is seldom organized around such accumulative interests; security, amenity, and autonomy are given political primacy. In short, because of the different functional relation that each group bears to domestic property, it can be said that their entrepreneurial interests may be the same, but their strategic interests are not.

The case study suggests that these differences are very real. The interests and actions of the acquisitive homeowners of the DSNA are *not* the same as the interests and actions of the household homeowners who have lived in the neighborhood most of their lives. For the former, the property they own and the place they live are as much a commodity as they are a home. For the latter, property and place function principally—even exclusively—as home and community, not as a source of financial gain.

Still, it must be acknowledged that the line dividing these two interest groups is not as definite as my "ideal" classification would suggest. It is not as clear-cut, for example, as the tenurial line dividing the resident owners of the CLC from the other homeowners, or the functional line dividing landlords from owner-occupiers. Of all the distinctions that have been theoretically drawn between the various property interest groups, the boundary between the owner-occupiers of household property and the owner-occupiers of acquisitive property is certainly the most permeable, the most blurred. The case study of the West End has provided evidence that the boundary is there, but it is obvious that much more research must still be done before we can determine the structural and demographic specifics of where that boundary falls, who is found on either side, and why.[2]

THE GENESIS AND DEVELOPMENT OF COLLECTIVE ACTION

A three-stage model of collective action has been proposed as a means of systematically analyzing the formation and development of locality-based interest groups. While the question of whether this model can explain group formation and collective action among the interest groups of private capital remains unanswered, since the West End

2. Two lines of investigation may prove particularly fruitful. Within the West End, elderly homeowners and women homeowners have tended to be less "interested" in the accumulative potential of their homes than those who are middle-aged or male. Age and gender, in other words, may prove to be key factors in differentiating homeowner groups.

case study provided only historical profiles of these capitalist groups, a wealth of material was presented regarding group formation and collective action among the neighborhood's residential population. This evidence suggests that the model at hand, with some modification, may provide enough insight into the social variables that constitute and cause locality-based action to provide a fresh understanding of why such action does or does not occur at any particular time.

The development (or decline) of most of the neighborhood's interest groups has occurred within the model's "lower" stages: either as transitions between a quasi-group and an improvement group or as transitions between an improvement group and a conflict group. For example, the public tenants of Laurel Homes collectively organized and acted first as a housing improvement association and developed later into a conflict housing group. The "acquisitive" homeowners of the DSNA followed a similar progression. Park Town's residents and the neighborhood's long-time "household" homeowners, by contrast, developed active neighborhood improvement groups, contributed their support to the conflict-oriented program of the WECC, and then reversed developmental direction. Park Town's residents association turned inward, returning to an earlier organizational focus on maintaining and improving the property and place of Park Town alone (although individual residents *have* lent their support to the CLC). The neighborhood's household homeowners gradually abandoned the WECC, neglected their former block clubs, and lapsed, at last, into a quasi-group instead of an organized interest group (although some of them, too, have actively supported the CLC).

While each of these cases fits comfortably into the theoretical framework that has been proposed, it is the rise and fall of the WECC that most closely conforms to the model's three stages of locality-based action. The council formed and functioned in the 1950s and early 1960s as a neighborhood improvement association. It became a conflict group in the mid-1960s. By the start of the next decade, with the establishment of the West End Development Corporation and other locally controlled planning and service affiliates, the WECC had laid the foundation for becoming a radical housing group.

The direction of the council's development was then reversed, beginning in the mid-1970s. As its organizational affiliates and constituent interest groups began to pull away, as its membership declined, and as its former leaders moved on to other things, the WECC lost its impetus and began to founder. It returned to its earlier conflict orientation for a brief period in the early 1980s under Roger Bradley's leadership but then lapsed into organizational chaos. The latest chapter in the council's history brings the development of this locality-based organization full circle. With the help of city officials, the current leaders of the WECC are working (so far, unsuccessfully) to reestablish the council as a neighborhood improvement association, containing all of the West End's interest groups.

The evidence suggests, then, that a three-stage pattern of progression—or regression—has marked the development not only of individual property interest groups but of interest-group clusters like the West End Community Council. The model before us would seem to be a reasonably accurate description of the formation and development of these locality-based groups. If we are to move beyond the descriptive to the explanatory, however, some refinement in the model is necessary. If we are truly to account for the "comings and goings" of the organized groups of the homeplace, in other words, we must know more about the "empirical conditions" of consciousness and organization that make such locality-based action a reality.

The three-stage model of collective action assumes that domestic property interest groups will form, act, and develop if these empirical conditions are present; groups will fail to form, fail to act, or reverse the direction of their development if these conditions are absent or later withdrawn. The time has come to look more closely at the most significant of these conditions, drawing upon both the West End case study and the research of others to refine the proposed model of locality-based action.

Empirical Conditions of Housing Consciousness

The fundamental problem in explaining the genesis and development of political consciousness is, according to Issac Balbus (1971: 171), "the systematic specification of variables which determine the conversion of latent interests to manifest interests and quasi-groups to interest groups, i.e., variables which determine the conditions under which individuals whose life-chances are similarly affected by similar objective conditions will become aware of their common interest and unite to defend it." Balbus is referring here to the two-stage formation of "classes" (in the Marxist sense), not to the formation and three-stage development of domestic property interest groups. Nevertheless, the central role that he assigns to "variables which determine the conversion of latent interests to manifest interests" is just as relevant to the analysis of housing consciousness as it is to the analysis of class consciousness.

Three conversion variables appear to be particularly significant in engendering housing consciousness: the instability of domestic property interests, the interaction of one property interest group with another, and ideologies of property and place that consolidate group identity. The genesis and development of housing consciousness will depend, in large measure, on the presence of these conditions. Conversely, the stability of property interests, the isolation of a group from other property interest groups, or the presence of ideologies that confuse group identity or obscure what Weber called the "transparency of the connections between the causes and consequences" of one's property position will tend to undermine, retard, or prevent housing consciousness.

The stability of one's tenurial and functional relation to domestic property, accompanied by the stability of the advantages intrinsic to that position, fosters the illusion that one's stake in domestic property is a private, autonomous affair. As Marx (1972a:41) observed, capitalist society imposes and enforces a practical isolation on individuals, such that "an individual [is] separated from the community, withdrawn into himself, wholly preoccupied with his private interest and acting in accord with his private caprice." Consequently, one is encouraged "to enjoy one's fortune and to dispose of it as one will, without regard for other men and independently of society" (ibid.: 40). The stability of one's property position and property interests reinforces this atomizing tendency of capitalist society. As long as one's own control over domestic property is certain and as long as the advantages that one expects to derive from that tenurial relation are stable and secure, one can enjoy property "without regard for other men," believing that those advantages exist "independently of society."

Instability shatters this solipsistic illusion. Uncertainty of tenure, changes in land use and building function, fluctuations in the security, amenity, autonomy, legacy, liquidity, or equity that one expected to enjoy in holding a stake in domestic property—all are threats to individual well-being; all make manifest the precarious dependency of one's interests on "society" and on "other men." Experiencing such instability, recognizing or anticipating threats to their own well-being, individuals are awakened to the objective, relational interests that are theirs; they are made aware of the social and locational "connections" that link their fates together. As Schmalenbach (1961:334) observed, people tend to take their "communities" for granted—until they are jolted by a destabilizing disturbance: "One is usually not fully aware of [those communities to which one belongs]. They are given. They simply exist. . . . Only through contrasts and disturbances does a community become an object of attention for its members." I would argue that this is especially true for the "communities" of interest that exist on the basis of property and place. Instability will often engender housing consciousness.

The case study has demonstrated, time and again, that this is so.[3] Threatened interests—or opportunities to benefit from fluctuating interests—have repeatedly sparked consciousness into becoming the "engine" of group formation and interest group development. The deteriorating health and housing of the West End and the economic insecurity of its residents gave rise to a "passion for organizational affiliation" (Miller, 1972:61) in the 1920s, resulting in numerous neighborhood improvement groups. The CMHA's proposal to demolish blocks D and E, in the 1930s, prompted the formation of the West End Property Owners Association. Twice, in the late 1950s and in the mid-1960s, the city's efforts to raze parts of Liberty-Dalton resulted in the political mobilization of much of the West End's population. Throughout the 1960s, in fact, the continuing threat of urban renewal was to stimulate and sustain the organization of numerous block clubs, as well as the development of the WECC. Meanwhile, public tenants were experiencing instability of their own, as federal cutbacks hastened the decline of their residential security and amenity. The Laurel Homes residents council developed into a conflict housing group in response to this threat, and PHACT's membership soared. In the 1980s the threat of gentrification pushed many long-time home-

3. Added to the evidence of the West End is a great deal of research in other localities documenting the importance of "instability," "uncertainty," and "threats" in promoting consciousness and solidarity among property interest groups. Thus Gray (1982:280) contends that "housing struggles typically only take place when . . . people experience a real threat to their material housing conditions." Cox and McCarthy (1982:196–97) conclude that neighborhood activism is a response to "some threat to the neighborhood in which activists live"—a response to "a serious disturbance in the use values enjoyed by labor in the living place." In an earlier article (1980:26), they noted that "a good deal of resident activism is anticipatory . . . called into being in the expectation of some future threat." Tilly (1974:219) suggests that "communities act" only when tenurial control over land is insecure and property values are rising. Blum and Kingston (1984:175) suggest that perceived "threats" to "the material incentives that accompany homeownership" may explain the social interaction and political activism of owner-occupiers, who "share an important economic fate with their neighbors." See Agnew (1978:133) and Ineichen (1972:411), as well. They explain homeowner activism in terms of "threatened" property values.

owners and private tenants into the ranks of the CLC, while the threatened loss of historic structures (combined with the opportunity to profit from fluctuating property values) engendered and sustained the DSNA. Political consciousness, in every case, has been sown and nurtured in the soil of instability.

Consciousness of common—and contentious—interests can also be awakened by the interaction of one property interest group with another, particularly if there is overt conflict between the members of these groups. There is no "disturbance" quite like conflict with another group for making individuals aware of the collective, contentious character of their interests.[4] In addition to awakening political consciousness, interaction can lead to the development of consciousness. Interaction between property interest groups that have attained different *levels* of housing consciousness can spur the consciousness of the less developed group into "catching up" with that of the more developed group. This should be especially true where the relations between such groups are antagonistic, although it can occur between compatible groups as well.

Thus, in the West End, the interaction of the founders of the CLC with both the preservationists of the MPA and the acquisitive homeowners of the DSNA helped to provoke the initial formation of the CLC. Later, the opposition of the CLC to the activities of the MPA and the DSNA helped to spur the development of these latter groups: the MPA moved to organize a housing improvement association of its own among the residents of its rehabilitated properties; the DSNA began increasingly to act like a conflict group.

Beyond the effects of instability and interaction, housing consciousness is partially a consequence of current ideologies that explain and justify the kinds of relations that people "properly" have to property and place—and "properly" have with one another *because* of that relation to property and place. Rose, Saunders, Newby, and Bell (1976:700) have described this ideological element well in noting the presence of various "justificatory theories" surrounding the ownership of agricultural land in Britian:

---

4. Conflict provokes a recognition of common interests and a commitment to common purposes in the face of an "enemy" with different interests. This effect is described well by Boulding (1962:162): "A strong enemy . . . is a great unifying force; in the face of a common threat and the overriding common purpose of victory or survival, the diverse ends and conflicting interests of the population fall into the background and are swallowed up into the single, measurable, overriding end of winning the conflict."

[W]hen we speak of the "ideology of landownership" we are referring to those ideas espoused by and for land-owners which seek to explain and justify the economic and political advantages which landownership commands. This need not imply that such an ideology is necessarily consciously evolved as a means of justifying a privileged position. Rather, it is likely that landowners will be in a position to dip into a coherent repertoire of ready-made justificatory statements embedded within a "sub-universe of meaning" on the rare occasions when they are called upon to do so.

Ideas that "explain and justify the economic and political advantages" that people command by virtue of their different property positions are not the domain of landowners alone. Every property interest group may develop a set of ideas and beliefs that (1) define the advantages that are "rightfully" theirs as a result of their particular relation to domestic property, (2) justify the particular uses to which their property is put, and (3) explain the nature of the particular threats that make their interests so precarious and contentious. Since domestic property is inextricably situated within a particular locality, ideologies of property tend to extend to "place" as well: legitimizing the different accommodative or accumulative uses to which the "communal living space" is put by different property interest groups; explaining the causes of neighborhood problems; and justifying particular courses of action in solving those problems.

Ideologies of property and place, such as those articulated by the CLC and the DSNA, are part of what Weber described as "general cultural conditions, especially . . . those of an intellectual sort" that are capable of fostering the "transparency" of one's material situation—engendering, thereby, collective action that is "oriented to a rationally motivated adjustment of interests" (Gerth and Mills, 1958: 183–84). These ideas and beliefs tend to reveal the character and "connections" of one's property position. They tend to accentuate the commonality and contrast of property interests, within and between different domestic property positions. They help to promote both collective consciousness and conflict consciousness.[5]

5. Despite their contribution to interest group identity, ideologies of property and place can also function to retard the development of consciousness. This is, in fact, the more familiar role that an "ideology" is thought to play: obscuring the interests and connections of structural positions, not making them more "transparent"; masking the contrasts and blunting the antagonisms between interest groups, not making them more apparent. The obscuring, masking function of ideologies of property and place, as well as their awakening, unifying function, will be examined more closely in the next chapter.

Instability, interaction, and ideology are the primary empirical conditions of consciousness, promoting—or, in their absence, preventing—the "conversion" of the latent interests of property positions into the manifest interests of property groups. As such, these three conditions underlie the genesis of *both* collective consciousness and conflict consciousness. These first two levels of housing consciousness differ in degree, not in kind. Conflict consciousness is merely a deepening and clarification of the cognizance of common interests and relational connections that collective consciousness has already achieved.[6]

This is not the case for the third level of housing consciousness. The conditions underlying the genesis of radical consciousness are somewhat different than those involved in the formation of collective and conflict consciousness (cf. Giddens, 1973:113). Instability, interaction, and ideology play a part, but they will usually *not* be sufficient to awaken radical consciousness. Three additional conditions appear to be necessary: (1) the upward mobility of the "least advantaged" interest groups on the "tenure ladder" must be no longer possible or credible; (2) a counter-ideology must be available to explain and justify an overall reorganization in the institutional mediation of property; and (3) actual conflict between organized interest groups must have continued for a long time.

Mobility is an impediment to housing consciousness, a fact recognized since the earliest attempts to explain housing struggles in terms of "housing classes." Thus, as John Rex (1968:216) was to observe, to the extent that mobility is "credible," "disadvantaged groups come to see the position of the privileged as legitimate and the system of class conflict tends to be transformed into a status system. Potentially class conscious attitudes amongst the housing classes may therefore be blurred." The homeless seek to become tenants; public tenants seek to become private tenants; tenants of all kinds seek to become homeowners; and homeowners strive constantly for "better" housing in "better" neighborhoods, while seeking to convert their holdings into financial gain as assiduously as the most avaricious speculator. To the extent that mobility to the next rung of the tenure ladder is a realistic—or, at least, a *believable*—prospect, there is little incentive

6. Giddens (1973:112) has described the connection between these two levels of consciousness as a "maieutic" one, borrowing a term derived from the Greek word for "midwife." The term refers to the Socratic method of helping a person to become fully aware of ideas or memories that he or she already possesses in an underdeveloped or unarticulated form.

for "disadvantaged" interest groups to embrace radical housing goals. Collective consciousness or conflict consciousness *can* develop in the face of mobility, because people have a strategic interest in making the most of what is already theirs and in turning aside any threats to their position. *Radical* consciousness cannot develop, however, because the prospect of transcending one's current property situation makes the possibility of transforming the entire institution of property seem unnecessary and unwise. Property institutions that are preceived to be "working" are believed to require no major overhaul.

The most important component of this "working" system in the United States has been the popular aspiration and national goal of homeownership for every citizen who is willing to wait and work for it. Whenever this kind of mobility becomes unrealistic or unbelievable, however, more people become willing to question the legitimacy of existing property relations and to consider alternative tenurial and functional arrangements. "Radical" consciousness may be the result, arising out of the growing realization that an "entitlement" has been taken away. The radical potential of such a realization is implicit in Stone's (1980:95) provocative question: "Homeownership became a symbol of status and almost a civil right for anyone who saved up for the downpayment. Homeownership was also considered a hedge against inflation and a way to accumulate wealth. Having created the expectation, fostered the hope, and promoted the dream, what would be the consequences if capitalism could no longer deliver the goods?"

Radical consciousness becomes even more likely if, at the same time that people are becoming convinced that the current system of property relations is no longer "delivering the goods," an interest group discovers or develops a new conception of property and place—that is, an alternative system of ideas, beliefs, and expectations that explain and justify a new set of tenurial and functional relations. This counter-ideology says what is "wrong" with the institutional arrangements under which people currently control and use domestic property. Furthermore, it says what kinds of control people *ought* to exercise, and what new functions property *ought* to serve.[7] What currently exists is stripped of legitimacy; what might exist is portrayed as possible, necessary, and urgent. A counter-ideology is an endorsement—

7. Moorhouse and Chamberlain (1974:387) speak of a "counter-ideology" in terms of "attitudes 'deviant' to dominant values concerning the ownership and rights of property." The formulation that I am suggesting goes further than this. A counter-ideology does not merely deviate from a dominant justificatory scheme, it opposes that scheme, providing both a critique of present property relations and a vision of a more

and a blueprint—for the radical restructuring of domestic property relations. It is an essential ingredient in awakening and maintaining radical housing consciousness.

Counter-ideologies played a crucial role in furthering the radical housing programs of both the WECC and the CLC. Ideas of "black power" and "community control," woven into the WECC's collective consciousness and common goals by Mallory, Lewis, and others during the 1960s, helped to transform the council from a conflict housing group into a radical housing group. Similarly, ideas of "common ownership," "social justice," and "social property," rooted in the religious traditions of the CLC's founders, helped to create the fertile ground into which the "radical" proposal for a community land trust was planted and from out of which the CLC was to grow. Radical consciousness, in other words, for both the WECC and the CLC, was partially a product of counter-ideologies of property and place.

Finally, the case study suggests that the genesis of radical consciousness depends upon *sustained* conflict between property interest groups. This is not merely "interaction," but a rancorous struggle for power, dominance, and material resources, with one group defending or promoting its property interests to the detriment of another's. Sustained conflict tends eventually to engender a recognition of the need to reorganize the domestic property relations on which this conflict is based.[8] Such a radical perception occurs because (1) one of the combatants realizes that transforming the institutional mediation of property will undermine the political position of its opposition; (2) one of the combatants recognizes the need to consolidate and institutionalize whatever gains have been won by months (or years) of struggle; or (3)

"just," "moral," and/or "effective" alternative. Susan and Norman Fainstein (1985:5) come closer to this notion in positing, as one "cause" of urban social movements, "alternative political ideas which can create an oppositional consciousness among a significant sector of the citizenry."

8. To suggest that radical housing consciousness—and, by extension, a radical housing group—is politically constituted by sustained conflict is to echo E. P. Thompson's (1978:149) contention that the "highest" stage of political consciousness and political organization is a *later* product of political struggle. Thus: "Classes do not exist as separate entities, look around, find an enemy class and then start to struggle. On the contrary, people find themselves in a society structured in determined ways. . . . They experience exploitation. . . . They identify points of antagonistic interest, they commence to struggle around these issues and in the process of struggling they discover themselves as classes, they come to know this discovery as class consciousness." In a similar vein, Sabia (1988:62) has argued that Marx himself believed that class solidarity and class revolution would emerge only after workers' interactions and struggles "at places of work, residence, and recreation" had deepened "their sense of common identity and of sharing a common fate."

political and economic elites have been moved to propose a restructuring of local property relations as a means of purchasing social peace, after a period of local conflict.

The time element seems especially important here. Conflict must have continued long enough for a warring group to have exhausted many of its other strategic options for overcoming its opponent(s), long enough for there to be gains in need of consolidating, or long enough for a local conflict to become an object of concern for political and economic elites. The West End provides two examples. The West End Community Council's bid to institutionalize "community control" of property development and social services occurred after years of sustained conflict with extralocal elites had achieved only limited success in halting the destruction and exploitation of the neighborhood. This "radical" approach was proposed by Mallory as a means of protecting the gains of the West End Task Force, gains that had been wrested from a power structure tired of fighting the WECC. Similarly, the decision by founders of the Community Land Cooperative to institutionalize a new form of social property in the West End came after years of struggle by these experienced activists to promote civil rights, prevent displacement, and preserve the neighborhood. After years of conflict, there was recognition that a more "radical" approach was required if the neighborhood's housing problems were to be adequately addressed.

As necessary as these empirical conditions of consciousness might be in providing the impetus for the formation and development of property interest groups, these conditions do not, by themselves, explain the appearance of some groups and the absence or disappearance of others. (Note, for example, that instability of property interests during the early days of urban renewal did *not* provoke the kinds of collective action that later appeared in the 1960s.) Consciousness must be complemented by organization. Extending the metaphor that was used before, the "engine" of consciousness must be fueled by empirical conditions of organization. Without this "fuel," organized groups either never get started, idle in place after reaching one plateau or another, or roll back down the developmental slope.

Empirical Conditions of Organization

The place of residence was described earlier as a "recruiting field for groups," a site where tenurial and functional relations of domestic property differentiate a number of "quasi-groups," each having a characteristic set of domestic property interests. If the individuals who belong to these quasi-groups become conscious of their common interests, organized groups may emerge. Then again, they may not, for there are social, political, and technical conditions that intervene in this process of group formation. Domestic property interest groups do not form—or, if they do, they do not develop or last—unless these empirical conditions of organization are present. Let us consider the most important of them.[9]

Social conditions of organization   The proposition that various "social conditions" facilitate the formation and maintenance of groups has a long sociological pedigree, dating back to the work of both Marx and Weber. Marx, for instance, attributed the failure of the French peasantry to organize itself into a class to the extreme isolation in which peasants were forced to live and work, an isolation that was "increased by France's bad means of communication" in the early nineteenth century (Marx, 1972c:515). In a similar vein, Weber was to note that "class-conscious organization succeeds most easily" when large numbers of people in the same situation are concentrated in the same place, "as in a 'workshop community'" (Roth and Wittich, 1978:305).

The observations of Tilly and Logan should be added, as well, for they speak specifically to group formation on the basis of territory. Thus Tilly (1974:219) claims that "communities act" when they are "homogeneous with respect to the main divisions of power at the regional or national level," a homogeneity that is often "a by-product of segregation by occupation, race, religion, or something else." Logan (1978:410) claims that

> movements [of place] are strengthened by the normal overlap of stratification of place with the geographic segregation of persons by class and status. . . . Place may so overlap with class and status (race, religion, culture, language) that it may provide an ecological support for organization as well as a symbolic sense of community, at the same time as being itself an objective basis for common action.

9. Dahrendorf's description of "empirical conditions of conflict group formation" (1959:182–89) provides a general framework for the present discussion. Nevertheless, much of what is included here under "social," "political," and "technical" conditions of organization is drawn from other sources, including the West End case study. It should be noted, moreover, that these conditions are presumed to underlie the formation and maintenance not only of "conflict groups," but of all *three* "levels" of interest-group development that are posited by the present model of locality-based action.

Social conditions of organization, therefore, are a matter of both proximity and homogeneity. Whatever closes the physical and social distance that separates similarly situated individuals will make it easier for them to form a group. Thus, in the West End, as urban renewal took larger bites out of the neighborhood, concentrating those who remained into a smaller area, and as whites and affluent blacks took leave of the neighborhood in larger numbers, the West End's population gradually drew closer together: spatially, racially, and economically. This was to make political organization easier to achieve from the early 1960s to the present.

A third social condition was suggested by the West End case study: the spatial *"fixity"* of a population. Individuals who have occupied the same property position, lived in the same place, and interacted with the same collection of people over a long period of time—and who have every reason to expect such place-bound interactions to continue long into the future—are far easier to organize than those who have recently arrived or will soon depart. The relatively "fixed" population of Laurel Homes, for instance, may partially account for the success that activists have had in sustaining an interest group organization among these public tenants; conversely, the relative transience of the neighborhood's private tenants has helped to make them a very difficult population to organize.

Fixity is also relevant to consciousness, since the recognition of common property interests is almost certainly affected by the length of time that one has had those interests. Furthermore, the disruption of fixity—for example, the threatened displacement of a stable population—can push consciousness toward "conflict" or even "radical" stages of awareness. I include fixity among the empirical conditions of *organization*, however, because group formation and group maintenance in residential neighborhoods is so crucially dependent upon a population's relatively permanent, predictable presence in a particular place. Transient populations are not easily transformed into organized interest groups.

Political conditions of organization Interest groups cannot form —or do so only with great difficulty—under conditions of active repression, disruption, or manipulation by political and economic elites. A climate of political permissibility is crucial for groups to form—and for locality-based groups like the ones in the West End to survive.

It is not necessary, however, to go to repressive extremes to create inhospitable political conditions for group formation. Indeed, at the neighborhood level, the organization of property interest groups is likely to be inhibited less by the repressive actions of political and economic elites, enforcing organizational scarcity, than by the competitive actions of other locality-based groups, representing an organizational *surfeit*. A neighborhood with a multitude of organized groups may so exhaust the locality's limited pool of volunteers, leaders, and financial support that the formation and sustenance of property interest groups (or a "cluster" of such groups) becomes extremely difficult, if not impossible. This certainly contributed to the decline of the WECC. The council experienced a gradual depletion in its leadership caused, in part, by the proliferation of public advisory groups, created through the War on Poverty, and of organizational spinoffs from the council itself.

Technical conditions of organization   Dahrendorf, drawing upon Malinowski's analysis of institutional prerequisites, lists four "technical conditions of organization." In Malinowski's formulation: "Without a charter, certain norms, a personnel, and certain material requisites, interest groups cannot be formed, even if it is justified to assume that quasi-groups exist" (Dahrendorf, 1959:185).

Regarding "norms" and "material requisites," very little explanation is required. An organization clearly requires some sort of normative structure, whether embodied in formal bylaws, policies, and procedures or in informal patterns of behavior that establish stable standards for incorporating new members, appointing leaders, and making group decisions. Likewise, an organization clearly requires some sort of material support—money, land, buildings, vehicles—the level and nature of which depend on the group's size, goals, and activities. Without an internal structure and without material resources, an interest group can neither come into being nor be sustained.

"Personnel" refers, in the most general sense, to the people who constitute an interest group. Obviously, a group must have members. On the other hand, an unorganized collectivity has "members" as well, so it is not merely the presence of people that fosters group formation. Personnel refers to a specific kind of people, those who make up the leadership of an organization: "It is, indeed, not the total membership of an interest group which is in question here, but that sector of the membership which can be described as the leading group or cadre. For an organized interest group to emerge from a quasi-group, there have to be certain persons who make this organization their business, who carry it out practically and take the lead" (ibid.).

The availability of organizers, founders, and leaders is a technical prerequisite for the organization, development, and maintenance of property interest groups. A collectivity must discover potential leaders if it is to *organize* as an interest group, something that the West End's private tenants, for example, have never been able to do. An interest group must develop new leaders and retain experienced leaders if it is to *survive* as an organization, something that the wecc, for example, did very well during the 1960s, but has done very poorly ever since.

Of all the technical conditions of organization underlying the genesis and development of locality-based collective action, the West End case study has suggested that leadership may be among the most important. Unfortunately, it is also the organizational condition that is the most theoretically elusive and empirically unpredictable. Consider a single example, the contrast in organizational development between the residents councils of Laurel Homes and Lincoln Court. The populations from which these organized groups draw their members are demographically identical. The objective interests of these populations are the same, as are the threats to their interests emanating from Washington or the cmha. The same array of social, political, and technical conditions permit, promote, and sustain both organizations—with one difference. The leadership of the Laurel Homes council is politically conscious and organizationally sophisticated in a way that the leadership of the Lincoln Court council is not. As a result, the former has functioned for nearly ten years as a conflict group, while the latter has remained a poorly organized improvement group. The centrality of leadership, in differentiating the development and effectiveness of these two locality-based groups, should be obvious. But how is one to explain the appearance of a Shirley Colburt in Laurel Homes, but not in Lincoln Court? Similarly, how does one explain the appearance and influence of a William Mallory, a Richard Lewis, a Jerry Bates, or a Maurice McCrackin in spurring the development of organizations like the wecc, wedco, the dsna, or the CLC? These are questions for which the present model of locality-based action cannot provide an answer, even if it *does* posit leadership as a technical prerequisite of organization.[10]

Finally, there is what Malinowski referred to as the "charter" of an

10. The answer obviously lies outside of the model, in the fact that people have interests, affiliations, ideas, and life experiences other than those that emanate out of their relation to domestic property. Social phenomena can seldom be completely described or explained by one attribute.

organization, "the system of values for the pursuit of which human beings organize" (ibid.). This is where consciousness and organization become practically indistinguishable, however, for the charter of an organized interest group consists of those "manifest interests" that are articulated and codified as the organization's purposes, its mission, its goals. Should the consciousness of the organization's members—or, more crucially, the consciousness of the organization's leaders—change or develop, so too will the raison d'être of the organization itself.[11] Because this charter gives coherence and direction to the organization's programs and activities, any change in consciousness will also change the character of the action that an interest group is prepared to undertake. Keeping in mind the other empirical conditions of organization, it can thus be said, somewhat simplistically, that without consciousness, there is no charter; without a charter, there is no organization; without an organization, there is no collective action; and when consciousness changes, so too will the organization and collective action of a domestic property interest group.

Empirical Anomalies

The West End case study has generally supported both the plausibility and worth of the locality-based model of collective action proposed in Part I, while allowing us to refine that model through the specification of empirical conditions of consciousness and organization. At the same time, however, the case study has revealed a couple of unexpected, unexplained anomalies that do not easily fit into the present theoretical framework. These should be acknowledged before we reexamine the typology of intergroup conflict.

Despite the case study's general confirmation of a three-stage pattern of interest-group development, there have been two significant exceptions. The West End Property Owners Association, which sprang into being to resist the efforts of the CMHA to demolish blocks D and E, acted consciously and contentiously as a conflict group from its very inception. The Community Land Cooperative was organized, from the very beginning, as a radical housing group. Neither organization passed through earlier stages of development—although in the

11. There can be a considerable lag between the changing of the leaders' consciousness and the changing of an organization's charter. Once manifest interests have become codified in an organization's public purposes, pronouncements, and programs, they take on a life of their own. Changing the mission of an established organization can be a formidable, time-consuming task.

latter case, a three-stage evolution apparently occurred in the housing consciousness of the CLC's founders *before* they brought the land cooperative into being.

What these exceptions imply for a model of locality-based action is that threats to domestic property interests may sometimes loom so large and so urgent as to provoke a leap in consciousness, calling forth from an unorganized quasi-group an organized property interest group that is originally established at a "higher" level of development than the housing improvement association. Furthermore, the origins of the CLC seem to suggest that such a leap in consciousness may sometimes occur among people who do not themselves possess a direct material stake in the property under siege. Group formation and collective action on behalf of endangered property interests may sometimes occur on the basis of social, political, or religous values that are held in common by an organization's founding members. The conditions that give rise to such developmental "leaps"—and the special problems of sustainability that seem to accompany them—require further theoretical and empirical work.

Second, several of the neighborhood's organized groups have displayed a tendency to "straddle" one or more of the theoretical lines separating the three stages of interest group development. The CLC is the most obvious example, where the consciousness and collective action of an improvement group, a conflict group, and a radical group are manifested, at one and the same time, within the same organization. Similarly, organized groups such as the WECC, the Laurel Homes residents council, and the DSNA did not entirely abandon the activities of their earlier stage(s) of development once they reached a "higher" stage of consciousness and action. This suggests that the "real life" boundaries between developmental stages may be less distinct and more permeable than previously, "ideally" presumed.[12]

Questions such as these do not invalidate the model at hand. They do indicate, however, that some of its parts are in need of greater specification. They set the agenda for future research.

12. Alternatively, these developmental stages may be just as distinct as earlier presumed, but their activities may be more "cumulative." A sustainable conflict group, in other words, may be one that has managed to retain many of the celebratory elements of a housing improvement group. A sustainable radical group may be one that has managed to incorporate many of the oppositional *and* celebratory elements of "lower" developmental stages. I have already indicated, in the case of the CLC, that such "layering" of activities across various stages may create organizational difficulties. Skillfully done, however, such "layering" may actually promote organizational solidarity and stability.

THE PRODUCTION AND PATTERN OF INTERGROUP
CONFLICT

The same interests of domestic property that constitute a basis for the
differentiation and development of locality-based groups have been
said to constitute a basis, too, for the frequent conflict among these
groups. The social relations that have been shown to exist among the
locality-based organizations of the West End in the 1980s provide
considerable support for this thesis. Such intergroup conflict has been
shown to conform to a somewhat predictable two-by-two pattern of
conflict between groups with different property interests at the same
level of political consciousness; between groups with the same interests at different levels of consciousness; between groups with different
interests at different levels of consciousness; and between groups with
the same interests at the same level of consciousness.

Contentious relations such as those between the CLC and the DSNA
can be explained almost entirely in terms of antagonistic property
interests. The incompatibility of different property interests also accounts, in large measure, for the conflict between the public tenants
and the CMHA, the breakdown in the proposed alliance between the
CLC and Miami Purchase, the fragility of the present alliance between the WECC and the DSNA, and the undercurrent of tension that
persists in the otherwise peaceful, mutually protective alliance between Miami Purchase and the DSNA. Different relations to domestic
property, in each of these cases, provide an objective, material basis
for political relations that are marked by underlying tension or outright hostility.

Intergroup conflict, however, is not merely a matter of opposing
interests that are objectively "impressed" upon individuals by the
property positions that are theirs. It also arises from opposing perceptions of what those interests are or should be. This means that conflict can arise between two organizations that embody the same domestic property interests or speak on behalf of the same property
interest group, but exhibit different levels of political consciousness.

One example is the escalating conflict between PHACT and the Lincoln Court residents council. A second might be the strained relations
between the CLC and the current incarnation of the WECC. Both the
CLC and the WECC have a following among the neighborhood's private tenants; both purport to speak on their behalf; but one is a radical housing group, with a strong dose of conflict consciousness, while
the other is currently reconstituting itself as a neighborhood improve-

ment association, with a welcome extended to all of the neighborhood's interest groups. The CLC would defend tenant interests by expanding the supply of social property and protesting the spread of gentrification. The WECC would defend tenant interests by making peace with the neighborhood's competing factions and petitioning the city for additional funds for subsidized housing in the West End. So different are the political perceptions of these two organizations that they now cooperate on nothing at all, despite the similarities in their social base.

Different levels of political consciousness may also explain part of the political strain between Miami Purchase and the DSNA. The tension in their alliance is due in part to the mild incompatibility of their property interests. Specifically, the MPPF is not as single-mindedly dedicated to enhancing the exchange value of domestic property as the DSNA. Equally significant, however, is the tension generated by the organizations' different perceptions of their strategic interests. Both the DSNA and the MPPF have been attacked by the CLC and by certain unorganized fragments of the WECC for their preservationist and promotional activities. The response of the DSNA to these attacks has been to become more of a conflict group. The MPPF, on the other hand, has responded by attempting to cooperate with the CLC and—when that strategy failed—by quietly building a housing improvement association among the new homeowners in recently renovated MPPF properties. Such political passivity is a source of irritation and aggravation for the leaders of the DSNA. They have come to realize that that are "dealing with a lot of factions that keep trying to put roadblocks in your way." They are fighting for their financial lives. Consequently, the refusal of the MPPF to recognize the precarious, contentious nature of the interests they share with the DSNA—and to *act* as if they are in a fight—has contributed to the tension that lies beneath the surface of the DSNA/MPPF alliance.

Since intergroup conflict can apparently arise out of either a difference in (objective) property interests or a difference in the (subjective) perception of those interests, a residentially diverse neighborhood such as the West End will occasionally produce a situation in which there are differences in *both* the property interests *and* the level of political consciousness between two organized groups. This was, in fact, what happened in the early relations between the CLC and the DSNA; in the continuing relations between the CLC and the MPPF; and, to a somewhat lesser degree, in the current relations between the DSNA and the WECC.

The conflict between the CLC and the DSNA was, at first, a lopsided battle with only one belligerent fully engaged, a battle that was being haphazardly waged between a radical housing group with conflict consciousness and a neighborhood improvement association with little idea of what the fuss was all about. Continuing opposition from the CLC, combined with emotional denunciations in monthly meetings of the WECC, provoked a gradual change in the DSNA's perception of its own interests and its own political situation vis-à-vis other property interest groups. The DSNA has now become as much of a housing conflict group as the CLC.

Relations between the CLC and the MPPF, by contrast, have also been characterized by unequal levels of political consciousness and by direct political attack, but the reaction of the MPPF has been not to become more like the conflict group that the CLC *is* but like the neighborhood improvement association that the DSNA *was*. Thus the conflict with the CLC has transformed a neighborhood improvement association into a conflict housing group (in the case of the DSNA) and has transformed a regionally based nonprofit developer into something of a locality-based neighborhood improvement association (in the case of the MPPF).

The current detente between the DSNA and the WECC is another example of groups with opposing interests at different levels of political consciousness. In this case, a conflict housing group (the DSNA) and a neighborhood improvement association (the WECC) have reached an expedient accommodation despite their differences. Cooperation, not conflict, is the public character of their present relations. This is an uneasy alliance, however, one that is made fragile by the incompatible interests of each organization's principal constituency, but made possible by the differences in each organization's political consciousness; an alliance that exists despite a difference in (objective) interests and because of the difference in (subjective) perceptions of those interests. The danger here, for the WECC, is that the more politically astute, more conflictually oriented DSNA will succeed in taking over the leadership and the organizational agenda of the community council. The danger for the DSNA is that episodes like the popular furor over the police station arch will gradually transform the political consciousness of the community council, revealing the DSNA as an enemy and a threat, not as an ally. Should the WECC ever become a politically conscious defender of tenant interests, developing into a conflict group like the DSNA, its alliance with the DSNA would probably become untenable.

There is one other variety of intergroup conflict that our investigation of the West End has revealed, one that runs counter to the property interest explanation developed to this point. Some neighborhood conflicts occur even though the property interests and the political consciousness of two interacting organizations are the same. The present rivalry between PHACT and the Laurel Homes residents council fits this troublesome category. So do the political hostilities that sometimes surfaced between the CLC and the WECC in the early 1980s, when the WECC was more of a conflict group than it is today. In the West End, these conflicts have primarily been struggles over "turf"— competitions between like-minded organizations for the right to represent the same interest group. Intergroup conflict of this sort is an abrupt reminder that the interests of domestic property, as useful as they may be in explaining group formation and intergroup conflict, are not the *only* factor affecting cooperation and conflict among locality-based organizations. Whether for reasons of turf, race, religion, ethnicity, or simply the incompatible personalities or ambitions of local leaders, locality-based conflict sometimes occurs between two organizations whose social base, property interests, and political consciousness are exactly the same.

In summary, the four varieties of intergroup conflict that have been revealed by the case study of group formation and intergroup relations in the West End tend to follow a predictable pattern. This pattern generally conforms to the two-by-two typology that was introduced in Chapter 6, with each type of conflict classified in terms of a particular political configuration of property interests and housing consciousness, existing between any two locality-based organizations (see Figure 12).

This typology requires several clarifications and comments. First, it should be noted that the interests that are at issue between two organizations like the CLC and the DSNA are not merely "different." They are relationally different and contentiously different. The fact that interests are not the same is less significant in explaining conflict than the fact that the two groups are drawn into hostile interaction because they discover that their interests are precariously, antagonistically interdependent. One organization cannot promote the interests of its constituency without threatening the interests of the other's constituency.

Second, it is somewhat misleading to suggest, as this typology seems to do, that political consciousness is something separate and independent from property interests. They are objective and subjec-

Domestic Property Interests

		Different	Same
		(A) CLC/MPPF	(C) PHACT/Lincoln Court
	Different	DSNA/WECC	residents council
Level of		CLC/DSNA*	DSNA/MPFF
Political			CLC/WECC
Consciousness			
		(B) CLC/DSNA	(D) PHACT/Laurel Homes
	Same		residents council
			CLC/WECC*

*Early 1980s

Figure 12. A typology of West End conflict

tive dimensions of the *same* social reality—that is, two dimensions of a group's structural relation to domestic property. Even so, the case study shows that a group's perception of its property interests can be just as important as its interests themselves in shaping its political relations with other groups. Furthermore, factors that affect those perceptions—affecting, thereby, a group's level of political consciousness—operate somewhat independently of a group's property interests. This is why "level of political consciousness" is cross-tabulated with "domestic property interests" as a seemingly separate social variable.

Third, while the typology distinguishes among various origins of intergroup conflict, it does not distinguish among various degrees of conflict. Contentious relations ranging from mild tension (for example, DSNA/MPPF), to a quietly mounted organizational putsch (for example, PHACT/Lincoln Court residents council), to angry protests and public denunciations (for example, CLC/DSNA) are all treated equivalently as representative cases of "intergroup conflict." Theoretically, there has been no need to make such distinctions among escalating degrees of belligerency or rancor. Our primary focus, after all, has been to discover the structural lines along which locality-based organizations act and interact in oppositional ways, not to explain the various forms that such political behavior may take.[13] Even so, it must

13. While noting the typology's limits in explaining the "form" that local conflicts may take, I should also repeat my earlier warning about the political "content" of such conflicts; that is, neither the typology presented here nor the three-stage model of locality-based action discussed earlier is able to explain when or why the politics of place will sometimes have "liberal" or "progressive" goals—and sometimes "conservative" or "reactionary" ones. I shall say more about this issue in the next two chapters.

be acknowledged that degrees of conflict do exist and that they are an important variable in intergroup relations and neighborhood politics.

It must also be admitted, moreover, that neither the present typology of intergroup conflict nor the case study from which it is drawn provide much help in explaining this variable—that is, in understanding *why* the degree of conflict is greater or lesser from one situation to another. What *can* be said is that intergroup conflicts in Cell C, where the property interests are the same but the level of political consciousness is different, are the *least* likely to exhibit the sort of overt hostility, personal vilification, and unconventional political behavior that William Gamson (1966) described as "rancorous conflict." Characterized more by an undercurrent of tension than by a gathering wave of animosity, these Type C conflicts are also the least likely to be played out in the public eye. By contrast, intergroup conflict in Cell B, where property interests are different but the level of political consciousness is the same, are the *most* likely to be rancorous, public, and frequent (*if* consciousness has reached either a "conflict" or "radical" stage of development). Aside from these generalizations, all that can really be said is that rancorous conflict cannot be entirely excluded from any cell, nor can the possibility of even the most rancorous relations being transformed into a tense (but relatively peaceful) detente. Specifying the conditions under which conflict varies, from one degree of belligerency or accommodation to another, is beyond the scope of this book.

TOWARD A THEORY OF LOCALITY-BASED ACTION

Collective action organized at the place of residence is neither a random nor exceptional event. As Katznelson (for one) has pointed out, locality-based movements and protests have become a "major characteristic of political life throughout the West in the past quarter of a century" (1981:210). Previous explanations have proved inadequate to the theoretical task of saying why, how, and when locality-based action occurs. A new theory is clearly needed.

Such a theory must differentiate multiple, material bases, within the locality for the collective action that is organized there. It must specify the reciprocal "moments" and "empirical conditions" through which locality-based groups come into being and develop or decline. It must identify the causes of conflict or cooperation among them. The theoretical framework that was proposed in Part I and refined here, in combining a *static* model of property positions with a *dynamic* model of group formation and intergroup conflict, was designed to meet these requirements.

Its success in doing so was given a preliminary test in the case study of Part II. For the most part, this theoretical framework has proven to be a fairly accurate *description* of the principal cleavages and conflicts of Cincinnati's West End. Furthermore, in facilitating a systematic analysis of the interests and conditions that engender these social phenomena, the framework has provided a degree of *explanation*, as well. Indeed, I believe that no other "explanation" of locality-based action would have done as well in describing and explaining the "comings and goings," the politics and conflicts of the neighborhood's organized groups.

The static and dynamic models that have been constructed here cannot yet be said to represent a finished theory of locality-based action. There is much theoretical and empirical work that remains to be done, particularly with regard to the multiple conditions underlying the twin "moments" of consciousness and organization. Nevertheless, enough of a fit *has* been discovered between the proposed framework and the examined facts to suggest that I am probably on the right track. There is reason to believe that further research into the social relations of domestic property will eventually yield a better description—and better explanation—of the politics of place than we have had heretofore.

12

Domestic Property Analysis: Theoretical Implications

> I see no incompatibility between adopting a Marxist approach
> to urban protest movements and complementing it with an-
> alyses which explicate some of the questions which have not
> received due attention in the studies so far.
>
> —C. G. PICKVANCE (1977:175)

Despite the need for further theoretical and empirical work, the analytic approach developed here has shown considerable promise. There
is reason to believe that a better understanding of collective action,
occurring on the territorial basis of an urban neighborhood like the
West End, *can* be achieved by analyzing such action in terms of the
differentiation, development, and conflict of domestic property interest groups.

Given the theoretical promise and empirical plausibility of this particular approach, it is reasonable to ask whether the examination of
interests and conditions underlying locality-based action might contribute to a better understanding of other theoretical and practical
problems touching upon the place of residence. In other words, if
domestic property analysis can shed such light on the whys and ways
in which "communities act," then perhaps it can illuminate other aspects of urban development and urban political life in which these
"communities" play a part.

The next two chapters will explore this possibility. Admittedly,
such a line of inquiry is rather speculative, since it moves beyond both
the framework and facts of this book. There is, however, much to be
gained by considering how the analysis developed here might be applied to such related issues as the theory of urban development, the

theory of capitalist reproduction, and the practice of neighborhood politics and planning. There is an advantage in addressing the provocative question that arises soon after our original question has been answered: place-bound "communities" (and their constituent groups) do "act"—so what?

THE THEORY OF URBAN DEVELOPMENT

The analysis of domestic property interests and domestic property interest groups has the potential of being a neighborhood-level *complement* to a recent strain of neo-Marxist scholarship that attempts to understand, on a more macro level, urban development and urban political movements in advanced capitalist societies. This potential is most apparent in the work of David Harvey (1974; 1978; 1981; 1985), Neil Smith (1979; 1982), and John Mollenkopf (1981a; 1981b, 1983), three theorists who give particular attention to the ways in which various "crises" of capitalist accumulation and urban development are played out within the urban neighborhood.

Harvey and Smith: The "Locational Seesaw" of Capitalist Development

Harvey and Smith have sought to reveal the accumulative processes that determine and differentiate capitalist investment in urban neighborhoods. They have asked two basic questions: Why is capital invested in the "non-productive" streets, parks, utilities, offices, shops, and housing of a city's built environment? Why is capital invested in some neighborhoods and not in others? Their answers provide a theoretical context within which threats to domestic property interests appear as the patterned, predictable products of capitalist development.[1]

David Harvey's answer to the question of capitalist investment in the built environment is that such investment is a temporary solution to the crisis of "overaccumulation" in productive, industrial sectors of the economy—the "primary circuit of capital." Overinvestment in industrial enterprises tends to produce glutted markets, falling rates of

---

1. This is the other side to the complementary relationship that is being explored here: even as domestic property analysis can explicate the process by which locality-based groups come to participate in urban conflicts that the neo-Marxists regard as inevitable, neo-Marxist analysis can explicate the process by which property interests come to fluctuate in the face of economic and political factors originating outside of the local neighborhood.

profit, surplus labor, and surplus capital. One solution to this crisis is to switch capital investment into the built environment of urban neighborhoods—the "secondary circuit of capital"—siphoning off overaccumulation and solving the problem of rising surpluses and falling profits. In the residential urban neighborhood, capitalists discover new opportunities for accumulation.

This merely shifts the crisis to another sector, however, since overaccumulation eventually occurs in the secondary circuit as well. The same contradictory tendencies that appeared in the industrial sector reappear in the built environment, "although they are even more exaggerated here because of the generally long amortization time involved, the fixing in space of the asset, and the composite nature of the commodity involved" (Harvey, 1981:113). The problem is that the physical structures that are created in the course of capitalist investment in the built environment last so long that they act as *barriers* to further accumulation. Thus, even as some "fractions" of capital are reaping profits from their past investment in the built environment, other "fractions" have an interest in razing these buildings to make way for new investment.

As long as there are alternative opportunities for real estate investment and development, however, the buildings of the past are not razed. Barriers to development in one neighborhood lead investors to look elsewhere, particularly to neighborhoods with vacant land and buildings that can be cheaply acquired and demolished. The prime locations for such reinvestment, according to Smith (1979:545; 1982:149), are those residential neighborhoods where previous investors have removed so much value from the built environment that the return on investment from *current* land uses is substantially lower than the return that is possible under a *different* use. When "devalorization" has reached this point, reinvestment by speculators, developers, and financiers—often with the help of public agencies—will either raze the neighborhood's former structures to make way for new commercial and industrial uses (as occurred in Queensgate I and in Liberty-Dalton) or upgrade those structures for the use and profit of a more affluent population (as occurred in the gentrifying blocks of the upper West End).

Capitalist investment in the built environment, therefore, is spatially uneven, moving from one neighborhood to another in long cycles of development, devalorization, destruction, and reinvestment. Harvey summarizes this "contradictory character of investments in the built environment" in the following way:

Capitalist development has therefore to negotiate a knife-edge path between preserving the exchange values of past capitalist investments in the built environment and destroying the value of these investments in order to open up fresh room for accumulation. Under capitalism there is, then, a perpetual struggle in which capital builds a physical landscape appropriate to its own condition at a particular moment in time, only to have to destroy it, usually in the course of a crisis, at a subsequent point in time. (1981:113)

This development process, as it moves restlessly from neighborhood to neighborhood, is described by Smith as a "locational seesaw":

The logic behind uneven development is that the development of one area creates barriers to further development, thus leading to underdevelopment, and that the underdevelopment of one area creates opportunities for a new phase of development. Geographically, this leads to the possibility of what we might call a "locational seesaw": the successive development, underdevelopment, and redevelopment of given areas as capital jumps from one place to another, then back again, both creating and destroying its own opportuities for development. (1982:151)

For both Harvey and Smith, it is not only past investment in the built environment that "contradicts" further capitalist development, neighborhood by neighborhood, but the present resistance of the "working class" to the "violence which the capitalist form of accumulation inevitably inflicts upon it" (Harvey, 1981:114). This, too, is part of the "logic behind uneven development": the residents of some neighborhoods resist the disruptions and depradations of the locational seesaw; they act collectively and contentiously to erect political barriers to future development. Such political struggle around the built environment is as much a product of the "capitalist form of accumulation" as the locational seesaw itself. Conflict is instrinsic to the urban development process. Conflict is inevitable.

Harvey and Smith make a substantial contribution to understanding the political economy within which neighborhoods are developed (and underdeveloped), property interests are affected for better or for worse, and "communities" do or do not act. Theirs are fruitful analyses of what Pahl (1975:241) has called "the encapsulating social structure and its relations to the means of production." Less fruitful is their understanding of these products of urban development—the neighborhoods, groups, and conflicts that arise within the encapsulating structure of urban capitalism. It is at this more micro level that their analyses—especially Harvey's analysis—begin to break down.

Harvey seems to assume that if capitalist relations create the underlying conditions for community action and urban conflict, then capitalist relations must also constitute an objective *basis* for the groups and struggles that emerge. As Harvey (1978:30) puts it; "Conflicts in the living space are, we can conclude, mere reflections of the underlying tension between capital and labor. . . . The surface appearance of conflicts around the built environment—the struggles against the landlord or against urban renewal—conceals a hidden essence which is nothing more than the struggle between capital and labor." The problem here is that the cleavages and conflicts of urban neighborhoods cannot be reduced to such a simple dichotomy. Residential neighborhoods do exist within the encapsulating structure of capitalism, but these localities also contain a material base and social structures of their own. Since the social relations of the homeplace do not exactly replicate the social relations of the workplace, the political movements and urban conflicts that emanate from the place of residence will often have a logic that is somewhat different and somewhat independent from the logic of class struggle. Even if the fluctuations and disruptions of the locational seesaw are the principal empirical condition for community action, the formation, mobilization, and conflict of local groups are not "mere reflections" of the struggle between labor and capital. These locality-based struggles are something different, something more.[2]

Domestic property analysis provides a means of acknowledging and explicating this "different" basis for collective, conflictual behavior that does not require, at the same time, a complete rejection of Harvey's and Smith's neo-Marxist analyses of the accumulative process that "encapsulates" and engenders such locality-based action. The analysis of domestic property interests and groups assumes that people experience the effects of urban development not as workers, but as the interested incumbents of domestic property positions, situated within a specific territorial place. Their domestic property interests, being inherently relational and precarious, are extraordinarily

2. Despite his earlier characterization of locality-based conflicts as "nothing more" than conflicts between capital and labor, Harvey has more recently acknowledged that "community" struggles and "community" consciousness can have a "real material basis in daily life" (1985:251). These community phenomena are still deemed to have only a residual, reproductive significance, however. In Harvey's words, they are "fetishes" that obscure the inner workings and meanings of capitalism.

sensitive to any fluctuations in the neighborhood's economic, political, or social environment. Such interests become the *primary conduit* by which the contradictions of capitalism are transmitted into the place of residence and translated into the lived experience of most people. Neo-Marxist analysis explains how and why these contradictions exist. Domestic property analysis explains how and why they can (sometimes) lead to collective action and urban conflict.

Not only do the neo-Marxists err in reducing all movements and conflicts of the "living space" to class conflicts, but in ignoring the entire question of how the groups who engage in such action come into being in the first place. Between the accumulative crises of the capitalist structure and the collective outcomes of neighborhood resistance, the problem of group formation is mysteriously suspended like an unopened "black box." How the "social base" of urban neighborhoods is transformed into the "social force" of urban movements is left largely unexamined. Pickvance has described this weakness well:

> In most of the studies of urban social movements so far very little attention has been paid to the process of mobilization. The issues at stake and social base affected are said to be determined by structural contradictions, and the social force appears from the social base at the wave of the magic wand of organization. This appears to me to ignore what is not only a major theoretical problem but also a major problem for political practice, namely how, in Marxian terms, does a class in itself become a class for itself? (1977:179)

Chiding his neo-Marxist colleagues for ignoring such issues, Pickvance goes on to recommend that neo-Marxist analysis be complemented by "some non-Marxist analyses" to "explicate some of the questions which have not received due attention in the studies so far" (ibid.:175). I suggest that domestic property analysis, with its special focus on group formation and intergroup conflict in the residential urban neighborhood, may provide some of the "non-Marxist" (or quasi-Marxist) answers that are now overlooked in most neo-Marxist urban theory. In short, these theoretical approaches are complementary, each adding a piece that the other one lacks.[3]

---

3. Before these theoretical approaches can be made truly complementary, however, a major piece of theoretical and empirical work remains. The *articulation* of the interests, consciousness, and politics of the homeplace with the interests, consciousness, and politics of the workplace must be spelled out in greater detail, specifying not only how the contradictions of a capitalist economy affect domestic property interests, but how the class structure of a capitalist society assigns different groups to different

Mollenkopf: The Dynamic Tension of Accumulation and Community

Where Harvey and presumably Smith are inclined to treat urban conflict as "nothing more than the struggle between capital and labor," Mollenkopf recognizes a different sort of "underlying tension.". Like Harvey and Smith, he acknowledges the dominant role of capitalist accumulation in urban development, but he argues that cities contain and concentrate a second set of relationships as well, those of social interaction and community formation. Since "accumulation" and "community" each operate by a "distinct, unequal, and ultimately opposing logic," these two sets of urban relationships are in constant tension, a tension that "deeply permeates urban institutions, urban form, and urban life" (1981a:320). The antagonistic, asymmetric interaction of accumulation and community is what propels urban development forward, "in a manner resembling the old-fashioned pump-handled railroad cart," producing alternate cycles of growth and conflict.[4]

The inevitable conflicts and crises of urban development, therefore, are not a function of the accumulative process alone, but of the periodic collision of accumulation and community. Urbanization engenders communal forms that initially allow and promote economic growth, both by promoting stable social units and by winning popular allegiance for the "rules of the game" that govern the economic and political life of capitalist society. Eventually, however, communal relationships and communal forms become an impediment to further economic expansion. A city's leading actors tend to respond to these barriers to accumulation "by undermining prevailing communal forms while simultaneously erecting new, more accommodating communal forms" (ibid.:331). But the attempt to remove or reorganize "community" on behalf of "accumulation" is frequently opposed by those who are wedded to the "old" communal forms. Conflict is the result:

domestic property positions. Further work must also be done to examine the role of the homeplace in reproducing the capitalist relations of the workplace, a problem discussed more fully in the second half of this chapter.

4. *Accumulation*, for Mollenkopf, refers to "how a society creates, expands, and distributes its means of well-being"; "market values, particularly profit maximization, occupy an overriding place." *Community* refers to neighborhoods in which ethnicity, class, communal institutions and other building blocks have created an overlapping set of bonds through the years. Market values "play relatively little role in shaping community interactions. Instead, nonmarket values like reciprocity, mutual support, and informal helping patterns are central" (Mollenkopf, 1981a:320).

The urban population built communities based to varying degrees on reciprocity rather than exchange and profit. Though subordinated to the patterns of economic growth and hardly opposed to the principal of material well-being, these emerging neighborhoods sought life beyond work. These communities typically became the main source of resistance, when economic elites felt that economic expansion could only be achieved by reorganizing social life. Thus, as cities concentrated relations both of accumulation and community, they intensified the potential for conflict. (ibid.322)

Suspended between accumulation and community is urban government—mediating, moderating, and channeling the volatile interaction between these antagonistic urban forces. Those actors for whom accumulation is paramount attempt to enlist the aid of government agencies in "progrowth coalitions," dedicated to removing all impediments to economic expansion. Those actors for whom community is paramount attempt to enlist the aid of government in the fight to preserve their neighborhoods in the face of downtown business expansion and capitalist development. Politics, as Mollenkopf notes, "necessarily comes to the fore." Economic accumulation may play the dominant role in shaping and constraining the choices made by political actors, but local government is firmly rooted in the "ethnic and kinship bonds, geographic propinquity, voluntary associations, [and] shared political convictions" of community (ibid.:321). Therefore, nothing guarantees that either the laws of the marketplace or the power of capitalist elites will completely or always prevail in urban politics.

There are several places where Mollenkopf's analysis and domestic property analysis either overlap or complement one another. The theoretical convergence of these two approaches is most apparent in the tension that is posited between "accumulation" and "community" in Mollenkopf's formulation, and the tension that has been posited between interests of exchange (accumulation) and those of use (accommodation) in this book.[5] To the extent that these analytic approaches are describing essentially the same sort of structural antagonism or

5. As noted in Chapter 1, this posited antagonism between "use" and "exchange" is a familiar theme in contemporary urban studies, a concept that is unique to neither Mollenkopf nor myself. Most recently, Logan and Molotch (1987) have made this theme the theoretical linchpin of their "political economy of place." Fashioned along conceptual lines that closely resemble Mollenkopf's theory of urban development, Logan and Molotch's theory has the same potential for serving as a macro level complement to domestic property analysis. Their theory has many of the same weaknesses (and strengths) found in Mollenkopf.

"underlying tension," there is the potential for extending Mollenkopf's analysis "downward," into the local neighborhood, and for extending domestic property analysis "upward," beyond its current neighborhood focus. Thus, just as urban government is suspended between accumulation and community, so too are many of the institutions, interests, and ideologies of individual neighborhoods. Just as the cleavages and conflicts of the residential locality can be largely described in terms of the antagonistic interests of exchange and use, so too can many of the cleavages and conflicts of the city as a whole. The overlap of these two approaches provides easy access for each to enter the level of analysis initially explored by the other.[6]

Second, the emphasis that Mollenkopf places upon political alliances and social networks makes "political interests" an unavoidable part of his theory. Thus, in describing the development of U.S. cities since the early nineteenth century in terms of the tension between accumulation and community, he endeavors "to clarify the actors at work on each side, the strategies they adopted in pursuing their interests, and the resulting impact on the nature of our cities" (ibid.:323–24). It is unclear, however, what the connection might be between the interests that his actors are pursuing and the two sets of urban relationships that are presumed to be in opposition. The "political interests" that are brought to the fore by his theory, in other words, are not theoretically grounded in the processes of economic accumulation and community formation that form the dynamic basis for that theory. Indeed, at one point, sounding more like a pluralist than a neo-Marxist, Mollenkopf seems to suggest that interests are constituted by the political process itself, with *no* structural underpinning in either accumulation or community:

Political movements and alliances are rarely based on structural distinctions in any clear way. Instead, potential political alliances and the in-

---

6. Both approaches have already been extended somewhat beyond their initial focus by their authors. Thus Mollenkopf (1981b; 1983) looked at neighborhood-based opposition to urban renewal in the course of examining urban development in Boston and San Francisco. Likewise, this study of neighborhood-based action in Cincinnati's West End opened with an overview of the city's development and the progrowth coalition that redeveloped the neighborhood. My point is that Mollenkopf's theory of urban development loses some of its effectiveness when applied to the neighborhood, while my own theory of domestic property interests and groups becomes less effective when removed too far from the neighborhood. Combining these two approaches would allow the researcher to move more easily and effectively from one level of analysis to another.

terests which undergird them arise through the operation of specific institutions such as the post-war development agencies. The source of inputs, the way institutions allocate them and the constituencies to which institutions respond each provide the basis for political mobilization and alliance formation. (ibid.:333)

Without a clearer idea of the ways in which political interests might be linked to the processes which, in tandem and in tension, "propel urban development forward," Mollenkopf inadvertently divorces the theoretical and empirical problems of group formation, collective action, and intergroup conflict from the "volatile interaction" of accumulation and community. In short, he leaves a yawning gap between his theory of collective action, such as it is, and his theory of urban development.

Domestic property analysis can help to close this gap. Interests of domestic property provide a set of "structural distinctions" that are capable of linking citywide processes of economic accumulation and community formation with locality-based political movements and alliances. The objective antagonism and organized conflict of these property interests also add a degree of specificity and concretness to the "antagonistic interdependence" and "ensuing tension" that Mollenkopf presumes to exist between accumulation and community. This is not to suggest that economic accumulation and community formation, or the interaction between them, can be exclusively or exhaustively described in terms of property interests of exchange and use. Domestic property interests do describe, however, a material and political dimension that has particular significance for collective action. Such interests and action provide a theoretical grounding for the coalitions and conflicts that "necessarily come to the fore," along with politics, in Mollenkopf's theory of urban development.

Finally, domestic property analysis theoretically and empirically complements Mollenkopf's notion of the urban residential neighborhood as a set of institutions, ideas, and relationships that sometimes support and sometimes impede economic accumulation. He does little to develop this theme, but what he does say about it anticipates discussions of capitalist reproduction and resistance that are taken up in the next section. Let us move, then, from considering the implications of locality-based interests and action for a theory of urban development to considering their implications for a theory of capitalist reproduction.

THE THEORY OF CAPITALIST REPRODUCTION

The concept of "reproduction," as used in social theory, is rooted in Marx's (1967:578) observation that "capitalist production . . . produces not only commodities, not only surplus value, but it also produces and reproduces the capitalist relation." It is not only the replacement and resupply of the means of production that is at issue here nor the sustenance of the bodies, skills, and families of the producers themselves. Equally important is the maintenance and renewal of the relations of domination and exploitation that characterize capitalist society. The reproduction of such relations occurs primarily within the workplace, where the fundamental relation between capital and labor is established, but not in the workplace alone. Capitalist reproduction is also a product of noneconomic factors such as ideology, private property, and the State. It also occurs within sites *outside* of the workplace, especially within social sites like the family, the public school, and the residential neighborhood.[7]

It is the last of these "social sites" that concerns us here. A diverse body of social theory, developed mainly by neo-Marxists, regards the institutions, ideas, and conflicts of the homeplace as conducive to the on-going maintenance of capitalist society. The theoretical framework and case findings of this book, which propose domestic property interests and domestic property interest groups as the principal units of analysis, can be used to complement and confirm this notion of the residential neighborhood as a site of capitalist reproduction. This same analytic perspective can be brought to bear on the opposite proposition: that residential neighborhoods might sometimes serve as social sites of *resistance* to capitalist relations of accumulation and domination. Consideration will be given to both.

The Homeplace as a Site of Capitalist Reproduction

Aside from institutions of socialization such as families, schools, and churches, the institution of the homeplace that has long been regarded as one of the most conducive to capitalist reproduction is

---

7. Lefevre (1973:51) describes well the kinds of questions that have informed the work of a recent generation of neo-Marxist scholars who have begun looking outside of the workplace for structures of capitalist reproduction: "Can the relations of exploitation and domination, of authority and power (implying relations between those who

the owner-occupation of domestic property. Homeownership is said to exert an immobilizing, pacifying, conservatizing influence over the political behavior of subordinate classes. As Harvey has put it: "a worker mortgaged to the hilt is, for the most part, a pillar of social stability" (1978:15).[8] Since some workers own their homes and some do not, homeownership also serves to fragment working class solidarity. Disparate interests of property undermine and replace common interests of class,[9] particularly among workers of different races and different status. Homeownership can lead even nonbigoted workers to practice racial or social exclusion in their neighborhoods, acting in biased defense of their property values.[10] Furthermore, since those who own their homes can use this property as a sort of private insurance or retirement plan, working class support for the public provision of social security and other services of the welfare state is undermined.[11]

Arguments such as these do not claim that private homeownership replicates capitalist relations per se but that the diffusion of homeownership so completely encumbers, distracts, and divides those who might otherwise challenge capitalism that they are made politically quiescent, politically impotent. Homeownership, in other words, is a pervasive and effective means of social control.

This property institution is also presumed to play a more direct role in the reproduction of capitalist relations. Homeownership, it is claimed, is a powerful means of inculcating widespead respect for private property and popular allegience to the stability and values of the status quo.[12] It is also described as a powerful ideological means of justifying the prerogatives and property of private capital. This happens in two ways. Capitalists intentionally blur the distinctions between the private property of the owner-occupier and the private property of landlords, developers, financiers, industrialists, and spec-

---

make decisions and those who carry them out), be perpetuated in the workplace and in units of production alone? Do they not imply conditions exterior to the conditions of work? And, if this is so, then where, how, and why does this reproduction take place, since it coincides neither with production as such, nor with the reproduction of the human and material means of production?"

8. See also Engels (1935:50), Angotti (1977:43), Stone (1980:89), Harvey (1974:244), Agnew (1978:142), and Perin (1977:73).

9. See, for example, Clarke and Ginsburg (1975:4, 17, 25), Ball (1976:29), Edel (1982:211), Harvey (1978:15), and Dunleavy (1979:423).

10. See, for example, Perin (1977:161) and LeGates and Murphy (1981:266).

11. See, in particular, Kemeny (1980; 1977).

12. Such an argument is made by Bell (1977:39), Blum and Kingston (1984), Couper and Brindley (1975:571), and Wright (1981:65, 126).

ulators, using the ideas, sentiments, and beliefs that surround the property of the homeowner to legitimate the very different property of the capitalist: "In such cases, the assumption is implicitly drawn that if *any* form of private property is intrinsically just, or even natural, then so too are *all* forms" (Rose, Saunders, Newby, and Bell, 1976:710).

Second, homeownership is made such a righteous, uncontested ideal of the American Dream that alternative conceptions of tenure are all but excluded from the marketplace of ideas (Duncan, 1982:126). Alternative forms of housing tenure, particularly those of "social property" that happen to lie in between the more familiar dichotomies of renting versus owning or private housing versus public housing, are not allowed the benefit of public debate.[13]

Residential neighborhoods are often said by neo-Marxists to contain two other sets of ideas that perpetuate capitalist relations, each involving the ideological use of "community." Ideas of community are used, first of all, to support the extension of capitalist relations into the homeplace. Capitalists, according to this argument, have a vested interest in inculcating a perception of the "communal living space" that defines and values a locality not as a place-bound *community* of "mutually supporting ties of trust, friendship, sociability, and predictability," but as a consumable, disposable *commodity*. By "imposing upon labor its own definitions of the meaning of the communal living space," capital thus removes an important barrier to the "colonization of urban land as a means of accumulation" (Cox, 1981:432–34).

Second, it is argued that community has been used not only to facilitate the penetration of capitalist relations into the place of residence but to blunt any potential opposition to them. Ideas of community mask the inevitable cleavages and conflicts of capitalist society. The residential neighborhood—and, by extension, the larger society—is portrayed as a harmonious whole, "where diversity and political con-

13. Economic and political elites of countries like the United States, Britain, and Australia have been as convinced of the "goodness and righteousness" of homeownership as have the members of subordinate groups. Consequently, homeownership—and public policies promoting this particular form of housing tenure—have been vigorously and vocally supported by dominant groups as a bulwark against "bolshevism," "socialism," "unionism," and social unrest (Dean, 1945; Jennings, 1938; Dreier, 1982b; Kemeny, 1977; Bell, 1977; and Ball, 1976). Such loyalty to the "ideology of homeownership" by economic and political elites lends credence to the thesis of Abercrombie and Turner (1978:159) that dominant ideologies may have "a greater impact on the dominant classes than on the dominated."

flict are somehow non-existent" (Clark, 1982:136). Bell and Newby put it this way: "This ideological usage of 'community' has emphasized a common adherence to territory, a solidarity of place, to both elites and subordinates alike. It has denied the existence of any conflict of interest, but has instead interpreted relationships as being characterized by harmony, reciprocity, stability, and affection" (1978:286). The recognition and articulation of conflicting interests is made more difficult by such a climate of denial, as is the mobilization of any collective challenge to capitalist projects and prerogatives.

Beyond the institutions and ideas of the residential neighborhood, whatever *conflicts* arise within this social site are presumed to protect and perpetuate capitalist relations. Locality-based conflicts, according to Katznelson (1981), are the mainstay of a system of "city trenches" in the United States, defending capitalism against frontal assault by subordinate classes and groups. The boundaries of conflict are those of the local neighborhood. Struggles are turned inward, pitting groups that inhabit the same territory against each other instead of against the powers-that-be. The basic political and economic structures of capitalist society are left untouched, intact.

These are themes that are repeated, with only slight variation, among Marxists and non-Marxists alike. Thus Goering (1979:512) notes the frequency with which neighborhood groups fight with each other for scarce resources rather than uniting to demand fundamental changes in a system that distributes resources, services, and life chances so unequally. Sennett (1977:295) notes that when locality-based groups do confront City Hall, they typically fight "to be left alone, to be exempted or shielded from the political process, rather than to change the political process itself." Taub et al. (1977) suggest that many neighborhood groups are the passive *products* of this political process: "externally induced" by City Hall to help legitimize the power of economic and political elites.[14]

These diverse theoretical strands, portraying the place of residence as a social site for the reproduction of capitalist relations, are poten-

14. Harvey (1974:250–51; 1981:115), Molotch (1979:290), Saunders (1981:276), and Katznelson (1981:44) take this argument one step further, asserting that *any* opposition to the existing system of exploitation and domination will be doomed if it is organized on the basis of the local neighborhood. Locality-based struggles, according to this view, are internally fragmented, strategically limited, politically isolated affairs that serve merely to siphon off the tensions that build up in the workplace and transform the structural conflict between capital and labor into a political contest between citizens and the state—a struggle that is far less likely to have radical or revolutionary results.

tially complemented and partially confirmed by the sort of domestic property analysis that has been developed and applied in the preceding pages. The property interests, interest groups, and intergroup relations that are engendered by domestic property positions provide a theoretical framework within which these "reproductive" institutions, ideas, and conflicts of the homeplace can be seen in a new light. In particular, homeowner support for capitalist prerogatives, local ideological support for capitalist relations, and the political fragmentation of potential opposition to capitalist domination are substantiated and explained.

The accumulative property interests of the homeowner groups that I have characterized as the "owner-occupiers of household property" and the "owner-occupiers of acquisitive property" provide a way of explaining why homeowners might be found supporting the accumulative use of domestic property by private capital. These same interests drive a political wedge between residents who own their homes and those who do not, even if both belong to the same economic class. Furthermore, the relational precariousness of homeowner interests—particularly those of equity and liquidity—*can* turn homeowners into routine, even if sometimes reluctant, defenders of the racial, social, economic, and political status quo. Neighborhood changes that might cause fluctuations in their property interests are dreaded, denounced, and opposed.

Property interests that are objectively constituted and subjectively perceived also help to explain the fragmentation and limitations of political struggles organized at the place of residence. On occasion, when an event like urban renewal poses a ubiquitous threat to the interests of *every* group, residential communities do act collectively and contentiously in opposition to the plans of economic and political elites. Such opposition is likely to be short-lived, however, because the solidarity of interest-group clusters like the WECC is made terribly fragile by the different—and often conflicting—interests of its constituent groups. Domestic property interests explain (and confirm) the tendency of community action to fracture into internecine conflicts.

These separately organized interest groups also tend to adopt and promulgate ideas of property and place that are part of the general cultural, ideological milieu. Although they tailor these ideas to fit their own political purposes, local property interest groups often end up revitalizing and "reproducing" ideas that are particularly conducive to the protection and extension of capitalist relations. Thus, in a neighborhood like the West End, ideas of homeownership that emphasize the public benefits of a private interest in equity and liquidity, ideas of The Market that reify and celebrate the performance of an unfettered market in real estate, and ideas of community that focus on the commodified artifacts of the built environment to the exclusion of indigenous social bonds all contribute to a definition of the communal living space that justifies and encourages the "colonization of urban land as a means of accumulation." Ideas of a pluralist neighborhood, moreover, such as those proclaimed by the Dayton Street Neighborhood Association, can make conflict consciousness and radical consciousness more difficult to achieve, simply by masking the cleavages and conflicts intrinsic to domestic property relations.

My argument, then, is that the interests, groups, and ideologies brought to light by domestic property analysis can be used in support of a theory of capitalist reproduction that regards the institutions, ideas, and conflicts of residential neighborhoods as conducive to the maintenance of capitalist society. On the other hand, domestic property analysis may also be used to elucidate a very different perspective on the place of residence. There are interests and ideas endemic to the homeplace that are *not* conducive to capitalist accumulation. "Communities act," on occasion, to impede rather than encourage the penetration and expansion of capitalist relations. Residential neighborhoods can sometimes function, in other words, as social sites of *resistance*. Domestic property analysis may help to reveal when and why.

Resistance amid Reproduction: The "Relatively Autonomous" Homeplace

A developing body of social theory begins with the basic assumption that "mechanisms of social and cultural reproduction are never complete and always meet with partially realized elements of opposition" (Giroux, 1983:259). Not only is the generalization of capitalist relations never entirely complete, leaving some institutions and social sites with relative autonomy within the capitalist system, but the mechanisms of reproduction are themselves *contradictory*. They are fraught with the same kinds of internal tensions, subject to the same destabilizing crises, and spark the same sorts of spontaneous acts of resistance as the mechanisms of production and accumulation that characterize capitalist society—a fact that is frequently forgotten in many accounts of capitalist reproduction. As Michael Apple has pointed out:

The reproduction account is too simple in another way. It undertheorizes and hence neglects the fact that capitalist social relations are inherently *contradictory* in some very important ways—that is, just as in the economic arena where the capitalist accumulation process and the "need" to expand markets and profits generates contradictions within a society . . . so too will similar contradictions emerge in other dominant institutions. (1981:30)

The dominant institutions receiving the most attention from Giroux, Apple, and other authors of "resistance theory" are those of schooling and education.[15] Their notions of the "incompleteness" and "contradictions" of capitalist reproduction are, however, applicable to other social sites as well, including the residential neighborhood.

When Giroux (1983:260) and others speak of schools as being "relatively autonomous institutions that . . . provide spaces for oppositional behavior," they reject any simple or complete correspondence between the structures, processes, and values of these institutions and the structures, processes, and values of the underlying economy. Thus: "Schools are not solely determined by the logic of the workplace or the dominant society; they are not merely economic institutions but are also political, cultural, and ideological sites that exist somewhat independently of the capitalist market economy" (ibid.).

Mollenkopf, for one, has described a similar sort of noncorrespondence existing between the community of the urban neighborhood and the accumulation of the capitalist economy: "each operates by a distinct, unequal and ultimately opposing logic" (1981a:320). Like the schools of resistance theory, residential neighborhoods may be encapsulated and penetrated by capitalist relations, but they also exist somewhat independently of the capitalist economy. They have a logic of their own—that is, a set of relations and an internal dynamic that is distinct from those of capitalist accumulation and ultimately opposed to them.

This is hardly a new idea. There is a long sociological tradition documenting and analyzing the essential antagonism between community relations and market relations. Marx and Weber, in particular, noted the tendency of the developing capitalist economy to dissolve the personal, affective bonds of community. As Marx (1971:66)

---

15. Joining Giroux (1981; 1983) and Apple (1981; 1982) in this theoretical endeavor to discover and explain oppositional, counterhegemonic, nonreproductive elements in educational institutions are such theorists as Willis (1981; 1983), Wexler (1983), and Dale (1982).

observed, "the social relations of individuals have become transformed [by capitalism] into the social connections of material things."
Weber expressed essentially the same idea:[16]

> The market economy as such is the most impersonal relationship of
> practical life into which humans can enter with one another. . . . The
> reason for the impersonality of the market is its matter-of-factness, its
> orientation to the commodity and only to that. Where the market is
> allowed to follow its own autonomous tendencies, its participants do
> not look towards the persons of each other but only toward the econ-
> omy; there are no obligations of brotherliness or reverance, and none
> of those spontaneous human relations that are sustained by personal
> unions. They all would just obstruct the free development of the bare
> market relationship, and its specific interests serve, in turn, to weaken
> the sentiments on which these obstructions rest. (Roth and Wittich,
> 1978:636)

Weber clearly contrasts the "interests" of the marketplace with the
"sentiments" of community, noting the antagonistic, obstructionist
interaction between them. Indeed, for Weber, the interests and classes
of the capitalist economy become sovereign only when "all other determinants of reciprocal relations are, as far as possible, eliminated in
their significance" (ibid.:930). The only real difference between this
traditional sociological treatment and that of modern theorists like
Mollenkopf and Cox lies in the latter's insistence that sentimental ties
of reciprocity and sociability are not *completely* eliminated by capitalist development.[17] On the contrary, they are believed still to play a
role in urban politics and urban development. Community sentiments
still exist in the urban neighborhood and, on occasion, they still "obstruct the free development of the bare market relationship."

Domestic property analysis provides a different, though complementary, explanation for the incompleteness of capitalist reproduc-

16. Marx and Weber were joined, of course, by Tonnies, Durkheim, and others.
What distinguishes the work of Marx and Weber is the emphasis they placed not
merely on the dissolution of communal bonds, but on their replacement by relations of
market exchange. They specifically link the transformation of community to the development of capitalism.

17. Weber, like Marx before him, recognized the tendency of market relations to
generalize, sweeping away communal relations of reciprocity, "brotherliness," and
"reverence." Unlike Marx, however, there is always in Weber a hint that these nonmarket relationships just might be more obstinate and more persistent than the victo-
rious march of capitalism, rationalization, and secularization might otherwise indicate.

tion in residential neighborhoods and for the contradictions that arise within these social sites. This is not to deny the significance of neighborly sentiments, values, and relationships in making the "logic" of community antagonistic to that of capitalist accumulation. It is to suggest, however, that the material stake that people have in domestic property may also contribute to the failure of capitalist relations to completely penetrate and dominate residential communities. Social *sentiments* are not alone in establishing reciprocal relations among neighbors and in obstructing the free development of capitalist structures, processes, and values. The relational *interests* of domestic property, along with the conflicts and ideologies that they engender, may do so as well.

Because domestic property constitutes the material base of residential neighborhoods, these localities contain a contradictory set of material and political interests. Some of these property interests are compatible with capitalist accumulation. Residents who have a material stake in the equity and liquidity of domestic property will be collectively oriented toward political action and cultural ideas that support the accumulative use of property and place. Indeed, this was one of the reasons given earlier for homeownership being a "reproductive" institution. Other interests of domestic property, however, referred to previously as "accommodative" interests, are less compatible with capitalist accumulation. They are, in fact, generally antagonistic, predisposing those who possess these interests toward actions and ideas that support *non*accumulative uses of property and place; predisposing those who possess these interests to resist the actions and ideas of those with accumulative interests. Interests of accommodation, therefore, create a basis for a set of social relationships, political struggles, and counterhegemonic ideas that obstruct the free development of capitalist relations. Doing so, these accommodative interests may create, in the language of resistance theory, "relatively autonomous spaces" that will often be more congenial to resistance than to reproduction.

These "spaces" are created not only for tenants or the homeless, who have no accumulative interests, but for homeowners as well. As invested and "interested" as most owner-occupiers may be in the accumulative potential of their homes, the fact remains that they are also interested in the security, amenity, and autonomy of the property and place in which they live. Given that these interests are *other* than those of accumulation, some owner-occupiers will come to view their homes and their neighborhoods as something of a haven against the marketplace, rather than as an extension of it.[18] Given that these interests are *opposed* to those of accumulation, some owner-occupiers will come to act against any agents of the marketplace who would undermine their security, amenity, or autonomy in pursuit of real estate profits.[19]

Homeownership, then, may sometimes be less conducive to capitalist reproduction than its accumulative advantages would portend. Note, too, that when homeowners, tenants, or other locality-based groups act to obstruct the extension or development of market relationships, it is not only because a sentimental attachment to community has been disrupted, but because material interests of accommodation have been put at risk.

The *conflicts* that emerge from the contradiction between accommodative and accumulative interests may also be less protective of the capitalist status quo than has been assumed heretofore. Let me suggest three sets of circumstances under which this may be so.

First, in anticipating or experiencing threats to their accommodative interests—or merely in recognizing a collective interest in improving their security, amenity, or autonomy—neighborhood residents organize groups that can become relatively autonomous incubators of resistance to capitalist reproduction and development. Even the most politically quiescent neighborhood improvement association becomes a site where acommodative interests of property and sentimental bonds of community overlap, strengthening the sorts of communal

18. David Rose, for instance, has described the aspiration for homeownership in the working class as the "struggle for a separate sphere." Rather than integrating the worker into a capitalist society, homeownership has been "used to create a space for life-outside-capitalist-production. A sense of security, autonomy, and control over life at home, in the family, in the community, acccompanied homeownership. . . . These were not purely illusory benefits, nor was anything inherently 'reactionary' or 'divisive' about them" (quoted in Gray, 1982:283).

19. Cox and McCarthy (1982:200) have suggested that such use interests, especially autonomy, may be more useful in explaining the typically high rates of activism among owner-occupiers than their interests in exchange: "The typical activist views the ownership of his home not so much in terms of investment or exchange value, but rather as a means by which he can exert *control* over a fundamental use value—the living space. It is infringements upon the ability to control the use value of the living space that may provide the link between homeownership and neighborhood activism." The opposition of long-time homeowners in the West End to historic designation and gentrification has suggested that use interests may occasionally take precedence over exchange interests even when the defense of the former is to the long-term detriment of the latter.

relationships that Marx and Weber, Mollenkopf and Cox deem so inimical to capitalist relations.[20]

Conflict housing groups, go even futher, for they directly disrupt the stability and social peace that capitalist investment requires. Such disruptions may, in provoking the mediation of political authorities, force concessions from economic elites that block or alter the path of capitalist development. Furthermore, in struggling to defend accommodative interests, these property interest groups will sometimes develop radical alternatives to the present structure of property relations—institutions that consciously and structurally *exclude* most accumulative uses of property and place.

Second, as fragmenting as these locality-based groups and conflicts may be, there is the ever-present possibility, given the spatial segregation of social groups within the United States, for the politics of place to overlap those of race or class. When this occurs, as it did in Cincinnati and numerous other American cities during the 1960s, it can spur great leaps in political consciousness, forging links of solidarity among disparate groups and distant neighborhoods and pushing the conflicts of the place of residence out of the "city trenches" that protect the centers of power in capitalist society.

Third, in a more day-to-day fashion, these interest groups and locality-based conflicts of domestic property nourish ideas of property and place that repudiate what Cox (1981:432) has called "a meaning system, both normative and cognitive," that defines the communal living space primarily—or exclusively—as a commodified "consumption artifact." The kind of counter-ideology articulated by the Community Land Cooperative in its ongoing struggle with the DSNA, the MPPF, and other interest groups who would further gentrify and commodify the West End provides a perfect example. Domestic property, according to the CLC, should be reserved for the accommodative use

---

20. Such organizational affiliations and communal bonds may become the basis for collective resistance not only in the place of residence, but in the place of work as well. This may be particularly true for women. Many of the patterns of domination and exploitation that women experience in the capitalist workplace are replicated and reinforced through similar patterns in the family, church, and community. But there is also reason to expect that the social networks and voluntary organizations of the homeplace (in which women are typically more "invested" than men) will sometimes serve as important sources of support for the collective, oppositional activity of women in the workplace. References to the homeplace providing such support can be found in Frankel (1984) and in Sacks (1984). For a discussion of other nonworkplace "incubators" of resistance to capitalist relations, see Dreier (1980).

and political empowerment of those in need of shelter, not for the accumulative use and economic enrichment of those in search of profits. The extension and development of The Market and the activities of those who "irresponsibily" act in its name should be regarded and resisted as threats to the security and community of those who have made the neighborhood their long-term home. "Community" should be conceived as a place-bound network of mutuality and neighborliness, not as a built environment of historic structures and commodified "housing packages." Justice should precede pluralism in any society where property and power are so unequally distributed. Conflict, in an unjust society, should be both encouraged and affirmed.

Ideas such as these are mirror images of those that legitimate the accumulative use and capitalist penetration of residential neighborhoods. In fact, such ideas are more conducive to the production and reproduction of oppositional behavior than they are to the reproduction of capitalist relations.

As sketchy as this picture may be, it does suggest that domestic property analysis may provide a new way of studying and interpreting the long-noted tendency of community relations to obstruct market relations. Clearly, the systemic antagonism between the logic of community and the logic of accumulation that Mollenkopf and others have described is *not* reducible to the locality-based antagonism between accommodative and accumulative property interests. On the other hand, the organizations, conflicts, and ideas that appear at the cusp of this latter contradiction *do* shed new light on the incompatibility of many residential settings to the reproduction of capitalist relations. They do suggest, in their appearance and operation, that the residential neighborhood may be a social site not only for reproduction but for resistance as well. It is an expanded theory of capitalist reproduction, therefore, to which domestic property analysis may make its greatest contribution—a theory in which, as Apple (1982:8) has put it, "reproduction and contestation go hand in hand."

13

Neighborhood Politics
and Planning

To organize a community you must understand that in a highly
mobile, urbanized society the word "community" means
community of interests, *not* physical community. The
exceptions are ethnic ghettos where segregation has
resulted in physical communities that coincide with their
community of interests, or, during political campaigns, political
districts that are based on geographical demarcations.
—SAUL ALINSKY (1971:120)

Professional agitator and political mentor to an entire generation of
community organizers, neighborhood planners, and grassroots "radicals" of every stripe, Saul Alinsky was right to advise his colleagues to
base their local organizing efforts upon the shared "interests" of residential populations. Political action in the place of residence *is* a function of the interests that people objectively possess, subjectively recognize, and collectively act upon. Alinsky, however, was wrong to
assume such interests to lack a "physical," spatial component outside
of the ethnic ghetto or political ward. Some of the most politically
significant (and politically volatile) interests that people possess are
tied to land and buildings that they personally use for shelter or
profit. Domestic property has a physical, spatial dimension—as does
the "community of interests" that people share by virtue of their common relation to that property. These interests are indigenous to a
particular locality. They are affected by what happens in and to that
locality. They are a large part of what makes collective action in the
place of residence both a strategic possibility and, under the right
conditions of consciousness and organization, a political reality.

These interests are also what makes locality-based action somewhat understandable, somewhat predictable, and somewhat susceptible to practical manipulation and management. By examining the interests and conditions that engender locality-based action, the "disinterested" researcher may find new ways of explaining why locality-based groups come into being, why they develop (or decline), and why they act as they do. A similar examination may allow the "interested" practitioner to find new ways of intervening in the organization, behavior, and interaction of these groups. In short, a better understanding of the interests (and conditions) that produce and pattern locality-based action may contribute not only to a better theory of collective action in the place of residence, but to a better practice of neighborhood politics and planning.

ELUSIVE SOLIDARITY

Aside from challenging Alinsky's assumption that mobility and urbanization have put an end to most interests of "physical" community, domestic property analysis both challenges and corrects a popular brand of urban theory and neighborhood practice that assumes a simple, dichotomous split in the interests of urban populations. On a citywide scale, this popular perspective focuses on the domination of urban politics by capitalist elites or procapitalist "growth coalitions" while anticipating the formation, in times of crisis, of broad, anticapitalist alliances among the urban consumers of housing, public transportation, and other "means of collective consumption" (cf. Castells, 1977, 1978). At the neighborhood level, a similar perspective tends to reduce all political conflict into a struggle between "accumulation" and "community" (cf. Mollenkopf, 1981a) or between "place entrepreneurs" and "community residents" (cf. Logan and Molotch, 1987).

Domestic property analysis reveals a more complicated, more "fractured" political landscape. True, it does posit a tendency for domestic property interests and domestic property interest groups to diverge and conflict along an axis created by the antagonism of accumulation and accommodation, but domestic property analysis also reveals a complex mosaic of objectively different and conflicting interests on both sides of this political divide. The cleavages created by this interest mosaic can make solidarity an elusive goal—whatever a locality's long-term tendancy toward political bifurcation. They can impart a fragility to capitalist coalitions, a fragility to community coalitions, even a fragility to organizations made up exclusively of homeowners or tenants that is underestimated or overlooked by all who presume only two sets of interests in the urban neighborhood. Political practice in the fractured community can succeed only by taking such "elusive solidarity" into account.

Part of this organizational fragility is undoubtedly due to the sheer number of empirical conditions that must be present to engender and sustain locality-based collective action, whether that action is undertaken by a single property interest group or by a cluster of these groups.[1] The modification or removal of any of these conditions can erode whatever solidarity has been achieved, leading to the decline or demise of whatever organization has been developed to promote a collectivity's interests. Contributing even more to organizational fragility, however, when *multiple* groups have joined together, are the numerous objective and subjective differences that exist among the domestic property interests of the local population. Forging and maintaining any urban coalition in the face of such differences can be a difficult task indeed.

As for the maintenance of capitalist coalitions, very little attention has been given to the presence of "objectively different and conflicting" interests within the ranks of private capital. Most of my attention has been focused on differences and divisions existing within the ranks of residential populations. Nevertheless, the West End case study does give a glimpse of competing interests among Cincinnati's capitalists, at least insofar as the neighborhood's physical redevelopment was concerned. From the City Plan of 1925 until the urban renewal of the 1950s, there was continuous tension between those capitalist interest groups that would keep the West End a densely populated residential slum and those that would convert most of this territory to commercial and industrial use. On the side of slum per-

1. It is worth repeating an earlier observation about the formation and development of these coalitions (or "clusters") of property interest groups, made in regard to the rise and fall of the West End Community Council. Such coalitions, when organized around one or more of the property interests that are shared by a coalition's constituent groups, tend to behave and develop along the same lines as a *single* property interest group. Thus the three-stage model that was designed to explain the genesis and development of collective action by an individual interest group like private tenants or acquisitive owner-occupiers also tends to be applicable to the genesis and development of organized clusters like homeowner associations, capitalist growth coalitions, or local community councils. Similarly, what has been said about the production and patterning of locality-based conflict among individual property interest groups tends also to describe conflicts among organized clusters of these groups.

petuation were the landlords and developers who were reaping exhorbitant profits by subdividing and renting minimally maintained West End tenements. Here too were real estate brokers and mortgage bankers who opposed urban renewal out of a dual fear that tens of thousands of displaced blacks would either overrun nearby neighborhoods, threatening local property values, or overrule the popular consensus against public housing, which the real estate industry had lobbied so long and so hard to create. On the side of redevelopment were the industrialists, commercial bankers, and larger developers, who finally succeeded in rebuilding most of the West End in their own image, for their own interests.

Even within this redevelopment camp, however, political consensus proved difficult to maintain—so much so that the growth coalition that led the campaign to bulldoze and rebuild the West End was unable to finish the job. There were many reasons for this, not the least of which was the organized resistance of West End residents. But it is important to note that the coalition itself did not survive the 1960s. After twenty years of advocacy on behalf of Cincinnati's master plan, the captains of industry that had led the Citizens Development Committee handed over the Committee's staff and agenda to the Chamber of Commerce, a group of commercial capitalists with different interests and different priorities than those that had united and motivated the original members of the CDC. So weakened, so fractured was Cincinnati's growth coalition by 1967 that a project the size of Queensgate II could not even be launched, let alone completed. Queensgate II lies largely undeveloped to the present day.

If it is politically unwise to assume a unitary interest among those who have an entrepreneurial stake in capital accumulation, it is equally imprudent to assume a single "community" interest among those who dwell within the same neighborhood. Even when a neighborhood's residential population is not otherwise divided by race, class, ethnicity, or other social attributes, its interests will be materially and politically divided by the cross-cutting cleavages of domestic property. These cleavages may be politically insignificant only when (1) a neighborhood has but a single property interest group, (2) an external event like urban renewal threatens the interests of all of a neighborhood's property groups, or (3) racial, occupational, ethnic, or other social solidarities are actively mobilized, bridging the gap between different property interest groups.

Such atypical circumstances might sometimes allow local organizers and planners temporarily to cultivate undivided, community-wide support. More likely and lasting, however, are circumstances in which domestic property cleavages *cannot* be politically avoided or ignored. The fragmentation of the WECC, for example, occurred despite nearly ten years of solidarity. When the external threat of urban renewal and the unifying passions of the civil rights movement passed from the scene, the council's organizers could no longer paper over the political stresses created by the neighborhood's underlying structure of domestic property. Likewise, the latest attempt by the city's neighborhood planners to resurrect the WECC as the lone "spokesman" for the West End has been stymied, so far, by deep divisions separating different property interest groups. The city's planners have yet to discover a common political ground among the neighborhood's contending groups.[2]

Domestic property analysis suggests, moreover, that solidarity may be elusive not only within the accumulative ranks of capitalist growth coalitions and within the accommodative ranks of community coalitions, but within the ranks of homeowners and tenants as well. Social scientists, city planners, and community activists are nearly unanimous in regarding homeowners as a single interest group. Tenants, too, tend to be treated as if they all possessed the same interests. Domestic property analysis challenges the accuracy of both assessments and the adequacy of any political strategy based on them.

The diverse interests and diverse interest groups engendered by the various (objective) relations that a population bears to domestic property, accompanied by a population's different (subjective) assessments of what those relations are (or should be), can cause great difficulty in attaining and sustaining any number of seemingly "natural" political alliances, coalitions, or groups. Solidarity in the fractured community can be an elusive goal. Domestic property analysis can provide considerable insight into why.

SELECTIVE SOLIDARITY

Elusive as it may be, political solidarity in the place of residence is neither impossible nor infrequent. Property interest groups do form. On occasion, they even join together in cooperative action, pursuing

2. If it is imprudent and impractical to assume only two sets of interests in the urban neighborhood, as many neo-Marxist and "growth coalition" theorists do, it is even more simplistic and ineffective to assume only one set. It is not uncommon, however, to find municipal planners and social reformers pursuing strategies of neigh-

common goals. Communities do act. Therefore, despite my emphasis on the divisiveness of domestic property interests in the present study, property interests can occasionally lead two or more groups into alliance. Just as interests that are "objectively different and conflicting" can provide a basis for intergroup conflict, interests that are similar and compatible can provide a basis for intergroup cooperation.

This is not to suggest that the practitioner of neighborhood politics or planning should ignore the lesson of elusive solidarity; indeed, for every property interest that would draw two or more locality-based groups together, there is usually another interest threatening to drive them apart. There is too much diversity in the interests possessed and perceived by various groups for the practitioner to act as if the interests of any two groups are altogether the same. There is nearly always a difference, always a tension.

But there is also nearly always a way of using those interests (and ideas) that groups do have in common to forge alliances that succeed and endure for a time. The strategies that accomplish this political goal are derived from a general approach to community organizing that might be called "selective solidarity": the practice of building neighborhood organizations on the basis of one or more property interests that are similar for two or more groups, while avoiding—or neutralizing—those interests that are different.

The success of this rather obvious approach depends upon an accurate analysis of the interests and conditions that underlie the "comings and goings" of locality-based groups. The organizer or planner who would foster collective action is little different than the social researcher who would study and explain it. The practitioner, however, seeks not only to understand these locality-based groups but to influence their development and behavior. By evaluating the objective, relational interests that distinguish and motivate the members of a residential neighborhood, the practitioner can select those issues that cut across existing cleavages; he or she can work with and not against the political grain of the population that he or she would organizationally shape in a certain way. By recognizing the prerequisites of consciousness and organization, moreover, the practitioner can work with those conditions that facilitate the formation and maintenance of

borhood planning and community development that make precisely this assumption of a single neighborhood interest. These practitioners act as if the only barriers to political consensus and common action in a given neighborhood were the lack of coordination among various public and private parties and the lack of rational design in the delivery of various public or private services.

locality-based organizations (or coalitions) and against those that make them so difficult to establish and sustain.

This general approach can be strategically applied to any number of neighborhood issues that form the politics of place. I have chosen two such issues for the sake of illustration, what I shall call the "politics of community" and the "politics of homeownership."

The Politics of Community

What is usually described as "community action" tends in reality to be collective action by a coalition of separate property interest groups that have managed to unite, for a time, into a single neighborhood organization, community council, or residents association, with membership open to all who live within a certain geographical area. These "community" organizations typically form and act on the basis of interests that their members share in the accommodative use of property and place (although in neighborhoods where homeowners are the primary interest group, accumulative interests may also be involved). Common interests of security, amenity, and autonomy typically determine the organization's charter, program, and course of action. These interests tend to be the basis, as well, for the organization's conflictual—or cooperative—relations with other groups, inside and outside the neighborhood.

Building and sustaining neighborhood-wide, multigroup coalitions can be furthered by at least four political strategies, each of which attempts to neutralize the interest-based cleavages that exist among a "community" organization's constituent groups. The first of these is a planning strategy that eliminates intergroup conflict by eliminating (or preventing) any interest-group diversity that might otherwise develop within a given locality. A locality with a *single* property interest group is much easier to forge into a single community organization than a locality with a half dozen of these groups. Thus a planning strategy that prevents homeowner-driven gentrification in a neighborhood where nearly all of the housing units have long been occupied by private tenants may preserve a "community" with a single set of tenant interests. Conversely, a planning strategy that encourages homeowner gentrification of a tenant-dominated neighborhood or one that erects zoning barriers around a homeowner-dominated neighborhood to exclude the construction of multi-unit housing may promote a community with a single set of homeowner interests. Either strategy results in a residential population that is easier to form into a single community organization.

Community activists might also pursue a strategy of "common threat": building an organization around carefully selected issues, problems, or events that negatively affect the property interests of everyone with a residential stake in the same locality. Identifying threats that touch nearly all of a neighborhood's residents and transforming them into issues for common action was, in fact, the core of Alinsky's particular approach to community organizing:

> In the beginning the organizer's first job is to create the issues or problems. It sounds mad to say that a community such as a low-income ghetto or even a middle-class community has no issues per se. The reader may feel that this statement borders on lunacy, particularly with respect to low-income communities. The simple fact is that in any communty, regardless of how poor, people may have serious problems— but they do not have issues, they have a bad scene. (1971:119)

A strategy of common threat is most likely to be successful when combined with a third strategy, that of mobilizing a neighborhood's various property interest groups on the basis of racial, religious, or other common attributes, temporarily bridging the gap and mitigating the tension existing among groups with different property interests. The collapse of the West End Community Council notwithstanding, such bridges can be sustained for many years—particularly when buttressed by a common threat that is perceived not only as an attack upon a population's property interests but upon its identity or survival as a racial, religious, or ethnic community.[3]

Finally, rather than focusing on a common threat, the organizer or planner might pursue a strategy of "public amenity organizing." Except in neighborhoods like the West End, where every improvement will be seen by the indigenous population as another step toward gentrification, there are usually opportunities for all property groups to work together on such politically neutral endeavors as improving a playground, cleaning up vacant lots, or planting trees and flowers in public spaces. To the extent that the benefits of these amenity improvements are shared by all, with harm to none, the divisiveness of

3. This sort of multilayered perception of a common threat is precisely what occurred in the West End during the heyday of the West End Community Council, when urban renewal was increasingly portrayed not only as a physical threat to domestic property but as a racist threat to a community and culture that a beleaguered black population had gradually built up over several generations.

different property interests can be put aside in cooperative community action.

Employing such strategies, organizers and planners may be able to create circumstances in which community-wide support for their programs and plans is not undermined or contested by the fractious relations of multiple property interest groups. There is, however, an alternative tack. Instead of adopting a posture of political neutrality in attempting to forge all of these groups into a single association, organizers and planners can foster solidarity among a smaller subset of a neighborhood's groups—promoting the interests of one segment of the community over those of another.

Practitioners can, in a phrase, *choose sides.* They can practice their craft on behalf of these programs, policies, and plans that support accumulative uses of domestic property or on behalf of those that support accommodative uses. While I recognize that describing the practitioner's choice in this way risks reviving the kind of simplistic dichotomy that I have just rejected, one cannot ignore that a general divide in the interests and groups that make up a neighborhood's political life does exist, one that makes it very difficult—perhaps impossible—for organizers and planners to ply their trade on both sides at once.

The choice to work for accumulative interests and groups has, in effect, already been made by city planners who endorse the return of urban renewal land to the marketplace, tax holidays for inner-city developers, or low-interest rehabilitation loans for landlords and "back-to-the-city" homeowners. This choice is also unintentionally made by community organizers who fight the interest groups of private capital, in the words of Kevin Cox (1981:438), "on capital's own terrain"—endorsing strategies which assume that "the community can only be saved by treating the communal living space as a commodity": "Banks redlining the area, for example, have to be convinced that the neighborhood is a good investment. . . . Community organizations form their own realty organizations. . . . And those whose greatest concern is community have to appeal for the support of those whose primary interest is neighborhood-as-commodity through a scenario terminating in massive property value impacts."

I prefer to focus on the other side of the political divide, since my own choices have led me to work almost exclusively in support of organizations that defend locality-based interests of accommodation. To the extent that these accommodative strategies impede or contest the more accumulative uses to which domestic property is routinely put—and to the extent that they also disrupt the capitalist domination of a community's physical development, social relations, and social meanings—these strategies contribute to what may be called "radical reform." As such, they fall within the purview of what Kraushaar, among others, has described as "progressive planning."[4]

The first of these "progressive" accommodative strategies—indeed, the essence of all accommodative strategies—is the defense of *security of tenure* for all residents as the primary interest of domestic property and the bottom-line political demand of locality-based activism. The right to stay put can be deemed a prerequisite for every one of the other advantages of accommodation. The stability and "rootedness" that security allows, moreover, tends to be an important precondition of political participation and organization at the neighborhood level (cf. Rich and Wandersman, 1983). A residential population that lacks such spatial "fixity" is enormously difficult to organize. Any measure that enhances security of tenure, therefore, particularly for groups without equity, should have the dual effect of impeding accumulative uses of domestic property and making the formation and maintenance of locality-based organizations easier to achieve.[5]

Second, intergroup conflict, played out in public, can be a remarkably effective accommodative strategy. Not only can it raise the political consciousness of powerless people trapped in the passivity of a "bad scene," conflict can discourage those who would exploit or underwrite the potential profitability of such a scene. Conflict can give pause to prospective lenders and turn away prospective investors,

4. Kraushaar (1988:91) has defined "progressive planning" as activity pursued in conscious furtherance of "radical reform," defining the latter in terms of changes that increase the "democratic rights and power of 'average' citizens in their daily lives as workers and consumers." Radical reform, in the current context, refers to the empowerment of average citizens in their daily lives as consumers of housing and as residents of local neighborhoods. Kraushaar correctly calls attention to the special dilemma at the heart of such radical reform: "Radical reform takes as its objectives fundamental political and economic changes, which it seeks to attain without crises or revolution. But radical reform sees the existing economic and institutional mechanisms of society as a primary cause of inequity and inequality. Therefore I use the term 'radical reform' deliberately, to reflect the contradictions inherent in its objectives and activities."

5. Examples include just-cause eviction statutes, rent control ordinances, rent stabilization agreements, condominium and cooperative conversion regulations, and various forms of housing tenure that grant tenants greater security and greater managerial control over their units. Not to be discounted, moreover, are the relocation strictures and benefits that have been built into the Uniform Relocation Act and the federal Community Development Block Grant Program in recent years. These promote tenant security by significantly increasing the financial cost to public agencies of displacing families.

leading both to seek more stable, peaceful locales.[6] Conflict can cause politicians and government officials to temper their support for the projects and plans of private capital. In short, anything that makes the tension between accommodative and accumulative interests more acute and the conflict between interest groups more overt can poison the investment climate that makes accumulative uses of domestic property both possible and desirable.

Third, community organizing and neighborhood planning can strengthen institutions, practices, and rituals that reproduce, within the "cultural terrain" of residential neighborhoods, *not* the ideologies of capitalist accumulation, but oppositional ideas of property and place.[7] In the words of Giroux, the essential task of such a strategy would be:

> to analyze what counter-hegemonic elements such cultural fields con-
> tain, and how they tend to become incorporated into the dominant
> culture and subsequently stripped of their political possibilities. Implicit
> in such an analysis is the need to develop strategies . . . in which oppo-
> sitional cultures might be rescued from the processes of incorporation
> in order to provide the basis for a viable political force. (1983:285)

Counted among these "counter-hegemonic elements" are ideas of domestic property that elevate accommodation over accumulation: ideas (and models) that treat housing as a social good instead of a speculative commodity, ideas (and practices) that treat housing as a human right instead of a precarious privilege.[8]

Included, as well, among the "counter-hegemonic elements" of the homeplace are those nonmarket sentiments, practices, and attach-

---

6. There is little doubt, for example, that the ongoing conflict between the CLC and the DSNA has played a significant role in slowing the pace of gentrification in the upper West End.

7. Not least important, in this regard, is the need to sustain such oppositional elements within a neighborhood's own organizations. "Counter-hegemonic" rituals of stewardship, neighborliness, and mutual aid, like those celebrated by neighborhood improvement associations, are often put aside by organizations that have reached a more conflictual or radical level of development—or they are simply overlooked amidst the ongoing struggle to overcome an opponent or develop a particular piece of property. Similarly, "counter-ideologies" of property and place like those proclaimed by the Community Land Cooperative can lose their clarity and force as one generation succeeds another in occupying the social property that has been created. Such rituals and ideas need rescuing again and again.

8. A discussion of the ideological and practical challenge that a "right to housing" poses for the hegemonic ideas of "housing as property" and "housing as commodity" appears in Davis (1990).

ments that bind person to person, and person to place. Such "spontaneous human relations," as Max Weber noted, can serve as "obstruc-
tions" to the free development of the "bare market relationship"
(Roth and Wittich, 1978:636) within a neighborhood. What this
means for progressive practice, I believe, is that *cultural* rituals that
strengthen and celebrate the bonds among neighbors may be as important a part of an accommodative strategy as *political* "rituals"
that create issues and heighten conflict.

Neighborhood women often play a special role in both. Indeed,
anyone who has practiced organizing or planning at the neighborhood level for any length of time has probably discovered that women
make up the majority of most locality-based organizations that promote accommodative interests and ideas. Conversely, organizations
representing acquisitive homeowners, landlords, developers, and
others who have a more accumulative stake in domestic property tend
to be dominated by men.[9] Many explanations can be offered for this
remarkably consistent pattern, including the feminization of poverty,
the predominance of female-headed households among public and
private tenants, and the exclusion of women from activities that center on business and finance. But something else is going on here, as
well. Interests, ideas, and relationships that define the place of residence as "community," rather than "commodity," tend to spark the
political mobilization of women, when threatened, more often than
they spur the mobilization of men. Furthermore, to the extent that
there exists an "oppositional culture" within the terrain of the local
neighborhood, the bearers of that tradition, more often than not, are
the locality's women. These are personal observations that have not
been tested by systematic research, but I believe these patterns to be
pervasive enough to recommend the practical wisdom of taking them
into account.

Finally, and most important over the long run, a progressive politics of community depends upon the forging of new political alliances,
within the neighborhood and without, enlisting new institutions and
new interest groups in the defense of accommodative uses of property
and place. Included in such alliances should be institutions like
churches, charities, and religious orders for whom "stability," "community," "justice," and even "social property" are often familiar
values and goals. Progressive practitioners must also find ways of

---

9. Realtors are a notable exception. Although the larger interest group of which
realtors are a part, the "speculators," is dominated by men, women are well represented within the ranks of licensed real estate brokers.

reaching beyond those property interest groups like tenants and the homeless, which have no stake in accumulation, to include those residential groups who have an interest in *both* accommodation and accumulation. In other words, a progressive politics of community requires organizers and planners to regard homeowners in a new political light, an unconventional perspective to which domestic property analysis gives considerable credence.

The Politics of Homeownership

Homeowners have been typically regarded by most community theorists and practitioners as a single interest group whose obsession with the rise and fall of their property values makes them politically active to an unusual degree but predictably conservative. Far from being considered a potential ally of tenants, churches, or other groups and institutions struggling to defend accommodative interests of domestic property, homeowners have been treated as part of the problem—an impediment (or threat) to accommodative interests, despite their own stake in the security, autonomy, and amenity of property and place.

Domestic property analysis challenges this popular notion. Just as it repudiates a unitary "consumer" interest for those who collectively consume urban services and a unitary "community" interest for those who reside in a particular locality, domestic property analysis repudiates a unitary "homeowner" interest for those who tenurially and functionally relate to domestic property as owner-occupiers. Three homeowner interest groups have been identified: owner-occupiers of acquisitive property, owner-occupiers of household property, and owner-occupiers of social property. By acknowledging the differences among these homeowner groups, private activists and public officials of any ideological stripe should be better able to assess the differential impact of proposed programs, plans, or policies on each—and to anticipate the political response of each. Practitioners with a more progressive bent should be able to take selective advantage of such differences, both in promoting accommodative uses of property and place and in resisting accumulative uses that undermine security and threaten community.

The material and political differences existing between two of these groups, the acquisitive homeowners and the social homeowners, have already been discussed in some detail, particularly with regard to the contentious relations between these groups in the West End. Less has been said about the politically conflicted "middle ground" that the homeowners of household property tend to occupy in many urban neighborhoods. Their particular situation deserves a closer look, using the West End for illustration.

West End homeowners who have little or no strategic interest in the accumulative uses of their domestic property currently have no organizational base of their own, their former block clubs having all but disappeared by the 1980s. Nevertheless, they cannot be politically disregarded. These household homeowners are sometimes found in public conflict with the acquisitive homeowners of the DSNA and, to the extent that individual household homeowners do participate politically in the neighborhood, they tend to support either the social homeowners of the CLC or the tenants of the WECC. Of greater political significance, however, is the fact that the aging members of this quasi-group of household homeowners control a significant number of residential parcels in the upper West End. Whatever happens to these parcels—that is, whether they go to resident owners of the CLC, to supporters of the DSNA, or to owner-occupiers with strategic interests that are more accommodative than accumulative—will significantly affect both the current balance of political power and the future development of the neighborhood.

This middle group may be politically pivotal in another way. During the next few years, the Miami Purchase Preservation Fund, with the assistance of several city agencies, may succeed in rehabilitating a large number of housing units. The people who occupy these units will swell the ranks of West End homeowners who have neither a CLC-style limitation on their accumulative interests nor a DSNA-style emphasis on accumulation. Whether or not these owner-occupiers actually organize as a separate political group, as the MPPA has planned, the political choices they make, either supporting positions of the CLC or those of the DSNA, may tip the balance in the ongoing struggle between these organized conflict groups.

Generalizing from the case at hand, it can be said that urban neighborhoods sometimes contain a group of household homeowners that are (1) politically situated between more accommodative or accumulative homeowner groups and (2) contentiously oriented toward one extreme or the other, depending upon local circumstances. In a neighborhood like the West End, this middle group of owner-occupiers is rather small; in other neighborhoods, household homeowners may constitute the bulk of the residential population. In either case, their political role is likely to be significant. Depending upon which groups regularly receive their support, which groups eventually acquire their property, and which interests they personally and collectively defend, this pivotal group of owner-occupiers can tilt the balance of a neighborhood's politics, preserving the character of a place of residence for either accommodation or accumulation.

Every owner-occupier is somewhat pivotal in this regard, of course, since all have both an accommodative and accumulative stake. But social homeowners, like those of the CLC, or acquisitive homeowners, like those of the DSNA, are already materially and politically oriented in a single direction. They are predisposed, by their property positions, toward cooperation with some groups and toward conflict with others. By contrast, household homeowners in the middle can— and do—go either way. They will sometimes be found fighting to defend what Cox (1981) has called "the communal living space as community." They will sometimes be found fighting to promote the "communal living space as commodity." Their interests are ambiguous—and often contradictory. So, too, is the pattern of action and conflict that their property interests produce.

For those practitioners with a particular bias toward defending the accommodative interests of residential groups and promoting the communal relations of residential neighborhoods *against* the accumulative interests and commodity relations of private capital, the ambiguity of the property positions occupied by each of these homeowner groups suggest three progressive strategies.

Household homeowners, teetering on the point of the political fulcrum between accommodation and accumulation, can be tipped away from private capital by organizational and cultural strategies that (1) strengthen their communal ties with neighbors who do *not* possess domestic property and (2) enhance and celebrate accommodative uses of property and place. This means, in particular, abandoning a political perspective and practical strategy of automatically relegating all homeowners to the political camp of private capital. This means finding new ways to integrate household homeowners into collective activities that preserve the use and meaning of the "communal living space as community." Since the elderly represent a rather high percentage of owner-occupiers in many neighborhoods—and may make up the *majority* of a locality's household homeowners—this strategy may be especially effective when tailored to their situation. Women, too, tend to be overrepresented among those owner-occupiers whose interest in domestic property is more accommodative than accumulative. Addressing the special needs of women, children, and the elderly, therefore, may be an accommodative strategy with some likelihood of success in drawing household homeowners into common cause with their nonacquisitive neighbors.

As for acquisitive homeowners, a political and ideological wedge can be driven between their interests and those of private capital. Despite their interest in financial gain, the accommodative interests of acquisitive homeowners can sometimes be mobilized against capitalist interest groups. Opportunities may also exist for separating the accumulative interests of this homeowner group from those of landlords, developers, or financiers. This is primarily a matter of identifying where the interests of acquisitive homeowners diverge from those of private capital and selecting issues and activities that exacerbate those differences. Such a strategy only becomes possible, of course, for the practitioner who refuses to treat all homeowners as if their "conservative" accumulative interests must make them them the inevitable allies of private capital.

Finally, the politics of homeownership can be given an accommodative, anticapital bias by expanding the proportion of owner-occupied property that has been "decommodified"—expanding, in effect, the local stock of social property. Limited equity housing cooperatives and community land trusts are the two examples of social property that have been prominently mentioned here, but any measure, public or private, that restricts or removes the homeowner's stake in accumulation tends to bring accommodative interests to the fore, while simultaneously closing the political gap between neighbors who own domestic property and those who do not. Social property, in other words, is a political strategy for making homeownership a bulwark of community relations instead of a mainstay of commodity relations—a source of solidarity within the residential neighborhood, instead of a source of financial competition and political fragmentation.[10]

AGENCY AND STRUCTURE

The locality-based model of collective action proposed in this book has a number of practical implications for the formation, development, and maintenance of locality-based organizations. The most im-

10. An expanding supply of social property can also help stabilize some of the more transient segments of a neighborhood's population, granting more households the right to stay put. Such spatial fixity, combined with the organizational umbrella that is part of most models of social property, makes organizing social homeowners for collective action an easier task than organizing private tenants.

portant of these have to do with the model's specification of objective property interests as the basis for group formation and collective action, its identification of empirical conditions underlying consciousness and organization, and its integration of consciousness and organization in a dynamic, staged sequence of organizational development or decline.

Aside from directing the practitioner's attention to the interests and conditions that bring locality-based groups into being, the three-stage model of collective action introduces a dynamic, developmental element into organizational analysis and planning that is often overlooked. The model's assumption of two moments of collective action and three levels of interest-group development raises a number of practical questions for the community organizer or neighborhood planner who would act in support of the collective action of a particular locality-based organization. For example, what sort of organization is the practitioner trying to promote: an improvement group, a conflict group, or a radical group? Can consciousness and organization be brought into alignment to attain and sustain that preferred level of development? What are the drawbacks to remaining at the present level of development? What are the advantages to moving to a "higher" level of development—or returning to a "lower" level? What are the dangers of straddling more than one level at once?

The three-stage model, in raising questions like these, forces the practitioner to treat the locality-based organization as a changing—and changeable—entity, the development or decline of which follows the complex interaction of consciousness, organization, and collective action. To ignore this developmental dynamic is to lessen the practitioner's chances of successfully intervening in the creation, guidance, and support of locality-based groups.

Such talk of practical intervention in the politics of place is an appropriate, even if somewhat ironic, note on which to end the discussion of locality-based collective action. It is appropriate to conclude in this way for the simple reason that this is where I originally began. Confronted with the political fact that "even in big cities people continue to act collectively at times on the basis of common territory," existing theories of collective action seemed inadequate to the task of explaining why "communities act." So I sought to develop a theoretical framework that might provide a better understanding of the conditions under which such locality-based action occurs. Confronted with the political fact that in neighborhoods like the West End people continue to act contentiously, even when they share a common territory, existing theories of community action seemed inadequate to the task of explaining why residential "communities" are so frequently fractured and fractious. So I sought to develop a theoretical framework that might provide a better understanding of the conditions under which such intergroup conflict occurs. As an organizer and planner personally confronted with the practical task of intervening in the development of locality-based organizations like those in the West End, I discovered among practitioners of my craft an inadequate appreciation for the developmental dynamic that shapes and forms such organizations. So I sought an understanding of locality-based collective action that could account not only for its genesis, but for its development or decline as well.

If such mention of politics and practice also seems an ironic note on which to end, it is because so much of what has been said herein has seemed to exclude human agency. Collective action, intergroup conflict, and interest-group development in the place of residence have been "explained" less in terms of the volitionally directed wants and actions of individuals than in terms of the objectively constituted interests and "action orientations" of domestic property positions. Even making the conversion process the theoretical linchpin of the current analysis has seemed to salvage little role for human agency, since the subjective recognition of objective interests relies so heavily upon empirical conditions like instability, interaction, ideology, and the rest.

Nevertheless, among all of the structures, interests, and conditions that have been said to engender locality-based action, there is still a place for human agency. Not only are the empirical conditions of collective action somewhat susceptible to manipulation by individual practitioners, operating inside or outside of the locality, but the values, experience, attitudes, and purposive activity of individual actors are always interposed between the structural determinants and collective outcomes of group formation. Human individuality and instrumentality, in other words, *mediate* between the structure of domestic property and the formation, development, and behavior of locality-based groups.

In short, as much as we may look to an underlying structure of objective interests and empirical conditions to understand the continuing tendency of people to act collectively on the basis of a common territory, human agency is never entirely absent. There is ample room, in theory and in practice, for the mediation and intervention of individual actors. "Communities" do act, but this seldom precludes the political possibility of individuals acting as well.

Appendix A
Sources and Methods

The study of Cincinnati's West End combines historical narrative, ethnographic description, and sociological analysis to examine the formation, interaction, development, and demise of organized groups of a particular kind: those with a membership and leadership recruited from a single neighborhood and those with a conscious, collective purpose of protecting and promoting the material well-being of those who reside in that neighborhood. Such a focus on what I have called "locality-based" organizations raises significant issues regarding the sources and methods used in researching and preparing the case study.

The documentary record. The case study makes extensive use of available written records, including census reports, city plans, scholarly studies, newspaper articles, the publications of municipal agencies, and the corporate documents and promotional materials of West End organizations. The papers of the Citizens Development Committee and the Cincinnati Metropolitan Housing Authority, contained in the archives of the Cincinnati Historical Society, proved especially helpful in the historical investigation of the "besieged community," presented in Chapter 7.

Such written records were necessarily relegated to a more secondary, confirmatory role in Chapters 8, 9, and 10, for three reasons.

First, the public record of social relations within black communities is rather sparse. Municipal agencies and metropolitan newspapers tend to focus almost exclusively on the social pathologies of neighborhoods like the West End, generally ignoring their organizations, personalities, and politics. Second, the record-keeping of voluntary, locality-based organizations tends to be sporadic at best. There are often few written records to examine. Finally, the evolution of political consciousness, the "comings and goings" of locality-based groups, and the tensions that arise among them seldom leave a written trail. These are not events that are normally the "stuff" of documentation, particularly when they occur within a low-income neighborhood like the West End.

Consequently, the primary sources of information for what I have called the "mobilized community," the "fractured community," and the "contested community" have been the oral histories and personal insights of people who were or are a part of these communities of interest.

I have also relied upon my own observations of the neighborhood's political and organizational life. For most of 1983, as a regional representative for the Massachusetts-based Institute for Community Economics, I lived and worked in the West End. Operating out of the rectory of St. Joseph's Church on Ezzard Charles Drive, I provided technical assistance to nonprofit housing development organizations in Cincinnati and, on occasion, in neighboring states. The organization with which I worked most closely was the Community Land Cooperative of Cincinnati (CLC).

As a professional consultant to the CLC, I had privileged access to the leaders, documents, members, and meetings of this grassroots organization, as well as a vantage point from which to observe its interaction with other organizations and groups. Thus whatever information I have gleaned from other sources pertaining to the neighborhood's recent history has been supplemented by my own field notes, observations, and impressions. Despite this involvement, I have made a rigorous effort to cast the many organizations, persons, and events that appear herein in a light that is equally critical and equally fair to all.

Selection of informants. The necessity of depending upon local informants for much of my information about the internal politics of the West End required me to make decisions about who might possess the most accurate information and how particular individuals should be selected for interview from this larger pool of presumably well-informed people.

I decided to interview local "influentials"; that is, leaders of the neighborhood's organized groups, past and present, and other individuals who were described by these organizational leaders as having played a pivotal role in the neighborhood's recent history. While I recognized that the accounts of these influentials might deviate in some respects from the interpretation of recent events that more rank-and-file residents might offer, I believed that the people who would be the best able to identify the material interests, collective purposes, and "empirical conditions" underlying the genesis and development of the neighborhood's locality-based groups would be those who had been the most influential in building and guiding these organizations.

My original plan, after compiling a list of every locality-based organization that had been politically active in the West End between 1960 and 1985, was to interview every person who had served as an officer, staff member, or board member in any such group. I then planned to interview several people inside and outside the West End who had played a significant role in the neighborhood's physical and political development but who had not been a positional leader of one of its organized groups.

The number of people eventually interviewed, as might have been expected, was less than intended. When practical, I adhered to my original plan of interviewing every "influential" within a given organization. I was particularly successful with the leaders of the DSNA and the CLC. For the neighborhood's other organizations, my ability to contact everyone I had listed was constrained by circumstances beyond my control. Their current whereabouts were unknown, or they had left the city, or they had died. Among the "influentials" whom I *most* regret missing were Allen Davis, Roger Bradley, Dorothy Ratterman, Robert Beck, James Rankin, Harry Martin, and "Babe" West. I would gladly have included all of these West End leaders had circumstances allowed.

The oral record. I conducted forty-four interviews with forty different "influentials"; four were interviewed twice, at an interval of six months. All interviews were guided, in part, by questions prepared beforehand. All questions were verbally presented to the interviewee. Except for the short list of prepared questions, tailored to the informant's experience, each interview's content was open-ended, as was its length. Each lasted from one to two hours. The purpose was described to each informant as "research for a book about organizations and tensions in changing neighborhoods like the West End."

All interviews were recorded on audio tape with the assent of the interviewee. They were later transcribed, indexed, and cross-referenced with the transcripts from other interviews for eventual retrieval, comparison, and corroboration. The information provided by these "influentials" was verified, whenever possible, by documentary records.

Despite my year's residence in the West End, which ended a year and a half before these formal interviews began, only persons who were connected to the CLC or PHACT had had previous contact with me. My prior association with the CLC opened many doors among local and extralocal informants who regard the CLC (or its leaders) with respect—without closing any doors among those for whom the CLC is an object of suspicion, antagonism, or scorn.

Missing cases. A problem with focusing on the organized groups of the West End has been that the interview data provided for one of the locality's largest "quasi-groups" was less abundant than anticipated. With no leaders of their own outside of the West End Community Council or the Ministerial Alliance, few private tenants were included among the formal interviews. Much of my information about the material interests and "empirical conditions" underlying the tenants' property position was gathered, therefore, from the leaders of organizations advocating on behalf of private tenants—or, in some cases, from the leaders of organizations for whom private tenants are seen as either an obstacle to progress or an opportunity for profit. Such information was supplemented by my own encounters and conversations with a number of private tenants. However, the rule that I had adopted of interviewing only "influentials" led me not to commit these conversations to tape. Tenant voices, as a result, are underrepresented.

Interaction between theory and case study. The presentation adopted herein implies that an abstract theory was developed as a purely intellectual exercise (Part I), then tested against the concrete events of the West End (Part II), and finally refined on the basis of the case study's empirical findings (Part III). It is fair to say that the evolution of my thinking did, in fact, follow this general progression, but there was far more interaction between theory and case than this much-too-tidy, three-step format might suggest.

This book grew out of the challenge posed by the locality-based politics of the West End to the "explanations" of community action that I had explored as a doctoral student in sociology and urban planning two years prior to my arrival in Cincinnati. The politics, organizations, and conflicts of this urban neighborhood simply did not fit any of the theoretical explanations with which I was familiar. Nor did these theories provide much practical help in understanding the needs and behavior of the locality-based housing groups (like the CLC) with which I was working. A new "explanation" of group formation and intergroup conflict in the place of residence was clearly needed.

I developed the conceptual outlines for such a explanation while still in Cincinnati. This theoretical work continued over the next year and a half in Boston and in Burlington, Vermont, during employment as an organizer and trainer for several nonprofit housing providers.

By the end of 1984, I had decided to conduct an intensive study of the West End to see how well my evolving ideas might fare in describing and explaining the day-to-day political life of an inner-city neighborhood. I spent several weeks in Cincinnati in the fall of 1984 gathering materials on the history and development of the West End, as well as cataloguing the many locality-based groups that had arisen there over the years. I returned in January and June of 1985 to collect corporate documents, membership lists, and promotional materials from as many of these groups as possible, while conducting formal interviews with as many "influentials" as I could find.

By the fall of that year, Part I had been written and the transcript for the Cincinnati interviews had been completed. The case study of Part II was written the following spring. The entire manuscript was finished by May 1986. It then lay dormant for nearly eighteen months, until being substantially revised for publication—a weekend-by-weekend chore slowly accomplished during my first year as housing director for the City of Burlington.

What should be obvious from this short account is that proposed theory and observed fact have gone hand-in-hand from the very beginning. There has been little separation between my evolving theory of locality-based action and my ongoing exposure—as consultant, researcher, and city official—to locality-based groups in the West End, Boston, and Burlington. The result is a grounded explanation (although some might say a "tainted" explanation) for group formation and intergroup conflict in the place of residence that has been shaped and refined by a particular set of social facts. How well that explanation will stand the test of other facts from other cities is a question that can only be answered by further research.

Appendix B
Names and Affiliations
of Interviewees

Name	Date of Interview(s)	Relation to West End Property	Affiliation(s)
Gerald Bates	January 1985	Homeowner, Landlord, Developer	President, DSNA
Brenda Brown	January 1985	Resident owner, CLC	Board, CLC
Shirley Colburt	June 1985	Public tenant	President, Laurel Homes residents council; ex-secretary, WECC
Adele Cramer	January 1985 June 1985	—	Director, MPPF
Richard Folden	June 1985	Homeowner	Development committee, MPPF; Building committee, WECC
Daniel Goepper	January 1985 June 1985	—	Planner, Department of Neighborhood Housing and Conservation
Hubert Guest	June 1985	—	Director, City Planning Department; ex-director, Model Cities; ex-director, WETF

Name	Date of Interview(s)	Relation to West End Property	Affiliation(s)
Paul Henry	June 1985	—	Professor, University of Cincinnati; ex-trainer, CHART
David Hewer	January 1985	Homeowner, landlord, developer, realtor	Ex-president, DSNA
Bruce Hinkley	January 1985	—	Secretary, CLC; pastor, York Street Methodist Church
R. Jerome Jenkins	January 1985	—	Director, Seven Hills Neighborhood Houses; ex-member, WETF
Clinton Johnson	January 1985		Community Development Director, CAC; ex-staff, WEDCO; ex-member, WETF
James Jones	January 1985	Ex–Park Town	Director, WEDCO; ex-president, Park Town; ex-member, WETF
Norman Kattleman	January 1985	Landlord	Secretary, DSNA
Helen Lee	January 1985	—	Ex-director, Findlay Street Neighborhood House
Richard Lewis	June 1985	Ex–Park Town	Ex-director, WEDCO; ex-member, WETF
Michael Lundy	January 1985	Landlord	Vice president, DSNA
Beth McClure	January 1985	—	Resident applicant committee, CLC
Ann Renee McConn	June 1985	—	Ex-director, Neighborhood Support Program; ex-director, SNAP
Maurice McCrackin	January 1985 June 1985	Private tenant	Pastor, Community Church of Cincinnati; board, CLC
William Mallory	January 1985	Homeowner, ex–Park Town	State representative; ex-president, WECC; ex-member, WETF
Judy Martinez	January 1985	—	Organizer, PHACT
Terry Meehan	June 1985	—	Ex-pastor, St. Joseph Catholic Church; ex-staff, CLC

Name	Date of Interview(s)	Relation to West End Property	Affiliation(s)
Shirlene Minefield	June 1985	Public tenant	Outreach worker, St. Joseph Catholic Church; member, PHACT
Chandler Nesbitt	January 1985	Park Town	Treasurer, Park Town; resident applicant committee, CLC
Michael Painter	January 1985	Homeowner, landlord, developer, realtor	Treasurer, DSNA
Mary Partee	June 1985	Public tenant	Board, CMHA
Wilma Payton	January 1985	Homeowner	—
Vonnie Robbins	January 1985	Resident owner, CLC	Board, CLC; treasurer, WECC
Lucy Roberts	January 1985	Public tenant	Organizer, PHACT
Charlene Robinson	January 1985	Resident owner, CLC	Outreach worker, CLC
Pauline Robinson	January 1985	Park Town	Ex-director, Findlay Street Neighborhood House
Richard Sellers	January 1985	—	Pastor, West Cincinnati Presbyterian Church; board, MPPF
Frank Simmons	January 1985	—	Director, Findlay Street Neighborhood House
Betty Warren	January 1985	Park Town	Ex-president, WECC; ex-chair, WEDCO
Willie Watts	January 1985	Park Town	Director, CLC
Barbara Wheeler	January 1985	Private tenant	Staff, Dominican Social Services Project; vice-president, CLC; ex-president, CLC
Dwight Wilkins	January 1985	—	Board, CLC
Connie Wilson	June 1985	—	Board, MPPF; ex-director, MPPF
Diann Wright	January 1985 June 1985	Private tenant	President, WECC

Bibliography

General

Abercrombie, Nicholas, and Bryan S. Turner. 1978. "The dominant ideology thesis." *British Journal of Sociology* 29 (June): 149–70.

Achtenberg, Emily, and Peter Marcuse. 1983. "Towards the decommodification of housing: A political analysis and a progressive program." Pp. 202–31 in Chester Hartman, ed., *America's Housing Crisis: What Is To Be Done?* Boston: Routledge and Kegan Paul.

Agnew, John. 1982. "Home ownership and identity in capitalist societies." Pp. 60–97 in James S. Duncan, ed., *Housing and Identity: Cross-cultural Perspectives.* New York: Holmes and Meir.

——. 1981. "Homeownership and the capitalist social order." Pp. 457–80 in Michael Dear and Allen J. Scott, eds., *Urbanization and Urban Planning in Capitalist Society.* New York: Methuen.

——. 1978. "Market relations and locational conflict in cross-national perspective." Pp. 128–43 in Kevin R. Cox, ed., *Urbanization and Conflict in Market Societies.* Chicago: Maaroufa Press.

Alford, Robert R., and Harry M. Scoble. 1968. "Sources of local political involvement." *American Political Science Review* 62 (December): 1192–1206.

Alinsky, Saul D. 1971. *Rules for Radicals.* New York: Random House.

Angotti, Thomas. 1977. "The housing question: Engels and after." *Monthly Review* 29 (5): 39–51.

Appelbaum, Richard P., and John I. Gilderbloom. 1986. "Supply-side economics and rents: Are rental housing markets truly competitive?" Pp. 165–79 in

Rachel G. Bratt, Chester Hartman, and Ann Meyerson, eds., *Critical Perspectives on Housing*. Philadelphia: Temple University Press.

Apple, Michael W. 1982. "Reproduction and contradiction in education: An introduction." Pp. 1–31 in Michael W. Apple, ed., *Cultural and Economic Reproduction in Education*. Boston: Routledge and Kegan Paul.

——. 1981. "Reproduction, contestation, and curriculum: An essay in self-criticism." *Interchange* 12 (2–3): 27–47.

Auger, Deborah A. 1979. "The politics of revitalization in gentrifying neighborhoods." *Journal of the American Planning Association* 45 (October): 515–22.

Bachrach, Peter, and Morton Baratz. 1962. "Two faces of power." *American Political Science Review* 56 (December): 947–52.

Balbus, Isaac D. 1971. "The concept of interest in pluralist and marxian analysis." *Politics and Society* 1 (February): 151–77.

Ball, Michael. 1976. "Owner-occupation." Pp. 24–29 in *Housing and Class in Britain*. Papers presented at the Political Economy of Housing Workshop of the Conference of Socialist Economists, London.

Barbalet, Jack M. 1980. "Principals of stratification in Max Weber: An interpretation and critique." *British Journal of Sociology* 31 (3): 401–18.

Barry, Brian. 1969. "The public interest." Pp. 159–77 in William E. Connolly, ed., *The Bias of Pluralism*. New York: Atherton Press.

——. 1965. "The concept of interest." Pp. 173–86 in *Political Argument*. New York: The Humanities Press.

——. 1962. "The use and abuse of 'the public interest.'" Pp. 191–204 in Carl Friedrich, ed., *The Public Interest*, Nomos Series, no. 5. New York: Atherton Press.

Barton, Stephen E. 1977. "The urban housing problem: Marxist theory and community organizing." *Review of Radical Political Economics* 9 (Winter): 16–30.

Bell, Colin. 1977. "On housing classes." *Australian and New Zealand Journal of Sociology* 13 (February): 36–40.

Bell, Colin, and Howard Newby. 1978. "Community, communion, class and community action: The sources of the new urban politics." Pp. 283–301 in D. T. Herbert and R. J. Johnson, eds., *Social Areas in Cities*. New York: John Wiley and Sons.

Benn, S. I. 1960. "Interests in politics." *Proceedings of the Aristotelian Society* 60: 123–40.

Bentham, Jeremy. 1948. *An Introduction to the Principles of Morals and Legislation*. New York: Hafner.

Benton, Ted. 1981. "Objective interests and the sociology of power." *Sociology* 15 (May): 161–84.

Blum, Arthur, and Ibrahim Ragab. 1985. "Developmental stages of neighborhood organizations." *Social Policy* 15 (Spring): 21–28.

Blum, Terry C., and Paul W. Kingston. 1984. "Homeownership and social attachment." *Sociological Perspectives* 27 (April): 159–80.

Boulding, Kenneth E. 1962. *Conflict and Defense: A General Theory*. New York: Harper & Row.

Carey, George W. 1976. "Land tenure, speculation, and the state of the aging metropolis." *Geographical Review* 66 (July): 253–65.

Castells, Manuel. 1983. *The City and the Grassroots*. Berkeley: University of California Press.

——. 1978. *City, Class, and Power*. New York: St. Martin's Press.

———. 1977. *The Urban Question*. Cambridge: MIT Press.

Clark, David B. 1973. "The concept of community: A re-examination." *Sociological Review* 21 (August): 397–416.

Clark, Gordon L. 1982. "Rights, property, and community." *Economic Geography* 58 (April): 120–38.

Clarke, Simon, and Norman Ginsburg. 1975. "The political economy of housing." Pp. 3–33 in *Political Economy and the Housing Question*. Papers presented at the Housing Workshop of the Conference of Socialist Economists, London.

Cohen, Jean L. 1983. "Rethinking social movements." *Berkeley Journal of Sociology* 28: 97–113.

Connerly, Charles E. 1986. "The impact of neighborhood social relations on prospective mobility." *Social Science Quarterly* 67 (March): 186–94.

Connolly, William E. 1972."On 'interests' in politics." *Politics and Society* 2 (Summer): 450–77.

Couper, Mary, and Timothy Brindley. 1975. "Housing classes and housing values." *Sociological Review* 23 (August): 563–75.

Cox, Kevin R. 1982. "Housing tenure and neighborhood activism." *Urban Affairs Quarterly* 18 (September): 107–29.

———. 1981. "Capitalism and conflict around the communal living space." Pp. 431–55 in Michael Dear and Allen J. Scott, eds., *Urbanization and Urban Planning in Capitalist Society*. New York: Methuen.

———. 1978. "Local interests and urban political processes in market societies." Pp. 94–108 in Kevin R. Cox, ed., *Urbanization and Conflict in Market Societies*. Chicago: Maaroufa Press.

Cox, Kevin R., and Jeffery J. McCarthy. 1982. "Neighborhood activism as a politics of turf: A critical analysis." Pp. 196–219 in Kevin Cox and R. J. Johnston, eds., *Conflict, Politics, and the Urban Scene*. New York: St. Martin's Press.

———. 1980. "Neighborhood activism in the American city: Behavioral relationships and evaluation." *Urban Geography* 1 (1): 22–38.

Cullingworth, J. B. 1979. "Owner-occupation." Pp. 98–115 in *Essays on Housing Policy: The British Scene*. London: George Allen and Unwin.

Dahrendorf, Ralf. 1959. *Class and Class Conflict in Industrial Society*. Stanford: Stanford University Press.

Dale, Roger. 1982. "Education and the capitalist state: contributions and contradictions." Pp. 127–61 in Michael Apple, ed., *Cultural and Economic Reproduction in Education*. Boston: Routledge and Kegan Paul.

Davis, John Emmeus. 1990. "Reconcilable differences: housing and human rights in the United States." *Peace and Democracy News* (Bulletin of the Campaign for Peace and Democracy/East and West), 4 (1–2).

———. 1986. "In the interest of property: group formation and inter-group conflict in the residential urban neighborhood." Ph.D. diss., Cornell University.

———. 1984. "Reallocating equity: A land trust model of land reform." Pp. 209–32 in Charles C. Geisler and Frank J. Popper, eds., *Land Reform, American Style*. Totowa, N.J.: Rowman and Allanheld.

Dean, John. 1945. *Home Ownership: Is It Sound?* New York: Harper & Row.

Dear, Michael J., and Jonathan Long. 1978. "Community strategies in locational conflict." Pp. 113–27 in Kevin R. Cox, ed., *Urbanization and Conflict in Market Societies*. Chicago: Maaroufa Press.

Dennis, Norman. 1968. "The popularity of the neighborhood community idea." Pp. 74–92 in R. E. Pahl, ed., *Readings in Urban Sociology*. New York: Pergamon Press.

Dolbeare, Cushing. 1986. "How the tax system subsidizes housing for the affluent." Pp. 264–71 in Rachel G. Bratt, Chester Hartman, and Ann Meyerson, eds., *Critical Perspectives on Housing*. Philadelphia: Temple University Press.

Dreier, Peter. 1982a. "The housing crisis: dreams and nightmares." *The Nation* (August 21–28): 141–44.

——. 1982b. "The status of tenants in the United States." *Social Problems* 30 (December): 179–98.

——. 1980. "Socialist incubators." *Social Policy* 11 (May/June): 29–34.

Duncan, Nancy G. 1982. "Home ownership and social theory." Pp. 98–134 in James S. Duncan, ed., *Housing and Identity: Cross-cultural Perspectives*. New York: Holmes and Meir.

Dunleavy, Patrick. 1980. *Urban Political Analysis: The Politics of Collective Consumption*. London: Macmillan.

——. 1979. "The urban basis of political alignment: Social class, domestic property ownership, and state intervention in consumption processes." *British Journal of Political Science* 9 (October): 409–43.

Edel, Matthew. 1982. "Home ownership and working class unity." *International Journal of Urban and Regional Research* 6 (2): 205–21.

——. 1977. "Rent theory and working class strategy: Marx, George, and the urban crisis." *Review of Radical Political Economics* 9 (Winter): 1–15.

Effrat, Marcia Pelly. 1973. "Approaches to community: Conflicts and complementarities." *Sociological Inquiry* 43 (3–4):1–34.

Elster, Jon. 1985. *Making Sense of Marx*. Cambridge: Cambridge University Press.

Engels, Frederick. 1935. *The Housing Question*. New York: International Publishers.

Fainstein, Susan, and Norman Fainstein. 1985. "Economic restructuring and the rise of urban social movements." Paper presented at the Fifth Urban Change and Conflict Conference, University of Sussex.

——. 1983. "Regime strategies, communal resistance, and economic forces." Pp. 245–82 in Susan S. Fainstein et al., eds. *Restructuring the City: The Political Economy of Urban Redevelopment*. New York: Longman.

Feagin, Joe R. 1982. "Urban real estate speculation in the United States: Implications for social science and urban planning." *International Journal of Urban and Regional Research* 6 (1): 35–59.

Feit, Ronnie, and Jan Peterson. 1985. "Neighborhood women look at housing." Pp. 177–90 in Eugenie Ladner Birch, ed., *The Unsheltered Woman: Women and Housing in the 80s*. New Brunswick, N.J.: Center for Urban Policy Research, Rutgers University.

Flathman, Richard E. 1966. "The concept of interest and the public interest." Pp. 14–31 in *The Public Interest*. New York: John Wiley and Sons.

Fletcher, Colin. 1976. "The relevance of domestic property to sociological understanding." *Sociology* 10 (September): 451–68.

Form, William H. 1954. "The place of social structure in the determination of land use: Some implications for a theory of urban ecology." *Social Forces* 32 (May): 317–23.

Frankel, Linda. 1984. "Southern textile women: generations of survival and struggle." Pp. 39–60 in Karen Brodkin Sacks and Dorothy Remy, eds., *My Troubles Are Going to Have Trouble with Me*. New Brunswick, N.J.: Rutgers University Press.

Fried, Charles. 1963. "Two concepts of interests: Some reflections on the Supreme Court's balancing test." *Harvard Law Review* 76:755–78.

Frieden, Bernard J., and Arthur P. Solomon. 1977. *The Nation's Housing: 1975–1985*. Cambridge: Joint Center for Urban Studies of MIT and Harvard University.

Friedland, Roger. 1982. *Power and Crisis in the City*. London: Macmillan.

Galster, George C., and Garry W. Hesser. 1982. "The social neighborhood: An unspecified factor in homeowner maintenance." *Urban Affairs Quarterly* 18 (December): 235–54.

Gamson, William A. 1966. "Rancorous conflict in community politics." *American Sociological Review* 31 (February): 71–81.

Gaventa, John. 1980. *Power and Powerlessness: Quiescence and Rebellion in an Appalachian Valley*. Urbana: University of Illinois Press.

George, Henry. 1975. *Progress and Poverty*. New York: Robert Schalkenbach Foundation.

Gerth, Hans H., and C. Wright Mills, eds. 1958. *From Max Weber: Essays in Sociology*. New York: Oxford University Press.

Giddens, Anthony. 1979. "Ideology and consciousness." Pp. 165–97 in *Central Problems in Social Theory*. Berkeley: University of California Press.

———. 1973. *The Class Structure of the Advanced Societies*. New York: Harper & Row.

Giroux, Henry A. 1983. "Theories of reproduction and resistance in the new sociology of education: a critical analysis." *Harvard Educational Review* 53 (August): 257–93.

———. 1981. "Hegemony, resistance, and the paradox of educational reform." *Interchange* 12 (2–3): 3–26.

Goering, John M. 1979. "The national neighborhood movement: A preliminary analysis and critique." *Journal of the American Planning Association* 45 (October): 506–14.

Gray, Fred. 1982. "Owner-occupation and social relations." Pp. 267–91 in Stephen Merrett, *Owner-Occupation in Great Britain*. London: Routledge and Kegan Paul.

Haddon, R. 1970. "A minority in a welfare state." *New Atlantis* 2:80–133.

Harloe, Michael. 1984. "Sector and class: A critical comment." *International Journal of Urban and Regional Research* 8 (2): 228–37.

Hartman, Chester. 1984. "The right to stay put." Pp. 302–18 in Charles C. Geisler and Frank J. Popper, eds., *Land Reform, American Style*. Totowa, N.J.: Rowman and Allanheld.

Harvey, David. 1985. "The urbanization of consciousness." Pp. 250–76 in his *Consciousness and the Urban Experience*. Baltimore: Johns Hopkins University Press.

———. 1981. "The urban process under capitalism: A framework for analysis." Pp. 91–121 in Michael Dear and Allen J. Scott, eds., *Urbanization and Urban Planning in Capitalist Society*. New York: Methuen.

———. 1978. "Labor, capital, and class struggle around the built environment in advanced capitalist societies." Pp. 9–37 in Kevin R. Cox, ed., *Urbanization and Conflict in Market Societies*. Chicago: Maaroufa Press.

——. 1974. "Class-monopoly rent, finance capital and the urban revolution." *Regional Studies* 8:239–55.

Held, Virginia. 1970. "The public interest in relation to individual interests." Pp. 18–48 in *The Public Interest and Individual Interests*. New York: Basic Books.

Hillery, George A. 1955. "Definitions of community: Areas of agreement." *Rural Sociology* 20 (2): 111–23.

Ineichen, Bernard. 1972. "Home ownership and manual workers' life-styles." *Sociological Review* 20 (August): 391–412.

Institute for Community Economics. 1982. *The Community Land Trust Handbook*. Emmaus, Pa.: Rodale Press.

Jacobs, Jane. 1961. *The Life and Death of Great American Cities*. New York: Random House.

Janowitz, Morris. 1952. *The Community Press in an Urban Setting*. New York: Free Press.

Jaret, Charles. 1983. "Recent neo-Marxist urban analysis." *Annual Review of Sociology* 9:499–525.

Jennings, Walter W. 1938. "The value of home-owning as exemplified in American history." *Social Science* 13 (January): 5–15.

Katznelson, Ira. 1981. *City Trenches: Urban Politics and the Patterning of Class in the United States*. New York: Pantheon Books.

Katznelson, Ira, Kathleen Gille, and Margaret Weir. 1982. "Race and schooling: Reflections on the social bases of urban movements." *Urban Affairs Annual Reviews* 22: 215–35.

Keith, Nathaniel. 1973. *Politics and the Housing Crisis Since 1930*. New York: Universe Books.

Keller, Susan. 1968. *The Urban Neighborhood*. New York: Random House.

Kemeny, Jim. 1982. "A critique and reformulation of the new urban sociology." *Acta Sociologica* 25 (4): 419–30.

——. 1981. *The Myth of Home Ownership: Private Versus Public Choices in Housing Tenure*. London: Routledge and Kegan Paul.

——. 1980. "Home ownership and privatization." *International Journal of Urban and Regional Research* 4 (September): 372–87.

——. 1977. "A political sociology of home ownership in Australia." *Australian and New Zealand Journal of Sociology* 13 (February): 47–52.

Kingston, Paul W., John L. P. Thompson, and Douglas M. Eichar. 1984. "The politics of homeownership." *American Politics Quarterly* 12 (April): 131–50.

Kirkpartick, David. 1981. "Limiting equity in housing cooperatives: choices and tradeoffs." *Economic Development and Law Center Report* 11 (January/March): 1–9.

Kotler, Milton. 1969. *Neighborhood Government*. New York: Bobbs-Merrill.

Kraushaar, Robert. 1988. "Outside the whale: Progressive planning and the dilemmas of radical reform." *APA Journal* 54 (Winter): 91–100.

Lefevre, Henri. 1973. "Reproduction of the relations of production." Pp. 42–91 in Henri Lefevre, The Survival of Capitalism. New York: St. Martin's Press.

LeGates, Richard, and Chester Hartman. 1981. "Displacement." *Clearinghouse Review* (National Clearinghouse for Legal Services) 15 (July): 207–49.

LeGates, Richard, and Karen Murphy. 1981. "Austerity, shelter, and social conflict in the United States." *International Journal of Urban and Regional Research* 5 (2): 255–75.

Ley, David, and John Mercer. 1980. "Locational conflict and the politics of consumption." *Economic Geography* 56 (April): 89–109.

Logan, John R. 1978. "Growth, politics, and the stratification of places." *American Journal of Sociology* 84 (2): 404–15.

Logan, John R., and Harvey L. Molotch. 1987. *Urban Fortunes: The Political Economy of Place.* Berkeley: University of California Press.

Lukes, Steven. 1974. *Power: A Radical View.* London: Macmillan.

Luria, Daniel D. 1976. "Wealth, capital, and power: The social meaning of home ownership." *Journal of Interdisciplinary History* 7 (2): 261–82.

Macpherson, C. B. 1973. "A political theory of property." Pp. 120–140 in C. B. Macpherson, *Democratic Theory: Essays in Retrieval.* Oxford: Clarendon Press.

Marcuse, Peter. 1980. "Ideologies of ownership and property rights." Pp. 39–50 in Richard Plunz, ed., *Housing Form and Public Policy in the United States.* New York: Praeger.

———. 1972. "Homeownership for low-income families: Financial implications." *Land Economics* 48 (May): 134–43.

Marx, Karl. 1972a. "On the Jewish question." Pp. 24–51 in Robert C. Tucker, ed., *The Marx-Engels Reader.* New York: W. W. Norton.

———. 1972b. "The German ideology." Pp. 110–64 in Robert C. Tucker (ed.), *The Marx-Engels Reader.* New York: W. W. Norton.

———. 1972c. "The eighteenth brumaire of Louis Bonaparte." Pp. 436–525 in Robert C. Tucker, ed., *The Marx-Engels Reader.* New York: W. W. Norton.

———. 1971. *The Grundrisse.* New York: Harper & Row.

———. 1967. *Capital.* Vol. 1 New York: International Publishers.

Mayer, Martin. 1978. *The Builders: Houses, People, Neighborhoods, Governments, Money.* New York: W. W. Norton.

Mollenkopf, John H. 1983. *The Contested City.* Princeton: Princeton University Press.

———. 1981a. "Community and accumulation." Pp. 319–37 in Michael Dear and Allen J. Scott, eds., *Urbanization and Urban Planning in Capitalist Society.* New York: Methuen.

———. 1981b. "Neighborhood political development and the politics of urban growth." *International Journal of Urban and Regional Research* 5 (1): 15–39.

Molotch, Harvey. 1979. "Capital and neighborhood in the United States: Some conceptual links." *Urban Affairs Quarterly* 14 (March): 289–312.

———. 1976. "The city as a growth machine: Toward a political economy of place." *American Journal of Sociology* 82 (September): 309–31.

Moore, Robert. 1977. "Becoming a sociologist in Sparkbrook." Pp. 87–107 in Colin Bell and Howard Newby, eds., *Doing Sociological Research.* New York: Free Press.

Moorehouse, H. F. and C. W. Chamberlain. 1974. "Lower class attitudes to property: Aspects of the counter-ideology." *Sociology* 8 (September): 387–405.

Neuwirth, Gertrud. 1969. "A Weberian outline of a theory of community: Its application to the 'Dark Ghetto'." *British Journal of Sociology* 20 (2): 148–61.

Nisbet, Robert A. 1953. *The Quest for Community.* New York: Oxford University Press.

O'Brien, David J. 1975. *Neighborhood Organization and Interest-Group Processes*. Princeton: Princeton University Press.

——. 1974. "The public goods dilemma and the 'apathy' of the poor toward the neighborhood organization." *Social Service Review* 48 (June): 229–44.

Ollman, Bertell. 1976. *Alienation: Marx's Conception of Man in Capitalist Society*. New York: Cambridge University Press.

——. 1972. "Toward class consciousness next time: Marx and the working class." *Politics and Society* 3 (1): 1–24.

——. 1968. "Marx's use of 'class'." *American Journal of Sociology* 63 (March): 573–80.

Olson, Mancur. 1965. *The Logic of Collective Action*. Cambridge: Harvard University Press.

Orbell, John M., and Toru Uno. 1972. "A theory of neighborhood problem solving." *American Political Science Review* 66 (June): 471–89.

Pahl, R. E. 1975. *Whose City? And Further Essays on Urban Society*. Baltimore: Penguin Books.

Parcel, Toby L. 1982. "Wealth accumulation of black and white men: The case of housing equity." *Social Problems* 30 (December): 199–211.

Park, Robert E. 1952. *Human Communities*. Glencoe, Ill.: Free Press.

Parkin, Robert. 1979. *Marxism and Class Theory: A Bourgeois Critique*. New York: Columbia University Press.

Perin, Constance. 1977. *Everything in Its Place: Social Order and Land Use in America*. Princeton: Princeton University Press.

Pickvance, C. G. 1977. "From 'social base' to 'social force': Some analytic issues in the study of urban protest." Pp. 175–86 in Michael Harloe, ed., *Captive Cities*. New York: John Wiley.

——. 1976. "Housing: reproduction of capital and reproduction of labor power." Pp. 271–89 in John Walton and Louis Masotti, eds., *The City in Comparative Perspective*. New York: John Wiley.

——. 1975. "On the study of urban movements." *Sociological Review* 23 (February): 29–49.

Plamenatz, John. 1963. *Man and Society*. Vol. 2. New York: McGraw-Hill.

——. 1954. "Interests." *Political Studies* 2 (1): 1–8.

Plant, Raymond. 1978. "Community: concept, conception, and ideology." *Politics and Society* 8 (1): 79–107.

Pratt, Geraldine. 1982. "Class analysis and urban domestic property: A critical reexamination." *International Journal of Urban and Regional Research* 6 (4): 481–501.

Qadeer, M. A. 1981. "The nature of urban land." *American Journal of Economics and Sociology* 40 (2): 165–82.

Rakoff, Robert. 1977. "Ideology in everyday life: The meaning of the house." *Politics and Society* 7 (1): 85–104.

Redfield, Robert. 1941. *The Folk Culture of the Yucatan*. Chicago: University of Chicago Press.

Rex, John A. 1971. "The concept of housing class and the sociology of race relations." *Race* 12 (January): 293–301.

——. 1968. "The sociology of a zone of transition." Pp. 211–31 in R. E. Pahl, ed., *Readings in Urban Sociology*. New York: Pergamon Press.

Rex, John A., and Robert Moore. 1967. *Race, Community, and Conflict*. New York: Oxford University Press.

Rich, Richard C. 1980. "A political-economy approach to the study of neighborhood organizations." *American Journal of Political Science* 24 (November): 559–92.

Rich, Richard C., and Abraham Wandersman. 1983. "Participation in block organizations." *Social Policy* 14 (Summer): 45–47.

Rose, David, Peter Saunders, Howard Newby, and Colin Bell. 1976. "Ideologies of property: A case study." *Sociological Review* 24 (November): 699–730.

Rossi, Peter, and Robert Dentler. 1961. *The Politics of Urban Renewal*. New York: Free Press.

Roth, Guenther, and Claus Wittich, eds. 1978. *Max Weber: Economy and Society*. Berkeley: University of California Press.

Roweis, Shoukry T., and Allen J. Scott. 1978. "The urban land question." Pp. 39–75 in Kevin R. Cox, ed., *Urbanization and Conflict in Market Societies*. Chicago: Maaroufa Press.

Sabia, Daniel R. 1988. "Rationality, collective action, and Karl Marx." *American Journal of Political Science* 32 (1): 50–71.

Sacks, Karen Brodkin. 1984. "Generations of working-class families." Pp. 15–40 in Karen Brodkin Sacks and Dorothy Remy, eds., *My Troubles Are Going to Have Trouble with Me*. New Brunswick, N.J.: Rutgers University Press.

Saunders, Peter. 1984. "Beyond housing classes: The sociological significance of private property rights in means of consumption." *International Journal of Urban and Regional Research* 8 (2): 202–25.

———. 1981. *Social Theory and the Urban Question*. New York: Holmes and Meier Publishers.

———. 1979. *Urban Politics: A Sociological Interpretation*. London: Hutchinson and Company.

———. 1978. "Domestic property and social class." *International Journal of Urban and Regional Research* 2 (June): 233–51.

Schmalenbach, Herman. 1961. "The sociological category of communion." Pp. 331–47 in Talcott Parsons et al., eds., *Theories of Society*, Vol. 1. New York: Free Press.

Schmidt, Walter S. 1935. "Private versus public enterprise in housing." *Journal of Land and Public Utility Economics* 11 (August): 342–51.

Scott, William. 1977. *In Pursuit of Happiness: American Conceptions of Property from the Seventeenth to the Twentieth Century*. Bloomington: Indiana University Press.

Sennett, Richard. 1977. *The Fall of Public Man*. New York: Alfred A. Knopf.

———. 1970. *The Uses of Disorder*. New York: Alfred A. Knopf.

Shlay, Anne B., and Denise DiGregorio. 1983. "Same city, different worlds: Examining gender and work based differences in perceptions of neighborhood desireability." Paper presented at the 78th annual meeting of the American Sociological Association, Detroit (August 31–September 4).

Smith, Neil. 1982. "Gentrification and uneven development." *Economic Geography* 58 (April): 139–55.

———. 1979. "Toward a theory of gentrification: A back to the city movement of capital not people." *Journal of the American Planning Association* 45 (October): 538–48.

Stacey, Margaret. 1969. "The myth of community studies." *British Journal of Sociology* 20 (June): 134–47.

Stein, Maurice. 1960. *The Eclipse of Community*. New York: Harper & Row.

Steinberger, Peter J. 1984. "Urban politics and communality." *Urban Affairs Quarterly* 20 (September): 4–21.

Stone, Clarence N. 1976. *Economic Growth and Neighborhood Discontent: System Bias in the Urban Renewal Program of Atlanta*. Chapel Hill: University of North Carolina Press.

Stone, Michael E. 1980. "Housing and the American economy: A Marxist analysis." Pp. 81–108 in Pierre Clavel, John Forester, and William W. Goldsmith, eds., *Urban and Regional Planning in an Age of Austerity*. New York: Pergamon Press.

———. 1978. "Housing, mortgage lending, and the contradictions of capitalism." Pp. 179–207 in William K. Tabb and Larry Sawers, eds., *Marxism and the Metropolis*. New York: Oxford University Press.

Taub, Richard P., et al. 1977. "Urban voluntary associations, locality based and externally induced." *American Journal of Sociology* 83 (September): 425–42.

Tawney, R. H. 1920. *The Acquisitive Society*. New York: Harcourt Brace Jovanovich.

Thompson, E. P. 1978. "Eighteenth-century society: Class conflict without class?" *Social History* 3 (May): 133–65.

Tilly, Charles. 1978. *From Mobilization to Revolution*. Reading, Mass.: Addison-Wesley.

———. 1974. "Do communities act?" Pp. 209–40 in Marcia Pelly Effrat, ed., *The Community: Approaches and Applications*. New York: Free Press.

Tonnies, Ferdinand. 1963. *Community and Society*. New York: Harper Tourchbooks.

Van Gunsteren, Herman. 1979. "Public and private." *Social Research* 46 (Summer): 255–71.

Wall, Grenville. 1975. "The concept of interest in politics." *Politics and Society* 5 (4): 487–510.

Warren, Roland. 1963. *The Community in America*. Chicago: Rand McNally.

Webber, Melvin M. 1964. "The urban place and the nonplace urban realm." Pp. 79–153 in Melvin M. Webber et al., eds., *Explorations into Urban Structure*. Philadelphia: University of Pennsylvania Press.

———. 1963. "Order in diversity: Community without propinquity." Pp. 23–54 in L. Wingo, ed., *Cities and Space*. Baltimore: Johns Hopkins University Press.

Weiner, Richard R. 1981. *Cultural Marxism and Political Sociology*. Beverly Hills, Calif.: Sage Publications.

Wellman, Barry, and Barry Leighton. 1979. "Networks, neighborhoods, and communities: Approaches to the study of the community question." *Urban Affairs Quarterly* 14 (March): 363–89.

Wexler, Philip. 1983. "Movement, class, and education." Pp. 17–39 in Len Barton and Stephen Walker, eds., *Race, Class, and Education*. London: Croom Helm.

Williams, Raymond. 1976. *Keywords*. New York: Oxford University Press.

Willis, Paul. 1983. "Cultural production and theories of reproduction." Pp. 107–38 in Len Barton and Stephen Walker, eds., *Race, Class, and Education*. London: Croom Helm.

———. 1981. "Cultural production is different from cultural reproduction is different from social production is different from reproduction." *Interchange* 12 (2–3): 48–67.

Wirth, Louis. 1938. "Urbanism as a way of life." *American Journal of Sociology* 44 (July): 3–24.

Wolf, Peter. 1981. *Land in America: Its Value, Use, and Control.* New York: Pantheon Books.

Wright, Gwendolyn. 1981. *Building the Dream: A Social History of Housing in America.* New York: Pantheon Books.

Yearwood, Richard. 1968. "Land, speculation, and development: American attitudes." *Plan* 9 (March): 15–23.

Cincinnati

Bodamer, Richard. 1965. "The Liberty-Dalton redevelopment project proposal." M.C.P. thesis, University of Cincinnati.

Brown, Luther. 1975. "The fight for survival: A case study of the West End Development Corporation." M.C.P. thesis, University of Cincinnati.

Cincinnati Human Relations Commission. 1981. "Neighborhood opinion poll: Dayton and York Streets." Cincinnati: Ohio: CHRC (November).

Cincinnati Metropolitan Housing Authority Archives. Cincinnati Historical Society, Cincinnati.

Citizens Development Committee Archives. Cincinnati Historical Society, Cincinnati.

Citizens Planning Association Archives. Cincinnati Historical Society, Cincinnati.

City Demonstration Agency. 1970. "Cincinnati Model Cities: Mid-planning statement." Cincinnati: CDA (March).

City Planning Commission. 1972a. *West End Development Plan.* Cincinnati: City Planning Commission.

——. 1972b. *West End: Existing Conditions.* Cincinnati: City Planning Commission.

——. 1966. *A Program for the West End.* Cincinnati: City Planning Commission.

——. 1965. *Dayton Street Preservation Area Study.* Cincinnati: City Planning Commission.

——. 1959. *Master Plan for Redevelopment of the Kenyon-Barr Urban Renewal Area.* Cincinnati: City Planning Commission.

——. 1951. *Redevelopment of Blighted Areas.* Cincinnati: City Planning Commission.

——. 1950. *Program of Capital Improvements for the City of Cincinnati, 1951–1955.* Cincinnati: City Planning Commission.

——. 1948. *City Plan.* Cincinnati: City Planning Commission.

——. 1946a. *Residential Areas: An Analysis of Land Requirements for Residential Development, 1945 to 1970.* Cincinnati: City Planning Commission.

——. 1946b. *Industrial Land Use: Present and Future.* Cincinnati: City Planning Commission.

——. 1925. *The Official City Plan of Cincinnati, Ohio.* Cincinnati: City Planning Commission.

City Planning Department. Building Permit Files. Office of Planning and Management Support, Cincinnati.

Community Land Cooperative. 1983. "A grant proposal submitted to the Public

Welfare Foundation by the Community Land Cooperative of Cincinnati" (May).

Costello, Kevin Patrick. 1982. "An analysis and evaluation of local preservation efforts in Cincinnati, Ohio." M.C.P. thesis, University of Cincinnati.

Creahan, Tom. 1973. "Preliminary analysis of the Liberty-Dalton project." Cincinnati: Unreleased report by the Department of Urban Development, City of Cincinnati.

Department of Neighborhood Housing and Conservation. 1982a. *Linn Street Urban Design Plan*. Cincinnati: DNHC.

———. 1982b. *Citizen Services Survey '81: West End Neighborhood Report*. Cincinnati: DNHC.

Department of Urban Development. 1972. *Urban Design Plan for Queensgate II*, Appendix ND-401A. Cincinnati: Department of Urban Development.

Fairbanks, Robert B. 1981. "Better housing movements and the city: Definitions and responses to Cincinnati's low cost housing problems, 1910–1954." Ph.D. diss., University of Cincinnati.

Fairbanks, Robert B., and Zane L. Miller. 1984. "The martial metropolis: housing, planning, and race in Cincinnati, 1940–55." Pp. 191–222 in Roger W. Lotchin, ed., *The Martial Metropolis: U.S. Cities in War and Peace*. New York: Praeger.

Hamilton County Department of Public Welfare. 1933. *A Survey of Housing Conditions in the Basin of the City of Cincinnati*. Cincinnati: DPW.

Jenkins, Roger Jerome. 1974. "Images of the future—a case study of the University of Cincinnati's inter-disciplinary planning team's interface with the Queensgate II urban renewal project no. A9." Ph.D. diss., University of Cincinnati.

Jenkins, Roger Jerome, and Richard W. Lewis. 1982. "Queensgate II and 'the Movement': A view from the community." Pp. 105–21 in Zane L. Miller and Thomas H. Jenkins, eds., *The Planning Partnership*. Beverly Hills, Calif.: Sage Publications.

Jenkins, Thomas H. 1982. "The West End Task Force: Community participation and policy planning." Pp. 83–103 in Zane L. Miller and Thomas H. Jenkins, eds., *The Planning Partnership*. Beverly Hills, Calif.: Sage Publications.

Koehler, Lyle. 1983. "Cincinnati's black peoples: A chronology and bibliography." Cincinnati: Unpublished manuscript, Urban Studies Collection of the University of Cincinnati, Archival Collections.

McCrackin, Maurice. 1982. Interview. Pp. 93–96 in Institute for Community Economics, *The Community Land Trust Handbook*. Emmaus, Pa.: Rodale Press.

Marquette, Bleecker. 1972. *Health, Housing and Other Things*. Cincinnati.

Meehan, Terry, and Willie Watts. 1981. "Memorandum to members of the Community Land Cooperative board."

Miller, Zane L. 1982. "Queensgate II: A history of a neighborhood." Pp. 51–79 in Zane L. Miller and Thomas H. Jenkins, eds., *The Planning Partnership*. Beverly Hills, Calif.: Sage Publications.

———. 1972. "A history of the Cincinnati model neighborhood," Working Paper No. 3. Institute for Metropolitan Studies, University of Cincinnati.

Miller, Zane L., and Hayden B. May. 1982. "Housing: The critical nexus." Pp. 141–56 in Zane L. Miller and Thomas H. Jenkins, eds., *The Planning Partnership*. Beverly Hills, Calif.: Sage Publications.

Miller, Zane L., and Thomas H. Jenkins, eds. 1982. *The Planning Partnership.* Beverly Hills, Calif.: Sage Publications.

Ross, D. Reid. 1957. "The effect of planned public improvement programs on the low rent housing supply." Cincinnati: Unpublished report, Better Housing League.

Stimson, George P. n.d. "They cared. . . . Citizens Planning Association, 1944–1948/Citizens Development Committee, 1948–1968." Cincinnati: Unpublished manuscript, Cincinnati Historical Society.

Taylor, Henry Louis, Jr. 1979. "The building of a black suburb: The Lincoln Heights, Ohio story." Ph.D. diss., University of New York at Buffalo.

Tillery, Tyrone. 1971. "Cincinnati blacks and the Great Depression, 1929–1938." M.A. thesis, University of Cincinnati.

Topps, Shaun Christopher. 1982. "The Community Land Cooperative of Cincinnati residential property owners study." Cincinnati: Unpublished report, Community Land Cooperative.

University of Cincinnati School of Planning. 1983. "West End north frame plan." Cincinnati: Unpublished report, Community Land Cooperative.

Urban Redevelopment Division. 1956. "The Kenyon-Barr urban renewal project." Cincinnati: Unpublished report to the Cincinnati City Council (February 1).

Washington, Michael L. 1984. "The black struggle for desegregated quality education, 1954–1974." Ed.D. thesis, University of Cincinnati.

West End Task Force. 1968. *A Community Organizes for Planning: Progress Report of the West End Task Force.* Cincinnati: West End Task Force.

——. 1966a. "General information: Dayton-Findlay I." Cincinnati: Unpublished report, West End Task Force (October).

——. 1966b. "General information: Dayton-Findlay II." Cincinnati: Unpublished report: West End Task Force (August).

Wheeler, Barbara. 1983. "Letter to Ginger Brockwell, Director of Miami Purchase Preservation Fund" (April 6).

Index

Accommodation. *See* Function of property

Accumulation: as basis for property classes, 30–31, 38; capitalist, 25, 62, 69, 286–88, 291–92; sources of, 30–31, 33–36. *See also* Equity; Function of property

Achtenberg, Emily, and Peter Marcuse, 47, 53

Acquisitive homeowners, 68, 181, 188–91, 322. *See also* Dayton Street Neighborhood Association; Differentiation: of owner-occupiers; Homeowners

Alinsky, Saul, 307–8, 314

Amenity: characteristics, 51–53; in charter of local associations, 313; interest of acquisitive homeowners 227–28; interest of property capitalists, 70; interest of social homeowners, 206, 208; interest of tenants, 74, 194, 198, 200; organizing around, 87, 314–15; threats to, 52–53, 194, 200

Apple, Michael, 306, 310

Autonomy: characteristics, 53–56; in charter of local associations, 313; effect of historic preservation, 192n; as "home rule," 40, 54; interest of ac-

quisitive homeowners, 218; interest of social homeowners, 67, 147, 206, 208; interest of tenants, 74–76, 198–99, 200–201; organizing around, 316n; threats to, 192n

Balbus, Isaac, 15, 18n, 80, 263

Bates, Gerald, 183, 217–18, 275

Bell, Colin, 34, 296n, 297n; and Howard Newby, 298

Better Housing League of Cincinnati: as critic of tenant relocation, 135, 137n; founding of, 113–14; member of West End Task Force, 143. *See also* Marquette, Bleeker

Blacks (race): bourgeoisie, 112–13; causes of ghetto in West End, 110–12, 121; displacement of, 119–20n; employment, 110, 116; homeowners, 110, 112–13, 119, 151–52, 165, 171, 177, 179, 185–88, 191–92; memory of "community lost," 140, 142, 145; migration to Cincinnati, 103; neighborhood ties, 69, 177, 179; population in West End, 106, 130, 148, 179; in public housing, 120–21; settlement in West End, 107; West End as center

347

Library of Congress Cataloging-in-Publication Data
Davis, John Emmeus, 1949–
  Contested ground : collective action and the urban neighborhood /
John E. Davis.
    p. cm.
  Includes bibliographical references.
  ISBN 0-8014-2215-9 (alk. paper). — ISBN 0-8014-9905-4 (pbk. : alk.
paper)
    1. Neighborhood—United States. 2. Community power—United
States. 3. Community development, Urban—United States. I. Title.
  HT123.D39 1991
  307.3'36216'0973—dc20   90-42034